D1453219

BRITISH FOREIGN POLICY SINCE SUEZ

1956–1968

BRITISH FOREIGN POLICY SINCE SUEZ

1956-1968

by

Donald D Maclean

HODDER AND STOUGHTON

Printed in Great Britain for Hodder and Stoughton Limited,
St. Paul's House, Warwick Lane, London, E.C.4, by
Ebenezer Baylis and Son Limited,
The Trinity Press, Worcester, and London

Contents

8 *Contents*

Foreword

Foreign policy is an emotive subject and with very good reason: human society has developed to a stage in which the fate of man now depends directly and literally on the way in which the leading powers, capitalist and socialist, conduct their relations with each other and with the smaller countries. Value judgments neither should nor can be avoided in discussing the subject.

On the other hand, besides what one may feel about the rightness or wrongness of foreign policy actions, there is the question of what, like it or not, is actually happening in international affairs; of the direction in which the foreign policy of various countries, great and small, is moving; of the factors responsible for that movement, and of the eventual consequences for us all to which it is likely to lead.

In the period preceding the Second World War, those who hated the Nazis and all they stood for had a much clearer idea of what was to come than those who, in one degree or another, sympathised with them. The assumptions about Germany's intentions made by, say, Neville Chamberlain and Sir Horace Wilson, were wildly wrong and poles apart from those made by anti-Fascists of all persuasions. Nonetheless, the latter's conception of what was in the making, while right in the main, proved in the test of subsequent events also to be considerably out of focus.

The stakes are even higher now, which makes it more important than ever that the largest possible number of people should have the clearest possible idea of the processes now at work in international affairs, so that they can the better define their attitude to foreign policy questions and, if they wish, try to influence their solution.

When, after having spent the first sixteen years of my working life in the Diplomatic Service, I found myself faced with the necessity of finding a new profession, I decided, after some casting about, that what I was best qualified to do was to contribute to this much wider problem by making a continuous study, as objectively as possible, of the process of development of contemporary British foreign policy. Although Britain's capacity to determine what happens in international affairs is smaller than it was even twenty years ago, her influence for good or ill is still great and the way she exercises it still affects the lives not only of the British people, but of hundreds of millions besides. The task of attempting to produce even a slightly clearer picture of what British policy-makers are aiming at and of what factors are at work seemed, and still seems to me, eminently worth while. I have been engaged on this job for the last fifteen years, at first working on a journal concerned with international affairs and for most of the time as a member of one of the institutes of the Academy of Sciences, the Institute of World Economics and International Relations, specifically concerned with the whole subject, which is where I am still working.

The present book sums up the results of this work so far. Its particular object is to elucidate the direction in which contemporary British foreign policy has been and is moving by analysing both the attitude of those responsible for the main problems confronting them and the actual course of British diplomacy in certain key areas. A number of others have set their hand to clarifying special aspects of post-war British foreign policy and there are also one or two general accounts, but there has not been, so far as I know, an attempt to solve the particular problem dealt with here.

In order to have a hope of identifying long-term trends, one has to go back some distance in time, but not, I think, all the way back to the beginning of the post-war period.

It is already possible to distinguish two phases in international relations since the war, the dividing line falling somewhere around the mid-fifties, when a number of qualitative changes took place, setting the scene in which we now find ourselves. Among the most important of these were the attainment by the Soviet Union of nuclear parity with the United States, the re-emergence of France, West Germany, Italy and Japan as major independent factors in foreign affairs and the opening of the final stage in the dissolution of the colonial system, signalised by the failure of the Anglo-French attack on Egypt. For this reason, the book concentrates on the period since the mid-fifties, though excursions are made deeper into the past where this seems necessary. The cut-off date, 1968, is arbitrary, but where possible, I have included material relating to 1969.

The study is divided into three parts, dealing with the main groups of problems facing British diplomacy, i.e., those arising in Britain's relations with the other Western powers, with the third world and with the Communist powers. Although its basic structure is, thus, not chronological, within each part the main object has been to bring out the evolution of British policy, its nature and causes.

Partly because of the nature of the book and partly for reasons of time and space, I have not tried to cover every problem and every part of the world. I have also not ventured far into certain germane, but specialised and debatable questions, such as the economic consequences for Britain of the dissolution of the colonial empire, on which I cannot give a qualified opinion. I hope, however, that all the essential pieces in the picture are, in one form or another, present.

The work is based on documentary material, primarily the published speeches, statements, diplomatic correspondence, etc., of the Government, its members and advisers, supplemented by semi-documentary material in the shape of politicians' and officials' memoirs and those of their American and other opposite numbers and also officially authorised publications.

In the category of semi-documentary material I also include works such as Schlesinger's account of Kennedy's presidency and studies published by Anthony Nutting, Christopher Mayhew, Robert Scott, Michael Wright, Charles Johnston and other ministers and officials, written in the light of recent and direct access to official information.

As many as possible of the growing number of professional studies of various aspects of British post-war policy have been read or consulted, details of which are given in the footnotes and some of which are discussed in the text.

I should like to express my thanks to my colleagues in the Institute of World Economics and International Relations for much helpful discussion of the problems raised here. The views expressed are, however, mine only.

D. D. MACLEAN.

Moscow. September 3, 1969.

Publisher's Foreword

Since the announcement of the publication of this book has already, not surprisingly, caused comment in the press and its eventual appearance is likely to cause more, it was thought sensible to add a word of comment from the publishers. We had heard about the existence of this book in draft for many months before it proved possible for me to go to Moscow, read it, make contracts to cover its publication in the western world and return with the typescript. We have the author's word that the book is his own, that it was at no point revised or redrafted by any higher authority in the Soviet Union.

The author states in his Foreword that the subject of the book is one on which he has been engaged for the last fifteen years. The result of these years of careful observation and of publication in specialist journals is very far from being written for any *ad hoc* purpose of publicity or personal gain.

The usual practice would have been to publish first in Russia and then to submit the book to the West via the main Russian literary agency. That this practice was not adopted in this case was entirely the decision of Donald Maclean, who preferred to make his own arrangements as regards publication. The book will appear in Russian after its British and American editions have come out. Since it was written while the author was employed (as he still is) in the Academy of Sciences, Maclean declined to accept further reward by way of royalties on other earnings and has given all such earnings to a charity of his nomination, after any necessary tax deductions have been made.

As to the contents of the book the reader, whether or not he is an expert in the subject, will make up his own mind. But I think it worth adding that despite severe criticism of the leaders of the British Government in the period under review, the author is far from intending his book to be an attack on Britain, or the Government. It is a survey, not a polemic. It also illuminates Russian attitudes to Britain and the rest of the world. Despite the controversy

13

with which his name is associated the auther's purpose in publishing his book in the West is a constructive rather than a controversial one.

Robin Denniston
Hodder & Stoughton Ltd.
February 1970

PART I

POLICY TOWARDS THE OTHER WESTERN POWERS

CHAPTER ONE

New Patterns in Western Relationships

Twilight of Western Unity

In the period we are considering, the question of relations with the other Western powers has grown more and more complicated and occupied an ever-increasing place in British foreign policy as a whole.

For two main reasons, one of the results of the Second World War was temporarily to lower tension between the capitalist great powers.

In the first place, in the early post-war years, since Germany, Italy and Japan were semi-prostrate after their defeat, their capacity to pursue their own ends in international affairs was strictly limited, while the voice of France was also reduced almost to a whisper. In the late forties and early fifties, there were in effect only two great powers in the West—the United States, which emerged from the war as a super-power, in a different category from all the rest, and Britain, which, although financially dependent on Washington, was far and away the strongest of the powers of second rank. The world-wide struggle for advantage between the capitalist states was for a time fought out chiefly between these two very unequal contestants.

Secondly, the increase in the strength of the Soviet Union, the establishment of Communist régimes in Eastern Europe and the wave of pro-Communist feeling in France, Italy, Greece and continental Europe generally which followed the war, gave rise to strong centripetal tendencies in the Western world. For a time, fear of Communism dominated the diplomacy of all the main Western countries, drew them into an alliance against the Soviet Union and Communism generally, and dampened down conflicts between them.

As one of the leading Foreign Office officials of those years puts it, so far as British diplomacy was concerned, the mechanism of the balance of power in the old sense had been made inoperative by the world cleavage between capitalism and socialism. Isolation was out of the question, and separate alliances could serve no purpose. Hence the emergence of what he calls "the conception of the Western

17

community", based on American military power and embodied in NATO and other Western organisations.[1]

By the second post-war decade this situation had radically altered.

Not only France, but West Germany, Italy and Japan, having recovered economically and regained a substantial part of their freedom of action, were once more independent forces to be reckoned with in world affairs and were striving actively on every front to further their own particular interests.

At the same time, fear of Communism, with its unifying influence on Western diplomacy, had begun to weaken. For reasons discussed elsewhere, all the chief Western powers, each in its own way, began to pay more attention to normalising their relations with Communist Europe and less to conducting a holy war against it.

The change in the balance of economic strength between the powers can be seen in broad outline from the tables,[2] on this page and p. 19.

As these figures show, in 1947 the two chief Western victor powers, the United States and Britain, between them accounted for 43% of all exports of the capitalist world. Ten years later this figure had dropped to 30·1% and by 1967 had fallen further to 23·8%. The corresponding figures for the defeated powers plus France rose from 7·3% in 1947 to 20·5% in 1957 and then to 27·6% in 1967 (Table 2).

Table 1
Percentage of Industrial Production
of Capitalist World

	1948	1950	1957	1958	1961	1963	1964	1965	1966	1967
Britain	11·9	11·6	9·7	9·8	9·2	8·5	8·5	8·2	7·7	7·6
United States	55·8	54·6	48·9	46·6	44·7	44·9	44·1	44·9	46·0	45·0
West Germany	4·2	6·6	9·0	9·5	9·9	9·4	9·4	9·3	8·9	8·5
France	4·4	4·4	4·8	5·0	4·8	4·7	4·7	4·5	4·4	4·5
Italy	2·2	2·5	2·9	3·1	3·6	3·7	3·5	3·4	3·6	3·8
Japan	1·3	1·6	3·5	3·5	5·1	5·4	5·8	5·6	6·0	6·9

[1] Lord Strang. *Britain in World Affairs*. London. 1961. pp. 342–343.
[2] Unless otherwise stated, all economic statistics in this book are drawn from publications of the Institute of World Economics and International Relations, Moscow.

Table 2

Percentage of Exports of Capitalist World

	1947	1953	1957	1958	1962	1963	1964	1965	1966	1967
Britain	10·0	9·7	9·3	9·4	8·7	8·5	8·2	8·0	7·8	7·3
United States	33·0	21·3	20·8	18·7	17·5	17·3	17·3	16·5	16·6	16·5
West Germany	0·5	6·0	9·1	9·7	10·8	10·9	10·7	10·9	11·2	11·5
France	4·1	5·2	5·4	5·7	6·0	6·0	5·9	6·1	6·0	6·0
Italy	1·4	2·1	2·6	2·7	3·8	3·8	3·9	4·4	4·5	4·6
Japan	1·3	2·4	3·4	3·5	4·0	4·1	4·7	5·1	5·4	5·5

Table 3

Gold and Foreign Currency Reserves

(million dollars at year's end)

	1948	1953	1959	1961	1963	1964	1965	1966	1967
Britain	2,009	2,546	2,750	3,324	2,657	2,315	3,004	3,099	2,695
United States	24,399	22,091	19,507	17,063	15,808	15,903	14,846	14,881	14,830
West Germany	295	1,736	4,533	6,542	7,098	6,969	6,353	8,028	8,152
France	553	829	1,720	2,939	4,457	5,105	5,459	6,733	6,994
Italy	n.a.	768	2,953	3,419	3,180	3,678	4,251	4,910	5,463
Japan	n.a.	892	1,321	1,486	1,878	1,799	1,897	2,119	2,030

In 1953 the gold and foreign currency reserves of the United States were still more than five times as large as those of the defeated powers plus France. Ten years later this group's holdings exceeded those of the United States and by 1967 the latter had fallen still further behind (Table 3).

As regards shares of the industrial production of the capitalist world, although in the mid-sixties the United States (but not Britain) recovered some ground, much the same pattern can be seen. In 1948 the two powers accounted for 67·7%. Ten years later this figure had dropped to 56·4% and by 1967 to 52·6%. The corresponding figures for the defeated powers plus France were 12·1% rising to 21·1% and then to 23·7% (Table 1).

The direction of change in the military field has been the same, though the military strength of the United States has remained greater than that of all the other capitalist powers put together.

For seven years after the Second World War, the United States enjoyed a complete monopoly of nuclear weapons among the Western powers. From 1952, when the first British nuclear device was exploded, she shared this privileged position with Britain. This joint Anglo-Saxon monopoly was broken by the first French atomic test in 1960. The first British and French delivery systems became operational in 1955 and 1964 respectively.

As regards conventional forces, for a short time after the war the United States and Britain possessed the only substantial independent military forces in the Western world. The French and Italian armed forces were, however, built up fairly quickly, followed by those of West Germany, the turning point here being the Paris Agreements of 1954 removing the Western ban on German rearmament. In rough quantitive terms, the new balance reached between the six leading capitalist powers by 1967–1968 can be seen from the following figures.[1]

Table 4

	Regular Armed Forces (1968)	Trained Reservists (1968)	Defence Expenditure (mill. doll.) (1967)	Defence expenditure as percentage of GNP (1967)
United States	3,500,000	994,100	73,000	9·8
France	505,000	400,000	5,502	5·3
West Germany	456,000	750,000	6,000	4·8
Britain	427,000	170,000	5,340	5·7
Italy	365,000	600,000	1,890	2·9
Japan	250,000	30,000	1,068	·9

With the return of the ex-Axis powers and France to the arena and the weakening of the influence of anti-Communism on the foreign policy of all the Western powers, new patterns began to emerge in Western relations.

All six leading powers, and lesser powers such as Canada, Australia,

[1] Drawn from *The Military Balance 1968–1969*. The Institute for Strategic Studies. London. 1968.

Belgium, Holland, Norway, Denmark, Spain, Portugal, Greece and Turkey, remained bound together in a system of anti-Communist military alliances headed by the United States either through multilateral organisations such as NATO, SEATO, CENTO and ANZUS or through bilateral agreements with Washington or both. At the same time fissiparous tendencies appeared within the Western community so strong as to render the term itself almost meaningless.

This is not to say that antagonistic politico-military alliances of the type which preceded the First and Second World Wars have already reappeared and that events are once more moving towards armed conflict between the chief capitalist powers. Bearing in mind the entirely different world balance between capitalism and socialism, and also the nature of modern weapons, it seems unlikely that a third cataclysm of this kind will occur.

There are, nevertheless, widening rifts, the main line of division running between the United States, on one side, and the continental Western European powers, on the other, with Britain now wavering between the two. This basic pattern is overlaid by a great many other lines of alliance and conflict, but over the last ten years it has emerged more and more clearly through the tangle of intra-Western relationships.

So far, the growth of opposing groups has proceeded fastest in the economic field. From small beginnings in the first half of the fifties the European Economic Community has emerged as a powerful and increasingly autarchic bloc, which, although still much weaker than the United States in industrial strength, is already bearing down heavily on the United States (and Britain) in the world market and challenging the hegemony of the dollar (Table 5).

Table 5
(*figures for 1966*)

	Population	% of capitalist world industrial production	% of capitalist world exports	gold & foreign currency reserves (mill. doll.)
U.S.	196,000,000	45·5	16·8	14,556
EEC	181,110,000	19·3	21·9[1]	20,186

It cannot be said that this development yet has a clearly defined parallel in the politico-military field. Through NATO and a network

[1] West Germany, France and Italy, without Benelux.

of bilateral agreements with Washington, most of Western Europe still forms part of a single military system controlled by the United States.

NATO is, however, beginning to disintegrate, France having withdrawn from its military organisations and expelled its headquarters and military formations from French territory. Moreover, the general trend towards Western European separatism has given rise to a variety of projects for closer co-ordination of the foreign and military policies of the Six, some version of which is likely sooner or later to be realised.

As regards nuclear weapons, a peculiar situation has arisen over the French striking force. France having, despite American disapproval, developed its own war-heads and delivery systems, has so far refused to integrate its force into the Anglo-American system of joint targeting against Eastern Europe or to subordinate it in any way to American or NATO control. It remains at present a weapon pointing West as well as East and the nucleus of a potential Western European nuclear force fulfilling the same dual—political rather than military—function.

All in all, it is not too much to say that twilight is falling on Western unity and that, overlaying the basic conflict between the capitalist and socialist systems, new lines of battle are being drawn between the the Western powers.

The Question of Partners

In the new situation, London has had to conduct its relations with the other chief Western powers from a position of increasing weakness.

A glance back at Tables 1 and 2 will show that Britain is the only one of the leading capitalist powers whose share both of industrial production and of the capitalist world market has during the whole post-war period fallen in an almost unbroken curve. As regards gold and foreign exchange reserves, at the end of the fifties and the beginning of the sixties, as shown in Table 3, first West Germany, then Italy and then France all established and held a firm lead over Britain. Whereas by the end of the first post-war decade, all the Western European powers and Japan had achieved or were about to achieve solvency, Britain alone continued for another ten years and more to be subject to recurrent balance of payments crises, forcing her to seek a series of massive foreign loans, mainly from the United States, and culminating in the enforced devaluation of sterling in November 1967.

From the second half of the fifties, financial weakness imposed stricter limits on military expenditure than those observed by other powers. As a result, while Britain retained a certain lead over France in the field of nuclear weapons, her advantage is not so great as appears at first sight. In 1960, owing to acute financial difficulties, the future development of the British striking force became dependent on American delivery systems, while France, despite the immense cost, has so far continued to rely on her own resources. As regards conventional forces, as shown in Table 4, in terms of size both France and West Germany have overtaken Britain. Throughout the period under review, owing to its financial weakness, London has found itself obliged to plead with Bonn to pay at least part of the foreign exchange costs of British forces stationed in West Germany.

The decline in Britain's weight among the Western powers has forced British diplomacy on to the defensive in its dealings with the United States, France, West Germany and with the Six as a group. It has also rendered peculiarly intractable what seems to me to have been the central question in intra-Western relations facing London during the period we are considering, namely the question of partners or, more precisely, the choice between a transatlantic and a cross-Channel orientation. Twenty years ago this problem was a mere speck on the horizon. Today it casts its shadow over every aspect of British foreign policy.

Shortly after the Second World War Churchill proclaimed the comfortable theory, usually known as the "three circles" theory, that Britain was assured of a unique influence in international affairs owing to her triple role as main partner of the United States, chief Western European power and leader of the Commonwealth, the assumption being that all three roles could be harmoniously combined.[1]

At the time, and during the first post-war decade, the idea had something in it, since Britain was then indeed the leader among the Western European powers and this pre-eminence was indeed successfully combined with maintenance of a special relationship with the United States and with the preservation of the imperial preference system, the sterling area and other mechanisms assuring Britain a privileged position in the Commonwealth.

But with the increasing weight of France and West Germany in international affairs and particularly with the establishment and consolidation of the European Economic Community, it became

[1] Speech at the Annual Conference of the Conservative Party. October 9, 1948. Winston S. Churchill. Speeches 1947 and 1948. *Europe Unite*, London. 1950. pp. 417–418.

more and more apparent that London was no longer strong enough to ride three horses at once and had to decide which of them was likely to carry it farthest.

The decision to give priority to London's Western European interests over the preservation of special trading and financial links with the Commonwealth was taken by the Macmillan Government in the early sixties. As recalled in more detail below, the British delegation at the Brussels negotiations in 1961–62 found itself forced to offer the liquidation of imperial preference and a major reduction in Britain's trade with the Commonwealth as part of the entrance fee to the EEC.

But the question of priority as between Western Europe and the United States remained unresolved and, indeed, unacknowledged, since for most of the period under review, successive Governments behaved as if there were no incompatibility between preserving the Anglo-American special relationship and securing entry to the Common Market.

Thus, Macmillan and his colleagues, when they prolonged the Anglo-American nuclear partnership under the terms of the Nassau Agreement of December 1962 apparently did not realise that by so doing they were driving the last nail into the coffin of their own project of joining the Six.

Four years later, at the preliminary stage of London's second attempt to achieve this object, the Labour Foreign Secretary (George Brown), when challenged on the point, declared that the Government was resolutely opposed to the view that if Britain joined the EEC, she must change her relationship with the United States.[1]

It is true that the Government in the following year reversed its position, Lord Chalfont, the minister in charge of the proposed negotiations with the EEC, declaring that in future there must be less and less of a special relationship between the United States and Britain and more and more of a relationship between the United States and Western Europe of which Britain was going to be a member.[2] This statement was not, however, accompanied by concrete actions to give it substance and seems to have been no more than a hasty tactical move designed to avert the then already imminent second French veto.

Although Conservative and Labour Governments alike behaved as if there were no dilemma, there was nevertheless a distinct

[1] *Hansard.* November 16, 1966. Col. 455.
[2] Statement on television by Lord Chalfont on October 9, 1967. *The Times*, October 10, 1967.

evolution of opinion in policy-making circles away from the idea
that the Anglo-American special relationship was forever sacrosanct
and towards the idea that Britain's fate might after all be bound up
first and foremost with the recapture of a leading position in Western
Europe through membership of the Common Market. The turning
point here was the failure of the first British application to join the
EEC, which, by the terms in which the French Government rejected
the application,[1] brought the dilemma fully to the surface and made
it easily visible to those who were willing to see.

This process of evolution can perhaps best be illustrated by the
gradual shift in the interpretation given in official and semi-official
quarters to the doctrine of interdependence, which during the last
decade and more has been used by all leading foreign affairs
practitioners and theoreticians as an umbrella to shelter various
prescriptions for settling the increasingly acute problem of Britain's
relations with the other Western powers.

The doctrine of interdependence was jointly proclaimed by
Eisenhower and Macmillan in Washington in their Declaration of
Common Purpose of October 25, 1957. "The concept of national
self-sufficiency is now out of date," it said. "The countries of the free
world are now interdependent, and only in genuine partnership, by
combining their resources and sharing tasks in many fields, can
progress and safety be found."[2]

As can be seen from the use of the phrase "countries of the free
world" and the reference to "safety", in form the new doctrine
embraced all the members of the anti-Communist alliance. In
substance, however, it was intended to explain and justify a new
stage in the Anglo-American partnership.

The Declaration went on to make clear that, whatever other
powers might decide to do, the President and the Prime Minister had
resolved to put interdependence into practice on a bilateral basis.
"For our part," they said, "we have agreed that our two countries
will henceforth act in accordance with this principle." Concretely,
Eisenhower promised in the Declaration to secure an amendment of
the U.S. Atomic Energy Act, permitting the restoration of Anglo-
American co-operation over nuclear weapons.

Thus at this stage the doctrine had a strong transatlantic military

[1] Particularly de Gaulle's statement at his press conference on January 14, 1963, that if
Britain were admitted, the cohesion of the EEC would be destroyed and "it would
ultimately appear as a colossal Atlantic Community dependent on and directed by
America, which would soon swallow up the European Community".

[2] *Documents on International Affairs, 1957.* Royal Institute of International Affairs. London.
1960. pp. 700–703. Future references to this series will be indicated by the word *Documents*
and the appropriate year.

bias and, in London's eyes, had no particular relevance to the
problem of Britain's relations, political, economic or military, with
Western Europe.

Four years later, while still using it primarily for its original
purpose, the Government was giving the conception of interdependence a rather wider interpretation.

In a disquisition on the subject in 1961, Douglas-Home, then
Foreign Secretary, gave first place to military interdependence in
general and its Anglo-American version in particular. "Interdependence between Britain and the United States," he wrote, "is
the kernel of the defence of the free world. There is the industrial
potential and the wealth and the manpower which alone can match
and surpass the resources of the Communists."

But since preparations were by then afoot for the first attempt to
join the Common Market, the necessity for interdependence between
Britain and Western Europe (and the Commonwealth) was also given
some recognition. "In the context of our conscious search for interdependence," said Home, "must also be counted our efforts to come
closer to Europe. Britain in order to live must go where the markets
are best . . . There is no greater British and Commonwealth interest
than the economic, political and military cohesion of the
Continent."[1]

After the collapse of the Brussels negotiations, a primarily cross-
Channel interpretation began to make serious headway.

Thus, Kenneth Younger, Director of the Royal Institute of
International Affairs and a former Minister at the Foreign Office,
in a study of the courses open to British diplomacy after the Brussels
débâcle, published in 1964, suggested that of the various forms of
interdependence, the form which Britain must choose might well be
integration with Western Europe. He developed the idea that in the
modern world there are industrial and scientific fields, civil as well as
military, in which no power the size of Britain can hope any longer to
compete with larger rivals and that her Western European neighbours are her best partners.[2]

Younger offered up a prayer that events will not develop in such
a way as to compel Britain to choose between Western Europe and
the United States. On the other hand, he specifically demanded the
abandonment of the original *raison d'être* of the doctrine of interdependence, namely the special bilateral relationship between
Britain and the United States in the field of nuclear weapons, and the

[1] The Earl of Home. *Great Britain's Foreign Policy*. London. 1961. pp 8–9.
[2] Kenneth Younger. *Changing Perspectives in British Foreign Policy*. London. 1964. p. 13.

substitution for it of a similar arrangement between Britain and her European neighbours. "If she makes the other choice, of continuing to claim a special relationship with the United States, not shared by others, for the purpose of maintaining a measure of independence for her own national nuclear forces," he wrote, "she must expect to pay the price of having no influence upon the policies of Europe."[1]

In 1965, the Government, in the person of the Prime Minister, in advancing the thesis that the future of NATO depended on "wholehearted acceptance of the fact of interdependence", far from stressing Anglo-American versions thereof, accused U.S. arms manufacturers of failing to observe its principles and of pursuing their own selfish advantage to the detriment of Britain and the rest of Western Europe. Trust and interdependence between the Governments of Europe and those of North America are one thing, Wilson said, but subordination to individual national industries quite another.[2]

We may also recall here that the project for a Western European technological community launched by the Government towards the end of 1967 not only made no provision for U.S. participation, but contained clearly audible anti-American overtones. The widening technological lead of the U.S. over Western Europe was advanced as a prime reason for new and far-reaching forms of technological co-operation between Britain and the continental powers leading to the creation of a European-scale industry capable of competing on equal terms with American industry. Echoing one of de Gaulle's favourite themes, Wilson declared that "there would be no future for the countries of Europe, including Britain, if American business and industry were allowed to dominate their growth industries and determine the pace and direction of Europe's industrial advance".[3]

By the end of the period under review, the Government was, to all appearances, giving a clear priority to partnership with the other Western European powers over partnership with the United States. Thus, at the beginning of 1969, the Chancellor of the Exchequer declared that he believed in close Anglo-American ties, but that they should be on a basis of an approach to equality. Between Western Europe as a whole and the United States this could exist. "But between any individual country — Britain or any other — and

---

[1] *Ibid.* pp. 103–104, 109–110.
[2] Speech to the London meeting of the North Atlantic Council on May 11, 1965. *Commonwealth Survey.* May 25, 1965.
[3] Speech at the Guildhall on November 13, 1967. *Survey of British and Commonwealth Affairs.* November 24, 1967.

the United States it is not possible." It was now generally accepted, he continued, that Britain's future role lay in association with other European states of comparable power and status.[1]

If, however, one looks at policy as it is actually being conducted, it can be seen that transatlantic and cross-Channel tendencies within it are still in deep conflict, taking the form chiefly of conflict between the establishment's politico-economic aims centred on the EEC and its politico-military aims centred on NATO and with it the American alliance.

NATO Dilemma

As already mentioned, the strains now developing in the relations between the Western powers have produced a major fissure in the central Western alliance, NATO, and posed in an acute form the question of the future politico-military relationship between the United States, on one side, and the Western European powers, including Britain, on the other.

Following a whole series of preliminary moves stretching back to 1958, the French Government in February 1966 announced its decision to withdraw from the military organisation of the alliance and to request the other members, meaning chiefly the United States, to remove their troops and bases from French territory and also NATO's European military headquarters.

By 1967, with certain relatively minor exceptions, all French forces had been withdrawn from NATO command and all French personnel from NATO's military staffs, American forces and bases had been transferred mainly to West Germany, Britain and the United States, and NATO headquarters had been moved to Belgium together with the NATO Council, i.e., its political staff. French troops remained in West Germany, but no longer as an arm of the alliance, but in virtue of a separate bilateral agreement between France and the Federal Republic.

Since France did not denounce the North Atlantic Treaty itself, the obligation upon her and upon the United States to come to each other's aid in the event of aggression remained in force. The avowed object of her policy was, however, to substitute a Western European military system controlled by the Western European powers for the existing Atlantic military system controlled by the United States. Implicitly, and later explicitly, the French governing élite contem-

---

[1] Speech to the Consultative Assembly of the Council of Europe on January 29, 1969. *Ibid.* February 28, 1969.

plated British participation in the proposed Western European system if London was prepared to dissolve its military partnership with Washington inside and outside NATO. In his confidential approach to Ambassador Soames in February 1969, de Gaulle in effect proposed a deal under which Britain would agree to come into an exclusively Western European politico-military grouping and to the dissolution of the military organisation of NATO in exchange for admission to a substantially revised European Economic Community.[1]

The French withdrawal from the military organisation of NATO, and its implied invitation to the other European members to do the same, struck a heavy blow at the basic structure of European security nurtured with such care by every post-war government from Attlee's to Wilson's and at the same time made more complicated than ever the problem of reconciling partnership with the United States with partnership with France and the continental powers.

As suggested in more detail in Chapter 3 of this book, European security as viewed by those in authority contains within it two separate, though inter-connected, elements, one dominant—security against the spread of Communism, and one subordinate—security against too great an increase in the power and freedom of action of capitalist Germany. They regard American military power as essential for maintaining European security in both its meanings, especially the first, and NATO as the best mechanism through which that power can be applied for this double purpose.

By the time of the 1966–1967 crisis, the view in high quarters of the way in which NATO should fulfil its chief, anti-Communist, function was a great deal more moderate than the highly belligerent doctrine which held the field when the North Atlantic Treaty was signed in 1949. But there was, and still is, no disposition to consider that there is no longer any need for this function as such. On the contrary the Government insisted, and insists, on NATO's preservation as an essential counter-weight to Soviet military power in Europe.

The same applies to NATO's other function, that of holding West Germany in a lover's, but also a wrestler's embrace. The thoughts now current on the subject in establishment circles can be seen from a particularly frank discussion of the role of the British Army of the Rhine (BAOR) by the military correspondent of *The Times*, who was presumably expressing not only his own personal ideas.

Whatever NATO might decide about the nature of the Soviet

---

[1] For the Foreign Secretary's account of this proposal, and of his rejection of it, see *Hansard*, February 24, 1969. Cols. 1088–1089.

threat, he wrote in the spring of 1968, Britain had an interest in future developments in West and East Germany, which transcended the current pre-occupation with the Communists. BAOR provided an instrument with which to maintain that interest. The presence of non-German troops in the Federal Republic was as relevant to the German as to the Russian threat. BAOR had to be able "in the last resort to restrain the Germans from any unconsidered move eastward".[1]

Both functions of NATO appear plainly in a more measured pronouncement by one of the most influential of the recent generation of British military leaders, General Hackett, written in his capacity of commander of the Northern Army Group of NATO and designed to rally British public opinion behind NATO and to influence it in favour of maintaining NATO's military strength, particularly that of the BAOR.

Firstly, arguing that, with the present instability in Central and Eastern Europe, a military emergency might develop, the General declared that "reduction of Western forces to a very low level might offer the USSR temptations to military adventure". The West had to maintain a sufficient force "to make sure the Soviet forces, even though superior in strength to our own, would not be able to guide events in the sole interests of the USSR". Secondly, he urged that it was NATO's task to "ensure that the legitimate defensive requirements of the Federal Republic of Germany are met in a military system which the Germans themselves do not dominate".[2]

In its practical diplomacy the Government, with the support of the Conservative opposition, sprang to the defence of NATO as soon as the French decision of 1966 became known. The Foreign Secretary (George Brown) immediately denounced the French move as an extremely serious blow directed "at that integrated system of defence upon which the security of the West and the freedom of mankind depends".[3] A few days later a Government statement appeared declaring that members of NATO, such as Britain, who believed in the need for an integrated defence organisation as a deterrent to aggression, were determined to ensure NATO's continued existence.[4]

In a major statement of future military policy in July 1967, the Government declared that it was "essential to maintain both the military efficiency and the political solidarity of NATO" and that for

[1] *The Times.* April 1 and 3, 1968.
[2] Letter in *The Times* of February 6, 1968.
[3] Speech at Glasgow on March 14, 1966. *Commonwealth Survey,* April 1, 1966.
[4] Published on March 18, 1966. *Ibid.*

this purpose Britain must continue to make a substantial contribution to NATO's forces.[1]

In May 1968 a measure was announced designed to reinforce NATO and Britain's influence within it. In addition to the 50,000 men of the BAOR and the RAF units stationed in West Germany and to the air, naval and army units in Britain already assigned to NATO, the Government offered to place under NATO command two new forces, drawn from those returning from East of Suez – a mobile task force of 20,000 men, with its own air transport, to be stationed in Britain, and an amphibious force to be stationed in European waters.[2]

While the proposed base or bases for the latter force were not named, it was given to be understood that they would be in the Mediterranean on NATO's southern flank, the idea being to provide an extra counter-force to Soviet naval forces in the Eastern Mediterranean.

This determination to keep NATO in being, and in particular to avoid being separated from the United States (and Canada) on matters touching European security, was also reflected fairly clearly in London's response to proposals from the Soviet Union and other states of Eastern Europe for improving relations between the capitalist and socialist halves of the continent.

When in July 1966 the parties to the Warsaw Pact, at their Bucharest meeting, proposed the liquidation of both the Warsaw and the North Atlantic Pacts, the Government rejected the suggestion outright. Referring directly to this proposal, the Foreign Secretary declared that, if national armies were not to be abolished, "it does not make either military or political sense to abolish the alliances" and that if in present-day Europe the military sides of the two alliances were to be dismantled, leaving only separate and independent national armies, "this would be more likely to create dangers than to remove them". He accepted in principle the suggestion in the Bucharest Declaration that an East-West conference on European security should be held, but insisted that the United States and Canada must participate.[3]

The latter point was made again, though more discreetly, by the Prime Minister the following year. When Kosygin, the Soviet Prime Minister, visited Wilson in London in February 1967, they agreed,

---

[1] *Supplementary Statement on Defence*. Command 3357. July 18, 1967.
[2] Statement by the Minister of Defence at a press conference in Brussels on May 10, 1968. *Survey of British and Commonwealth Affairs*. May 24, 1968.
[3] Speech by George Brown on November 21, 1966. *Commonwealth Survey*. December 23, 1966.

according to the communiqué, that a conference on European
security would be valuable and that all the countries of Europe
should take part. But in a statement to Parliament a few days later,
Wilson, clearly referring to U.S. participation, underlined the
Government's concern to see that "all countries which have a stake
in European security" should be enabled to play a full part.[1]

The Conservative leadership showed itself to be no less wary than
the Government of any idea that the United States should withdraw
from Europe. "What is essential," said Edward Heath in March
1968, "is that the United States presence remains in Europe.
Nothing must be done to damage that."[2]

Thus, in the fluid situation created by the French withdrawal
from the NATO military organisation, the policy-makers decided
that the country's best interest lay in not only preserving, but
strengthening NATO and increasing the British role within it. But
since they continued to give a high priority to obtaining membership
of the EEC, and since this could not be achieved without simultaneously establishing a closer politico-military relationship with
France and its other members, this decision, far from solving the
quandary in which British diplomacy found itself, deepened it.

Denis Healey, in announcing the offer to assign two new and
substantial task forces to NATO, said it would strengthen support in Europe for close co-operation between the EEC and Britain
in the face of the second French veto on the British application
for membership. This was no doubt true as far as it went, but the
calculation was one of a chess-player looking at only part of the
board and not at the disposition of the main pieces. By committing
more and more of its forces to NATO, the Government gained
extra leverage in Rome, Brussels, The Hague and with the Atlanti-
cists, though not the Gaullists, in Bonn. But it was also drifting
further along a collision course with Paris, upon whose attitude the
success or failure of all British attempts to gain entry into the
Common Market mainly depended.

Present Tactics

By the end of the period under review, there had emerged in the
upper echelons of the establishment three main schools of thought on
the question of how this contradiction can best be solved.

The majority view, reflected in official policy, favours an attempt

[1] *Hansard*. February 13, 1967. Col. 112.
[2] *The Times*. March 6, 1968.

to get out of the impasse by a structural change in NATO, leading to the formation within it of a European grouping, headed by Britain. Under this scheme of things, Britain, by going into the European Economic Community, would obtain a dominant influence over the process of Western European economic integration and the building of such political superstructure as that process makes necessary. At the same time, the drive towards Western European politico-military autarchy, led 'by France, would be blunted and diverted by the creation of a European sub-division of NATO, which would itself remain dominated by the United States. By this two-pronged operation Britain would acquire the leadership of Western Europe in the economic, military and political fields, while ensuring the continued presence of American military power.

When the Minister of Defence, towards the end of 1968, set out the nature and purpose of what is sometimes called "a European identity" within the Atlantic alliance, he said that the military security of Western Europe would depend for the foreseeable future on America's commitment to collective defence through NATO and that anything which might weaken that commitment would be disastrous. But closer co-operation between the West European powers within NATO would not weaken their links with the United States and would be welcomed in Washington. He asserted Britain's right to lead the proposed new grouping on the ground that she was the only European member of NATO with "responsibilities by land, sea and air on every part of the European front—in Scandinavia and in the Mediterranean as well as in Central Europe".

In outlining the fields in which the new grouping should operate, Healey cited the joint study then being made by the British and West German Governments, under the auspices of the NATO Nuclear Planning Group, of certain aspects of NATO's nuclear policy. He also referred to the negotiations then in progress between the British, West German, Italian, Dutch and Belgian Governments regarding the joint production of a new advanced combat aircraft for use by all five countries in the late seventies[1] which might, he said, lay the foundation for a general Western European approach to the problems of arms production as a whole. Looking further ahead, he spoke of closer co-operation among the European members of NATO in the day-to-day organisation and training of their forces, in the procurement of defence equipment, and in logistics.

Finally Healey defined two major questions on which a European

---

[1] These negotiations led to an Anglo-West German-Italian Agreement in May 1969 to proceed with the project on a tripartite basis. *Hansard.* May 14, 1969. Cols. 1411–1417.

grouping within NATO should express a common, collective point of view to the United States—first, the scale and nature of America's role in NATO in the seventies in the light of internal pressures on the U.S. Administration to diminish that role, and secondly, American policy in any negotiations with the Soviet Union in stopping the nuclear arms race between the two super-powers, regarding which the Western European countries "will have a vital common concern to ensure that their views and interests are not overlooked".[1] In a later speech, the same speaker went further, declaring that closer co-operation between the European members of NATO was "the only way in which Europe can play its necessary role in the dialogue with the United States and between the United States and Russia".[2]

The two minority schools of thought are not opposed in principle to this line of action, but both are inclined to regard it as unrealisable and for the same basic reason, namely, that in the light of ten years' experience of French policy, it is unlikely that France can be brought to admit Britain to the EEC unless Britain is prepared to swing over to a predominantly European orientation in her military as well as her economic policy. The solutions proposed by the two schools are, however, diametrically opposed.

Those who in this context may be called the Europeans recommend a major change in nuclear policy involving a switch from the present Anglo-American partnership to a new Anglo-French partnership, with which the other members of the Six, including West Germany, would be associated. The most authoritative advocates of this move are the leaders of the Conservative Party.

In May 1967, in connection with the Government's decision to make a second attempt to join the EEC, Edward Heath said that it should be possible for the British and French striking forces "to be held in trust for Europe" and that this need not run counter to the proposed treaty on non-proliferation since, as he understood it, the latter "would enable a united Europe to have its own nuclear force". Pressed to explain himself more clearly, he urged that the two nuclear powers in an enlarged EEC, Britain and France, should agree to form a committee within the framework of the EEC, similar to the McNamara Committee in NATO, in which the other members could deal with nuclear matters. "If this is done in NATO," he said, "I see no objection to its being done in the Community."[3]

When the second attempt to gain entry to the EEC had broken

[1] Speech to the British Atlantic Committee on November 6, 1968. *Survey of British and Commonwealth Affairs.* January 3, 1969.
[2] Speech to the European Atlantic Group on April 2, 1969. *Ibid.* May 9, 1969.
[3] *Hansard.* May 9, 1967. Col. 1299.

down in the face of another French veto, Heath reverted to this proposal, suggesting that if it had been adopted, this further French rebuff might have been avoided. The Government, he said, "should have been prepared to discuss an Anglo-French nuclear arrangement . . . and to discuss it with the United States in the context of the European Economic Community". To this he received from the Government spokesman the obvious answer that his plan ran counter to the Conservative's Party's own policy of support for NATO. "France," said the Minister of Defence, "is not prepared to be part of NATO, least of all in the nuclear field. It is clearly not possible to conceive of integrating nuclear forces with France so long as she holds her present views."[1]

Those who in this context may be called the Americans advocate switching the main emphasis in foreign economic policy away from the attempt to gain entry to the Common Market and towards the establishment of a North Atlantic Free Trade Area, consisting in the first place of the United States, Canada, Britain and the other members of EFTA. Under this plan of action, the present contradiction between politico-economic and politico-military aims would supposedly be solved not by Europeanising Britain's military policy, but by Americanising her economic policy.

In December 1966 a rather low horse-power group was set up, known as the Atlantic Trade Study to examine and popularise this idea. Apart from some well-known economists such as James Meade and Roy Harrod, its Committee consisted mainly of second-flight former ambassadors and representatives of financial and industrial interests, such as the Chartered Bank, the Bank of London and South America and the Bowater Paper Corporation, which, owing to the particular character of their business, had long been sceptical about the consequences to their affairs of British membership of the Common Market. The first study sponsored by the group was published in the autumn of 1967.[2]

But in the spring of 1968, after the second French veto, the idea of a North Atlantic Free Trade Area received more powerful support, expressed, for example, in a letter to *The Times* signed by Lords Sherfield, Caccia, Watkinson and Boyd, all four key establishment figures.[3] Some support was also forthcoming from both the left and right wings of the Labour Party. Frank Cousins, then Secretary of the Transport and General Workers' Union, signed the

---

[1] *Hansard.* March 5, 1968. Cols. 235–253.
[2] The Free Trade Area Option. *Opportunity for Britain.* London. 1967.
[3] *The Times.* April 30, 1968.

letter of the four lords. The project figures prominently in the proposals put forward by Douglas Jay, until 1967 President of the Board of Trade and, like Cousins, a consistent opponent of British membership of the EEC.[1]

The attainability or unattainability of the aims which the Government has set itself and the course which it adopts in the seventies depend on a whole complex of factors entering into Anglo-American and Anglo-continental Western European relations discussed in the next two chapters.

[1] Douglas Jay. *After the Common Market*. London. 1968. pp. 111–126.

CHAPTER TWO

Anglo-American Relations

The Special Relationship

In their policy towards the other Western powers, successive governments have so far given first place to ensuring the closest possible politico-military understanding with the United States. In order to steer its much stronger partner in the direction in which it wanted it to go, British diplomacy has striven for the maximum degree of consultation at all levels and covering all branches of the British and American state machines, political, military and economic, concerned directly or indirectly with international affairs.

Washington, though attaching a far lower priority to maintaining a close understanding with London, has on the whole also seen advantage in preserving a more intensive system of consultation and co-operation with Britain than with any other Western power.

This unwritten bilateral understanding between the two powers, generally known as the special relationship,[1] operating outside the network of Western multilateral alliances and organizations, has played a much bigger part in British foreign policy than all such alliances and organisations put together.

The existence of a special relationship and its far-reaching influence on British foreign policy is recognised by almost all serious students of Anglo-American relations. But there is a wide diversity of view, and indeed some confusion, about its nature and history.

The majority of British specialists make no clear distinction between Anglo-American relations in recent decades and Anglo-American relations from the founding of the American Republic and declare or imply that the special relationship has always existed.

An extreme case of this may be found in the work of H. C. Allen,

---

[1] The term acquired general currency after Churchill's Fulton speech in 1946, when he urged the continuation of "a special relationship between the British Commonwealth and Empire and the United States".

Professor of American History at London University, who regards the whole course of Anglo-American relations since the eighteenth century as a "ripening of friendship", a "persistent, even steady, progress from mistrust to cordiality".[1]

Another, and considerably more hard-headed and perceptive, student of these matters, having also suggested that the special relationship can be traced back to the battle of Yorktown, asserts that "at least since World War I, British governments have given the highest priority to establishing and maintaining close understanding with the U.S.A.". He goes on to declare that even in the heyday of American inter-war isolationism, there existed between London and Washington at most levels of government, political and bureaucratic, "a freer traffic of information and consultation than regularly obtained with any other extra-Commonwealth capital".[2]

A third and no less competent expert fixes on 1940 as the beginning of the period in which the United States has played a peculiarly important part in Britain's destiny. But she also traces what she calls the "unavowed alliance" back to the distant past, in this case the promulgation of the Monroe Doctrine in 1823.[3]

An exception is to be found in the study of Anglo-American relations prepared jointly at the beginning of the fifties by the two principal semi-official British and American bodies dealing with foreign relations.

This work assumes as a major premise that intimate co-operation in foreign policy between Britain and the United States covering the whole world and continuing over a considerable period of time is a new development. It notes that during the Second World War the two powers achieved an intimacy of co-operation never before realised or even approached, and regards their post-war relationship, when "to each the other is its most important single ally", as a continuation, at a lower level of intensity, of their war-time collaboration.[4]

To me it seems that this last approach is right and that the "special relationship" in the generally accepted sense of an unwritten bilateral politico-military alliance is a relatively new and clearly defined historical phenomenon, beginning in 1940, evolving through various stages and now possibly approaching its end.

During the first forty years of this century, if Britain can be said to

[1] H. C. Allen. *The Anglo-American Relationship Since 1783*. London. 1959. p. 27.
[2] H. G. Nicholas. *Britain and the United States*. London. 1963. pp. 23–24.
[3] Coral Bell. *The Debatable Alliance*. London. 1964. pp. 1–13.
[4] *Britain and the United States*. Council on Foreign Relations, New York and the Royal Institute of International Affairs. London. 1953. pp. vii and 7.

have had a special relationship with any great power, it was with France and not the United States.

France was Britain's partner in the Entente Cordiale of 1904 and her chief ally throughout the First World War. In the inter-war period, over almost every important international problem, including the most vital of all—what to do about Nazi Germany—British diplomacy was far more concerned with concerting its policy with the French than with the American Government.

Contrary to the above-quoted opinion, "the traffic of information and consultation" between London and Paris was then consistently heavier than between London and Washington. In the opening stage of the Second World War France and not the United States was once more Britain's chief ally.

In the critical years leading up to the Second World War British ministers, while acting in the closest partnership with their French colleagues, not only did not concert their foreign policy with Washington, but deliberately avoided a situation in which they would be obliged to do so. When in 1938 the Roosevelt Administration went out of its way to draw the Chamberlain Government into confidential, high-level consultation on the international situation, the latter, far from welcoming the opportunity, rejected it.

This episode is sometimes treated as if it were due mainly to a quirk in the character of the then British Prime Minister, to "a clash of temperaments and philosophies".[1] But, while the handling of Roosevelt's approach certainly owed something to Neville Chamberlain's peculiar pig-headedness, the relatively small importance then attached to foreign policy consultations with the American as compared with the French, or, for that matter the German or Italian, Governments was entirely consistent with the long-established priorities of British diplomacy.

The turning point came in the spring and early summer of 1940 with the German conquest of France, Belgium, Holland, Norway and Denmark and Italy's entry into the war on Germany's side. These events brought about the collapse of the British system of Western European alliances, compelled London to look to the United States for salvation, and brought to power the men—Churchill, Eden and others—who had already perceived more clearly than Chamberlain and his friends the fundamental importance of the American factor in the struggle with Germany.

These same events simultaneously brought the American policy-makers sharply up against the fact that, if the United States was to

[1] Nicholas. *op. cit.* p. 26.

avoid confrontation with a hostile combination of almost the whole
of the rest of the capitalist world, the country must move from a
policy of neutrality to one of alliance with Britain.

Out of the resulting reorientation of British and American
diplomacy grew the special relationship. Since this moment in 1940
it has, it seems to me, gone through three distinct phases.

In the first phase, from 1940 to 1945, the special relationship was
directed primarily towards the defeat of the Axis powers and was
essentially the product of the extreme exacerbation of antagonisms
within the capitalist world itself.

In this period the degree of co-operation between the two countries
reached its highest level. There were Anglo-American conflicts of
all kinds throughout the war period, but the pooling of military,
economic and financial resources and the co-ordination of policy was
carried to a point which has never been even approximately equalled
since.

A major part of the armed forces of the two countries were subordinated to a joint command in the field and at general staff level,
the development of the atomic bomb was conducted as a joint
operation, the allocation of munitions, food, shipping, and raw
materials was to a substantial extent determined by combined
boards, under Lend-Lease the United States took over most of
Britain's dollar expenditures and, at the top, all-important questions
affecting the partners were decided in the course of direct and continuous discussion between Roosevelt, Churchill and their closest
advisers.

In the second phase, coinciding with the first post-war decade,
anti-Communism became the main feature of the special relationship and the establishment of positions of strength against the Soviet
Union its main objective. It thus reflected the particularly acute tension between the Soviet Union and the Western powers characteristic
of international relations in that period.

With the end of the Second World War, on U.S. initiative, many
of the war-time forms of the special relationship came to an end,
among them Lend-Lease, the combined Anglo-American Boards
and military staffs, and Anglo-American co-operation in the manufacture of nuclear weapons. But the relationship itself survived as one
of the instruments of the anti-Communist policy of the two Governments, above all in Europe.

Britain became the main partner of the United States in the latter's
efforts, through the Marshall Plan, to put capitalism in Western
Europe back on its feet. U.S. nuclear bases were set up in Britain

directed against the Soviet Union. Washington and London together played the main role in the establishment and development of NATO, in the restoration and rearming of West Germany, in the suppression of the left-wing in Greece, and in the imposition of trade embargoes against the socialist states.

Even though the special relationship continued to exist in this period, it showed a marked tendency to grow weaker.

With the defeat of the Axis powers, the original motive force of the Anglo-American alliance disappeared. Anglo-American conflict became particularly sharp. While united in their efforts to stem the tide of Socialism, the two powers were at the same time engaged in a bitter struggle with each other — over tariffs, over atomic weapons, over the future of Palestine, over Iranian oil, over policy towards Egypt. The two Governments adopted different tactics towards the new Communist régime in China. Although they were allies in the Korean war, there was sharp conflict between them regarding its scope. An open political quarrel broke out between them over the question of Indo-China in 1954. Washington and London pursued opposing policies towards Western European economic and military integration.[1]

In its third phase, running from the mid-fifties to the mid-sixties, the special relationship retained its anti-Communist core, but underwent a further evolution under the influence of major changes in world affairs. This phase is discussed in detail in this book. In general the two powers drew closer together on all the main foreign policy fronts. But it seems possible that a fourth phase is about to begin, or may already have begun, in which this tendency will be reversed.

If the foregoing analysis is correct, the chief factors bringing the special relationship into existence, keeping it in being for a quarter of a century and determining changes in its aims, scope and intensity have been external. It is not the result of internal processes carrying the two countries towards some kind of permanent organic fusion. On the contrary, like other capitalist great-power alliances of the past, it has been basically a response to outside pressures — from the Axis powers, from the world Communist movement, from the independence movements in the colonial world and, more recently, again from the continental Western European powers. Nevertheless, specific internal factors — economic, cultural and political — have been of considerable importance in holding it together.

There is no parallel in the Anglo-American special relationship

---

[1] For a full analysis of Anglo-American conflicts in this period, see I. M. Lemin. *Anglo-American Contradictions after the Second World War*. Moscow. 1955.

with the process of economic integration which has taken place in continental Western Europe since the war, nor with the long-term tendency towards the formation of a single U.S.-Canadian market in North America. On the other hand, the degree of inter-penetration of the British and American economies is substantial.

U.S. direct investment in Britain by 1965 totalled $5,119,000,000, which was just over a tenth of all U.S. direct foreign investment and the largest in any one country except Canada. This total was a good deal larger than that for U.S. investment in either West Germany or France, but rather less than that for the EEC as a whole ($6,254,000,000).[1]

There are no comparable figures for British direct investment in the U.S., but official estimates of earnings suggest that, though three or four times smaller than U.S. investment in Britain, they also make up about a tenth of the country's total direct investment abroad. In 1964 earnings on direct British investments in the United States amounted to £46,200,000, which was about 12% of earnings from all such investments abroad and more than earnings from any other one country except the South African Republic and Australia. This figure is more than three times that for earnings on British direct investments in the EEC countries (£12,900,000). These British earnings from the U.S. were heavily outweighed by U.S. earnings on U.S. investment in Britain, which in the same year totalled £153,500,000.[2]

As for foreign trade, the importance to Britain of the U.S. market has been rising fairly sharply. In 1955 the U.S. took 7% of all British exports and in 1966, 12½%. This latter figure represents less than a third of the share taken by Western Europe, but was the highest percentage for any one country.

The British market is considerably less important to the U.S., taking only 5·7% of all U.S. exports in 1966, as compared with 20% taken by Canada and 7·8% by Japan. Nevertheless, Britain was in that year the biggest single market for U.S. exports in Europe, though closely followed by West Germany.

In the field of government finance, there has been a peculiarly close and, owing to the enormous difference in the economic strength of the two countries, a peculiarly unequal, partnership throughout the whole course of the special relationship.

During the war period, as we have recalled, the U.S. carried a

---

[1] *Survey of Current Business.* U.S. Department of Commerce. September 1966.
[2] *Board of Trade Journal.* June 10, 1966. The figures for British earnings exclude oil, and those for U.S. earnings, oil and insurance.

major part of Britain's overseas expenditures through the mechanism of Lend-Lease. In the early post-war years Britain's deficit was mainly financed first by the American Loan of 1946 and then under the Marshall Plan. Thereafter, with each successive balance of payments crisis and accompanying threat to the stability of the pound, massive credits were organised and provided mainly by the U.S. financial authorities.

More than the two-way export of capital, more than a relatively high level of trade, this debtor-creditor relationship has played a major part in the Anglo-American alliance as a whole.

Not only has it been used by the U.S. oligarchy to squeeze major concessions out of London on particular issues, as in the Anglo-American Loan Agreement of 1946, but it has given every British Government since the war an extra and very tangible reason for being wary of any course in international affairs running directly counter to that of the U.S.

It is characteristic of this situation that on the most notable occasion when this risk was run, namely in the attack on Egypt in 1956, Washington's threat of withholding financial aid was one of the main factors compelling the evacuation of British troops.

How long this factor will continue to operate depends mainly on how long Britain remains, in the economic sense, the sick man among the Western powers and also on whether, as seems now to be happening, the Six replace the United States as her principal creditor.

The influence of cultural and psychological factors is sometimes regarded as the key to the special relationship. Thus one of the above-quoted experts declares that "the cultural has probably been the most important of all the ties binding Great Britain to the United States".[1]

This approach, it seems to me, confuses rather than clarifies the problem. The cultural tie is by its nature a permanent one going back to the foundation of the American state and certain to remain for centuries to come. If it were really of decisive significance in binding the two states together, history would not show much the same sort of wide and long-term fluctuations in Anglo-American as, say, in Anglo-French relations.

But it is, of course, true that the use of a common language, the deep inter-penetration of the two cultures, the extensive network of friendships, inter-marriages and other personal ties between the two élites make for quicker and easier understanding in the literal sense of the word. Moreover, psychologically, consciousness of a common

[1] Allen. *op. cit.* p. 129.

cultural heritage and, for many American and British citizens, a common ethnic origin predisposes large numbers of people in all classes of society in both countries to regard friendship and alliance as natural and right.

In the last twenty-five years these factors, while not an essential element in the special relationship, have certainly helped to strengthen it. The use of a common language has eased the whole process of consultation and co-operation, which, remembering the military aspect, involves literally thousands of people on both sides.

At the top level, the wheels of the Anglo-American partnership have been oiled by the development of a more than purely business relationship between the two sets of leaders—not only between Churchill, Roosevelt and Hopkins, but also between Acheson and Bevin,[1] between Eisenhower, Eden and Macmillan,[2] and between Kennedy and Macmillan,[3] in the last case reinforced by a family connection.

It is possible to find examples of persistently bad personal relations between leading figures of the period. According to their own accounts, at least two British Foreign Secretaries, Morrison and Eden, mistrusted Dulles.[4] Eden, scenting trouble to come, even urged Eisenhower point-blank not to appoint Dulles Secretary of State at all.[5] The latter, for his part, seems to have disliked and despised Eden.[6] This situation has, however, been the exception rather than the rule.

As regards internal political changes, it is generally supposed, probably rightly, that opposition to any form of pro-British orientation in American foreign policy is stronger in the Republican than in the Democratic Party. But, in practice, the traditional anti-Britishness of the Republicans has had no serious adverse influence on the special relationship. Indeed, its basic phases show no correspondence with alternations between Democratic and Republican Administrations.

For most of the critical period of the alliance, i.e., the first post-war decade, when, on American initiative, many forms of Anglo-American co-operation were terminated or attenuated, a Democratic and not a Republican Administration was in office.

[1] See Dean Acheson. *Sketches from Life*. London. 1961. pp. 11–36.
[2] See, for example, Dwight Eisenhower. *Waging Peace*. London. pp. 120–121.
[3] A. M. Schlesinger. *A Thousand Days. John F. Kennedy in the White House*. London. 1965. pp. 339–341. Harold Macmillan. *Winds of Change*. London. 1966. p. 29.
[4] Herbert Morrison. *An Autobiography*. London. 1960. p. 280; and Anthony Eden. *Full Circle*. London. 1960. p. 63.
[5] Eisenhower. *Mandate for Change*. p. 142.
[6] See Robert Murphy. *Diplomat among Warriors*. London. 1964. pp. 467–468

The abrupt cutting off of Lend-Lease, the harsh terms of the Anglo-American Loan Agreement, the MacMahon Act putting an end to the joint nuclear weapons programme, the refusal to form a common front over the Palestine question and many other actions of a piece with certain aspects of the subsequent foreign policy of the Republicans were all the work of the Truman Administration before its demise in 1952.

Conversely, the following phase of recovery and strengthening of the partnership, running from the mid-fifties to the mid-sixties, began and developed during Eisenhower's second Republican Administration from 1956 to 1960. In particular, one of the key events in this process, the Declaration of Common Purpose of 1957 and the accompanying restoration of Anglo-American co-operation in the military uses of nuclear energy, was brought about by Eisenhower and his advisers.

In any case, even if it is true that the Democratic Party as a whole is more favourably disposed to alliance with Britain than the Republican Party, there are scarcely less wide differences of view on this subject within the leadership of the Democratic Party itself.

Thus one of the most swingeing American attacks in recent times on British foreign policy, and the special relationship, was made by Dean Acheson, a former Democratic Secretary of State and at the time employed as an adviser by a Democratic President (Kennedy). Britain, he declared in furious tones, should give up attempting to play a role separate from Europe, a role based on an imaginary special relationship with the United States and on the leadership of an almost non-existent Commonwealth.[1]

On the other hand, one of the most emphatic American reaffirmations of the importance of the special relationship also came from a Democrat, namely President Johnson.

In greeting Sir Alec Douglas-Home on the latter's first pilgrimage to the White House as Prime Minister, he pointed out that the tradition of meetings between American Presidents and British Prime Ministers had remained unbroken for more than a quarter of a century. During these years there had been differences, but the differences had passed away because of a very special reason. There was, he said, an invisible cord between the two countries, much as between two brothers who may differ, but whose ties are too strong ever to break.[2]

[1] See Acheson's speech at West Point. December 5, 1962. *New York Times*. December 7 and 8, 1962.
[2] Speech in Washington. February 12, 1964. *Commonwealth Survey*. March 3, 1964.

Judging by experience so far and by the present political outlook in the United States, no internal political change there is likely by itself to cause a major change in Anglo-American relations in the next few years.

On the British side the situation has been more complicated, since the special relationship has for twenty years been a highly controversial issue in the political life of the country. Even so, there has been basic agreement between the leaderships of the Conservative and Labour Parties regarding the necessity and key importance of the American alliance. Compare, for example, Douglas-Home's "fundamentally on the Anglo-American alliance depends the freedom of mankind"[1] with Gordon Walker's "the prime concern of a Labour Government would be the maintenance of the Western Alliance—and, above all, Britain's close relationship with the United States".[2] The main battle has been fought not between the two leaderships, but within the Labour Party and the trade union movement and, to a lesser extent and for different reasons, within the Conservative Party.

Opposition to the special relationship point of view from the left has arisen principally from the aggressiveness of American foreign policy, has focused on the military aspects of the alliance, and ebbed and flowed in accordance with various phases in Washington's politico-military strategy.

In the particular situation which existed at the end of the fifties, it became increasingly clear to a very large number of people that, whatever the Government might say, alliance with the United States carried with it a direct threat of the total destruction of the British Isles.

U.S. nuclear bombers were on round-the-clock patrol over Britain. U.S. nuclear Thor rockets were being installed. In 1960 it was announced that an American Polaris submarine base was to be set up at Holy Loch. Anglo-American strategic doctrine dictated the immediate use of nuclear weapons in the event of war with the Soviet Union, but at the same time it was known and officially acknowledged that there was no means of fending off the inevitable Soviet counterblow.

From 1958 onwards public demand for dissociation in one form or another from American military plans and preparations for nuclear

---

[1] Speech at the Conservative Party Annual Conference reported in *The Times*, October 14, 1960.
[2] The Labour Party's Defense and Foreign Policy. *Foreign Affairs*. New York. April 1964.

war mounted steeply and only relaxed when, in 1960–1961, simultaneously with the advent of the Kennedy Administration, Washington itself recognised the suicidal character of its policy.

In 1958 the annual conference of the Labour Party passed a resolution calling for an end to patrol flights of U.S. nuclear bombers over Britain and the postponement of the establishment of the U.S. Thor rocket bases. In the following year the Trades Union Congress, over the protests of the leadership, went further by opposing the latter bases unconditionally. In 1960, again against the wishes of the leadership, both the TUC and the Labour Party passed resolutions condemning all forms of Anglo-American as well as British preparations for nuclear war. In 1961, though these decisions were reversed, the Labour Party Conference condemned the establishment of a Polaris base on British soil, a similar motion being passed by the TUC in 1962.

During the same period, the Campaign for Nuclear Disarmament, founded in January 1958, developed from a small group into a mass movement, particularly among young people. Its main accent was on unilateral nuclear disarmament by Britain, but it was also aimed directly against the military side of the Anglo-American alliance. The Campaign's programme demanded a general refusal to allow American as well as British nuclear weapons to be used for the defence of Britain, including an immediate ban on patrol flights by U.S. nuclear bombers and on the establishment of U.S. nuclear missile bases in the country.[1]

Since 1965 opposition has been growing to the Government's support of the American invasion of Vietnam.

In that year resolutions at the TUC calling for the withdrawal of all foreign troops, and at the Labour Party Conference, demanding an end to the American bombing of North Vietnam, though they each received over 2,000,000 votes, were defeated. But in 1966, the TUC came out in favour of the cessation of American bombing and in 1967 went a step further by calling on the Government to dissociate itself altogether from American policy in Vietnam. The Labour Party Conference also changed its attitude in 1966 by asking the Government to bring pressure on Washington to cease the bombing and end the war, and in 1967 called on the Government to dissociate itself completely from the policy of the United States in Vietnam.

As regards the Conservative Party, in the first post-war decade

---

[1] Christopher Driver. *The Disarmers*. London. 1964. p. 47.

opposition to the special relationship came mainly from the ultra-colonialist lobby discussed below. These mastodons, since they give a particularly high priority to the preservation of the traditional British sphere of influence in the Commonwealth and colonial empire, were peculiarly sensitive to American attempts to penetrate and undermine it. In terms of the "three circles" theory, they placed the Commonwealth circle well above not only the European circle, but the Atlantic circle as well.

The opposition of this group to the American alliance was by no means unconditional, since it regarded the United States as a necessary partner in the confrontation between capitalism and Communism. On the other hand, to many of its adherents the American drive towards domination of the capitalist world appeared to be an even more direct threat to British interests than Communism.

As one of the group's spiritual fathers put it, in an attack on the terms of the Anglo-American Loan agreement and American economic and financial policy generally, Britain stands as one with America on the main issue of human freedom, but "we, for our part, are in less immediate danger from Communism, than from American economic aggression".[1]

The biggest political demonstration of anti-American feeling from this quarter took place immediately after the Suez crisis of 1956, owing to what was considered to be Washington's betrayal of its ally for its own advantage. Over a hundred Conservative M.P.s then put their signatures to a motion declaring that the attitude of the United States represented a grave threat to the Atlantic alliance.[2]

Since the early sixties, when the U.S. oligarchy began to regard partnership with London in the third world, and ipso facto the preservation of British influence and British bases there, with a more favourable eye, the influence in British political life of ultra-colonial anti-Americanism has declined, though it is not yet entirely exhausted.

As we have said, the special relationship and its evolution have depended, and no doubt will continue to depend, primarily on external and not internal factors. The influence on Anglo-American relations of two of the three most powerful external factors—Communism and the independence movements in the third world—is discussed below. The third—developments in continental Western Europe—is considered later as part of the question of British policy in Western Europe as a whole.

[1] L. S. Amery. *The Awakening*. London. 1948. p. xiv.
[2] *The Times*. November 29, 1956.

The Anti-Communist Factor

Although in the period under review the influence of anti-Communism on British and American foreign policy as a whole diminished, it has remained the most important single factor determining the continued existence of the alliance between the two countries. In particular, the core of the special relationship, the Anglo-American military arrangements directed against the Soviet Union and its Eastern European allies, has not only remained in being, but has been developed further still.

At the same time, as compared with the first post-war decade, there was a major change in British policy towards the Soviet Union and the other European Socialist states and consequently in the tactical aims of British diplomacy in its dealings with Washington over various aspects of this question. Since a similar evolution of American policy came some time later, until the beginning of the sixties there was a fairly wide gap between the British and American Governments in this field, which began to narrow roughly from the time when the Kennedy Administration took over.

Anti-Communism continued to play a far smaller part in determining British policy towards China than towards the Soviet Union, whereas Washington's anti-Communist crusade in the Far East went ahead at full blast. The wide divergence between British and American policies towards China characteristic of the first post-war decade, while somewhat diminishing, has remained down to the present, and has been little affected by the anti-Soviet line taken by Mao Tse-tung and his disciples and other symptoms of galloping chauvinism and xenophobia in Peking. With the acquisition by China of nuclear weapons in 1964, preliminary Anglo-American countermeasures were taken, but these fell far short of those already in force against the Soviet Union. Moreover, in view of London's subsequent decision to withdraw from all its main bases east of Suez, the fate of even these preliminary joint measures is now uncertain.

The Anglo-American alliance against the Soviet Union and Poland, Czechoslovakia, Hungary and her other European allies consists not only of undertakings to act together in the case of war with the Soviet Union, but of a long-established and constantly functioning system of military co-operation ready at any time to go into action. The system is specifically concerned with the use of nuclear weapons against targets in Eastern Europe and thus with the very existence of Britain, the United States, their allies and their opponents.

Anglo-American bilateral arrangements overlap with multilateral arrangements entered into by the two powers in their capacity
as founders and leaders of NATO, and also directed against the
European Communist states. But they nevertheless amount to an
alliance within an alliance and have not yet been seriously affected
by the efforts of other members of NATO to break down their
exclusively Anglo-American character.

This situation is connected with the fact that for some years the
United States and Britain were the only members of NATO possessing nuclear weapons. But it existed several years before Britain
exploded her first nuclear device in 1952 and has continued unchanged since France exploded hers in 1960.

American nuclear bomber bases were first set up in Britain during
the Berlin crisis of 1948, when, owing to the relatively short range of
bomber aircraft of that period, the U.S. authorities proposed to
London that two groups of B29s should be urgently transferred to
British airfields and targeted on the Soviet Union.

This proposal was at once accepted by the Attlee Government,
whose attitude was summed up by Cripps, then Chancellor of the
Exchequer, when he told the Americans that "Britain must be
regarded as the main base for the development of American power
and the chief offensive against Russia must be by air".[1] By July
sixty B29s, and by September ninety, had been moved to RAF
bases, mostly in East Anglia.[2]

Thereafter a whole network of U.S. nuclear bomber bases was
established in Britain, most of which is still in existence today. By
1954 there were at least fifteen air bases serviced by 45,000 U.S.
military personnel.[3] In 1959, in addition to what was already there,
the greater part of two hundred U.S. fighter-bombers armed with
nuclear weapons were transferred to Britain from France, where the
French Government had denied them lodgement.

As rockets began to replace bombers in the nuclear arsenals of the
world, American rocket bases were established in Britain in parallel
with the bomber bases.

Under an agreement of February 1958, American Thor intermediate range rockets were installed at launching sites in Britain, the
cost of the sites being borne by London and of the missiles by
Washington. The nuclear warheads remained under exclusively
American control, but it was agreed that the launching of the rockets

[1] *The Forrestal Diaries.* New York. 1951. p. 491.
[2] *The World Today.* August 1960.
[3] *Ibid.*

would be a matter for joint decision.[1] As Eisenhower, co-author with Macmillan of this agreement, records, its effect was "to put missiles of intermediate range within striking distance of the heartland of the Soviet Union".[2] It remained in force until the Thors became strategically obsolete and were withdrawn in 1963.[3]

Meanwhile, a base for American Polaris submarines, complete with parent ship and floating dock, had been established at Holy Loch on the Clyde. According to Macmillan's announcement concerning this new base on November 1, 1960, its use in periods of emergency would, as with the Thor bases, be a matter for joint consultation between the two Governments. The Prime Minister also said that, while this understanding could not apply to the submarines when on patrol possibly hundreds of miles from Holy Loch, he was sure that wherever they might happen to be, the U.S. Government would never decide to use them without "the fullest possible previous consultation".[4]

The year 1960 also saw the conclusion of an Anglo-American agreement to establish a joint ballistic early warning station at Fylingdales in Yorkshire, the equipment being mainly supplied by the United States and the site and buildings by Britain. The station, giving warning simultaneously to the American and British Air Commands of the approach of Soviet missiles, was commissioned in 1963.[5]

In 1961–62 the two Governments began an exchange of facilities for nuclear weapon tests, the British being allowed to use the American underground test site in Nevada, while the Americans were given the use of Christmas Island for high-altitude hydrogen bomb tests.

Though no exact date has been published, the British and American nuclear striking forces in Europe have been integrated for operational purposes since the second half of the fifties when the British force first came into service.

The fact that they were so integrated was first made public by the U.S. Secretary for Defence in June 1962, when he said that Britain's V-bomber forces with their nuclear weapons had long been organised as part of a thoroughly co-ordinated Anglo-American striking force and were targeted as such.[6] This was confirmed a few days later by

---

[1] *Documents* ... 1960. pp. 348–351.
[2] Eisenhower. *Waging Peace.* p. 124.
[3] The intention to close down the Thor bases was announced in London and Washington on August 1, 1962.
[4] *Documents* ... 1960. pp. 123–124.
[5] *Commonwealth Survey.* October 22, 1963.
[6] *The Times,* June 25, 1962.

the British Minister of Defence. Remarking that the Western deterrent must as a military necessity conform to a policy of common targeting, agreement on strategy and close day-to-day integration, he said that "Bomber Command has been operated in this fashion in full agreement with our American allies for a number of years".[1]

The British nuclear striking force, besides being integrated with the U.S. force for operational purposes, also came increasingly to rely on American delivery systems and, in at least one case, warheads as well.

This process began with the Eisenhower-Macmillan Declaration of Common Purpose of 1957 referred to in Chapter 1, containing a promise that American atomic energy legislation would be amended to permit a renewal of Anglo-American co-operation in the nuclear military field.

This promise was soon carried out and the new relationship was given formal shape in the Anglo-American Agreement for Co-operation on the Uses of Atomic Energy for Mutual Defence Purposes, signed in Washington on July 3, 1958.[2] In a special article it gave immediate satisfaction to a long-standing British request for permission to purchase from the U.S. a submarine nuclear propulsion plant.

When in 1960 the Macmillan Government was forced on financial grounds to abandon the Blue Streak rocket as a military weapon, it obtained Washington's consent to purchase first the Skybolt missile for use by British V-bombers and then Polaris missiles for use by British submarines.

The first transaction was a two-way deal, since, as Macmillan subsequently revealed, in return for Skybolt he granted facilities in Britain for American Polaris submarines (i.e., the Holy Loch base).[3] The second transaction, concluded at Nassau in December 1962, turned out to be more far-reaching than at first appeared, since it involved not only the Polaris delivery system, but the nuclear warhead. As Wilson put it two years later, shortly after taking office, the British Polaris programme could not provide an independent deterrent "because we are dependent on the Americans for the fissile material for the British warheads".[4]

The agreements regarding the Thor and Polaris bases provided specifically that they should not be used in an emergency (i.e., rockets would not be launched from them against the Soviet Union)

---

[1] Statement in London on June 27, 1962. *Commonwealth Survey.* July 3, 1962.
[2] *Documents* . . . 1958. pp. 361–369.
[3] *Hansard.* January 30, 1963. Col. 967.
[4] *Hansard.* December 17, 1964. Cols. 702–703.

except by mutual consent. This proviso applies also to the American bomber bases. Among other documents, the communiqué issued after talks between Eden and Dulles in Washington in March 1953 confirmed an already existing understanding that the use of U.S. bases in the United Kingdom in an emergency "would be a matter for joint decision by Her Majesty's Government and the United States Government in the light of the circumstances prevailing at the time".[1]

But it will also have been noted that these agreements do not cover the use of American Polaris submarines based on Holy Loch while operating on the high seas. This omission arises from a wider and unresolved problem which has faced successive British Governments in one form or another at least since the beginning of the fifties.

The presence of U.S. nuclear bases on British soil and other aspects of the Anglo-American alliance exposes Britain to the risk of nuclear counter-attack should the United States use nuclear weapons against the Soviet Union. This remains true whether the U.S. fires its first salvo from British bases, from a Polaris submarine in mid-Atlantic, from the United States or from some other quarter.

From the point of view of the British sponsors of the alliance, the logic of this situation requires that there should be a binding overall agreement that the United States will not in any circumstances use nuclear weapons against the Soviet Union without British consent. Washington has not been willing to tie its hands in this way, but, besides the guarantees relating specifically to the use of bases in Britain, gave unofficial assurances of a wider character.

At the earliest stage of Anglo-American co-operation in nuclear matters—during the manufacture of the first, wartime, atomic bombs—such a binding agreement existed and was applied. From the signing of the Quebec Agreement by Roosevelt and Churchill in August 1943 until its disavowal by the Truman Administration at the end of the war, both countries had a clear-cut obligation, set out in the second clause of the Agreement, not to use nuclear weapons against third parties without each other's consent.[2] This clause was strictly complied with before the American atomic attack on Hiroshima.[3]

The hiatus was subsequently partially filled by personal assurances from the President to the Prime Minister, given orally and requiring renewal with each change of President. While it is not clear when

[1] *Documents* . . . 1953. p. 213.
[2] For an official account of the conclusion of this agreement, and its text, see Margaret Gowing. *Britain and Atomic Energy 1939–1945*. London. 1964. pp. 164–171 and Appendix 4.
[3] *Ibid.* p. 372.

exactly this understanding was first reached, it was apparently initiated by Macmillan and Eisenhower, which means that it dates from somewhere between 1957 and 1960.

Speaking in the House of Commons on June 26, 1962, Macmillan said that "there is an understanding which I had with President Eisenhower and now have with President Kennedy that neither of us in any part of the world would think of using power of this kind without consultation with each other".[1] The following year, using more cautious wording, he claimed to have renewed this understanding with Kennedy during their Nassau meeting. "I agreed," said Macmillan, "to bring up to date the moral undertaking which we and the United States already have, that is not to use nuclear weapons anywhere in the world without prior consultation with each other, if circumstances permit."[2]

While Anglo-American military dispositions against the Soviet Union expanded in a steady upward curve from 1948 till the end of the period under review, a major change took place in the attitude of Britain's leaders to United States policy towards the Soviet Union and the European Socialist states.

Towards the end of and immediately after the Second World War, the British establishment was haunted by the fear that Washington would prolong into the post-war period Roosevelt's policy of co-operation with the Soviet Union, would underestimate the strength and influence of Communist ideas in Europe and, as a corollary of these errors, sacrifice the interests of its British partner and of European capitalism generally on the altar of a global understanding between the two super-powers.

Though such fears proved to be unfounded, they were not imaginary. This can be seen, for example, from Harry Hopkins's remark, just before leaving for the U.S.-Soviet talks in Moscow in May 1945 as Truman's personal representative. "It was of vital importance," he said, "that we not be manœuvred into a position where Great Britain had us lined up with them as a bloc against Russia to implement England's European policy."[3]

In this situation, British diplomacy, official and unofficial, bent itself to the task of persuading American opinion that a Communist take-over in Europe was imminent, of pushing the U.S. Government into the leadership of an anti-Soviet alliance, and of consolidating London's position as Washington's chief partner within it.

[1] *Hansard*. June 26, 1962. Col. 958.
[2] *Hansard*. January 30, 1963. Col. 968.
[3] *Forrestal Diaries*. p. 58.

This was the aim of Churchill's speech at Fulton in March 1946. This was also the aim of the diplomatic démarche in February 1947, inviting the United States to take over the cost of military and financial support for the anti-Communist régimes in Greece and Turkey.[1] Here, too, lies the explanation of why it was London and not Washington which took the initiative in 1948 in proposing the first sketch of a North Atlantic Treaty.[2]

The period in which London rather than Washington was the pace-maker in the anti-Communist crusade in Europe was, however, short, ending in the second half of 1948, when the United States took over the leadership of the negotiations leading up to the formation of NATO, and of the military and other measures taken to protect the position of the Western powers during the Berlin crisis of that year.

Gradually, as the post-war revolutionary tide in Western Europe receded and as the nuclear balance became steadily more favourable to the Soviet Union, British anxiety that American foreign policy was not sufficiently resolute in its anti-Communism gave way to preoccupations of precisely the opposite kind. A reversal of roles within the alliance took place, London increasingly acting as a brake upon Washington's aggressiveness, while the latter sought to block the efforts of its partner to lower the temperature in East-West relations.

By the early fifties, the two Governments were in open disagreement over the question of summit meetings with the Soviet leaders. In May 1953, Churchill, without consulting or informing Washington, publicly proposed such a meeting and was immediately disavowed.[3] At their meeting in Bermuda the same year he attempted to get Eisenhower to change his mind, but was unsuccessful.[4] In 1954, although he did not in the end go through with it, Churchill, still unable to budge the Americans, proposed to Moscow a meeting of the heads of the British and Soviet Governments only.[5] Eisenhower was finally persuaded to go to the Geneva summit meeting in 1955, but, while Eden then and there initiated another round by

---

[1] Cf. the following comment by Attlee, who was Prime Minister at the time: "By giving America notice at the right moment that we couldn't afford to stay ... we made the Americans face up to the facts in the Eastern Mediterranean. As a result we got the Truman Doctrine, a big step." Francis Williams. *A Pattern of Rulers.* p. 172.

[2] According to the *Forrestal Diaries* (pp. 392, 422–423), the British Government was already pressing for a formal anti-Soviet alliance in March of that year, but secured U.S. agreement in principle only in June. Attlee tells us that, "at first in the face of many American doubts", he and his colleagues worked patiently "for over a year" to achieve their aim. Francis Williams. *op. cit.* p. 174.

[3] *Documents . . .* 1953 .p. 57.

[4] Sherman Adams. *First Hand Report.* London. 1962. p. 97. Eisenhower. *Mandate for Change.* pp. 504–505.

[5] *Pravda.* March 18, 1955.

inviting the Soviet leaders to visit Britain, the Americans held aloof.

Differences on this subject persisted throughout the run-up to the second, and abortive, heads of government meeting in Paris in 1960. During the discussions between the President and the Prime Minister at Camp David in March 1959, Macmillan declared that he could not take the British people into war without trying the summit first, while Eisenhower answered that he would "not be dragooned into a summit meeting".[1]

A similar pattern emerged over the question of ending nuclear tests, the British side pressing the Americans to make concessions to the Soviet point of view, while Washington, until the closing months of the Eisenhower Administration, persistently held back.

The same dove-hawk relationship between London and Washington developed over the question of West Berlin, then one of the main causes of East-West tension. Since this subject is discussed in more detail in Chapter 3, here we will only note that, according to Eisenhower's own account, American policy was "to be adamant . . . towards the East Germans in matters so small as to seem almost totally inconsequential", while the British were more interested in the question of practical access to West Berlin and were not much worried by the implications of giving tacit recognition to the East German régime.[2]

This difference over Berlin persisted during the early months of the Kennedy régime, but, by and large, from the beginning of the sixties down to the end of the period we are considering, the divergencies in British and American policy towards the Soviet Union and the other European Communist states grew less. The main factor responsible for this was the shift in American politico-military strategy away from unrealistic, not to say suicidal, ideas of "rolling back Communism" towards recognition of the necessity of a *modus vivendi*, i.e., towards the position already occupied by London.

From the time of the Kennedy-Khrushchev meeting in Vienna in 1961, despite subsequent acute crises in East-West relations, the desirability and necessity of direct top-level communication with the Soviet leaders was accepted in Washington no less than in London.

Disagreements over nuclear tests continued longer, since right up to the last moment Macmillan attempted to dissuade Kennedy from the renewal of American tests in the spring of 1962.[3] Before then, however, the Kennedy Administration had already shifted its posi-

---

[1] Eisenhower. *Ibid.* pp. 354–355.
[2] Eisenhower. *Ibid.* pp. 339.
[3] A. M. Schlesinger. *A Thousand Days. John F. Kennedy in the White House.* London. 1965. pp. 430–434.

tion on terms for an eventual test-ban treaty nearer to that of the British Government and subsequently joined the latter in sponsoring the proposals which made possible the conclusion of the treaty signed in Moscow in August 1963.[1]

Fairly acute Anglo-American differences over restrictions on trade with the Soviet Union and Eastern Europe lasted well into the sixties. As late as November 1963, Ball, the U.S. Under-Secretary of State, made a last-ditch, but unsuccessful, attempt to hold London to the NATO rule, imposing a five-year maximum on commercial credit granted by its members to the Soviet Union.[2] But as Washington began more and more actively to encourage American commercial, scientific, cultural and other contacts with Socialist Europe, British and U.S. tactics converged.

It is one of the peculiarities of the special relationship that, although in the post-war period it has rested chiefly on the anti-Communism common to both powers, and although it operates on a world-wide basis, one of its weakest points has been and still is the wide divergence between their respective attitudes towards Communist China.

During and after the Second World War, the United States, as part of its attempt to secure domination of the Western Pacific, gave a very high priority first to preventing the Chinese Communists from gaining power, and, when this proved impossible, to preventing them from consolidating their position and eventually bringing about their overthrow.

Just how high this priority is can be seen from the fact that the only wars fought by the United States in the last twenty years have both been on China's borders and both have had the aim of preventing the establishment or consolidation of Communist régimes likely to align themselves with China. The Korean war led to a direct clash between American and Chinese armed forces. At one time it looked as though the war in Vietnam might lead to an even more serious military conflict between the two.

Throughout the period under review the United States refused to recognise the Chinese People's Republic, maintained a trade embargo against it, played the main part in preventing it from taking its seat in the United Nations, and recognised, financed and armed Chiang Kai-shek's rump régime on Formosa (Taiwan).

The American permanent military establishment in the Western

[1] For details of this switch, see Michael Wright. *Disarm and Verify*. 1969. pp. 127–129. Wright was a British delegate to the Geneva Test Ban Conference 1959–1963.
[2] *The Times*. November 19, 1963.

Pacific, directed chiefly against China, is of colossal proportions, resting on bases in Japan, Formosa, Okinawa, the Philippines, Australia, Thailand, South Korea and South Vietnam, and on a major part of the U.S. fleet on constant patrol in the area.

In contrast, the British policy-makers, concerned primarily with Europe and the Middle East, over the same period gave a relatively low priority to the Far East in their world strategy. They devoted much effort to keeping the Communists down in Malaya and Singapore, where they directly threatened British control, but as regards China itself, and its immediate neighbours Korea and Vietnam, despite tactical zigzags, they stuck fairly firmly to the idea that in the long run their interests would be best served by reaching a *modus vivendi* with China and in any case avoiding war with her.

This question is discussed in more detail in Part III. Here we will recall British recognition of Communist China in 1950, Attlee's intervention in Washington later the same year against escalating the Korean war, Churchill and Eden's veto in 1954 on the American plan for Anglo-American direct intervention in Indo-China, the unilateral relaxation of the embargo on trade with China in 1957 and the renewal since 1962 of British support for Peking's claim to take its place in the United Nations.

In view of this wide difference of approach, it is not surprising that until the early sixties there were not even the beginnings of Anglo-American military contingency planning in the Far East directed against China comparable to those in Europe directed against the Soviet Union.

Throughout the Truman and Eisenhower Administrations Washington was more inclined to regard Britain as a weak but tiresome rival in the Far East, ripe for expulsion with the other old colonial powers, France and Holland, rather than as a useful ally against Communism in the area.

The U.S. Government sought British support, when it needed it, as in the Korean war or the Vietnam and Laos crises of 1954 and 1960–61, but at the same time centred its long-term system of alliances on Japan and Australia to the exclusion of Britain. Over London's protests, Washington vetoed British membership of the Australian-New Zealand-United States (ANZUS) Pact of 1951 and even the presence of British observers at meetings of the ANZUS Council.

A change came with the stocktaking of America's foreign policy problems which followed from the advent of the Kennedy Administration. This stocktaking had now to include a reassessment of the value, from Washington's point of view, of Britain's military role in Asia, including the Far East. "The United States," said McNamara, "strongly favours continued deployment of British land, sea and air forces in a broad area of Asia . . . British withdrawals in Asia would constitute a virtual invitation to the Sino-Soviet bloc to move into a power vacuum."[1] In that year the two powers embarked together on joint measures to reinforce India's defences against China.

From the time of the detonation of the first Chinese atomic device in 1964, signs began to appear that Washington and London were contemplating joint nuclear counter-measures. London's short-lived "East of Suez" strategy included among its components plans for the construction of joint Anglo-American nuclear bases in British Indian Ocean Territory, specially carved out by London for this purpose in 1965.

At the same time, however, as Anglo-American military dispositions against China began to grow, the Wilson Government, over the objections of Washington, was step by step forced, chiefly by financial considerations, to cut back British establishments in the Far East. By 1968 it had reached the point of announcing a planned run-down in Singapore and Malaysia, leading to total evacuation by 1971, and also its withdrawal from the Anglo-American plan to build a base at Aldabra in British Indian Ocean Territory.

All in all, it seems probable that, while in the immediate future attempts at integration of American and British (and Australian) strategic measures against China will continue, British efforts to reach a stable *modus vivendi* with Peking will also go on and that the gap between British and American policies will only narrow if Washington eventually modifies the intensity of its East Asian anti-Communist crusade.

In contrast, it seems likely that the existing fairly close Anglo-American understanding over general tactics towards the Soviet Union and the other socialist states of Eastern Europe, and the existing arrangements for joint action in the event of war against them, will for the present remain in being.

Rivalry and Partnership in the Third World

If one were discussing the first and not the second post-war decade, the word "partnership" would have to be written in very small print

[1] *The Times*. February 16, 1962.

or omitted altogether. Right up to the Suez crisis of 1956 conflicts of interest in the third world were the most persistent of all causes of discord in Anglo-American relations. In the more recent period a new Anglo-American common front gradually took shape. Conflicts and disagreement continued, but of more limited scope and intensity.

The main reason for the high tension in Anglo-American relations over colonial and allied questions in the early post-war years is not far to seek. Britain emerged from the war still the possessor of a vast empire, including the whole of the Indian subcontinent, most of the Middle East and tropical Africa, and Malaya and other colonies in South-East Asia, but without the strength to hold more than part of it. The United States, on the other hand, finished the war immensely strengthened in comparison with all the other Western powers. It was in a position to launch and did launch a systematic attempt to bring their crumbling empires within the American sphere of influence.

This may sound like an over-simplification, since Washington's operations were conducted under anti-colonial slogans in which no doubt many of the main actors sincerely believed. But, regardless of what Roosevelt and others may personally have intended, a sustained drive in fact took place—in Saudi Arabia, Palestine, Egypt, Morocco, Algeria, Tunis, Vietnam, Laos, Thailand, Indonesia, the Congo and elsewhere—to substitute American for British, French, Dutch or Belgian influence.

U.S. policy undoubtedly hastened the break-up of the old colonial empires, but at the same time led to the introduction into great tracts of Asia and Africa of the same method of indirect American control already practised in the Philippines and Liberia and above all Latin America. In Indo-China it led eventually to crimes against the Vietnamese people far more terrible than those committed by the former colonial power.

At least until the end of the war, the decision-makers in London seem to have been under the illusion not only that they would be able to retain the empire intact, but that they could do so without American help and regardless of what Washington wanted. In the preliminary Anglo-American skirmishes of that period the line on the British side was to rebuff and evade American attempts to influence or even discuss imperial policy.

We may here recall that Churchill's declaration in 1942 that he had not "become the King's first Minister in order to preside over the liquidation of the British Empire" was aimed not at the leaders of the independence movements but at American critics of British colonial policy.[1]

Roosevelt's repeated advice to Churchill in the same year to make immediate political concessions to India's leaders was rejected out of hand and, according to Hopkins's account, aroused more anger than any recommendation made by the President to the Prime Minister throughout the entire course of the war. The only part of one of these messages with which Churchill agreed was, we learn, its admission that strictly speaking British policy in India was none of Roosevelt's business.[2]

When Roosevelt told Eden, during their Washington talks in 1943, that he doubted whether the British, French and Dutch colonies then occupied by the Japanese should be returned to their former owners, Eden left the impression, at least on Hopkins, that "the British are going to be pretty sticky about their former possessions in the Far East".[3]

At the Yalta Conference, when Stettinius, then U.S. Secretary of State, brought up the subject of the future role of the United Nations in dependent areas, Churchill is reported to have exploded and announced that the Government would never in any circumstances consent to the United Nations "thrusting interfering fingers into the very life of the British Empire", a reaction which caused Roosevelt for the time being to abandon his intention of challenging the Prime Minister on the subject of British and French imperial outposts.[4]

After the war, when the real power and sweep of the independence movement was borne in on the Government and its advisers, it became a great deal more interested in working out a common Anglo-American course of action. It found itself, however, in an awkward dilemma. Britain was obviously unable alone to maintain its positions for long. On the other hand, the United States was not only the power able to give the most effective help, but also the power most actively expanding its own positions at Britain's expense.

This dilemma was a general one, but was at its most acute in the Middle East, where from London's point of view, owing to the strength of nationalist feeling, it was immediately necessary to call in American help, but where the United States was determined to replace Britain as arbiter, patron and overlord. British diplomacy was torn between the desire, on the one hand, to involve the United States in its problems and, on the other, to assert its own

[1] W. S. Churchill. *The End of the Beginning. War Speeches.* Boston. 1943. p. 268.
[2] Sherwood. *op. cit.* pp. 515–517, 535–536.
[3] *Ibid.* pp. 714–717.
[4] *Ibid.* p. 854. Herbert Feis. *Churchill, Roosevelt, Stalin.* Princeton. 1957. p. 556.

continuing primacy in the area over a far more powerful rival.

In practice, for the first ten years after the war, Labour and Conservative Governments alike persistently attempted to form a common Anglo-American front, but one presided over by themselves, and were met with just as persistent refusal by the Truman and Eisenhower Administrations to pull British chestnuts out of the fire. In so far as Washington played along at all, as in Iran, it did so only when it was in a position to call the tune.

British efforts to secure an agreed line of action in Palestine ended in total failure and bad blood between the two Governments, Bevin in his frustration publicly accusing Truman of sabotaging British policy in order to gain for himself the votes of the Jewish population of New York.[1]

In Iran, where American influence was already strong, the British side had in effect to buy American agreement to come to the rescue of British Petroleum (then the Anglo-Iranian Oil Company) in its struggle with the Mussadiq Government. As Eden tells us, it was not until he proposed American participation in a new oil consortium that the State Department agreed to abandon its tactics of preserving neutrality between Mussadiq and London.[2]

While the U.S. Government did not altogether deny support to the efforts of the Foreign Office to set up a Middle East Defence Organisation on the lines of NATO, it refused to join it when it finally came into existence in the form of the Baghdad Pact of 1955, once more causing considerable bitterness in London. "Having played a considerable part to inspire the project," writes Eden, the father of this ill-fated plan, "the United States Government held back while Britain joined it alone of the Western powers. Worse still, they tried to take credit for this attitude in capitals like Cairo, which were hostile to the pact."[3]

In the dispute with Saudi Arabia over the Buraimi oasis, London's efforts to get Washington to call its Saudi protégés to order for a long while met with a blank negative. When Eden, during a visit to Washington in February 1956, tackled Eisenhower on the subject, he was informed that the United States sympathised with the Saudi claims and that public opinion thought that "the whole Arabian peninsula belonged, or ought to belong, to King Saud".[4]

---

[1] For Truman's account of this episode, see _Memoirs of Harry S. Truman_. Vol. II. New York. 1956. pp. 153–154.

[2] Eden. _op. cit._ pp. 198–202. Under the new oil agreement negotiated by the Americans with Mussadiq's successor in 1954, in concert with London, U.S. oil companies received a 40 per cent share in what had previously been the exclusive preserve of AIOC.

[3] _Ibid._ p. 336.

[4] _Ibid._ pp. 334–335.

The culmination of Anglo-American rivalry in the Middle East was, of course, the open breach between the two powers during and immediately after the Suez crisis of 1956, generally, and I think rightly, considered to be the most serious rift in Anglo-American relations in the whole post-war period.[1]

From the moment when the question of Britain's privileged position in Egypt entered its last and most acute phase following the Egyptian revolution of 1952, London, owing to its own weakness, found itself obliged to seek American co-operation over almost every step in its manœuvres to preserve first the military base in the Canal Zone and then its control over the Suez Canal itself. Washington, for its part, gave some measure of support to these manœuvres, but persistently refused to tie its hands by committing itself to a firm Anglo-American front, and, when the crunch came, dissociated itself from its would-be partner altogether.

Following Egyptian nationalisation of the Canal in July 1956, Dulles joined Eden in working out a whole series of measures designed to compel Egypt to abandon full control, but evaded all Eden's efforts to take him in tow, and publicly proclaimed that in questions such as this the approach of the two countries was different. Britain and the United States might be allies in NATO, he said, but where colonial problems were concerned "the United States plays a somewhat independent role".[2]

This "somewhat independent role" in practice meant that when the Anglo-Franco-Israeli attack on Egypt was launched the United States played one of the leading parts in securing United Nations condemnation of British aggression and in compelling British withdrawal. Anglo-American co-operation temporarily broke down altogether, Eisenhower even refusing Eden's request to be allowed to visit him for consultations until British forces had been withdrawn from Egyptian soil.[3]

During and after the crisis, bitterness and hostility temporarily seized the leaders on both sides of the Atlantic. Selwyn Lloyd, then Foreign Secretary, privately briefing Commonwealth representatives, attributed the failure of British post-war diplomacy in the Middle East primarily to misguided attempts to co-operate with the Americans. "It was a mistake to give up the Palestine Mandate for the sake of creating Israel," he said. "It was a mistake, too, to withdraw from the Suez Canal Zone [under the Anglo-Egyptian Agree-

[1] See, for example, Nicholas. *op. cit.* p. 105; Allen. *op. cit.* p. 243; Bell. *op. cit.* p. 46.
[2] *New York Times.* October 3, 1956.
[3] See, for example, Sherman Adams. *op. cit.* pp. 209–210.

ment of 1954—D.M.]. On both occasions we submitted to strong American pressure, and ever since we have striven hard to arrive at a common Anglo-American policy without success. We have to look after ourselves now."[1]

If this was plaintive, Dulles was insulting. Addressing the U.S. Senate on January 25, 1957, he said "if I were an American boy going to fight in the Middle East, I would rather not have a Britisher and a Frenchman, one on my right hand and one on my left".[2]

From the second half of the fifties onwards, co-operation between the two powers in pursuing their aims in the third world increased and conflicts between them diminished.

The main underlying reason for this was the change in the overall balance of strength between East and West, the development of closer co-operation between the socialist states, chiefly the Soviet Union, and the new sovereign states and independence movements of Asia and Africa, and the spread of nationalist, anti-imperialist ideas throughout the whole of the ex-colonial and colonial world. In this situation both powers became increasingly concerned with the common problem of keeping the third world within the Western, capitalist orbit and increasingly aware that its solution required them to act with and not against each other.

The change of attitude was far greater on the American than on the British side. London moved on from the idea that American co-operation in the third world was desirable to the conviction that it was essential—a change of emphasis rather than a change of direction. Washington, on the other hand, starting from the assumption that association with Britain, or any other colonial power, was a hindrance rather than a help, travelled most, if not all, of the way to the opposite conclusion that the balance of advantage lay after all in concerting American and British policies.

In 1953, Dulles, after a tour of the Middle East, told the Senate that because of her alliance with Britain and France the United States was suspected by the peoples of the area of seeking to preserve or restore colonial interests. "I am convinced that United States policy has become unnecessarily ambiguous in this matter," he said. " . . . Without breaking from the framework of Western unity, we can pursue our traditional dedication to political liberty."[3]

Ten years later, McNamara, addressing the same body on much the same subject, sang an entirely different tune. As we have seen,

[1] Terence Robertson. *Crisis*. London. 1965. p. 177.
[2] *The Times*. January 26, 1957.
[3] *Documents* . . . 1953. p. 264.

he declared that the United States strongly favoured the continued deployment of British land, sea and air forces in Asia. He went on to cite the despatch of British forces to Kuwait in 1961 as an example of the strategic value to the United States of the British military presence in the area.[1]

The development of a new Anglo-American partnership in the third world, overlaying, but not ending, the old rivalry, proceeded unevenly, starting in the Middle East and only later taking in Southern and South-East Asia and Africa.

The Suez débâcle, despite the bitterness towards the United States which it engendered, convinced London that the key to safety of its still substantial interests in the Middle East lay as much in Washington's as in its own hands and that, like it or not, American leadership in this area must in future be accepted. As *The Economist* put it at the time, and as the Government subsequently confirmed by its actions, it now became an essential task of British Middle Eastern diplomacy to persuade "the United States Government that British interests . . . are worth the while of the United States, in its own ultimate interest, to respect and preserve".[2]

For Washington the turning point came with the failure of the Eisenhower Doctrine. Launched in January 1957 in the backwash of the Suez crisis and deliberately ignoring British and French views and interests, this was a single-handed attempt by Dulles and his men to establish the United States as the sole financial, military and political patron of all the Arab states. It turned out, however, to be a demonstration of weakness rather than strength, since it did nothing to stem the rising tide of Arab nationalism and left the United States floundering alone in hostile and at the time still unfamiliar seas.

The first major move towards a harmonisation of policies was made at the meeting between Eisenhower and Macmillan in Bermuda in March 1957. The communiqué issued after the meeting announced the decision of the U.S. Government "to participate actively in the Military Committee of the Baghdad Pact", thus ending Washington's game of cat and mouse with London's chief remaining politico-military instrument in the area.[3]

In the following year the new Anglo-American common front in the Middle East was seen in action when at the time of the revolution in Iraq, in July 1958, the two governments carried out co-ordinated landings in Jordan and the Lebanon. As Eisenhower's personal

---

[1] *The Times.* February 16, 1962.
[2] *The Economist.* December 8, 1956.
[3] *Documents . . .* 1957. pp. 381–382.

3

representative during this operation confirms, this was a combined Anglo-American enterprise not only politically but militarily. "American and British cooperated throughout the intervention," he writes. "The British navy provided support in the Mediterranean and made facilities in Cyprus available to us, while the United States gave logistic support by flying supplies into Jordan for the British contingent there."[1]

In London the fact that, in contrast to its behaviour during the Suez crisis, the United States Government had this time agreed to act together with the British Government was greeted with special satisfaction. Hence the cynical, and rather untypical, remark made by Macmillan, on the eve of the Anglo-American landings. It is sometimes better, he said, "to do the wrong thing together, than the right thing alone".[2]

In the Arabian peninsula, Washington, swinging away from the position that the British political and military presence there was in principle illegitimate, started to give London active assistance in maintaining its ground.

In the Persian Gulf the United States supported the despatch of British forces to Kuwait in 1961 in order to forestall an Iraqi take-over, and voted against an Egyptian resolution in the Security Council calling for the immediate withdrawal of British troops.[3]

On the other side of the peninsula, when, with the formation of the Yemeni Republic in 1962, the British position in the South Arabian Federation, centred on Aden, became highly vulnerable, Washington also rallied to London's aid. It is true that the United States recognised the new Republic, while Britain did not, but this did not prevent the Americans from at the same time firmly supporting retention of the Aden base.

For this we have the testimony of the Governor. Remarking that the divergence between American and British policies towards the Yemeni Republic presented an obvious danger to the British position in Aden, he recorded that "fortunately in this case realism seems to have triumphed over anti-colonial prejudice; anyhow the U.S. Government now left it in no doubt that they regarded the security of the Aden base as a matter of joint Anglo-American concern".[4]

U.S. diplomacy also came to the rescue in the United Nations. When in April 1964 the Security Council passed a resolution con-

[1] Robert Murphy. *op. cit.* p. 498.
[2] *Spectator.* July 25, 1958.
[3] *Documents* . . . 1961. p. 781.
[4] Charles Johnston. *The View from Steamer Point.* London. 1964. pp. 161–162.

demning British aggression against the Yemen, the U.S. delegate, who abstained, declared that his Government shared the British point of view that the resolution was inequitable and did not correspond to the facts.[1]

It would be misleading to speak of an Anglo-American common front during the Middle Eastern crisis in the summer of 1967, since the part played by Britain before, during and after the second Arab-Israeli war was insignificant compared to that of the United States. One may note, all the same, that on this occasion, in marked contrast to their behaviour during the Suez crisis a decade earlier, the two Governments remained in step.

In Southern Asia, India, Pakistan, Ceylon and Burma, so long as they were ruled from London, occupied the central position in Anglo-American conflicts in the third world. When, however, the Attlee Government conceded them independence, it at the same time satisfied Washington's principal demand, namely for access to the Indian sub-continent for American money, American goods, American ideas and American political and military influence.

Most of the heat was thus removed from the quarrel, but differences of approach persisted, the two powers changing places as regards tactics towards nationalist, anti-imperialist trends in the area.

During the fifties, American diplomacy, under Dulles's direction, far from continuing to pivot its tactics on the old conception of America's liberating role in this part of the world, directed its efforts towards dragging the new states into military alliances dominated by the United States. India, Ceylon and Burma's policy of neutralism in the cold war was denounced as immoral, and Pakistan, at that time willing to play Washington's game, was in 1954 bundled into a bilateral military pact with the United States and into SEATO.

British diplomacy was a good deal more cautious, seeking to persuade rather than bludgeon India into closer co-operation and, since British and Indian interests here coincided, welcoming her refusal to support Dulles's highly aggressive policies towards China and Vietnam.

Anglo-American politico-military partnership in this area dates from the early sixties. When the drastic deterioration in Chinese-Indian relations created a new situation, the Indian Government became anxious for American and British military help, while Pakistan effected a rapprochement with China and started to disentangle itself from Washington's embrace.

[1] *Commonwealth Survey*. April 14, 1964.

When, following the Chinese attack on her borders in 1962, India appealed to Washington and London for immediate help, the two powers, instead of responding separately, decided to join forces. American and British military and political emissaries were despatched to New Delhi, on the basis of whose report, Kennedy and Macmillan, at their Nassau meeting in December 1962, launched a joint programme of military assistance of a both short-term and long-term character.

In South-East Asia, throughout the post-war period, the degree of agreement and disagreement between London and Washington has been as much determined by differences in their respective attitudes to Communist China to the North as by harmony or disharmony between their immediate objectives within the area itself. Right up to the early sixties, the conflict between American attempts to browbeat, and British attempts to conciliate, Peking was reflected in a marked difference of approach to the problem of Indo-China both before and after the French withdrawal.

On top of this, British diplomacy in South-East Asia has all along been primarily concerned with one limited aim — the preservation of control over Malaysia and Singapore, where British business and military interests were mainly concentrated — while Washington hoped eventually to bring the whole area under its control.

These divergences led to the head-on collision over Indo-China in 1954 and the differences over Laos described in Part III of this book. As is there pointed out, when the British policy-makers finally switched over from opposing to supporting (though not participating in) direct American intervention in Vietnam and Laos, they did so as part of a general move towards military partnership with the United States East of Suez caused chiefly by China's emergence as a nuclear power.

The United States, for its part, showed considerable reluctance to provide corresponding support for British policy in Malaysia and Singapore.

When Indonesia launched her "confrontation" of Malaysia in 1963, London's reaction was to meet it with a massive display of armed force. Washington, on the other hand, being more interested in weaning Indonesia away from her then close relationship with Peking than in defending London's protégé, and conscious that not only Indonesia, but also the Philippines had territorial claims against Malaysia, kept clear of the conflict, hoping to act as mediator.

When, in January 1964, Robert Kennedy visited East and South

Asia as President Johnson's representative, his efforts to act as a peace-maker between Indonesia and Malaysia cut directly across London's policy and were publicly snubbed. A British official statement declared that Ministers were sceptical of the practical results of Kennedy's activities, that "plans to strengthen the British military position in South-East Asia" would not be altered, and that the Government had "made its position clear to Mr. Kennedy" during his subsequent visit to London.[1]

A reflection of this disagreement is to be found in the communiqué issued after the meeting between Home and Johnson in Washington in February 1964. It stressed the value of the military agreements, which the two Governments had concluded with South-East Asia states and of the military bases and forces which they maintained there, but avoided expressing U.S. support for British policy in Malaysia. The Prime Minister, for his part, re-emphasised "the United Kingdom's support for United States policy in Vietnam". But the President only reaffirmed "the support of the United States Government for the peaceful national independence of Malaysia".[2]

By the end of the year, however, when the alliance of the two powers in South-East Asia was once more confirmed at Wilson's talks with Johnson in Washington, a less unequal bargain appears to have been struck. At all events the communiqué this time, instead of using two different formulae, records only one, applying equally to Malaysia and Vietnam. "The President and the Prime Minister," it said, ". . . recognised the particular importance of the military effort which both their countries are making in support of the legitimate governments in South-East Asia, particularly in Malaysia and south Vietnam."[3]

In Africa south of the Sahara, where British economic and political positions remained, and remain, markedly stronger than those of the U.S., the political tactics used by Washington to penetrate the British sphere of influence were similar to those used in the Middle East. In particular at the beginning of the sixties, when, under pressure from the independence movements, the British (and French and Belgian) colonial empires were breaking up, the U.S. Government endeavoured to present itself to the African peoples as their disinterested friend in their struggle to end the domination of the old colonial powers.

[1] *Commonwealth Survey*. February 18, 1964.
[2] *Ibid.*
[3] *Commonwealth Survey*. December 22, 1964.

These tactics were openly employed by Mennen Williams (put in charge of African affairs in the State Department by Kennedy), when he visited East Africa at the beginning of 1961. Since the British Government was at this period engaged in complicated manœuvres to delay the political independence of Kenya, Uganda, Tanganyika and other British African colonies, Washington evidently saw a favourable opportunity for gaining political credit in this area by contrasting itself with London.

To the indignation of his colonial hosts, and particularly of the European settlers, Williams declared in Kenya that the United States "supports the theory of Africa for the Africans". In Tanganyika, when asked for his impression of British policy regarding independence for the countries of East Africa, he replied that he could not consider it satisfactory.[1]

During the Congo crisis of 1960–61, while both powers sought as a first priority to prevent the victory of the out-and-out radicals (led by Lumumba until he was murdered), they pursued different tactical lines, which at times collided fairly sharply. London being particularly concerned to protect the large British investment in Union Minière, supported Tshombe and the Katanga separatists, giving them direct help over the border from Northern Rhodesia, and acted in close concert with the French and Belgian Governments. Washington, which had wider aims in the Congo, worked through the Central Government, with which Tshombe was in conflict. This tactic enabled Washington to some extent to ingratiate itself with African and Asian opinion and to use the United Nations as a screen for its operations. As the then UN representative in Katanga puts it, U.S. policy "moved towards an 'Afro-Asian line' ('unity of the Congo') and away from an 'Anglo-French-Belgian line' ('order in Katanga')".[2]

The conflict between British and American tactics showed itself at the beginning of the crisis. When the vote was taken on the Security Council resolution of July 14, 1960, calling for the withdrawal of Belgian troops, the United States Government voted in favour, while the British Government abstained.

Anglo-American differences reached their high point in December 1961 when armed conflict was in progress between the Katanga separatists and UN forces. On the same day (December 13) as London, in an effort to save Tshombe, sent a special message to the

[1] For a summary of Williams's activities on this tour, see *Keesing's Contemporary Archives.* 1961. p. 18266.
[2] Conor O'Brien, *To Katanga and Back.* London 1962, p. 99.

UN Acting Secretary-General, calling for an immediate cease-fire in Katanga, the U.S. Government announced that it was opposed to a cease-fire "until the minimum objectives of the United Nations have been achieved".[1]

Subsequently, however, the general tendency was for the two powers to join forces in the Congo. In 1964 Tshombe, with the support of both the United States and British Governments, returned from exile to become the head of the central Congolese Government. In November of that year the two governments co-operated in a new invasion of the Congo by Belgian paratroops, the United States providing the aircraft and Britain the base from which they flew, Ascension Island.

The change in the attitude of the U.S. Government to the role of the old colonial powers in Africa, and that of Britain in particular, can be seen from a sort of *mea culpa* pronounced by Mennen Williams in March 1965. He claimed, it is true, that African states desired to "avoid exclusive relations with the former metropole" and that the United States can give them a "second 'great power' association, which will increase their sense of independence" and strengthen them in their dealings with the former metropolitan state. On the other hand, he went out of his way to recognise and approve the part played in Africa by the European powers, singling out Britain for a special accolade and reserving his disapproval only for Portugal and the South African Republic.[2]

In the situation which developed in Rhodesia following the unilateral declaration of independence by the Smith régime in November 1965, practical co-operation between London and Washington proved to be close. The decision to impose an embargo on the export of oil to Rhodesia was taken jointly by Wilson and Johnson during the former's visit to Washington in December 1965.[3] U.S. as well as British aircraft took part in the airlift of oil to Zambia to replace supplies formerly routed through Rhodesia.

In the deepening crisis in Southern Africa, it is likely that the two powers, caught in a cross-fire from African nationalism from one side, and Afrikaner aggressiveness from the other, will continue to act as partners, rather than play their own hands against each other.

At the time of writing, this is still true of the third world generally. But with the British military withdrawal East of Suez, and if the

[1] *Documents* ... 1961. p. 770.
[2] The Department of State Bulletin. April 12, 1965.
[3] *The Times*. December 18, 1965.

now incipient re-orientation of British foreign policy towards Europe takes place, the Anglo-American common front, constructed with such difficulty and effort, may, it seems to me, before long begin to crumble.

CHAPTER THREE

Britain and Western Europe

Decline of British Influence

In the years since the end of the Second World War, there has been a considerable shift in the main focus of British diplomacy in Western Europe.

In the first post-war decade—from military intervention against the Communists in Greece, through the Berlin airlift of 1948, the founding of NATO in 1949 and the legalisation of West German rearmament in 1954—the policy-makers in alliance with Washington were primarily concerned with preventing the establishment of Communist régimes within the area and with building up a politico-military front against the Soviet Union and the other Communist states of Eastern Europe.

In the later period which we are considering, while anti-Communism remained a major factor in British policy, the question of relations with the continental powers loomed larger and larger until it occupied the centre of the stage.

Throughout both periods there was a steady decline in British influence in Western European affairs. It is true that in the mid-fifties, when the plan for a European Defence Community collapsed and the diplomatic initiative in the question of rearming West Germany temporarily passed from American to British hands, it appeared for a moment that the tide had turned. But Eden's major contribution to the conclusion of the Paris Agreements of 1954, permitting the rearmament of West Germany on British terms and converting the Western European Union into a potentially more effective instrument of British policy, turned out to be not the beginning of a triumphant chapter in British diplomacy, but, so far as intra-Western relations are concerned, London's last successful intervention in this part of the world for many years to come.

There followed the failure in November 1958 of the British plan for an all-embracing Western European Free Trade Area and the collapse in January 1963 and November 1967 of the efforts of first the Macmillan Government and then the Wilson Government to secure entry into the European Economic Community. The Western European Union remained a side-show in international affairs, while NATO, the main transmission belt of not only U.S. but also British influence in Europe, with the withdrawal of France from its military mechanism and the expulsion of its high command and U.S. contingents from French territory, began to fall apart.

Britain has remained, it is true, the only nuclear power in Western Europe besides France, and her voice in NATO, whatever the pretensions of Bonn, has remained second only to that of the United States. Throughout the sixties, Britain has maintained an army of some 45,000 men in West Germany and, along with the United States and France, retained certain rights, and a contingent of troops, in West Berlin. Britain is the dominant power in the European Free Trade Association covering the Scandinavian countries, Switzerland, Austria and Portugal, with Finland as an associate member. Moreover, the diminution of British influence is a reversible process. As suggested below it seems possible that during the seventies London will acquire considerably more weight in continental affairs than it has today.

Nevertheless, excepting only countries lying on the periphery of Western Europe plus perhaps Holland, the strong position occupied by Britain at the end of the war and during the first post-war decade has been seriously eroded. In particular, her capacity to influence the course of action of the two chief continental powers, France and West Germany, has grown less and less.

Eden, realising that his hopes had been disappointed, wrote in 1960 that "the United Kingdom's relations with France and Germany are not as close and cordial as they have been and should be. To perfect these should be the principal task of Western statesmanship".[1] But as time went on these relations, far from improving, deteriorated further still. One result was that by the end of 1967 Wilson, Brown and their colleagues, like would-be customers at a pub after closing time, were reduced to banging on the closed door of the EEC, while the landlords made clear, France loudly and West Germany softly, that it would not, at any rate for some time, be opened.

Some of those chiefly responsible have attributed these defeats of British diplomacy to mistakes and miscalculations by themselves or others.

Harold Macmillan, in his memoirs, says that he will never cease to blame himself that he did not, when a member of the Churchill

[1] Eden. *op. cit.* p. 174.

Government, "raise as a matter of high principle the question of Britain joining actively at least in the preliminary talks which ultimately led to the Treaty of Rome".[1]

Sir Alec Douglas-Home, from the vantage point of 1962, remarked that as late as 1957, when he was himself already a leading member of the Government, "we could have had the leadership of Europe, but let it slip from our grasp".[2]

In the memoirs of Lord Kilmuir (Maxwell Fyfe), who was at one time the Churchill Government's chief emissary to the Council of Europe, Attlee and Eden are picked out for special blame, but the author considers that "the single act which, above all others, destroyed our name on the continent" was the decision announced by Eden in November 1951 that Britain would not become a member of the proposed European Defence Community.[3]

The principal British historian of British Western European policy in this period, Miriam Camps, also attributes its failure to underestimates, misjudgments, emotional blocs and other personal failings of the policy-makers. "All British Governments (Labour and Conservative)," she remarks severely, "should have given a far higher priority to European relationships during the earlier period when the leadership of the Continent was theirs for the asking."[4]

It is certainly true that successive governments and their advisers gravely misjudged the real balance of forces in Western Europe and did their own cause a good deal of harm both by saying "no" when they should have said "yes" and by ill-conceived initiatives resulting in failures, which weakened their future negotiating position still further.

To take only one example, and borrowing for a moment Mrs Camps' chalk and blackboard, the Government, when it had decided in 1966 to have another go at getting into the EEC, should, in the light of the collapse of the Brussels negotiations and all other known facts, have hinged the whole operation on an attempt to reach informal understanding with the French Government beforehand and, if this failed, put off the enterprise until this indispensable preliminary could be accomplished.

But for all that, there have been processes at work which, whether or not they were understood in Downing Street, have determined a falling-off in British influence in Western Europe.

During the first half of this century the basic pattern in the triangular relationship between the three main powers in Western Europe

[1] Harold Macmillan. *Winds of Change*. London. 1966. p. 23.
[2] Interview in *The Observer*, September 23, 1962.
[3] The Earl of Kilmuir. *Political Adventure*. London. 1964. pp. 186–188.
[4] M. Camps. *Britain and the European Community 1955–1963*. London. 1964. p. 507.

was an alignment of Britain and France against Germany. There were zigzags in the direction both of Anglo-German rapprochement at France's expense and of Franco-German rapprochement at Britain's expense, but when the decisive moments came, in 1914 and in 1939, Britain and France were on one side of the line and Germany on the other. This pattern continued for a short time after the Second World War and showed itself in the Anglo-French Treaty signed at Dunkirk in 1947, the principal clause of which provided for "measures of mutual assistance in the event of any renewal of German aggression".

Roughly since 1950, another pattern has imposed itself. There has been a reversal of alliances, France moving from a predominantly pro-British to a predominantly pro-West German orientation in its foreign policy. The old alignment within the triangle has been replaced by a new one, namely that of France and West Germany against Britain.

The truth or untruth of this proposition has been much discussed by specialists in the Soviet Union and no doubt elsewhere. The Franco-West Germany Treaty of Co-operation of January 1963 (the Elyseé Treaty), for instance, has in its time been interpreted as a flash-in-the-pan, a temporary patching over of deepening antagonisms between Bonn and Paris. Much colour was lent to this point of view by the deterioration of relations between the two governments during the Erhard interregnum between the Adenauer and Kiesinger régimes.

If, however, one looks at the course of events in the fifties and sixties as a whole, one can see a marked shift towards co-operation and alliance between France and West Germany, the main fruits of which were first the European Coal and Steel Community and then the European Economic Community, while the Elysée Treaty of 1963 appears as a sign-post on the same road.

Behind this change, there lies, on the French side, an endemic tendency in financial and business circles to favour partnership with their German opposite numbers. Without going back as far as the activities of the Comité des Forges, one may recall here that from the early summer of 1940 until the end of the war, all but a small fraction of the French big bourgeoisie went over from alliance with Britain to alliance with Germany.

On the West German side, the crushing defeat in 1945, the consolidation of the socialist system in Eastern Europe and the formation of a German socialist state in the Soviet Zone narrowed the territorial base of German capitalism, restricted its foreign policy choices, and impelled business and financial circles towards peaceful penetration of the Western European market through partnership with France. Moreover, the incorporation of Prussia, Saxony and the Protestant East in the German Democratic Republic (GDR) increased the political weight in capitalist Germany of the Catholic South and West and of politicians such as Adenauer (one of the leaders of the Rhineland separatists in 1918–1919) more disposed to alliance with France than were the leaders of the pre-war Reich, whether Nazi or pre-Nazi.

The demands of the technological revolution have worked in the same direction, accelerating the concentration of capital not only on a national but on a Franco-West German basis, and providing one of the main driving forces behind the formation of a common market between France and West Germany and their four associates.

For fifty years the influence of British diplomacy on the continent depended to a major degree on Britain's position as an arbiter between France and Germany. A situation in which over a longish period the relationship between Paris and Bonn has been closer than that between Paris and London or Bonn and London is new and embodies the traditional nightmare of British policy-makers, an unfriendly coalition of the chief continental powers. It is this new alignment which has, among other things, rendered fruitless all British attempts so far to use the West German Government as a lever to force the French Government to open the gate of the EEC.

British influence has also been seriously weakened by the incursion of the United States into Western Europe, an incursion which the British policy-makers themselves encouraged as part of their overall anti-Communist strategy.

Immediately after the Second World War there was a good deal of discussion in London of the possibility of attempting to build up a Western European third force, with Britain and France as its main members, which would be independent both of the United States and the Soviet Union and which would ensure Britain a leading position in the area for many years to come. In practice, this project never became part of the Government's policy. Instead the latter pursued the more modest tactic of endeavouring to achieve its aims in partnership with, rather than independently of, the United States.

The main reason for the adoption of this course was fear that, in the then existing situation, a group of this kind would be too weak to stem the European Communist movement without the backing of American military and economic power. As the Prime Minister of the day, Attlee, subsequently put it, "there wasn't either a material or a spiritual basis for it [a third force—D.M.] at that time. What remained of Europe wasn't strong enough to stand up to Russia by itself. You had to have a world force because you were up against a world force".[1]

British diplomacy actively promoted the strengthening of American influence in Western Europe, welcoming the Marshall Plan with open arms, accepting Washington's lead in West Germany and Berlin, hurrying on the conclusion of the NATO treaty and the assumption by the United States of a dominating military and political position in the whole area.

By doing so, the Attlee and Churchill Governments achieved part of their aims, since American power and money were indeed the main factor in stabilising the capitalist system in Western Europe and in preventing a victory of the left, particularly in Greece and Italy where the ruling class was approaching total political bankruptcy. Moreover, NATO, although American led, was from the first tailored to suit British as well as American requirements.

But the immense increase in American influence on the continent —spasmodic and marginal before the war—introduced a new factor into the balance of forces between the three chief Western European powers, which until the beginning of the sixties worked to Britain's disadvantage.

De Gaulle has popularised the conception of the "Anglo-Saxon" powers together attempting to establish their joint hegemony in Western Europe to the detriment of the continental powers. This is correct enough as regards nuclear weapons and NATO and in its own way also reflects the general situation which emerged in the sixties, when conflicts between the United States and Britain on one side, and France and West Germany on the other, developed in a number of fields. It is, however, a highly misleading formula if applied to the course of affairs in the post-war period as a whole. Throughout the fifties, the influence acquired by Washington in Paris, Bonn and Rome, which far outweighed that of London, was systematically used to frustrate some of the central aims of British diplomacy.

This applies above all to the question of Western European integration.

Until the beginning of the sixties, as is recalled in more detail below, Labour and Conservative Governments not only themselves refused to participate in supra-national organisations, but actively attempted to draw the states of Western Europe into other forms of

[1] Francis Williams. *op. cit.* p. 171.

co-operation, thereby in deed, if not in word, countering the various plans for economic, military and political integration favoured by the dominant political and business groups in France, West Germany, Italy and Benelux.

The Truman, Eisenhower and, for a short period, Kennedy Administrations, on the other hand, gave steady support to the supra-nationalists, thereby substantially increasing the latter's ability to advance their plans regardless of British wishes and contributing to the failure of a major part of London's counter projects.

Even though, in this case, the result was in the end favourable to London rather than Washington, this Anglo-American confrontation made itself strongly felt over the abortive attempt to establish the European Defence Community. Churchill, as he told Eisenhower, had from the first disliked "the sludgy amalgam" of EDC and did not blame the French for rejecting it, but only for inventing it.[1] Dulles, on the other hand, stood by EDC to the bitter end and, when its fate was sealed, told Eden by way of criticism of the latter's alternative plan for rearming the West Germans, that he would regard "any solution which did not provide for the creation of a supra-national institution as makeshift".[2]

In the economic field, this American line contributed directly to the quandary in which London has for the last ten years and more found itself in relation to the EEC.

The conflict between the attitudes of the two Governments towards economic integration can be traced right back to differences over the functions of the Organisation for European Economic Co-operation in the late forties and the desirability or otherwise of the European Coal and Steel Community set up at the beginning of the fifties.

Taking only the more recent period, the lines of battle over what was to become the EEC were drawn before the signing of the Rome Treaties in March 1957. Eden tells us that during a visit to Washington in 1956 he was unable to reach with the American leaders an agreed view of the plans for a European common market and atomic energy authority put forward by the Messina Conference of the Six the previous year, and remarks with a loftiness rather absurd in view of subsequent events that "the United States Government entertained for these proposals the same enthusiasm as they had shown towards the ill-fated European Defence Community".[3]

The failure at the end of 1958 of the British plan for a European

---

[1] Eisenhower. *Mandate for Change.* p. 405.
[2] Eden. *op. cit.* p. 159.
[3] *Op. cit.* p. 337.

Free Trade Area, designed, among other things, to prevent the formation of an autarchic bloc of the Six, was due to the opposition not
only of France and her partners, but also of the United States which,
during more than two years of negotiation, threw its weight against
London and with the Six. When all was over, Dillon, then U.S.
Under-Secretary of State, went out of his way to praise the EEC and,
blithely ignoring Britain's existence, declared that its establishment
"promises to expand intra-European trade to the benefit of all".[1]

The same thing happened over the Macmillan Government's
attempt to use the European Free Trade Association (the Seven, set
up at the end of 1959) as a means of forcing the Common Market
states to reopen negotiations. Washington once more used its influence to prevent so-called bridge-building between the Six and the
Seven. EFTA has survived so far, but not thanks to any support
from the United States.

Last but not least, London's ability to attain its aims in Western
Europe has been undermined by the persistent weakness of the
British economy as compared with that of France, West Germany,
Italy and the other continental countries. Changes in the main
indicators for all the chief capitalist powers were tabulated and
discussed in Chapter 1. The same tendencies with particular
application to the Western European powers can be seen from the
following table, showing the far higher rate of increase in industrial
production and income per head in the continental countries as
compared with Britain.

Table 6

	average annual increase in industrial production (%) 1956–1964	Increase in national income per head (%) 1958–1963[2]
Britain	2·8	26·2
West Germany	7·3	58·2
France	6·2	47·5
Italy	8·2	58·3
Belgium	3·7	25·8
Holland	5·2	41·0

This lag made itself felt most acutely in the chronic weakness of the
pound against the mark, franc and other Western European
currencies and in repeated balance of payments crises. In every
major political, military and economic negotiation between Britain

[1] *Documents on American Foreign Relations.* 1959. New York. 1960. p. 143.
[2] *Britain and Europe: the Future.* London. 1966. p. 47.

and the continental powers, British diplomacy conducted its affairs in the shadow of recent, current or imminent financial difficulties from which the other parties were relatively free.

The task of British diplomacy was further complicated by a major change in Britain's direct economic stake in the area.

As before, the capital investments of British industrial, commercial and financial interests in Western Euope are only a fairly small fraction of their overseas investments as a whole. A rough guide to proportions is given by the official estimates of earnings on direct overseas investments in 1965. These show figures of £252 million for the sterling area, £86 million for North America and only £30 million for Western Europe.[1]

But the situation as regards foreign trade radically altered during the second post-war decade. In the mid-fifties, as the following table shows, the sterling area was still far and away Britain's chief market, but by the mid-sixties it had been replaced by Western Europe. In the course of the period 1955–1968, the former's share of British exports dropped by some 20%, while Western Europe's share rose by some 10%.

Table 7

Share of British Exports (%)

	1950	1955	1960	1966	1968
Western Europe	26	28	32	38	37
Sterling Area	46	47	40	32	28

Thus British capitalism, on top of its political and military interests in "Western Europe, has acquired a greatly increased economic stake there and a highly vulnerable one so long as Britain remains excluded from the EEC".

There follows an attempt to analyse the course of British diplomacy on the two main questions confronting it in this part of the world, Western European integration and European security.

The Integration Problem

The steps taken by France and West Germany in partnership with Italy, the Netherlands, Belgium and Luxemburg to build an integrated economic and eventually political and military community

---

[1] *Board of Trade Journal.* June 30, 1967.

have faced British diplomacy with a problem which in the last decade has increasingly overshadowed all others with which it has had to deal in Western Europe.

Experience both of general tendencies within the capitalist system and of the history of the European Economic Community shows that economic integration is not a transitory phenomenon and that it corresponds to real changes in the Western European economy arising primarily from the scientific and technological revolution.

Political and military integration has lagged behind, witness the failure of the projected European Defence Community and of the plan contained in the Bonn Declaration of July 18, 1961, in which the heads of government of all six members of the EEC announced their decision to "give shape to the will for political union already implicit in the Treaties establishing the European Communities".[1]

But the EEC has from the beginning contained within its structure a regularly functioning Council of Ministers, Commission, Assembly and other political organs. Moreover, the Elysée Treaty of 1963 provides for a far-reaching system of political and military co-operation between France and West Germany intended eventually to include all members of the EEC.

The supra-national organs of the EEC and the inter-governmental organs of the Elysée Treaty system are in competition with each other, but both in their different ways are embryo forms of an integrated politico-military superstructure which the Six have been slowly, and with many backslidings, developing.

The essence of London's problem has been that the process of integration taking place on the continent has increasingly threatened to lead to the formation of a relatively stable and powerful bloc based on the two strongest continental powers, France and West Germany, which would gradually not only squeeze Britain out of Western Europe, or at best limit her influence to its periphery, but also undermine her politico-economic positions in all parts of the world.

The seriousness of the problem was realised in high quarters by the late fifties, when it became clear that the Six, from the small beginning of the European Coal and Steel Community, were going to advance to the formation of a full-scale common market.

Macmillan, then Prime Minister, speaking shortly after the signing of the Rome Treaties but before the EEC had been brought into existence, issued a general warning. "Let us be under no delusions," he said. "By far the biggest danger would be if this great European

[1] *Documents* . . . 1961. pp. 187–189.

unit came into being and we did nothing about it and were left outside."[1]

The nature of this danger was spelled out in more detail the same year in a study financed by most of the leading banks and firms in the country (and a number of trade unions). Once a continental common market is established which is not part of a wider free-trade area, it said, the United Kingdom's economic strength relative to the rest of the world declines. The Six would have a larger population, greater output and a bigger share in world trade than Britain where now individually they rank behind it.

The study went on to point out that the connection between economic and political strength was very close, that they were two faces of the same coin, and to ask what would be Britain's position if a political federation of the Six were established. "A third great power would be added to the USA and the USSR, less formidable than either but with a much greater claim to consideration than the UK." The latter would not retain a tithe of its former influence.[2]

It proved, however, easier to identify the danger than to find effective means of forfending it. For the last ten years and more, at first by sapping from without and then by attempting to secure entry to the fortress, successive governments have been extremely active in trying to prevent the development of the EEC as an autarchic bloc hostile to their interests, but have met with a series of reverses.

Besides the factors discussed at the beginning of this chapter, this failure arose in part from the peculiar structure of British capitalism itself. As compared with the other Western powers, the wealth and strength of Britain in the post-war period has rested to a unique degree on its overseas, extra-European positions—on the large accumulations of British capital in Australia, Canada, South Africa, Iraq, Iran, Kuwait, India, Malaysia, the Rhodesias, Ghana and Nigeria, on the sterling area and imperial preference system to which most of these countries belong, and on British political influence and connections in these and many other, mostly ex-colonial, countries.

Concern for the preservation of these positions and also of the Anglo-American special relationship presented not an imaginary but a real bar to British participation in plans for integration, fulfilled and unfulfilled, put forward by the continental powers. Participation would certainly have ensured Britain a leading place in Western European affairs and hampered or even prevented the evolution of a Franco-West German coalition. But no less certainly participation

[1] *The Times.* May 23, 1957.
[2] *Britain and Europe.* The Economist Intelligence Unit. London. 1957. p. 63.

would have restricted Britain's freedom of action in other parts of
the world and eroded her influence there. To take the most obvious
examples, membership of the proposed European Defence Community would have severely limited London's freedom to use its
armed forces outside Europe, and membership of the EEC from the
beginning implied sacrificing the imperial preference system.

During the fifties one government after another, largely for the
sake of preserving these massive extra-European interests, found
itself compelled to reject the one course of action which offered a
sure means of arresting the decline of British influence in Western
Europe. In the sixties, when London was attempting to join the
EEC, these same extra-European interests and accompanying
politico-military arrangements were once more the main impedi-
ment. When de Gaulle remarked that Britain was too much linked
with "the most diverse and often the most distant countries" and that
she must "transform herself" before she could fit into the Community,[1] he was, whatever his motives, pointing to a genuine
difficulty and not one invented just to suit France's own purposes.

As regards the course pursued by British diplomacy, up to the
beginning of the sixties London declined categorically to join any of
the continental integrated organisations and endeavoured to outflank
and undermine them by extending the scope and role of the Organisation for European Economic Co-operation[2] and NATO, in which
British influence was already strong, and by setting up the European
Free Trade Association as a rival bloc to the EEC.

The general line of refusal to take part in any form of integrated
organisation was early laid down. In 1950 Prime Minister Attlee, in
turning down an invitation from the French Government to join
in setting up the future European Coal and Steel Community, said
that a clear distinction must be made between "international"
arrangements, which the Government could accept, and "supra-
national" arrangements which it could not.[3] On the same occasion,
Sir Stafford Cripps, then Chancellor of the Exchequer, stated flatly
that participation in a Western European political federation "is
not compatible either with our Commonwealth ties, our obligations
as a member of the wider Atlantic Community, or as a world power".

This attitude was confirmed by the Conservative Government as
soon as it returned to power. Churchill told the U.S. Congress, in

---

[1] Press Conference on January 14, 1963. *L'Année Politique.* 1963. Paris. 1964. p. 400.

[2] The OEEC, to which almost all the Western European states belonged, was originally
set up under British leadership to administer the European end of the Marshall Plan and
remained in existence until 1961.

[3] *Keesing's Contemporary Archives.* 1950. pp. 10906–10908.

terms no less trenchant than Cripps's, that "the British Commonwealth of Nations, spread all over the world, is not prepared to become a state or group of states in any continental federal system on either side of the Atlantic".[1]

The belief that the rejection of integration could be successfully combined with the maintenance of Britain's influence on her neighbours can be seen from a speech of Eden's delivered almost simultaneously. Having, like Churchill, declared that Britain could not join a Western European federation because her interests lie "far beyond the continent of Europe", he underlined London's other military and economic contributions to the welfare and security of the areas and claimed that "our position on all this is well understood by our European friends", rashly adding, that after talks with the French Government on these matters, he did not think that there should be more misunderstandings.[2]

In the first half of the fifties London fought its main, and largely silent, diplomatic battle against the continental integrationists (and Washington) over the question of military integration and, owing to a favourable shift in the balance of political forces in France on this issue, scored its one and only victory of this kind.

When the plan for a European Defence Community was put forward by Pleven, then French Prime Minister, in October 1950, first the Attlee Government and then the Churchill Government immediately made clear that Britain would not be a member, but adopted an ambiguous attitude towards the plan as such.

London was just as anxious as Washington, Bonn and Paris to find a way of legitimising the rearmament of West Germany, and so long as the Pleven plan seemed to be the only way of doing this, supported it and, when the French Government and Assembly began to hesitate, joined the Americans in putting pressure on them to ratify the treaties under which the EDC was to be brought into being.

On the other hand, from the start both the Labour Government and its Conservative successor wanted the rearmament of West Germany to be brought about within the framework of NATO, and not of a new supra-national continental organisation.

So long as there was a united front of Washington, Paris and Bonn supporting EDC, London was not in a position to insist on its point of view. Nevertheless, alternative plans were drawn up at a very early stage and were put forward as soon as conditions became favourable.

[1] Speech on February 17, 1952. *Documents* . . . 1952. p. 52.
[2] Eden. *op. cit.* p. 36–37.

In December 1951, Eden, in a private note to Churchill, wrote that, if the Pleven plan failed, "we should try to work out a more modest scheme with our allies . . . without elaborate political superstructure". He warned that such an initiative would require careful timing since "if we move too soon, the Pleven plan will collapse, and we shall be told we have killed it". The Foreign Office, he concluded, had been instructed to set to work on these ideas.[1]

Two years later we find Eden trying out his scheme privately on Dulles during a NATO Council meeting in Paris in December 1953. Saying that he doubted whether the proposed EDC would in the end be accepted by the French, he asked Dulles whether, as an alternative, "we could not strengthen NATO obligations and machinery, and thus control Germany ourselves within NATO".[2]

When, in August 1954, the French Assembly finally rejected the EDC treaties, these plans, under Eden's guidance, came to fruition in the Paris Agreements of 1954, providing for NATO membership for a rearmed West Germany and assigning certain political and military functions to a non-integrated body, the Western European Union, consisting of Britain and the six signatories of the abortive EDC treaties.

In the second half of the fifties, the struggle shifted to the economic field, came right out into the open and led to an entirely different result.

When it became apparent, following the Messina Conference of 1955, that the Six were likely to form a common market despite Britain's refusal to join it, the Eden Government launched a counter-offensive in the shape of a proposal to establish a European Free Trade Area based on the OEEC and covering, besides Britain, most of the states of Western Europe, including the Six.

It was proposed that members would eliminate all tariffs and quantitive restrictions on trade in manufactured goods among themselves, but would remain free to pursue their own tariff policies in relation to non-members. The OEEC itself would become the administrative centre for the Free Trade Area, but it would acquire no supra-national powers such as those contemplated for the institutions of the EEC.

On London's initiative, the Council of OEEC in July 1956 set up a working party to study this and other plans; in February 1957 it decided that negotiations should be started for the establishment of a Free Trade Area, and in October 1957 convened for this purpose

[1] Eden. *op. cit.* p. 34.
[2] *Ibid.* p. 58.

an inter-governmental committee at ministerial level, with a British minister, Maudling, as its chairman. Negotiations continued until November 1958, when, with considerable recriminations on both sides, they broke down following a French statement, acquiesced in by the other members of the Six, that the British proposal was not acceptable.[1]

In putting forward this proposal, British diplomacy was pursuing two inter-connected purposes.

Firstly, British industry and finance would have obtained free access to a very large and rapidly expanding market commensurate in size with the changes of scale demanded by modern technology, and would have done so without sacrificing their existing protected market in the Commonwealth. Moreover, since foodstuffs were excluded from the plan, both the country's inflow of cheap food imports from outside Europe and the established system of subsidies to British agricultural interests would have remained untouched.

Secondly, the substitution of a free market in manufactured goods covering almost the whole of Western Europe for one confined to the EEC would have sapped the foundations of the latter and seriously weakened its cohesion. As a group, it would have tended in time to dissolve in a wider and looser system of Western European organisations based on the wider free trade area and in which British influence would have been as great, and probably greater, than that of France or West Germany. The long-term danger of the Six developing into a closed economic and political bloc would thus have been substantially diminished.

The first purpose is reflected in the Government's arguments for a Free Trade Area submitted to the OEEC in February 1957, which speak of "the pace of technical development which increasingly demands larger markets in order that its full benefits may be obtained" and urges that an FTA "will raise industrial efficiency by the encouragement it will afford to increased specialisation, large-scale production, and new technical and industrial development".[2]

The particular advantage expected for British firms was spelled out in the study to which we have already referred. According to the detailed calculations which it contained, the greater part of British industry stood to make substantial gains if an FTA were set up, and would lose heavily if it were not, i.e., if only a common market of the Six came into existence. Taking 1955 as the starting

[1] Statement to the press by Soustelle, then French Minister of Information. *L'Année Politique*. 1958. p. 482.
[2] *Documents* . . . 1957. pp. 433–441.

point, in the first case the British share of Western European imports of passenger cars would by 1970 rise from 16% to 20%, of commercial vehicles from 19% to 29%, of chemicals from 11% to 13%, of metal manufactures from 13% to 16%, and of electrical machinery, apparatus and appliances from 14% to 20%. In the second case, these shares would fall to 5%, 6%, 4%, 5% and 9% respectively.[1]

The second, and wider, political purpose was frankly admitted in a number of official warnings that unless a Free Trade Area linking Britain with the Six was established, the creation of the EEC would cause a political as well as an economic split in Western Europe. Thus, shortly after the signing of the Rome agreements giving birth to the EEC and Euratom, the President of the Board of Trade said that "although it is not military or hostile in its intent — six countries in Europe have signed a treaty to do exactly what, for a hundred years, we have always said we could not see done with safety to our own country" and went on to declare the Government's intention through the FTA to liberalise the EEC and "make it look outwards instead of inwards".[2]

The plan for a Free Trade Area offered certain economic advantages to the Six, particularly West Germany which had massive commercial interests to protect in Western Europe outside the EEC. In 1955, Britain, the Scandinavian countries, Austria and Switzerland took almost as large a share of West German exports as the Six — 28% as compared with 29%. In the Federal Republic, unlike France, there was a considerable section of business opinion, for whom Erhard, then Minister for Economics, was the spokesman, which favoured acceptance of the British proposal, or some variant of it.

As the negotiations drew to a close, London made a special effort to rally the West German Government to its cause as a counterweight to French opposition. Only a few weeks before the breakdown, the Prime Minister (Harold Macmillan), during a visit to Bonn, extracted Adenauer's agreement to a joint statement that "the two Heads of Government agreed that it was essential, in the interests of European unity, to bring the negotiations for a Free Trade Area to an early and satisfactory conclusion".[3]

But, as we have seen, West Germany, in common with the other members of the Six, acquiesced when the French veto was imposed. A month later, at a meeting with de Gaulle at Bad Kreuznach,

---

[1] *Britain and Europe, passim.* For purposes of these calculations Western Europe was taken to mean the Six plus the three Scandinavian countries, Austria and Switzerland.
[2] *The Times.* May 28, 1957.
[3] Anglo-West German Communiqué of October 9, 1958. *Documents . . . 1958.* p. 447.

Adenauer, in effect cancelling his recent agreement with Macmillan, subscribed to a communiqué making clear that both the French and West German Governments gave first priority to the development of economic and political co-operation within the framework of the Six and leaving vague, to put it mildly, what was to happen to the idea of a Free Trade Area.[1]

London's next move was to organise a free trade area without the Six in the form of the European Free Trade Association (EFTA) consisting of Britain, Sweden, Norway, Denmark, Switzerland, Austria and Portugal — the Seven — with Finland joining later as an associate member. The Convention establishing EFTA was initialled in Stockholm on November 20, 1959, and came into force on May 3, 1960.

A secondary object of this step was to consolidate British economic interests and political influence in the EFTA countries themselves, which were and are by no means inconsiderable. Although its future is uncertain, EFTA has so far served this purpose fairly well despite a series of shocks, including the imposition by Britain in 1964–1966 of a surcharge on the import of manufactured goods in contravention of the Stockholm Convention. In 1958–1966 EFTA's share of all British exports rose from 10% to 14·6%, not so far below the share of the EEC, 18·9%.

But the chief purpose was to strengthen Britain's hand in renewed attempts to persuade the Six to agree to some variant of its earlier proposal for an all-inclusive Western European free trade area. The formation of EFTA in some measure increased the interests of West German business circles in this proposal, since, unless an agreement between the Six and the Seven were reached, EFTA implied eventual discrimination against West German goods in what was, as we have seen, an important market. EFTA also offered an at least temporary means of keeping Denmark and Austria out of the orbit of the EEC, towards which both were and are drawn by their close economic ties with West Germany.

London's, and with it EFTA's, over-riding aim figured prominently in all the latter's pronouncements on policy during the first year of its existence.

When the Stockholm Convention was initialled the seven partners published a special resolution underlining the vital role of the OEEC, stating that they regarded their new Association "as a step toward an agreement between all member countries of the OEEC"

---

[1] France-West German Communiqué of November 26, 1959. *Documents* . . . 1958. pp. 459–460.

and expressing their readiness to initiate negotiations with the EEC as soon as the latter was willing.[1]

At its meeting in May 1960 the EFTA Council expressed its increasing concern "at the distortion of the European economy which will take place if the Six and the Seven continue to drift apart".[2] In February 1961 the Council declared "EFTA's wish to take part with the EEC in the creation of a single European market" and reaffirmed its willingness to start negotiations whenever the Six wished.[3]

These hopes were, however, disappointed. At the same time as EFTA was being brought into existence, a combination of factors altered the situation to London's disadvantage and forced the policy-makers, in a major switch of tactics, to apply for membership of the EEC.

In 1959–1960 — the years when the decision to change course was in the making — although Erhard and his friends kept up their campaign for some form of fusion between the Six and the Seven (hence their slogan "6 + 7 = 1"), the dominating forces within the Six — the French and West German Governments supported by the Commission — placed more and more emphasis on consolidating the EEC as a self-contained bloc and less and less on the need to create a free trade area with the other members of the OEEC, particularly Britain.

In this respect, the decision regarding the foreign relations of the EEC, taken by its Ministerial Council in November 1959, is typical. Such concessions over quotas and tariffs as were made to third countries were given to all members of GATT and not only to the other members of the OEEC. At the same time the disingenuous thesis was advanced that "the more the Community is strengthened internally, the more it will be able to follow liberal policies towards the outside world".[4]

Simultaneously, the United States Government was working out far-reaching plans for an Atlantic Community in which there would be room for the EEC, but none for the wider Western European free trade area desired by London. Whatever advantages British diplomacy saw in these American plans for its world strategy as a whole, they at this period served directly to weaken London's position vis-à-vis the Six.

[1] *Documents* . . . 1959. pp. 528–529.
[2] *Documents* . . . 1960. p. 155.
[3] *Documents* . . . 1960. pp. 163–164.
[4] *Documents* . . . 1959. pp. 529–532.

This can be illustrated by the fate of the OEEC, which since 1948 had been one of the chief instruments of British economic policy in Western Europe and the pivot of all British plans to set up an FTA. When, on Washington's initiative and as part of the proposed closer relationship between the U.S. and Western Europe, this body was converted into the Organisation for Economic Co-operation and Development (OECD) with the United States and Canada as additional members, few of its specifically Western European functions survived and London was thus deprived of one of its main strong-points in the area.[1]

Also at this period, mainly on French initiative, some progress was made towards the establishment of a closed circuit of political and military co-operation between the Six, a development which, although it in practice went little further than declarations of intent, was understandably viewed in London with scarcely less alarm than the formation of a closed economic bloc.

In September 1958 de Gaulle and Adenauer, at their meeting at Colombey-les-Deux-Eglises, announced boldly that close co-operation between France and West Germany—with no mention of Britain—was the foundation of "all constructive endeavour in Europe", that this co-operation should be put on an organised footing and that it should include in the first place their other closest partners in Europe.[2]

At the beginning of 1959, Debré, then French Prime Minister, in a major speech dealing with the future of the Six, declared that not only economic, but also close political co-operation between them was required, that this should be organised through regular and frequent consultations between the heads of government and that here lay the road to political unity between them.[3]

By 1960 these ideas, clothed in the form of a proposed system of standing political, military, cultural and other commissions with a central secretariat and of regular meetings of heads of government, ministers and officials, was being canvassed by de Gaulle both publicly[4] and privately with the heads of government of all the other members of the Six.

In February 1961 these proposals were discussed at a summit meeting of the Six in Paris, which set up the so-called Fouchet

---

[1] The Convention setting up the OECD and dissolving the OEEC was signed in Paris on December 14, 1960.

[2] *Documents* . . . 1958. p. 445.

[3] *Documents* . . . 1959. pp. 508–509.

[4] See, for example, his press conference on September 5, 1960. *Documents* . . . 1960. pp. 157–158.

Committee charged with producing an agreed system of political co-operation for submission to a further heads of government meeting. Although divisions were sufficiently deep to prevent firm commitments being made, the result was the above-mentioned Bonn Declaration of July 18, 1961.

One of the side-effects of these developments was to evoke cries of defiance from British statesmen, such as Macmillan's outburst in Washington in March 1960. According to reports leaked to the Press by American officials, he then told the U.S. Government that "should France and Germany go on the road towards a unified Western Europe, Britain in the long run had no other choice but to lead another peripheral alliance against them" and recalled for good measure that "in the time of Napoleon, Britain allied herself with Russia to break the French Emperor's ambitions".[1]

But the main effect was to force the Government to reconsider its attitude towards possible British membership of the EEC.

In exploring the ground afresh to see whether a satisfactory bargain regarding membership could be struck London conducted a series of soundings in the capitals of all the members of EEC including, of course, France. But at this stage, and indeed for some time to come, those responsible for British diplomacy hinged their operations on the apparently favourable attitude of Bonn, thus repeating the manœuvre employed unsuccessfully to bring the Six into a Free Trade Area.

At a meeting between Macmillan and Adenauer in Bonn in August 1960, it was agreed that the latter would act as Britain's broker with the other members of the Six. In the words of the communiqué, the two parties "agreed that it was essential in the interests of European unity that a solution be found for problems arising from the existence of two economic groupings in Europe" and had "undertaken to study, in co-operation with their respective partners, all possible solutions of these problems and to exchange ideas".[2]

In parallel, the Govenment made a direct, though unsuccessful, bid to secure a seat at the discussion on political, military and other forms of co-operation then in progress between the Six.

At a meeting of the Council of the Western European Union in February 1961, Edward Heath,[3] after having made clear that London

---

[1] *The Times.* March 31, April 1, 1960.
[2] *Keesing's Contemporary Archives.* 1960. p. 17661.
[3] In July 1960, as part of the Government's preparations for a new approach to the question of relations with the Six, Heath was appointed Lord Privy Seal and Minister of State at the Foreign Office with special responsibility for European affairs.

was now ready to make considerable concessions to secure an overall economic agreement with the EEC, said that no arrangement would be satisfactory to his Government which did not involve a political as well as an economic relationship with the Six. He claimed that the WEU Council was itself the proper forum for joint discussion of European political problems between Britain and the Six and complained that it had so far been wrongly ignored. Referring to the above-mentioned summit meetings of the EEC countries, he said, in an unabashed attempt at gate-crashing, that if the United Kingdom received a unanimous invitation from the Six to join them in such a meeting, it would be accepted.[1]

This same bid was repeated a year later, when the Brussels negotiations were already in progress, and with equally little success. Speaking once more in the Council of WEU on April 20, 1962, Heath, at the end of a long and rather vague exposition of British views on "European Political Union", said outright that the UK Government, as a future member of the EEC, "naturally expect to have the opportunity of consulting with the Six before a draft treaty of political union is agreed" and wished "to join with you now in your discussions about the future political framework of Europe".[2]

In the early months of 1961, the Government set about securing U.S. support for a British application to join the EEC and was in the main successful.

It would not be true to say that at this stage the U.S. authorities had transferred their sympathies from the Six to Britain, particularly as regards the sort of bargain which the latter wished to strike as a condition of agreeing to join the EEC. When in April 1961, during a visit to Washington, Macmillan sounded Kennedy on the American reaction to a British application for membership, he was apparently advised to apply without reservations, as desired by Paris and Bonn.[3] A year later, after the Brussels negotiations had begun, Kennedy warned Macmillan that the United States Government could not support British demands for a permanent privileged status in the common market for the goods of London's partners in the Commonwealth and EFTA.[4]

On the other hand, the U.S. Government certainly wanted Britain to become a member of the EEC.

At Macmillan's request, Kennedy informed General de Gaulle that that was the wish of the U.S. Government when he visited Paris

[1] *Documents* ... 1961. pp. 164–169.
[2] *Commonwealth Survey*. April 24, 1962.
[3] *The Economist*. April 15, 1961.
[4] Schlesinger. *op. cit.* pp. 720–721.

in June, 1961, i.e., even before the British Government had announced its decision to apply for membership.[1] As soon as the announcement was made in the following month, the President made a special statement declaring that "we welcome the project of Britain's participation in the institutions of the Treaty of Rome".[2] Moreover, British membership of the EEC became one of the assumptions of U.S. foreign policy during this period. Both Kennedy's plan for a grand Atlantic alliance launched in 1962 and the U.S. Trade Expansion Act of the same year were based on the assumption that the Brussels negotiations regarding British accession to the EEC would be successful.

The stormy course of the Government's attempts to secure the acquiescence of the other members of the Commonwealth in its decision to apply for membership of the EEC is described in Part II. A similar, and more successful, operation was conducted in respect of Britain's partners in EFTA.

At an EFTA Council meeting, in June 1961, London promised that its obligations under the Stockholm Convention would remain in force until agreements had been reached with the EEC "to meet the various legitimate interests of all members of EFTA and thus enable them all to participate from the same date in an integrated European market".[3] With this assurance that they would not be betrayed, all the other members decided to follow the British lead. In due course Norway and Denmark applied for full membership of the EEC and Sweden, Austria, Switzerland and Portugal for associate membership.

These preparations complete, Macmillan announced in the House of Commons that the Government had decided to open negotiations with the Six regarding possible membership of the EEC. Negotiations began in Brussels on November 8, 1961, and continued until January 29, 1963, when, on French insistence, they were finally broken off.

In announcing the decision to apply for membership of the EEC, Macmillan stated that Britain would only join "if satisfactory arrangements can be made to meet the special needs of the United Kingdom, of the Commonwealth and of the European Free Trade Association".[4] The fifteen months of negotiations between massed batteries of Ministers and officials at Brussels were devoted almost entirely to an attempt to reach agreement on what these "arrange-

[1] *Ibid.* p. 323.
[2] *The Department of State Bulletin.* August 28, 1961. p. 362.
[3] *Documents* . . . 1961. pp. 178–179.
[4] *Ibid.* pp. 189–191.

ments" should be, in particular what special régimes should be established for Commonwealth exports and for British agriculture.

These questions in themselves proved extremely hard to settle. Even though the initial British demands were progressively watered down, especially as regards the protection of the interests of the other members of the Commonwealth, by the end of 1962 there remained a thicket of unresolved problems, including the almost untouched question of how the interests of all the other members of EFTA were to be met.[1]

The Brussels negotiations, however, did not break down because of the intrinsic difficulty of reconciling the positions taken up by the two sides on the issues before them, but because of the irreconcilability of the policies of the principal parties — Britain, France and West Germany — on a much wider question, namely that of the nature and future of the European Economic Community itself.

London's attitude, shared by Washington, was that the Community should on no account develop as an autarchic, autonomous bloc, economic, political or military, and that British entry should ensure that this did not happen, since Britain would exert enough influence within the Community to tie it firmly into the wider Atlantic community then being actively promoted by the United States.

This point of view, often expressed in the form of euphemistic demands that the Community should be "outward-looking and not inward-looking", figured in practically all official British statements on the subject. We may note particularly Heath's statement in his speech to the Western European Union in April 1962, addressed point-blank to the six governments with which he was then negotiating in Brussels, and touching the sensitive subject of defence.

"We quite accept," said Heath, "that the European political union, if it is to be effective, will have a common concern for defence problems and that a European point of view on defence will emerge." It was essential, however, that the latter "should be directly related to the Atlantic alliance. We must make it clear beyond all doubt that the object of our common policy is to defend and strengthen the liberties for which the Atlantic alliance is the indispensable shield".[2]

It is true that this conception corresponded to that which had been earlier enshrined in the Bonn Declaration of July 1961, which spoke

---

[1] For a detailed and, it seems to me, fair account of the negotiations, see Camps, *op. cit.* pp. 367–413 and 455–499.
[2] *Commonwealth Survey.* April 24, 1962.

of "a united Europe, allied to the United States of America" and of furthering "the political union of Europe, thereby strengthening the Atlantic alliance". But it was already being publicly denounced by one of the parties to the Brussels negotiations, France, and treated with open suspicion by another, West Germany.

Less than a month after Heath's remarks to the WEU, de Gaulle, at his press conference of May 15, 1962, warned against the danger of France and the other members of the Six disappearing into "something quite different, much broader and much more extensive", i.e., an Atlantic Community, and following the lead "of some outsider", i.e., the United States.[1]

Simultaneously, Adenauer, in a speech in West Berlin on May 11, declared that Britain's interests were so different from those of the countries supporting a political union of Europe that he saw no prospect of her joining.[2] Despite an attempt by Macmillan, by means of a personal letter, to persuade the Chancellor to abandon this attitude, the latter reiterated it in a broadcast on August 29, saying that even if Britain did join the Common Market, she could not join a political union.[3]

Moreover, in the second half of 1962 — the period of Adenauer's triumphal visit to France (July) and of de Gaulle's even more triumphal visit to West Germany (September) — Paris and Bonn were preparing the ground for the conclusion of a bilateral politico-military agreement (the Elysée Treaty of January 22, 1963) with clearly audible anti-Atlantic overtones.

At this stage London, seriously disturbed by these developments, made a number of political gestures towards France, especially concerning nuclear matters, going beyond the abstract generalities hitherto used by Heath and others. Moreover, in doing so they diverged, at least on the surface, from the American line.

Only ten days after the U.S. Secretary of Defence, in his Ann Arbor speech, had launched a public attack on the danger, expense, built-in obsolescence and lack of credibility of limited, independent (i.e., French) nuclear forces,[4] Macmillan went out of his way to give his blessing in principle to French nuclear policy. "France is a nuclear power, and I think likely to remain one," he said, "and the British Government understand the reason."[5]

In September, Peter Thorneycroft, newly appointed Minister of

[1] Quoted in Camps. *op. cit.* p. 726.
[2] *The Times.* May 11, 1962.
[3] *The Times.* August 28 and 30, 1962.
[4] *Documents on American Foreign Relations 1962.* New York. 1963. pp. 230–236.
[5] Statement in the House of Commons. June 26, 1962.

Defence, was reported to have proposed to the U.S. Government that it accord to France the same privileged status in nuclear matters as Britain enjoyed.[1] In the following month his Ministry let it be known that he favoured the formation of a European nuclear deterrent (based on the British and French striking forces) which, while co-operating closely with the American striking force, would nevertheless be politically independent.[2]

In a statement in December to the Assembly of the WEU, a senior Minister (again Thorneycroft) came very near to endorsing de Gaulle's cherished conception of European separatism. After painting a glowing picture of the possible role of specifically European military forces acting in alliance with the United States, he went on to declare with some of the General's own fervour, that "Europe is potentially not a parish but a world power, and we must think of her defence along these lines".[3]

Such statements as these gave the impression that London was preparing to offer Paris bilateral co-operation in the nuclear field as a means of gaining admission into the EEC and of preventing the consolidation of a Paris-Bonn axis. But, whatever the hesitations in government circles, this was not what happened. Instead, as we have recalled elsewhere, Macmillan and his colleagues moved in precisely the opposite direction. In the quandary caused by the cancellation of the Skybolt programme, they concluded at Nassau in December 1962 a fresh deal with Kennedy which made the British nuclear force dependent on American goodwill and co-operation for years to come.

Most British specialists recognise, in one form or another, the connection between the Nassau Agreement and the French veto on British membership of the EEC shortly afterwards announced at de Gaulle's press conference on January 14, 1963 and, more generally, the conflict between French Europeanism and British Atlanticism.[4] But there has been, it seems to me, a general tendency to underestimate a no less important factor in the Brussels equation, namely the Franco-West German "special relationship".

In a passage, to which there are many parallels in the works of other authors, Mrs Camps asserts that the French Government broke off the Brussels negotiations "in the face of solid opposition

---

[1] *The Times.* September 11, 1962.
[2] *The Times.* October 10, 1962.
[3] *Commonwealth Survey.* January 15, 1963.
[4] See, for example, Coral Bell. *op. cit.* pp. 89–90; A. Buchan and P. Windsor. *Arms and Stability in Europe.* London. 1963. p. 194; Dorothy Pickles. *The Uneasy Entente.* London. 1966. p. 9.

4

from the five other members of the Community".[1] In other words, France was supposedly isolated.

This, however, ignores the fact that West Germany, by far the most influential of these other members, not only did not oppose the French action, but chose this moment to enter into a formal diplomatic alliance with France.

It is true that opinions were much divided in Bonn, but when Adenauer paid his visit to Paris from January 20 to January 23, he did not press for a withdrawal of the veto, as President Kennedy, among others, had urged him to do. He acquiesced in it and at the same time signed the Elysée Treaty.

We have already recalled that, in relying on the good offices of West Germany to ease its reception into the Common Market, the Macmillan Government was repeating the tactics used in the free trade area negotiations. It remains to add that not only the manœuvre, but also the result was the same in both cases, namely that when the decisive moment came Bonn sided with Paris and not with London.

In the years following the breakdown of the Brussels negotiations, the problem facing British diplomacy remained basically the same, but there were important changes in some of its components.

As regards the Six themselves, in the period coinciding with the chancellorship of Erhard in West Germany from October 1963 to December 1966, there was a marked deterioration in Franco-West German relations and, closely connected with it, a major crisis in the affairs of the EEC.

The shift in Bonn's foreign policy towards closer understanding with Washington and London and away from the pro-French orientation of Adenauer's day resulted in the near paralysis of the Elysée Treaty system of Franco-West German co-operation, not to speak of wider plans for systematising political, military, cultural and other forms of collaboration between all members of the Community.

Only eighteen months after its conclusion, de Gaulle was complaining publicly that the Elysée Treaty had not led to the emergence of a common Franco-West German policy because "Bonn has not so far believed that this policy should be European and independent".[2] This was met by a counter-statement from the Erhard régime that the Treaty had indeed not led to agreement on many important

[1] Camps. *op. cit.* p. 502.
[2] Press Conference of July 23, 1964. *L'Année Politique* 1969. Paris. 1965. p. 277.

matters, but that "a joint policy between two Governments cannot signify the acceptance of all the views of the other partner".[1]

Against this background of diverging French and West German foreign policies, a violent quarrel broke out in the EEC between France, on one side, and the other five, led by the West Germans, on the other, mainly over agricultural policy, the functions of the Commission and the powers of the Council of Ministers to take majority decisions. From July 1965 until January 1966, the French Government refused to attend meetings of the Council of Ministers and other organs of the Community, thus temporarily freezing its further development.

But, contrary to the opinion widely held at the time, these developments heralded neither the break-up of the Franco-West German alignment, nor the disintegration of the EEC by internal combustion.

From the moment when in December 1966 the Erhard régime was replaced by a government dominated by the pro-French wing of the Christian Democratic Party, led by Kiesinger and Strauss, West German policy moved back nearer to the course marked out in the late fifties and early sixties. The crisis in the EEC was settled even earlier, the French boycott ending in the first half of 1966, when the other five conceded the substance of the French demands.

Without going into the details of that settlement, it is necessary to mention the agreement reached on agricultural policy in May 1966, since it introduced a new factor into the problem of Britain's possible membership of the EEC.

Briefly, the EEC's new system of levies on food imports from outside the common market and fixed agricultural prices within it meant that, if Britain became a member, she would have to face a sharp rise in domestic food prices and a substantial extra burden on her balance of payments, arising from the foreign exchange cost of the levies payable to the Community. According to official British estimates, the cost of food to the British consumer would rise by 10–14%, equivalent to a rise in the cost of living of $2\frac{1}{2}$–$3\frac{1}{2}$%. The extra burden on the balance of payments was put at between £175,000,000 and £250,000,000 a year.[2]

These years also saw a widening of the breach between the United States and Western Europe, and a substantial diminution in American influence in Western European affairs.

Owing primarily to the active and persistent opposition of the French Government, Washington's plans for building what Kennedy

[1] *Commonwealth Survey.* September 15, 1964.
[2] *Hansard.* May 8, 1967. Cols. 1065–1070.

had called "a great new edifice", "a concrete Atlantic partnership" between America and a united Western Europe[1] came to nothing. NATO, instead of taking on a fresh lease of life as the military arm of a new Atlantic community, began to fall apart. American attempts, supported by Bonn, to bring into being a new Western European nuclear force (the MLF) as a component of a unified Atlantic force controlled by the Pentagon broke against French opposition and British obstruction.

The EEC, far from developing into a supporting pillar of a wider community headed by the United States, emerged more and more clearly as the latter's chief economic rival in the capitalist world, its members forming a single opposing bloc in the GATT negotiations in 1964–1967 concerning the reduction of tariffs (the Kennedy Round) and also to an increasing extent in the critical (still unfinished) struggle between all the main capitalist powers over the gold parity of the dollar.

Towards the end of 1966 President Johnson was still using the same, but now very hollow-sounding, phrases inherited from Kennedy's day. The new Europe, he said, "would be a stronger, increasingly united but open Europe—with Great Britain a part of it—and with close ties to America".[2] But American diplomacy in Western Europe lost both momentum and direction, the more so as in the mid-sixties American world strategy began to focus more and more upon East Asia rather than Europe.

We should also note that, in parallel with the similar development in Britain already discussed, some attention began to be paid in American political and business circles to the possibility of forming an Atlantic grouping without the Six, based initially on the United States, Canada, Britain and the other members of EFTA and taking the form in the first place of a free trade area in manufactured goods.[3]

In their practical diplomacy after the door was slammed in Brussels, the Conservative Government and its Labour successor for some three years perforce played a waiting game regarding relations with the EEC, and endeavoured to strengthen the position of British exports in the EFTA and Commonwealth markets and, in partnership with the United States, to diminish the discriminatory

[1] Speech at Philadelphia on July 4, 1962. *Documents on American Foreign Relations 1962.* New York. 1963. p. 226.
[2] Speech to the National Conference of Editorial Writers in New York on October 7, 1966. *The Department of State Bulletin.* October 24, 1966. p. 624.
[3] For details see Sperry Lea. *Americans for Free Trade. The Round Table.* London. January 1967; and a letter from Senator Javits and a large group of other signatories published in *The Times* on February 21, 1967.

effect of the common market's external tariff by bargaining with the Six within the framework of the Kennedy Round.

One of London's first moves was to set about reviving EFTA, which during the whole period of the Brussels negotiations had remained in a state of suspended animation. At its meeting in May 1963, in Lisbon, the EFTA Ministerial Council decided that tariffs on industrial goods traded between member countries should be eliminated by the end of 1966—three years earlier than originally planned. The following year, on British initiative, the Council was held at Prime Ministerial level. Wilson made clear on this occasion that London, in contrast to its previous tactics, now wished that any approach to the EEC should be made not by Britain alone but collectively by EFTA.

The Government also reversed its attitude towards the imperial preference system, which, under pressure of the Six, it had been ready to sacrifice as part of the price of securing admission to the EEC. At the Commonwealth Economic Consultative Council held in London in May 1963, great stress was put on the importance of developing intra-Commonwealth trade. The communiqué declared that the imperial preference system "had made, and continued to make, a major contribution to the economic development of the Commonwealth and to world trade, and any modifications would need to be considered in the light of compensating benefits which might be offered".[1] In January 1965 the Goverment announced the formation of a Commonwealth Exports Council to promote British exports to all parts of the Commonwealth.

This is not the place to examine British policy in the GATT negotiations, but we may recall the statement of a member of the Government as they got under way that "the Kennedy Round provides the best, possibly the only, chance of off-setting the disadvantages of tariff discrimination within Europe since the breakdown of Britain's negotiations with the Community".[2]

Meanwhile the question of British membership of the EEC was left dormant. In the general election campaign in the autumn of 1964, not only the Labour Party, the leadership of which had opposed the earlier attempt to secure entry, but also the Conservative leaders who had carried it out, treated the issue, in Douglas-Home's phrase, as a dead duck.

When asked to define his position shortly after assuming power,

[1] *Commonwealth Survey.* May 21, 1963.
[2] Speech by the Parliamentary Secretary to the Board of Trade at Zurich on May 6, 1964. *Ibid.* May 26, 1964.

Harold Wilson replied that "there is no reason to suppose that the circumstances which led to the breakdown of the Brussels negotiations have changed" and, reverting to the ideas and phraseology of the end of the fifties, said that the new Labour Government would "do all we can to build a bridge between EFTA and the EEC".[1]

Although there were signs in the winter of 1965–1966 that the Government was contemplating a change of policy, the official position remained substantially unchanged until after the general election in March 1966 was over.

But immediately after their re-election Wilson and his colleagues began clearing the decks for a new application to join the EEC, the first public move being the appointment of a new ministerial team to deal with relations with Western Europe, headed by George Brown, then Secretary of State for Economic Affairs and a well-known advocate of British membership.

In November 1966 the Prime Minister announced that he and Brown, who had meanwhile become Foreign Secretary, intended to engage in a series of discussions with each of the heads of government of the Six to see if it were likely that essential British and Commonwealth interests could be safeguarded should Britain accept the Treaty of Rome and join the EEC. After these discussions had been held, Wilson stated in May 1967 that the Government had decided to apply for membership.[2] Eight days later, with the support of the leadership of the Conservative Party, the Government obtained an overwhelming majority for this decision in the House of Commons (488 to 62). Formal letters applying for membership were delivered the next day, May 11.

While the underlying factors responsible for this decision were the same as those which moved the Macmillan Government five years earlier, the chief immediate cause was, it seems to me, the domestic economic impasse in which the policy-makers found themselves.

In the mid-sixties, the chronic sickness of the balance of payments entered a new and critical phase, marked no longer by periodic, but by continuous outsize deficits—£776 million in 1964, £342 million in 1965, £133 million in 1966 and £540 million in 1967—and culminating in the devaluation of sterling in November 1967.

At the same time industrial production was expanding at a snail's pace and far more slowly than that of all the other leading powers. In the three-year period 1964–1966 the British index rose by only 6 points, while that of Japan went up by 49, of Italy by 32, of

[1] *Hansard.* February 16, 1965. Col. 1003.
[2] *Hansard.* May 2, 1967. Col. 310.

the United States by 26, of France by 12 and of West Germany by 11.

The persistent failure to stabilise the balance of payments and get the economy on the march created, as is shown below, a new and serious obstacle to acceptance by the Six of British membership of the EEC, but it also blew a gaping hole in the arguments of those, inside and outside the Cabinet, in business and financial circles and in Whitehall, who had maintained that, since the country's troubles would be cured without any radical change in the structure of her external relations, the question of accession could be left to rest.

Developments on the other side of the Channel also played their part.

Firstly, during the period of Franco-West German estrangement and of acute internal conflict within the EEC, French diplomacy made a number of friendly gestures towards London, which, while calculated to neutralise the danger of a common front being formed by Britain and the other five members of the EEC and to exercise pressure upon Bonn, gave the Government some reason to believe that French opposition to British membership of the common market had relaxed.

At his Press conference on February 5, 1965, de Gaulle went out of his way to say that he believed it possible to draw France and Britain much closer together and to deal with all problems common to the two countries.[1] At the end of the year, he went further saying, in a television broadcast, that when, as he hoped, progress was made in organising political co-operation between the Six, Britain should and probably would join in.[2]

At a Council meeting of the Western European Union in March 1966, the French representative, according to the account given to the Press by the British Foreign Secretary, made clear that "France now believed it would be desirable for Britain to become a member of the EEC". In commenting on this incident in the House of Commons, the Prime Minister, while admitting that there might be various interpretations of what the French representative had said, claimed that from information available to him there was "a major change in the French position".[3]

Secondly, since the internal crisis of the EEC was settled on French terms, it became clear that politically the Community would for some time to come develop along lines favoured by London, i.e.,

---

[1] *Commonwealth Survey*. March 16, 1965.
[2] *The Times*. December 15, 1965.
[3] *Commonwealth Survey*. May 13, 1966.

towards a confederation in which the supra-national functions of its central organs would remain strictly limited.

In 1962, while the Brussels negotiations were in progress, the then Foreign Secretary defined very frankly the Government's attitude to the perpetual struggle within the Six between the supra-nationalists and their opponents. "If we act quickly now," he said, "we can go into Europe and help shape the political structure in the way which suits us best. De Gaulle doesn't want a tight European Federation, a Federal Europe—he wants a union of independent states. If we go in now, that is what it will be."[1] We may also recall that from 1962 onwards the draconian conditions for membership of the common market laid down by the Labour Party leadership included "freedom to pursue our own foreign policy" and "the right to plan our own economy".

In 1966, while there was no question of Britain "shaping" the political structure of the EEC, the at least temporary victory of the Gaullist conception of "l'Europe des patries" eased one of the main difficulties confronting British diplomacy and made the prospect of membership a good deal more attractive to former opponents in Britain both among the policy-makers and the public generally.

Thirdly, the evolution of French foreign policy since the early sixties away from the rigid position, maintained jointly with Bonn, over East-West relations in Europe, and the development of a sustained French offensive against American domination and against American aggression in Vietnam, played their part in reducing left-wing opposition in Britain to membership of the EEC. While the effect of this factor might have been negligible under a Conservative Government, it entered directly into the political arithmetic of the Wilson régime, dependent as it was and is upon the support of both left and right in the Labour Party and trade-union movement.

The fate of the second British application to join the EEC was the same as that of the first and for the same basic reason. At his Press conference on November 27, 1967, de Gaulle said that he was opposed to opening negotiations with Britain since to do so would lead to the break-up of the Community, and that the British people must first undertake the immense efforts which would one day transform their country into "one of the pillars of a European Europe". British membership would be incompatible with the attempt to make Europe "a counter-weight to the immense power of the United States" and independent of "a foreign economic, monetary and political system".[2]

---

[1] Lord Home in an interview published in *The Observer* of September 23, 1962.
[2] *Le Monde*. November 29, 1967.

At a meeting of the Council of Ministers of the EEC on December 18 and 19, the French representative, against the opposition of the other five members, insisted that negotiations with London should not be opened. As a result, the Council, while leaving the question of the British (and Norwegian, Danish and Irish) applications on its agenda, recorded its inability for the time being to take any decision upon it.[1]

In attempting to assess the situation as it stands at the moment, I think one must take as the starting point the long-term divisive process at work in the relations between the chief Western powers and the tendency for the latter to divide up into the counter-poised Western European and North American groupings discussed at the beginning of this book. Among its other consequences, this process has led to a situation in which the question of Britain's relations with the EEC forms an integral part of the wider question of her relations both with the other Western European powers and with the United States. What appears on the surface as a relatively limited problem, turning mainly on the economic advantages and disadvantages to the French, West German and British capitalist classes of British membership of a new form of privileged market is organically connected with the less visible, but far more important, problem of whether Britain will in future belong, economically, politically and militarily, to a Western European or a North American, Atlantic grouping.

The decision-takers have so far consistently aimed at membership of the EEC combined with the Anglo-American special relationship in the nuclear field and with American military domination of Western Europe through NATO. In doing so, they have been steering against an undertow in intra-Western relations which has proved far stronger than they reckoned and as a result they have twice been driven on to the rocks. The question is whether this is likely to happen again.

On the face of it, there is much to suggest that the answer must be "yes". Since de Gaulle's resignation in April 1969, the Government, cheered by the departure of their principal opponent in this matter, have been girding themselves for a third assault on the barricades, again without any overt sign of willingness to strengthen their politico-military ties with France and West Germany and to weaken them with the United States, especially in the nuclear field. As we have seen, the official response to continental pressure for a

[1] Statement issued to the Press on December 19, 1967.

4*

change of this kind so far consists of a proposal to form a British-led European group within NATO—NATO of which French forces and French military staff no longer form part.

In adopting this attitude Wilson and his colleagues are not only flying in the face of established French policy, but, like Macmillan and Heath before them, are also risking another collision with one fairly powerful school of thought in Bonn, once led by Adenauer and now by Strauss. The German Gaullists, it is true, are not yet ready to dispense with NATO any more than Britain's leaders are. But they want, nonetheless, to proceed forthwith with the building of an autonomous Western European military system, beginning with creation of a European nuclear force, based on French and British warheads and delivery systems.

Bearding the lion in his den, Strauss told a distinguished British audience gathered in the Palace of Westminster in May 1969 that the creation of a European defence organisation "is the only chance Western Europe has of becoming a potentially equal and autonomous partner of the United States within NATO" and that the first step could be for "Great Britain and France to pool their nuclear arms, creating the core of a European nuclear force to which the other European countries could make appropriate contributions".[1] Strauss's views are not shared by the West German Social Democrats now in power, nor for that matter by all groups within his own party. But judging by their frequent appearance in West German foreign policy over the last decade and more, they are, like de Gaulle's ideas, far more than the personal programme of one man.

The Government's present course also runs counter to that of the supra-nationalists, who are represented at or near the seat of power in all six countries of the EEC, but whose influence is perhaps strongest in Bonn. On them and their ideas, the Prime Minister, after some initial hesitation, turned his back at a rally in June 1969, intended to demonstrate the genuineness of Britain's determination to join the Community. "Whatever the future may hold," said Wilson, "the creation of supra-national, federal, political or defence institutions is not a reality in ten or twenty years."[2]

On the other hand, there are certain factors working in favour of a successful outcome some time during the present decade of British attempts to get into the EEC.

Firstly, the scientific and technological revolution lying at the root of the process of Western European integration, which has so far led

[1] *Survey of British and Commonwealth Affairs.* June 6, 1969.
[2] *The Times.* July 30, 1969.

to the organisation of two antagonistic trading blocs, one led by Britain, and the other by France and West Germany, as it develops further has the opposite effect of breaking down the barriers between the two organisations and impelling the members of both into one grouping. This applies particularly not only to Britain, the majority of whose industrial and financial leaders have long stood for a fusion of EFTA and the EEC, but also to West Germany. For more than a decade the top echelon of the German business world has considered the present boundaries of the Common Market to be too narrow to suit their interests and seen advantage in their expansion to include Britain and the other members of EFTA.

Secondly, the latest advances in the technique of nuclear warfare are slowly but surely pushing Britain nearer and nearer to the situation of the other Western European powers and undermining her present status of junior partner of the United States in nuclear affairs. Britain was able to participate as a principal and third party in the Soviet-American test-ban and non-proliferation negotiations, because she had weapons to test and to proliferate. She cannot claim a place at Soviet-American discussions on the question of anti-ballistic missile systems, because she has not the resources to build such a system, nor does the United States require British territory or British assistance to build its own.

One can see the incipient Europeanisation of Britain's status in this field in one aspect of Nixon's visit to London in February 1969, when the Government, as might any other Western European Government, pointed out to him that U.S.-Soviet talks on limiting anti-ballistic missile systems could affect the lives of millions of people in Western Europe and asked for an assurance that, should such talks take place, "Europe would be consulted".[1]

Thirdly, military withdrawal from east of Suez and the redisposition of the forces withdrawn in Europe and its surrounding seas has the effect of increasing Britain's real weight in Western European affairs and of giving British diplomacy a certain freedom of manœuvre vis-à-vis France and West Germany, which it has not for many years enjoyed. Perhaps even more important in the present context, it also leads, as we have already seen, to a weakening of the Anglo-American special relationship in an area of critical and increasing importance in world affairs, namely East Asia and the Western Pacific.

Fourthly, if, as seems quite possible, the British balance of payments is at last slowly emerging from its chronic crisis, the question

[1] *Survey of British and Commonwealth Affairs.* April 11, 1969.

of the cost to Britain, in the literal sense, of membership of the Common Market will become progressively less acute. At the time of the second attempt to gain entry, the Government, while realising and publicly stating that the country could only join with a strong balance of payments and stable pound, took the absurd position only a few months before the last and fatal run on the pound that these conditions were already being fulfilled and that this was fully realised by the Six.[1] It may be that what was then a myth, and one which even those in Brussels who favoured Britain's entry could not swallow,[2] will in a year or two's time bear some resemblance to the truth.

So far as practical policy is concerned, the main question, it seems to me, is whether the Government, by modifying its present opposition to any form of European separatism in the military, particularly nuclear, field, eventually lifts the particular latch which, judging by past experience, is the one that opens the door to the EEC. As we have seen, a proposal to France of nuclear marriage was once on the tip of the tongue of the Macmillan Government and now forms part of official Conservative policy. I cannot help thinking that Wilson and his colleagues must also have it at the back of their minds.

The last word here almost certainly lies with Washington both because the British striking force is now directly dependent on American components and because no Government, Labour or Tory, would in present circumstances make a move eventually affecting the whole balance within the Western alliance without the consent of its leader.

The views of the present American administration on Britain's place as between the United States and the continental powers were set out by Nixon in an interview published shortly after his election to the presidency. "While I favour closer Anglo-American relations," he said, "and even some short-term special arrangement between the two countries, I hope that Britain will be successful in forging closer ties to the Continent. I've said before: 'Britain belongs in Europe. Europe needs Britain and Britain needs Europe.'"[3] If this attitude is maintained, one of its consequences might be American consent to some form of hiving off of the Western European nuclear forces, and conventional forces as well, provided that this formed part of a wider operation resulting in British membership of the EEC.

[1] *Hansard.* May 8, 1967. Col. 1077.
[2] See, for example, the report of the EEC Commission of September 29, 1967. *Survey of British and Commonwealth Affairs.* November 24, 1967.
[3] *The Observer.* November 24, 1968.

Two Sides to Security

During the quarter of a century which has elapsed since the end of the last direct threat to the independence of the country, for all British governments the phrase "European security" has had two main meanings, one predominant and the other subsidiary.

In the first place and predominantly, it has meant the security of Britain and the rest of capitalist Western Europe against the Soviet Union and the rest of socialist Eastern Europe. During the Greek civil war in the forties, this conception was stretched to cover also security against the acquisition of state power by indigenous Communist-led movements within Western Europe.

In the second place, and very much in the second place, "European security" has meant security against renewed military aggression at some future date by German capitalism from its present base in West Germany.

In these twenty-five years there has been a shift, though a slow and hesitant one, in the practical interpretation given by British diplomacy to these two conceptions, and in the relative importance attached to each. This comes out fairly clearly if one compares the first with the second post-war decade.

Up till about 1955 the Attlee and Churchill Governments were obsessed with the idea of building up a massive military front against the Soviet Union and, for this purpose, strove hard, and successfully, to bring about the rearmament of West Germany. It is true that, as we have seen, they wanted this done within the framework of NATO and not of the proposed European Defence Community. It is also true, as shown by the terms of the Paris Agreements of 1954, that they did not wish West Germany to manufacture its own nuclear weapons. But subject to these provisos, the whole weight of British diplomacy was thrown in favour of the creation of a new Wehrmacht and against attempts from whatever quarter to stop or delay this process.

The idea of once more attempting to use Germany as a military counterforce to the Soviet Union, familiar from Neville Chamberlain's day, was circulating in high quarters before even the war in Europe was over.

A diary entry for 1944 by Field-Marshal Alanbrooke, then Chief of the General Staff, shows that when asked whether Germany should "be dismembered or gradually converted into an ally to meet the Russian threat", he suggested the latter. He felt certain, he wrote, "that we must from now onwards regard Germany in a very different light. Germany is no longer the dominating power in Europe . . . Russia is.[1]" We have it on Churchill's word that before the fighting was over he either told the British commander in the field (Field-Marshal Montgomery) "to be careful in collecting German arms, to stack them so that they could easily be issued again to the German soldiers with whom we should have to work if the Soviet advance continued", or had it in mind to do so.[2]

The decision openly to work for West German rearmament was taken in September 1950 at a meeting of the American, British and French Foreign Ministers in New York.

Ernest Bevin, the British representative on this occasion, once accused the pacifist, George Lansbury, of taking his conscience round from body to body, asking to be told what to do with it.[3] Over this question, he himself was guilty of the same misdemeanour.

Bevin displayed his tender conscience on the subject of German rearmament by telling the House of Commons in March 1950 that "all of us are against it. I repeat all of us are against it. It is a terrible decision to take.[4]" This was, however, a coy plea for sympathy and not a statement of policy. As informed accounts agree, at the New York meeting only a few months later he was determined that, terrible or not, West Germany should be rearmed, his only difference with the Americans being on the method.[5]

The Conservatives, when they returned to power in 1951, energetically set about achieving the objective already defined by their predecessors, Eden being, as we have recalled, the chief architect of the Paris Agreements, legalising West German rearmament and West German membership of NATO. He was himself, he tells us, the author of a Foreign Office statement, which sums up Government policy at this period. "The rejection of the Paris Agreements would not mean that German rearmament would not take place," it said. "The question is not whether the German Federal Republic will rearm, but how."[6]

In the second post-war decade, and indeed down to the present time, the main priorities remained the same, but the practical objectives of British diplomacy were modified.

As before, the chief aim was the preservation for an indefinite

---

[1] Arthur Bryant. *Triumph in the West.* 1943–1946. London. 1959. p. 242.
[2] Speech at Woodford on November 23, 1954. *Hansard.* December 1, 1954. Cols. 161–171.
[3] At the Annual Conference of the Labour Party in 1935, which resulted in Lansbury's replacement as leader by Attlee.
[4] *Documents* . . . 1949–1950. p. 315.
[5] For two eye-witness accounts, see I. Kirkpatrick. *The Inner Circle.* London. 1959. pp. 239–241, and Dean Acheson. *Sketches from Life.* London. 1961. pp. 31–34.
[6] Eden. *op. cit.* p. 171.

period of NATO, with a large West German contingent and backed up by an Anglo-American (90% American) nuclear force as a counter to Soviet military strength in Europe.

At the same time, within the limits set by pressures from its American and West German allies, successive Governments, both Conservative and Labour, tentatively promoted the idea of military disengagement rather than military confrontation in Europe and of reaching some form of stable *modus vivendi* between its socialist and capitalist halves, based on existing frontiers and on reduced force and armament levels.

It would be an exaggeration to say that official circles became less and less concerned with a possible military threat from socialist Europe and more and more concerned with a possible threat from West Germany and redirected their policy accordingly. On the other hand, the sort of European security system contemplated in London in this period certainly contained some provisions which had long figured in the foreign policy programme of the Soviet Union, Poland, Czechoslovakia and the other Eastern European states and which were not at all welcome to Bonn.

Moreover, in its official assessments of the danger to the security of Britain and the rest of Western Europe, the Government abandoned its well-worn thesis that, owing to the inherent aggressiveness of the Soviet Union, war in Europe was always just round the corner.

The Statement on the Defence Estimates 1965 stated, for example, that "bearing in mind the high risk that any conflict in Europe would escalate, deliberate aggression, even on a limited scale, is unlikely in this theatre.[1]" The Defence Review published in 1966, surveying British defence policy for the next several years, declared that, according to NATO's experience in the previous decade, "the danger of deliberate war in Europe at any level is small, so long as the potential aggressor believes that this is likely to lead to a nuclear response".[2]

The basic factors responsible for this evolution influenced the policy not only of Britain but of all the Western powers directly concerned with European security, and, for all their divergencies and differences of approach, produced a basically similar result in each case.

The attainment by the Soviet Union and its allies from the beginning of the fifties of a growing nuclear counter-strike capacity and with it an increasing degree of immunity from nuclear attack, and the emergence more and more distinctly of peaceful co-existence as

---

[1] Command 2592. 1965.
[2] Command 2901. 1966.

the main aim of their European policy, the passing of the post-war revolutionary crisis and the consolidation of capitalist régimes in most of Western Europe, and the growth of major politico-economic conflicts between the Western powers themselves, all helped in their various ways to demote the anti-Communist crusade from its dominating position in Western foreign policy and to open the road towards the stabilisation and normalisation of relations between the eastern and western halves of the continent.

Even though the process was a gradual one and no firm lines of demarcation can be drawn, I think it is possible nonetheless to discern some sort of turning points in 1955 in the case of Britain, in the formation of the Gaullist régime in 1958, when anti-American began to get the upper hand over anti-Soviet tendencies in French foreign policy, in the advent of the Kennedy Administration in the United States in 1960–1961, and in the succession to power of the Christian Democrat–Social Democrat coalition in West Germany in 1966, which, among other similar changes in foreign policy, made the first major break with the Hallstein doctrine by establishing diplomatic relations with Rumania.[1]

Besides these general factors affecting all the Western powers, the evolution of British policy was, and still is, influenced by a number of others peculiar to Britain. In the first place, the growth of autarchic integrationalist tendencies in continental Western Europe, the gradual squeezing out of British influence and the emergence in embryo of a new combination, with West Germany and France as its leaders, compelled the policy-makers to widen the angle from which they viewed the question of Euporean security to include their own highly unsatisfactory relationship with the Six.

Pure bluff though they were, all the hints issued by the Government from time to time of a possible radical change of policy regarding European security were linked with its own unsuccessful attempts either to dissolve or take over the leadership of the Six rather than with security questions *per se*.

The most striking example of this we have already quoted, namely Macmillan's cry in early 1960 that if France and West Germany continued upon their autarchic course, Britain would be compelled to lead a peripheral alliance against them. He made the same point in more cautious language the following year, in announcing the

---

[1] Since the Hallstein doctrine laid down that West Germany would not establish diplomatic relations with any state (except the Soviet Union) which recognised the German Democratic Republic, it meant in practice that Bonn, unlike London, Washington or Paris, refused to have diplomatic relations with any of the other socialist states of Eastern Europe.

Government's decision to apply for membership of the EEC. "If we cannot succeed in bringing this negotiation to a satisfactory conclusion," he said, ". . . the countries with whom we are to negotiate ought to be clear that . . . quite major changes may be made in the foreign policy and commitments of Great Britain."[1]

More recently, there occurred the so-called Chalfont affair, when in October 1967 the Minister in charge of Britain's second attempt to join the Six let it be known that, if the application were rejected, there would be a basic reappraisal of British foreign policy, covering such questions as the future presence of British forces on the continent, the Four-Power Agreements concerning Berlin, recognition of the East German Government and British membership of NATO.[2]

It is true that, since London's attempts first to set up a European Free Trade Zone and then to obtain entry to the EEC were pivoted on securing West German support, British diplomacy, in defining its attitude to various aspects of European security, continually found itself obliged to look over its shoulder at Bonn and to trim its sails in order to win the latter's good graces.

This vulnerability to West German pressure goes far to explain the peculiarly hesitant and self-contradictory character of British diplomacy to a whole series of proposals for reducing tension between Eastern and Western Europe. It also, incidentally, accounts for Macmillan's flight of oratory in praise of the Federal Republic at the UN Assembly in the autumn of 1960,[3] which formed a natural corollary to his August agreement with Adenauer that the latter would act as Britain's broker in securing membership of the Six.

It is also true that there was an inherent contradiction in the Government's threats of a revision of its European policy, rather similar to that in Dulles's famous, and equally ineffective, warning of "an agonising reappraisal" of American policy, if her allies, particularly France, refused to do what he wanted them to do.

In both cases, a supposedly punitive withdrawal from continental Western European affairs would have accelerated precisely these tendencies in French and West German policy which it was desired to arrest.

On the other hand, the steadily increasing pressure exerted by the continental powers on London's economic and political positions in Western Europe tended on the whole to make the policy-makers

---

[1] *Hansard.* July 31, 1961. Cols. 937–938.
[2] Accounts of Chalfont's remarks by the British journalists to whom they were addressed, while basically the same, vary in detail. The foregoing is based on those in the *Financial Times* of October 28 and 31 and *The Observer* of October 29, 1967.
[3] *The Times.* September 30, 1960.

more and not less interested in developing some sort of *modus vivendi* with the Soviet Union and its allies, if only as a form of reinsurance.

Secondly, Britain's chronic economic and financial difficulties gave rise to a persistent tendency in London to favour a reduction in the size, and with it the foreign exchange cost, of the British forces stationed in West Germany, which in turn coloured its attitude to the wider question of reducing force and armament levels in Central Europe generally and also caused sharp disagreements between the British and West German Governments.

In 1957–1958, in connection with severe balance of payments difficulties, the Macmillan Government, in the teeth of West German objections, reduced the British Army of the Rhine (BAOR) by one division and, after prolonged and acrimonious negotiations, extracted from Bonn, as a contribution to the future foreign exchange costs of the BAOR, three annual payments of £12,000,000 and an advance payment of £50,000,000 to be spent on arms orders in Britain.[1]

The balance of payments crisis in the summer of 1961 again precipitated a corresponding crisis over the size and cost of the BAOR. The above-mentioned three annual payments being by then exhausted, the Government abruptly announced that it was not prepared alone to bear the foreign exchange costs of its forces in West Germany in the following year or, in other words, that the BAOR would be further reduced unless Bonn agreed to make further contributions to its upkeep.[2] Faced with this ultimatum, the West Germany Government was forced into a new agreement on cost-sharing, renewed with variations and much back-biting in succeeding years.

In 1966–1967, when the pound was on its last legs before it was devalued, the Wilson Government secured new offset payments covering most of the foreign exchange costs of the British forces in West Germany (some £72,000,000 out of £82,000,000) this time from the United States as well as the Federal Republic, but also found itself obliged on financial grounds to make a cut in their size, withdrawing to Britain one brigade group of BAOR and one squadron of the RAF, Germany.[3]

Thirdly, ever since the Second World War—far more so than after the First—British public opinion has remained particularly

---

[1] For more details, see Foreign Office statement of May 29, 1958. *Documents* . . . 1958, pp. 359–361.

[2] Statement by the Chancellor of the Exchequer (Selwyn Lloyd) in the House of Commons on July 25, 1961. *Documents* . . . 1961. pp. 531–532.

[3] For details, see statement by the Minister of State for Foreign Affairs, George Thomson. *Hansard.* May 2, 1967. Cols. 332–339. Formal permission for the cuts was given at the NATO Council Session in December 1967.

sensitive to the danger of a revival of German militarism and of an eventual renewal of German aggression, and favourably inclined to the creation of a European security system which would effectively guard against it.

A fairly detailed study of British opinion and policy towards Germany by one leading British expert on foreign affairs complains that public opinion has throughout acted as a brake and limitation on the freedom of action of the Government to develop a more cordial and closer relationship with the Federal Republic. British relations with Germany, says the author, have therefore been formed "by an interaction between the traditional realism of Britain's political and professional diplomatic leadership and the emotional attitudes of hostility towards Germany of public opinion in Britain".[1]

While disagreeing with his idea of what has been realistic and what has been emotional, I think the author's definition of the role of public opinion on this question is about right. If only for electoral reasons, neither Conservative nor, still less, Labour Governments were able to ignore the fact that many features of West Germany's internal political development, her territorial claims and her demands for possession of or access to nuclear weapons aroused very little sympathy and often active and widespread criticism in all sections of British society.

We may note here the complaint of the West German Ambassador in London about what he calls the "over-sensitive" public reaction in Britain to events in his country and to the policy of his Government. "The anti-semitic incidents in Germany in 1960," he writes, "released a wave of indignation and excitement in Great Britain far greater than in any other Western country. Again, the news that the establishment of bases for the Bundeswehr in Spain was under consideration provoked an equally hostile response."[2]

After von Herwarth's time (he was Ambassador in London from 1955 till 1961), public disquiet of this kind continued unabated. In the first half of the sixties anxiety focused mainly on the danger that Bonn would somehow or other succeed in getting its finger on the nuclear trigger. More recently, public opinion has shown itself to be particularly sensitive (or "oversensitive" as Bonn would have it) to the growing influence of the neo-Nazi National Democratic Party.

This critical attitude was, and is, to be found in all parts of the political and social spectrum. It has been reflected and encouraged

[1] D. C. Watt. *Britain Looks to Germany*. London. 1965. p. 13.
[2] Hans von Herwarth. "Anglo-German Relations. A German View." *International Affairs*. London. October 1963.

by the Beaverbrook newspapers, more cautiously by the greater part of the serious Press, including *The Times*, once the arch-appeaser, by well-known experts on Germany, such as A. J. P. Taylor, and by High Tories, like Lord Hinchingbrooke. But it is most deeply rooted in the Labour movement.

In 1954, even though it was a Labour Government which in 1950 had decided in principle to promote the rearmament of West Germany, both the trade union movement and the Labour Party were split down the middle when the time came for practical decisions.

At the Trades Union Congress in that year over 3,500,000 votes were cast against German rearmament compared with 4,000,000 in favour. At the Labour Party Conference a few weeks later the majority was narrower still, 3,270,000 votes in favour and 3,022,000 against. Moreover, Attlee and his friends obtained this Pyrrhic victory only because the delegation of one of the smaller unions, the Woodworkers, were persuaded at the last minute to ignore the clearly expressed decision of their own annual conference.[1]

When the Paris Agreements came up for Parliamentary approval in November 1954, opposition within the Parliamentary Labour Party, headed by Aneurin Bevan and, among others, Harold Wilson, was so strong that the pro-rearmament leadership, rather than face a major split, decided that the party should officially abstain.

Resolutions opposing the nuclear arming of West Germany were passed by the TUC in 1959, 1960 and again in 1964. In tune with this mood the leadership of the Labour Party when in opposition came out against the American plan for a multi-national nuclear force, its spokesman on foreign affairs, Gordon Walker, saying the plan "will not satisfy the appetites which it is designed to still, the appetites in Europe for independent nuclear weapons".[2] The Labour Party Election Manifesto in the autumn of 1964 also opposed the plan and gave a high priority to stopping the spread of nuclear weapons and creating a nuclear-free zone in Central Europe.[3]

So far as practical diplomacy is concerned, it is proposed first to examine Government policy on the central question of confrontation or disengagement between West and East in Europe and then on the question of West German claims to some form of nuclear status.

The conception in high quarters of the eventual consequences for

---

[1] For details of this incident, see Leslie Hunter, *The Road to Brighton Pier*. London. p. 74.
[2] *Hansard*. June 16, 1964. Cols. 1139–1152.
[3] "The New Britain", published in full in *The Times*. September 12, 1964.

Britain of continuous military pressure on the Soviet Union in Europe began to change fairly radically as early as the beginning of the fifties. There was, however, no major change in British policy on questions of European security until 1955.

The key question then, as now, was that of the relationship between the two Germanys, between which ran and runs the most sensitive part of the frontier between socialist and capitalist Europe.

Until 1955 British diplomacy proceeded from the doctrine, common to all the Western powers and most fanatically advocated by West Germany, that, since Germany must be reunited under Bonn's aegis and brought as a whole into the NATO system, any European settlement must provide not for a relaxation of tension on the frontier on either side of which the armed forces of the Western and Eastern alliances directly confronted each other, but for the liquidation of that frontier.

The British Government not only supported this doctrine, but was the author of its most elaborate and best-known monument, the so-called Eden plan, which formed the basis of the Western position at the Berlin Conference of the Soviet, American, British and French Foreign Ministers in January 1954, and was again put forward, with additional trimmings, by Eden at the Geneva Heads of Government Conference in July 1955.[1]

In its latter form the plan contained provisions for a demilitarised zone and limitation of armaments in Central Europe and for a European Security Pact, but all to become operative only after West Germany had swallowed up East Germany and a reunified capitalist Germany had joined NATO. The object was, thus, not to bring about any form of disengagement along the existing East-West frontier, but to move that frontier eastwards across the GDR and up to the Polish border. The plan was discussed by Eden and Adenauer at Chequers in June 1955 and received the latter's willing benediction.[2]

But later at the Geneva Conference, during the discussions not on Germany or European security, but on disarmament, Eden also put forward a different proposal with a different object, which had not been discussed with Adenauer at Chequers. It cut across the main British proposal and the accepted Western doctrine which lay behind it, and contained the seeds of a subsequent cluster of ideas, collectively known as disengagement, and centred on recognition in one form or another of the existing frontier between the two Germanys.

[1] *Documents* . . . 1955. p. 17–20.
[2] Eden. *op. cit.* pp. 293–294.

In the words of the British memorandum circulated to the Geneva Conference, this second plan provided for "the establishment of a system of joint inspection of the forces now confronting each other in Europe. In specified areas of agreed extent on either side of the line dividing Eastern and Western Europe joint inspection teams would operate by mutual consent".[1] In introducing this proposal, Eden said that it could be put into operation at once, that it was not connected with his main proposal, that the military commands on both sides could appoint the inspection teams and the specified areas could later be extended.[2]

By the time of the Geneva Conference of Foreign Ministers in October 1955, held to carry on the work of the Heads of Government Conference, this heretical plan had been dropped from the British brief and, so far as official policy is concerned, for the next two years there was a return to strict orthodoxy. In correspondence with Bulganin, then Soviet Prime Minister, in 1957, Macmillan, without directly denying that the second Eden proposal had ever been made, stated flatly that "all Western proposals for European security are contingent on a reunified Germany with a freely elected all-German Government free to choose its own foreign policy".[3]

The reasons for the quick change of front between July and October 1955 are not given in first-hand British sources so far published. Indeed, such a thick smoke-screen was immediately put down over the whole episode that some serious attempts to give an account of the known facts are not, so far as I can see, correct.

F. S. Northedge, for example, describes the main Eden plan in detail, remarking, incidentally, that the Russians had strong and understandable reasons for rejecting it. But he goes on to derive subsequent British proposals for disengagement from this same plan, ignoring the existence of their real fountain-head. In the process, he casts doubt on the veracity of Selwyn Lloyd, in this case unjustly, for subsequently telling the House of Commons that at the Geneva Conference of Heads of Government, Eden supported the idea not of demilitarisation, but of mutual inspection on either side of the existing dividing line in Germany and that his demilitarisation proposals were put forward on the assumption of a unified Germany.[4]

Despite this confusion, the same author gives the generally accepted and no doubt right reason for the sudden burial of the second Eden

---

[1] *Documents* ... 1955. p. 41.
[2] *Ibid.* p. 43.
[3] *Documents* ... 1957. p. 15.
[4] F. S. Northedge. *British Foreign Policy*. London. 1962. pp. 244–249. Selwyn Lloyd's statement is given in *Documents* ... 1957. p. 9. Footnote 1.

proposal, namely overwhelming opposition from Britain's partners, principally West Germany. The plan was subjected to a double anathema in Bonn, for it not only implied the perpetuation and stabilisation of the frontier between the two German republics, but also a potentially far-reaching and permanent new system of discrimination against the Federal Republic as compared with her allies. Her territory would have been opened to inspection by representatives of the Warsaw Pact countries, while that of France, Britain and the other members of NATO would not.

Although, as we have said, for the next two years this plan was studiously ignored and disowned by its authors, it marked the beginning of a persistent drift in British diplomacy towards, if not disengagement, then acceptance of the status quo in Central Europe and away from confrontation and active, as distinct from nominal, support for the reunification of Germany on Bonn's terms.

While the Government was still submitting to the gag imposed by its allies, the general idea of disengagement received a thorough airing in establishment circles. From early in 1957 a constellation of military experts met at Chatham House to examine the subject, producing a detailed review of its various aspects the following year, written by Michael Howard.[1] In the spring of 1957, Gaitskell, then leader of the Labour Party, put forward a plan providing for the withdrawal of all foreign troops from the frontier between East and West Germany and subsequently from the whole of Germany, Poland, Czechoslovakia and Hungary, and, if possible, Rumania and Bulgaria.[2] At the end of the same year, the BBC provided George Kennan with a forum for launching his own version of the same idea.

By the beginning of 1958, the Government was once more in the ring, expressing a more positive interest than its partners in the Rapacki plan, put forward by the Polish Foreign Minister at the UN Assembly in October 1957 and, in its early versions, proposing the establishment of a denuclearised zone on the territories of the two Germanys, Poland and Czechoslovakia.[3] Replying in January 1958 to a personal letter from Bulganin supporting this idea, Macmillan told him that "it is open to certain obvious objections, but the British Government are studying it with a view to seeing whether there are elements in it which could be made the basis of some alternative proposal".[4]

[1] Michael Howard. *Disengagement in Europe*. London. 1958.
[2] Hugh Gaitskell. *The Challenge of Co-existence*. London. 1957. pp. 56–58.
[3] *Documents . . .* 1957. pp. 155–159.
[4] *Ibid.* p. 64.

At the end of the year, although the Polish Government, apparently in response at least partly to British suggestions, had by then extended its plan to include a reduction of conventional weapons in the proposed atom-free zone, the Government bowed out of this particular negotiation, Selwyn Lloyd, with a nod in the direction of Bonn and Washington, saying that the Rapacki plan was discriminatory against the troops of certain countries and might lead to the United States abandoning not only Germany but Europe as well.[1]

But only three months later, the Government plunged more deeply than ever into the waters of disengagement. At the conclusion of his visit to Moscow in February-March 1959, and at a time when tension between East and West was rising over the question of Berlin, Macmillan joined Khrushchev in declaring in an Anglo-Soviet communiqué "that further study could usefully be made of the possibilities of increasing security by some method of limitation of forces and weapons, both conventional and nuclear, in an agreed area of Europe, coupled with an appropriate system of inspection".[2]

The Prime Minister thus became temporarily the co-sponsor with the Soviet Prime Minister of the central idea of the Rapacki plan, which, in deference to Bonn and Washington, he had only recently rejected.

This step aroused fury in Bonn and confirmed all its previous suspicions of British perfidy on the German question. Sir Christopher Steel, British Ambassador in Bonn at the time and himself apparently more sympathetic to the West German than the British point of view on this question, tells us that the idea of disengagement had always aroused particular apprehension and resentment in Bonn. It had been ill-received, he says, when Eden produced his plan at the end of the 1955 Geneva Conference. When, in the tense situation prevailing at the time of Macmillan's Moscow visit, an obvious allusion to disengagement appeared in the Anglo-Soviet communiqué, it "spread sinister mistrust".[3]

As regards the Berlin crisis itself, which dragged on with varying degrees of intensity from the autumn of 1958 until the end of 1961, the Government, while never publicly parting company from the joint position of the Western powers, was from beginning to end the most persistent advocate within their councils of a settlement by

[1] *Documents* . . . 1958. p. 136. Footnote 1.
[2] *Documents* . . . 1959. p. 12.
[3] Sir Christopher Steel. 'Anglo-German Relations. A British View.' *International Affairs.* London. October 1963.

negotiation, even if this meant a further measure of de facto recognition of the German Democratic Republic, and was the most persistent opponent of the use of force to maintain access to Berlin across the territory of the GDR from the Federal Republic.

Eisenhower tells us of a British paper communicated informally by the Foreign Secretary to the U.S. Ambassador in London, at the beginning of the crisis, suggesting that the West should be ready "not only to deal with the East German puppet government, but, eventually, to recognise it, rather than expose Berlin to the danger of a blockade". Selwyn Lloyd had at the same time implied, we are told, that there was no reason why dealing with East Germany should lead to the ejection of the Western garrisons from Berlin.[1]

According to the same source, at a discussion of the crisis in London in February 1959, Macmillan told Dulles flatly that "the status quo in Berlin could not endure indefinitely, certainly not after Adenauer had passed from the political scene" and expressed interest in a thinning out of military forces in Germany, leading eventually to some sort of neutralisation, like that of Austria.[2]

In April 1961, Macmillan and Home, at a meeting in Washington with Kennedy and his advisers on the Berlin question, reacted sharply against the thesis advanced by Acheson that there was no prospect of any agreement on either Berlin or Germany compatible with the interests of the West, and that the United States and her allies should therefore concentrate on military measures against East Germany and the Soviet Union, including the despatch of an American division across the GDR to Berlin.

Home objected that it would be easy to isolate a single division on the road to Berlin, and tried to turn the discussion from military to political issues. The Western position was too negative, he said. We were offering no alternative to Khrushchev's proposal of a peace conference and a treaty. We were in Berlin because of the right of conquest, but the right of conquest was wearing thin.[3]

At a meeting at ambassadorial level of the four Western powers in Washington in October 1961 as the crisis was drawing to its close, the British representative, according to the official record subsequently leaked to the Press, and the American representative, who had by now moved over to the British position, had a stand-up row with their West German and French colleagues on much the same lines. The Anglo-American side proposed plans for exploratory talks with the

---

[1] Eisenhower. *Waging Peace*. p. 333.
[2] *Ibid*. pp. 342–343.
[3] Schlesinger. *op. cit.* pp. 344–345.

Soviet Union over Berlin and Germany, which their opponents denounced as impermissible and unacceptable.[1]

None of the above-mentioned schemes for disengagement — neither Eden's, nor Rapacki's, nor Gaitskell's, nor Kennan's, nor Macmillan's and Khrushchev's — were put into effect. Nor, for that matter, was any new agreement concluded with the Soviet Union over West Berlin. But the guiding idea common to all these plans, namely that the first stretch of the road to a European settlement lay through the acceptance and not the denial of the existence of the two Germanys and the frontier between them, won a central and enduring place in the practice, though not the theory, of British diplomacy.

As shown below the Government moved on from attempts to secure partial disengagement along the existing frontier between the two Germanys to wider schemes for a dialogue and détente between NATO and the Warsaw Pact, of which the Federal Republic and the GDR respectively form key parts. Owing to the parallel, though unsynchronised, evolution of American, French and finally West German policy, the once heretical proposals of Eden and Macmillan in due course became, in generalised form, the new orthodoxy of the Western alliance as a whole.

Before, however, the NATO powers as a group had reached this stage, the whole perspective for European security was for several years overcast by the imminent danger that Bonn, aided by Washington, would succeed in prising open the door, supposedly locked by the Paris Agreements, leading towards ownership of nuclear weapons.

On this question British diplomacy pursued a course very similar both in its aims and in its hesitations to that followed over disengagement.

Despite the ban on the manufacture of nuclear weapons by West Germany contained in the Paris Agreements of 1954, it was only a year or two before the question of Bonn's future nuclear status began to move towards the centre of the problem of European security. In particular the Soviet Union, Poland and the other states of Eastern Europe quite rightly foresaw that the Agreements would not prevent the Federal Republic from pressing its allies hard for some form of nuclear weapons and that the latter, in the interests of propping up the anti-Communist front, would be inclined to give way. As we have seen, the Rapacki plan, put forward by Poland as early as the autumn of 1957, was designed primarily to meet this danger, the

[1] Extracts from the official record appeared in *Der Spiegel*. September 12, 1962. S. 18–23.

method proposed being the total denuclearisation of the two Germanys, Poland and Czechoslovakia.

All variants of this plan having come to nothing owing to the opposition of Bonn and Washington, events developed in precisely the way that had been feared in Moscow, Warsaw and the other Eastern European capitals and also, to some extent, in London. In 1960 the military and political leaders of West Germany placed their nuclear demands face up on the table, and at the same time the United States Government and the American NATO Supreme Commander in Europe came forward with compromise proposals conceding to Bonn for the first time and as a first step part-ownership of nuclear weapons.

Bonn's position was epitomised by the so-called Generals' memorandum of August 1960, written by the West German General Staff, approved by the Federal Government in a special communiqué issued by Andenauer and Strauss, and published in the Monthly Bulletin of the Bundeswehr.

This document, couched in language reminiscent of that used in their time by the Nazi leaders, stated unequivocally that the Bundeswehr must have nuclear weapons. The Federal Republic was, it said, in constant and deadly danger from Bolshevik aggression. German soldiers have the right to weapons at least equal to those of their opponents, the Bundeswehr must have armaments of the same effectiveness as its partners in the NATO shield force. "The Bundeswehr shares responsibility for the security of the Federal Republic. It cannot deny itself conscription, membership of NATO, nor atomic weapons."[1]

Reading this memorandum some ten years later, it seems at first sight to be merely a plea that the Bundeswehr should be equipped with the same weapons as other NATO forces in the field and as its Eastern European opponents. But this was not what the General Staff and Government were after. Under arrangements introduced in the second half of the fifties, West Germany's armed forces like the U.S., British and other NATO contingents, were already equipped with the same nuclear weapons. The catch was that the warheads for those weapons (as distinct from the aircraft, missiles and guns for their delivery), though physically present and ready for use, were kept in the ownership and custody of their supplier, the United States.

Thus, in the event of war between the NATO and Warsaw Pact countries, the Bundeswehr would have been at no disadvantage as compared with the BAOR or any other NATO contingent as far as

---

[1] *Documents . . . 1960.* pp. 119–122.

nuclear firepower is concerned. On the other hand, West Germany, unlike the three Western producers of nuclear warheads, the United States, Britain and France, had no power, physical or legal, to decide when its, and still less anyone's else's, nuclear weapons should be used.

The 1960 démarche of the Generals and politicians in Bonn was designed to put an end to this situation, to make a start with raising West Germany to the nuclear status of Britain and France, and was so understood by all parties concerned at the time.

The essence of the compromise proposal put forward by the United States in 1960 was that West Germany should become the owner jointly with other members of NATO, including initially the United States itself, of a new multilateral nuclear force (MLF), additional to existing Western striking forces and using weapons bought or otherwise acquired from U.S. current production.

Ostensibly, this proposal was designed to meet the wishes of the European members of NATO generally. In fact, since Britain and France were independent nuclear powers and Italy was no more than mildly interested, its only purpose was to give partial satisfaction to the demands of Bonn, which from start to finish was its main, and towards the end only, proponent among the European powers.

The plan appeared in two basically similar versions, one worked out in NATO's European headquarters and announced to the world by its American Supreme Commander, General Norstad, and the other put forward by the State Department.

In a speech in November 1960, Norstad said that, owing to the growing desire for a broader sharing in the control of nuclear weapons, "a great new question" had arisen within the alliance. He proposed therefore the creation of a "multilateral atomic authority, making NATO a fourth atomic power". He underlined that this authority would acquire control not only of missiles, aircraft and guns for delivering nuclear warheads to their target, but also the warheads themselves, which would not, as under existing arrangements, remain in the custody of the supplier country, the United States. All members of NATO would have an equal voice in the control of this new force.[1]

A month later, at the December 1960 meeting of the NATO Council, Christian Herter, then U.S. Secretary of State, in the words of the communiqué, "suggested the concept of an MRBM [medium-range ballistic missile — D.M.] multilateral force for consideration by the Alliance".[2] While Norstad had a land-based missile force in mind,

---

[1] *Documents* ... 1960. pp. 124–130.
[2] *Ibid.* pp. 131–132.

Herter suggested that the United States might provide five Polaris submarines by 1963, carrying a total of eighty missiles, if a system of multilateral control could be devised.[1]

The United States Government promoted this plan for the next five years and in doing so was trying to kill several birds with one stone. Firstly, the offer of an MLF in which West Germany would be one of the senior partners strengthened the hand of the pro-Americans in Bonn, and weakened that of the pro-French school. This factor assumed particular importance after the conclusion of the Franco-West German (Elysée) Treaty in January 1963. Secondly, the existence of such a force would in the long run undermine the independent status of the British and French nuclear forces, even if Britain and France did not at first take part in it. Thirdly, the proposed system of common ownership held out the prospect of transferring part of the cost of the American nuclear programme to the Western European powers without, at any rate in the initial stage, necessarily losing control of the weapons furnished to the new force.

The plan, however, ran counter to what later became key theses in the foreign policy programme of the Kennedy and Johnson Administrations—namely, that further proliferation within the alliance must be stopped, that control of existing Western nuclear forces must as far as possible be centralised in American hands, and that agreement with the Soviet Union should be sought on the terms of a world-wide non-proliferation treaty.

We may note here McNamara's insistence in his speech at Ann Arbor in June 1962 that the current strategic situation "magnifies the importance of unity of planning, concentration of executive authority and central direction" and requires that there be neither "proliferation of nuclear power with all its attendant dangers", nor "competing and conflicting strategies to meet the contingency of nuclear war".[2]

The proposal to create an MLF, even with the retention of an initial American veto on its use, worked in the opposite direction.

As we have seen, its central feature was a relaxation of American control over nuclear warheads made available to West Germany, and the introduction of a measure of West German control. On any realistic assessment, the hypothesis that the MLF might in the end swallow up the British and French independent forces weighed less than the certainty that it would open the door, however slightly, to West German ownership of nuclear weapons. Moreover, it became

[1] Schlesinger. *op. cit.* p. 725.
[2] *Loc. cit.*

clearer and clearer that there was no hope of concluding a non-proliferation agreement with the socialist states if the United States insisted on leaving a loop-hole for the MLF.

There were other reasons why the MLF plan came to nothing, chief among them outright opposition by France and quiet sabotage by Britain, but the main factor was that it no longer fitted the changed priorities of its principal begetter, the United States.

The attitude of the Macmillan, Home and Wilson Governments was unfavourable to the proposed MLF, though much less openly so than that of the French Government. Pompidou, the French Prime Minister, reached the point of saying publicly in November 1964 that the MLF showed signs of becoming a form of American-West German military alliance, incompatible with the Franco-West German Elysée Treaty, destructive of Europe, provocative to the Soviet Union and "directed more or less against France".[1] British diplomacy, on the other hand, while working against the plan, followed the precept in Clough's rhyme: "Thou shalt not kill, but need'st not strive—Officiously to keep alive."

Much as in the case of the still-born plan for a European Defence Community (EDC) in the early fifties, in the face of heavy American pressure London was not able to oppose the MLF idea as such, but, seeing in it primarily a threat to the independence of the British nuclear force and to Britain's privileged nuclear partnership with the United States, contributed to its failure by refusing to join it and later by putting forward counter-plans designed in fact, though not in name, to torpedo it. Again as in the case of the EDC, these counter-proposals were hinged on the co-ordination, as opposed to the integration, of existing forces within the existing structure of NATO.

The Macmillan Government, even before General Norstad's above-mentioned speech, publicly cast doubt on the MLF idea and made clear that it did not intend to concede to NATO more than nominal and partial control over the British striking force.

In a speech at the beginning of November 1960, the Minister of Defence, Harold Watkinson, said that the deterrent would not be able to fulfil its function "if there were too many fingers on the safety catch". Secondly, he said, Britain "had responsibilities outside NATO, for example, to the Central Treaty Organisation and SEATO and we could not put all our eggs in the NATO basket". He then put forward an alternative proposal which was to feature in London's tactics on this question for several years to come. The

---

[1] *The Times.* November 6, 1964.

Government, he said, might see no objection to simply attaching a NATO label to some part of the British striking force, i.e., assigning certain units nominally to NATO, while still retaining ultimate control over them.[1]

In the following year, the United States adopted this latter idea as part of its own policy, but combined it with continued support for an MLF. In a speech in Ottawa in May 1961, the President said that the United States would commit five Polaris submarines to the NATO command, but hoped also to establish "a NATO sea-borne force, which would be truly multilateral in ownership and control", once NATO's non-nuclear goals had been achieved.[2]

During Macmillan's visit to Washington the previous month, Kennedy, according to the Press, suggested to him that the independent British nuclear force was an obstacle to Western unity and urged him to hand it over to NATO.[3] Macmillan, however, declined to adopt any definite attitude, at least in public. He devoted a considerable part of a major foreign policy speech, delivered during his visit, to what he called "a certain unease in the NATO alliance" arising from the Anglo-American monopoly of nuclear weapons, admitted the necessity of building a new partnership in the nuclear field with the European members of NATO, but gave no clue as to what form it should take. The speech, moreover, contained a special passage justifying the existence of the independent British striking force.[4]

Anglo-American differences over the MLF came to a head at the Nassau meeting between Macmillan and Kennedy in December 1962, to which we have already referred, and were temporarily resolved in favour of London.

Macmillan went to Nassau determined above all to save the independent British striking force by purchasing Polaris missiles, Washington having suddenly stopped further work on the Skybolt system on which British forward planning was based. Kennedy went there not unwilling to meet this request, but anxious to use the opportunity to push Macmillan towards participation in an MLF.

In the result, Macmillan got his Polarises, agreed that they (when

---

[1] *The Times.* November 5, 1960.

[2] *Documents* . . . 1961. p. 66.

[3] *The Economist.* April 15, 1961. pp. 219–220. According to Schlesinger (*op. cit.* p. 723), Kennedy told Macmillan that "a British effort to maintain its deterrent through the sixties might both confirm de Gaulle in his course and hasten the day when Germany would demand nuclear weapons for themselves". This episode is, however, attributed to February 1962. It is not clear whether this is an error in dating, or whether the same démarche was made twice at the interval of a year.

[4] Speech at the Massachusetts Institute of Technology. *Documents* . . . 1961. pp. 71–73.

they became operational) and part of the British nuclear bomber force (immediately) should be assigned to NATO, but entered into no commitment regarding British membership of an MLF.

Read in isolation, the terms of the Nassau agreement are confusing, because paragraphs 7 and 9 appear to imply that the British side did assume such a commitment. In fact, however, the term "NATO multilateral nuclear force" was used in the agreement in the wide sense of a composite force of American, British and other national components which might or might not also contain an MLF in the narrow, and generally understood, sense. As regards the latter, though, this did not appear in the communiqué, Kennedy told Macmillan at Nassau that he intended to pursue separately "the formation of a mixed-manned nuclear force to be assigned to NATO and to which non-nuclear Powers [i.e., chiefly West Germany — D.M.] could contribute".[1]

Spurred on by fear, following the Elysée Treaty of January 1963, that West Germany might move irrevocably into the French orbit, Washington was not slow in returning to the charge.

In early June 1963, an American naval delegation, headed by Admiral Ricketts, descended on London for discussion of the military and technical aspects of a proposed "NATO multilateral, surface-ship nuclear force".[2] At the end of the month the President himself had another go at the Prime Minister during their talks at Birch Grove (Macmillan's country house), but obtained no more satisfaction than he had at Nassau.

Kennedy, fresh from a visit to Bonn, said that he and Adenauer had reaffirmed their agreement to try to bring into being a multi-lateral sea-borne medium-range missile force and to pursue this plan with other interested governments. The most he could extract from Macmillan was that this plan should be discussed as part of wider discussions on the problem of more closely associating NATO members with the nuclear deterrent of the alliance and "without prejudice to the question of British participation in such a force".[3]

Moreover, only a few days after Kennedy's departure, Macmillan publicly questioned whether NATO really needed an increase in its nuclear strength, whether the large sums required would not be better spent on modernising existing forces, and whether the MLF would in fact resolve the basic political problem which it was sup-

[1] Statement issued by the Prime Minister's Office on **October 1, 1963.** *Commonwealth Survey.* October 22, 1963.
[2] *Commonwealth Survey.* July 16, 1963. p. 614.
[3] *Ibid.* p. 618.

posed to meet.[1] During a visit to Washington in October 1963, the Foreign Secretary (Home) complained to Kennedy that, while his Government understood the point of the proposed MLF, they were bothered by the insistence with which the Americans were pushing it.[2]

The Conservative Government did, it is true, shortly make one concession to American pressure. It was announced in the Defence White Paper of February 1964 that, again without commitment, Britain would participate in an experiment in mixed-manning being organised by the Americans on an American warship.[3] But by the time they were driven from office in October of that year, the Conservative leaders had still not decided for or against participation in an MLF.

The advent of the Labour Government did not bring a change of policy, but it did bring a more active pursuit of the objective of its predecessors. Instead of playing cat and mouse with the proposed MLF, the new Government openly attempted to torpedo it by putting forward a rival plan for a NATO nuclear force, to be known as the Atlantic Nuclear Force (ANF), consisting chiefly of American and British (and French, if Paris wished) national components drawn from existing forces.

The plan for an ANF was put to President Johnson by Wilson during his visit to Washington in December 1964 and announced to the House of Commons on December 16, a few days later. The British component, as provided for under the Nassau Agreement, was to consist of part of the V-bomber force[4] and of the Polaris submarines when they came into operation. They were to remain irrevocably committed to the ANF for as long as NATO remained in existence. In order to make this possible, the Government renounced the right, reserved by Macmillan at Nassau, to withdraw them "where Her Majesty's Government may decide that supreme national interests are at stake". The American contribution would consist of an equal number of Polaris submarines. The whole force would come under a single authority on which all participants would be represented. Each would have a veto on the use of the force.

Nominally, the plan allowed room for an MLF, jointly owned and

[1] *Hansard.* July 3, 1963. Cols. 509–510.
[2] Schlesinger. *op. cit.* p. 747.
[3] Command 2270.
[4] Judging by the communiqué of the NATO Council meeting in Ottawa in May 1963 (*Commonwealth Survey.* July 16, 1963), V-bombers by then had already been, or were about to be, assigned to NATO, in accordance with Macmillan's promise at Nassau.

mix-manned by West Germany and the other non-nuclear members of NATO, as an extra component of the ANF. But the Government made plain that it not only would not itself take part, but was also actively opposed to the creation of an MLF in the form proposed by Bonn and Washington.

Only a few weeks after he had taken office, Harold Wilson announced the Government's belief that "a mixed-manned surface fleet adds nothing to Western strength, is likely to cause a dissipation of effort within the alliance, and may add to the difficulties of East-West agreement".[1] In the debate on the ANF, he said that if there were to be a mixed-manned component, it would have to be designed so as not to transgress the principle of non-dissemination and that a new strategic force of surface ships armed with Polaris missiles was the least desirable way of applying mixed-manning.[2]

The diversionary role of the ANF in relation to the MLF was more or less openly admitted by Denis Healey, Minister of Defence, and one of its authors, a few months later. Our proposals for an Atlantic Nuclear Force, he said, "have already saved the Western Alliance from what threatened to be a catastrophic crisis over the MLF . . . Now our proposals are the basis of all discussion inside the Atlantic Alliance about the central problem of atomic sharing".[3] His opposite number on the Conservative benches made the same point, though in a more critical spirit. "The only engagement which this nuclear force (the ANF) has ever been in," he said, "was to sink the MLF and that was apparently successful."[4]

The fate of the MLF, and with it Bonn's immediate hopes of securing a basic change in West Germany's nuclear status, was not, however, decided in London, but in Washington.

Partly owing to the widening rift in the alliance over the whole conception and partly because, as the Soviet Government had persistently pointed out, any form of West German ownership of nuclear warheads would make the conclusion of a world-wide non-proliferation treaty impossible, the U.S. Government, by with-drawing its support, let the idea wither on the vine. Instead, it began moving towards a less dangerous means of dealing with Bonn's demands, namely associating the Federal Republic and other non-nuclear members of NATO with nuclear decision-making in NATO without giving them ownership of nuclear warheads in any guise.

When confronted with the Labour Government's ANF plan, the

[1] *Hansard*. November 23, 1964. Col. 943.
[2] *Hansard*. December 16, 1964. Col. 937.
[3] *Hansard*. March 3, 1965. Cols. 1330–1331.
[4] *Hansard*. March 3, 1965. Col. 1369.

U.S. Government, far from rejecting it out of hand, accepted it for discussion alongside the existing proposal for an MLF. By the summer of 1965, McNamara had come out with his plan for a NATO body, subsequently known as the McNamara Committee, consisting of the United States, Britain, France, West Germany and Italy and charged with studying ways of extending consultation on nuclear matters. The deliberations of this body led eventually to the establishment, by a decision of the NATO Council in December 1966, of two permanent bodies for nuclear planning—a Nuclear Defence Affairs Committee, open to all NATO countries, and a Nuclear Planning Group of seven members, including the United States, Britain and West Germany.

This evolution in American diplomacy was supported and encouraged by the British Government, which at times continued to run ahead of its partner.

In July 1965 there appeared an article by the Director of the U.S. Arms Control and Disarmament Agency, posing in highly cautious and ambiguous language the question of priorities between the creation of an MLF and the conclusion of a non-proliferation treaty.[1] The Foreign Secretary (Michael Stewart), however, speaking on the same subject two months later, came out in favour of preference being given to non-proliferation.[2]

The draft treaty on non-proliferation tabled by the Americans at the Geneva Conference on Disarmament in August 1965 still contained, in Articles I and II, loopholes designed to permit the formation of an MLF. The British delegate, Lord Chalfont, in explaining why Britain was not this time a co-sponsor of the draft, urged that these two articles should be amended to exclude the creation of any association capable of using nuclear weapons without the consent of an existing nuclear power—"in other words, we would like to see dissemination interpreted in the strictest possible way".[3]

The hope in London that the new arrangements for consultation on nuclear matters within NATO would simultaneously dispose of the MLF and open the way to a non-proliferation treaty can be seen from a speech of Healey's shortly before the arrangements were officially confirmed. NATO, he said, was just about to solve its internal problem of nuclear sharing on the basis of consultation between the nuclear and non-nuclear members. The agreement about to be reached would "not only eliminate a dangerous threat

[1] William Foster. "New Directions in Arms Control and Disarmament". *Foreign Affairs.* New York. July 1965.
[2] *The Times.* October 8, 1965.
[3] *The Times.* August 18, 1965.

to NATO's political and military solidarity, it will also remove one major obstacle to the conclusion of a world-wide agreement against the proliferation of nuclear weapons".[1]

As a result of a further modification of U.S. policy, these hopes were eventually justified by the signature on July 1, 1968, by the Soviet Union, the United States, Britain and others of a Non-Proliferation Treaty in terms outlawing the nuclear armament of West Germany in any form, including that of an MLF.

The question of the nuclear status of the Federal Republic is now, as we have seen, presenting itself in a new shape. As a means of securing entry into the EEC, the Conservative leaders, and probably not they alone, advocate the formation of a Western European nuclear force, based on the French and British striking forces, with which West Germany would in some way be associated. This does not mean that the Government, whether Conservative or Labour, is likely to reverse course and actively promote an arrangement which would make it physically possible for Bonn of its own volition to use, or threaten to use, nuclear weapons. But it does point to the latent danger that, in search of a way out of the central dilemma in Britain's relations with the other Western powers, British diplomacy may start down the slippery slope leading in that direction.

---

[1] Speech to the British Atlantic Committee in London on October 27, 1966. *Commonwealth Survey*. November 11, 1966.

PART II

POLICY TOWARDS THE THIRD WORLD

Policy Towards the Third World[1]

Only twenty-five years ago, policy towards what is now generally known as the third world was not a recognised part of British foreign policy. It was divided into separate compartments, dealt with by different branches of the Government machine and thought of as having little connection with each other.

To take the most important divisions, policy in the African and South-East Asian colonies, handled by the Colonial Office, was one thing, policy in the Indian empire, dealt with by the India Office, was another, and Middle Eastern policy, run by the Foreign Office, was a third. Only the last segment was considered to be part of foreign policy, and even that was fragmented since Palestine and the Aden area were colonies in the fiefdom of the Colonial Office.

As the colonial system disintegrated, these dividing lines gradually shifted and grew fainter until today policy towards the whole of the third world is accepted as an integral part of foreign policy and dealt with as such by one centre, the new Foreign and Commonwealth Office, which came into being in October 1968 as a result of the amalgamation of the Foreign Office and the Commonwealth Office, the Colonial Office having disappeared in 1966.

Thus well into the sixties, policy towards the third world was conducted not within one but several organisational frameworks, colonial-administrative, Commonwealth and diplomatic. Nevertheless the main factors underlying its evolution were, it seems to me, everywhere the same and gave rise to one and the same general direction of change. At the same time, in the areas of maximum economic, political and military involvement—the Middle East, Africa South of the Sahara, South and South-East Asia—highly differentiated problems arose, evoking a no less highly differentiated response.

It is proposed to deal first with the general evolution of policy and then separately with these three geographical areas.

[1] The term is used to cover all countries of Asia, Africa and Latin America, which are not part of the socialist system.

CHAPTER FOUR

General Evolution of Policy

Winds of Change

It is often said that throughout the post-war period successive British Governments directed their policy towards bringing the colonial and semi-colonial peoples of Asia and Africa to self-government and independence and that by so doing they displayed a far-sighted and statesman-like liberalism. This thesis is not only part of the stock-in-trade of Labour and Conservative politicians and their speech-writers, but is advanced in good faith by acknowledged experts on British foreign policy.

This is the point of view of, for example, Lord Strang, who was Permanent Under-Secretary of State at the Foreign Office in 1949–1953. While he does not deny that *force majeure* has played its part, he speaks of "the liberal experiment upon which Great Britain has deliberately embarked as a central feature of her external policy" and dates it from the time of the first post-war Government. He regards this experiment as "a characteristic manifestation of national behaviour in the modern age, an act of faith, the expression of a deeply-rooted moral idea". He also asserts with evident sincerity that the transformation of the British Empire had been "achieved on the whole without violence and by consent".[1]

Looking back, particularly if one remembers the protracted war in Malaya, the wholesale, if short-lived, repression of the Kikuyu in Kenya, the assault on Egypt, the imposition of a white-dominated Federation on the Rhodesias and Nyasaland, and the attempt to hold on to sovereignty in Cyprus and Aden by force, I do not think that any reasonable person could accept Strang's picture as a true one.

What one sees is not the unfolding of a logical, long-term strategy based on moral principles, but the ups and downs of the struggle between the independence movements and the metropolitan power, between different groups within the British establishment, between

[1] *Op. cit.* pp. 342–343, 347, 361, 388.

London and the settlers and a prolonged and bewildering series of marches and counter-marches by the Government.

Moreover, it is an illusion to think that the concession of independence to the succession states of the Indian Empire in 1947–1948 signified a volte-face as regards the colonial and semi-colonial world generally.

During the six years of Labour rule after the war, no other country was even promised, much less granted, full independence, not even Egypt, which had been agitating against British military occupation since the end of the First World War.

The colonial doctrine of the succeeding Conservative administration was summed up as follows by Oliver Lyttelton (Lord Chandos), the minister responsible. "In the twentieth century," he wrote, " ... the consent of the governed must in some measure be engaged. But consent to what? The word must not be construed to mean that the tutelary power, in this instance Britain, can divest itself of responsibility."[1] To this period belongs Eden's statement (in 1951) to the Egyptian Foreign Minister that the British Government "could not meet the Egyptian demand for evacuation and that it was no good the Egyptian Minister expecting it".[2]

Nevertheless, I think it is true that, from the mid-fifties onwards, a combination of powerful factors bit by bit forced the policy-makers, after a slow start, to realise that the whole structure of direct and indirect Western rule in Asia and Africa was collapsing and that they were confronted with a new and basic foreign policy problem, namely the question of what the future relationship between Britain (and the other Western powers) and the third world was to be. In a long-drawn-out battle between old and no longer workable conceptions of what was to be done and new and more realistic ones, the latter gradually got the upper hand.

In the first place, the strength of the independence movement within Britain's colonies and client states had by the mid-fifties grown enormously—in Malaya, in Iran, in Egypt and the Sudan, in East and West Africa—and was putting a severe strain on the old political framework.

The physical impossibility of holding back this movement and the necessity of finding some compromise with it were advanced as general propositions by Lyttelton's successor, Alan Lennox-Boyd (Lord Boyd), also a far from liberal Colonial Secretary, at the end of 1956. "We have to handle the most powerful, swift and elemental

---

[1] *The Memoirs of Lord Chandos*. London. 1962. p. 385.
[2] Eden. *op. cit.* p. 228.

5*

of all political forces—nationalism," he said. "The blunt truth is that, although with tact and skill we can to some extent guide the force of nationalism, we cannot regulate it at our wish, and it is not to be repressed." In these circumstances, he continued, in many colonies the Government preferred the risk of conceding self-government "to the certainty of driving them to sever their connection with us".[1]

It is true that the "many colonies" consisted at the time only of Malaya and Ghana, which gained their sovereignty in the following year. Nevertheless, we already have here the doctrine which was shortly to dominate colonial practice as a whole.

Secondly, in the mid-fifties co-operation between the third world and the Communist world began to develop on an entirely new scale. In 1955, with the sale of Czechoslovak arms to Egypt, the Western monopoly in arms supplies to the Middle East was broken. The same year saw the conclusion of the Soviet-Indian Agreement regarding the construction of the Bhilai steel works. There followed, in 1958, the Soviet-Egyptian Agreement providing for financial and technical co-operation in the construction of the Aswan high dam. In the ten-year period 1955–1965 trade between the socialist states and the third world increased many times over. By 1965 Soviet credits and other financial assistance totalled about three and a half thousand million roubles. Young people from Asia, Africa and Latin America began to stream to the socialist countries in search of higher education and technical training, particularly after the opening of Lumumba University in Moscow in 1960.

The danger that the colonial peoples of Asia might join hands with the socialist states and fear that diehard attitudes and methods would increase this danger played their parts in the decision of the Labour Government to concede sovereignty to the Indian Empire after the war. "Communism . . . appears to many of the peoples of Asia as a liberating force," wrote Attlee of this period. "An attempt to maintain the old colonialism would, I am sure, have immensely aided the Communist attack in Asia."[2] Ten years later, when the danger had assumed far more concrete forms, coming to terms with the independence movement in order to swing it away from co-operation with the socialist states and isolate it from the influence of socialist ideas had become one of the main factors in government policy.

Preoccupation with this problem showed clearly in a statement

[1] *Overseas*. London. November. 1956.
[2] C. R. Attlee. *As It Happened*. London. 1964. p. 189.

of Macmillan's in 1957. "To my mind," he said, "it is absolutely essential that the growing nationalism of Asia and Africa . . . should be canalised into broader and safe channels, otherwise nationalism will turn to Communism."[1] And two years later, Andrew Cohen, one of the main architects of modern colonial policy in Africa urged that nationalism should be turned into an ally against Communism. "If we confuse nationalism with Communism," he wrote, "we are doing a most harmful thing, because successful co-operation with nationalism is our greatest bulwark against Communism in Africa."[2]

The classic statement of the point is contained in Macmillan's "winds of change" speech in Capetown in February 1960.

"The growth of national consciousness in Africa is a political fact and we must accept it as such," he said. "That means, I would judge, that we must come to terms with it. I sincerely believe that if we cannot do so we may imperil the precarious balance between East and West . . . The great issue in this second half of the twentieth century is whether the uncommitted peoples of Asia and Africa will swing to the East or to the West. Will they be drawn into the Communist camp?"[3]

Thirdly, a major part in forcing a general shift in London's approach to the third world was played by the tactics used by Washington.

At least until the end of the fifties, as we have already pointed out, one of the main manœuvres used by the United States to further its purposes in the Indian sub-continent, the Middle East and Africa was to present itself as the disinterested friend of the peoples of these areas in their struggle against the old colonial powers, chiefly Britain and France.

At various times during the nineteen-forties and nineteen-fifties, Washington made sustained efforts to get itself accepted as an unselfish sympathiser and chief patron by, among others, the Indian, Jewish, Moroccan, Tunisian, Iranian, Egyptian and East African peoples.

In view of the great disparity of strength between the two powers, this aspect of American diplomacy added immensely to the Government's difficulties in holding the line against the independence movement. A notorious example of this is, as we have also recalled, the Suez crisis of 1956, when Dulles's double game was one of the

[1] *The Times.* July 27, 1957.
[2] Andrew Cohen. *British Policy in Changing Africa.* London. 1959. p. 61.
[3] *Documents . . .* 1960. p. 345.

main causes of the collapse of the Anglo-French-Israeli onslaught on Egypt.

Fourthly, the process of national-liberation itself produced a chain reaction, making it harder and harder to maintain the old order. As various parts of the British, French, Dutch, Belgian and Portuguese empires broke free, the very fact of their independence acted as a powerful accelerator of independence movements among their neighbours.

Thus the course of events in Egypt between 1952 and 1956 altered the perspective for the independence movement throughout the Middle East and North Africa. The attainment of sovereignty by Ghana in 1957 played a similar role in West Africa. Moreover, the new sovereign states, with few exceptions, used their new status to work actively for the ending of colonialism everywhere.

The Bandung Conference, four of whose five sponsors[1] were former British colonies, gave a new stimulus to the anti-colonial movement on a world scale. By 1960 feeling in the United Nations against the colonial system had become so strong that 89 members voted in favour of a resolution demanding its speedy and total abolition, while the colonial powers, who abstained — the U.S., Britain, France, South Africa, Belgium, Portugal, Spain and Australia — found themselves isolated.

Moreover, the loss of certain colonies and semi-colonies directly — physically — diminished the capacity of the colonial powers to hold on to the others. This applies particularly to the long-term effects of the loss of India, Pakistan and Ceylon, which had formerly provided a substantial part of the troops, bases and resources enabling Britain to retain her grip upon Iran, the Persian Gulf, and the Arab countries, to the West, and Malaya and other colonial possessions, to the East. Among others, Churchill was very conscious of this factor. "Britain's power to influence the fortunes of the Middle East," he said, " . . . is far less now that we have laid aside our imperial responsibilities for India and its armies."[2] Similarly, the loss of the vast military base in the Suez Canal Zone seriously weakened British power not only in the Middle East, but in East Africa also.

Fifthly, experience in India, Pakistan and Ceylon and later in Malaya and Ghana showed that concessions of sovereignty, if made in time, did not lead to the extinction of British economic, political or even in some cases military influence. British capital investments

---

[1] India, Pakistan, Ceylon, Burma, and Indonesia.
[2] *Documents* . . . 1952. p. 51.

were scarcely touched and in total increased, special trade and financial arrangements remained in being, British cadres were retained, and all these states voluntarily joined the Commonwealth as independent members.

The moral to be drawn for the future was pointed out at the end of the fifties by, among others, Kenneth Younger, a former Minister at the Foreign Office. "It is indeed the Indian experience," he wrote, "which points most clearly to the way in which the colonial powers should react to this widespread revulsion against the old colonial system. Ten years of Indian independence have shown that the former imperial power may, if it knows how to adapt itself, derive great advantages from the closeness of the past relationship, once the strains of parting are over."[1]

The same point, though in rather more Pecksniffian language, is made in a special study of Anglo-Indian relations by the Zinkins. Discussing the transition to greater flexibility and liberalism in imperial policy generally, the authors stress that "partly it is the result of success in India . . . the great interests in the sub-continent have not been touched; it was natural to think that perhaps other people, shown the same trust, would behave with the same appreciation".[2]

As is shown in more detail later, this point of view was shared not only by industrial and financial circles generally, but also by many, though not all, firms specially concerned with doing business in the third world. Here we will only quote by way of example the views of the Booker-McConnell Group expressed in 1961, more than half of whose profits were then coming from British Guiana, the West Indies and Central Africa, and which was substantially increasing its investments there and in India and West Africa also. The achievement of independence by the colonial peoples might lead to a temporary fall in profits but was "both inevitable and desirable", said the Group's annual report. "We must make it clear to the peoples and politicians of the newly independent and emerging nations in which we operate that we understand and accept that these countries must fashion their own destinies."[3]

The Economist does not, of course, speak for the whole of the City, but its summing up of the situation, at the beginning of 1962, is also not without interest. "Where the colonial powers have bowed to reason—" it wrote, "in India, Malaya, the Philippines, Burma,

[1] *New Fabian Colonial Essays.* London. 1959. p. 52.
[2] Maurice and Taya Zinkin. *Britain and India.* London. 1964. p. 123.
[3] *The Times.* June 12, 1961.

West Africa, Tanganyika—they have enjoyed improved relations. It is where they have gone on trying to expectorate into the wind of change that unpleasant things have been flung into their faces."[1]

All these factors served to shift the whole angle from which the question of relations with the third world was viewed. At the beginning of the sixties, the conception of a new "North-South" problem of equal or even greater importance than the familiar "East-West problem" began to take firm root among those who have the decisive voice in Britain's affairs.

One of its earliest exponents was Lord Franks, formerly British Ambassador in Washington and subsequently Chairman of Lloyds Bank. "During the late forties and most of the fifties," he told his shareholders, "the great political and strategic problem of the world was that of East-West tension . . . It is no longer true that the East-West problem is the sole great issue, we now have a second problem of equal importance . . . I call it the North-South problem, and I mean by this phrase the general problems of the relationships of the industrialised nations of the north of the globe to the under-developed and developing countries that lie to the south, whether in Central and South America, in Africa, in the Middle East or South Asia or in the island archipelagos of the Pacific. In 1947 the balance of the world turned on the recovery of Western Europe; now it turns on a right relationship between the industrial North and the developing South."[2]

A variant of this theme was put forward at about the same time by one of the establishment's most respected ideologues, Barbara Ward. "The old polarisation between the classes in the domestic economy has given place to a new one in the developing world," she wrote. " . . . A division between the wealthy lands of the North, where the breakthrough to sustained growth has been achieved, and the under-developed lands of the South where partial mobilisation [of resources—D.M.] creates an explosive mixture of hope and frustration."[3]

The same basic idea was subsequently taken up by the spokesman of the Labour Party on foreign affairs, Gordon Walker. "A Labour Government would pay increasing attention to North-South relations," he wrote in 1964, "to the relations between the advanced countries of the Northern Hemisphere and the hungry nations in the Southern Hemisphere. This seems to us to be of more funda-

---

[1] *The Economist*. January 6, 1962.
[2] Statement to the shareholders of Lloyds Bank. *The Economist*. January 30, 1960.
[3] Barbara Ward. *India and the West*. London, 1961. p. 228.

mental importance to the world than the division between East and West."[1]

Finally, in recent years it has at last been borne in on the Government and its advisers that Britain cannot in the literal sense afford to maintain the military framework on which the patron-protégé relationship with many third world countries still rested, that the cost of bases and garrisons there places a burden on the balance of payments that it can no longer carry.

This can be seen particularly clearly from the recent history of the South-East Asian and Middle Eastern bases, which under the original version of the East of Suez doctrine appeared to be promised eternal life, but which under present plans are to be abandoned by the end of 1971.

While political considerations no doubt played the main part in this change of front and while the Government moved not in one jump, but several, from one position to the other, the final push was given by the balance of payments crisis and devaluation of sterling in November 1967. The decision to evacuate was taken as a direct result of that crisis and occupied first place in the series of measures announced by the Government to deal with its consequences.[2]

The actual process by which the authorities moved over to new tactics towards the third world was tortuous in the extreme.

In a study of colonial policy in this period, W. P. Kirkman, the former Africa correspondent of *The Times*, asks why, if in the end independence was to be granted, there was so much useless tacking to and fro to avoid this result, why there was so much shuffling and deceit in the handling both of the leaders of the independence movements and of their local opponents, settlers, sheiks and sultans as the case may be? The author's answer is, "A lack of understanding arising . . . from overwork and lack of time to think."[3] Elsewhere, with reference to Kenya, he remarks on the conflict between an intellectual grasp of the radical changes which had to be made and the emotional resistance to making them.[4]

This view of the matter is the antithesis of Strang's and the official version generally and much nearer the truth. In particular, "a lack of understanding" in the shape of underestimation of the strength of the revolt against foreign domination and racial discrimination, time and time again led the policy-makers, despite their

[1] *Foreign Affairs*. New York. April 1964.
[2] Command 3515. January 1968.
[3] W. P. Kirkman. *Unscrambling an Empire*. London. 1966. p. 203.
[4] *Ibid*. p. 56.

expertise on African and Asian matters, into gross miscalculation of the real balance of forces and into impasses from which they extricated themselves only with the greatest difficulty.

Nevertheless, it is possible, I think, through the mass of particular events, moves, statements, etc., to distinguish certain tactical changes of general application.

In the colonial field, the authorities sooner or later engaged in an exercise euphemistically known as "preparing the colonies for independence". In practice this meant the widespread use of armed force and the exploitation of ethnic, tribal, religious and class differences to try to ensure that, when political power finally did pass, it passed into the hands of social forces and leaders who were not only willing, but able, to preserve a close connection with Britain.

This was no easy task. On the one hand, the colonial administrations' old standbys, ranging from tribal chiefs, feudal rulers and police and military mercenaries to sections of the business community, professional politicians and hand-picked trade-union leaders, in most cases commanded too little support within their countries to retain control once British rule was withdrawn. On the other hand, the leaders of the liberation movements, who did command mass support among the people and who were capable of retaining power, all stood, in greater or less degree, for an independent course in both internal and external affairs.

In some cases, such as Malaya and Nigeria, where there were particularly powerful ethnic and tribal factors to be played upon, it did prove possible to hand over power to well-tried collaborators. But on the whole it proved necessary in the end to attempt to reach an understanding with elements of the independence movements themselves.

The timing of such operations was, as one leading colonial expert has pointed out, a delicate matter. It is the duty of the Colonial Governor, he wrote, to pick in good time the national leader to whom, from London's point of view, power should eventually pass, and exceptional skill and sense of timing is required to ensure that the transfer is carried out as desired. "Assuming that the Governor has spotted his Nehru or Nkrumah or Nyerere, for how long," he asked, "should he strengthen such a leader's hand by spells in prison, and how soon can the leader be made Prime Minister without being called a stooge?" A revolutionary leader who co-operates with the colonial power too soon, he remarked, will lose his followers. But, worse still, if an influential national leader is denied access to power for too long, he may thereby be forced into more violent attitudes or "be replaced by devils worse than himself".[1]

Spurred on by this and the other more general considerations which we have mentioned, the Government in one country after another tried to make allies out of its opponents. Former inhabitants of its colonial jails—Nkrumah (Ghana), Makarios (Cyprus), Banda (Malawi), Kenyatta (Kenya), Kaunda (Zambia)—like Nehru before them, were recognised as Prime Ministers and Presidents and received with all honours in London. The volte-face which this involved is particularly striking in the case of Makarios and Kenyatta, both of whom, besides being imprisoned, were at one time systematically reviled in official propaganda as blood-stained criminals.

As part of the process of "preparing the colonies for independence", wide use was made of federation of hitherto separate colonies, protectorates, emirates and other territorial units in order to tilt the internal political balance in the desired direction.

This is not to say that there was no objective basis for the many federal schemes promoted by Whitehall during this period. On the contrary, all of them were founded in one degree or another on real economic, cultural or ethnic links.

But in every case, except the abortive West Indian Federation, the particular form of federation selected and put through by London was so designed as to strengthen the hand of its chosen allies at the centre as a counter-balance to the less co-operative forces at work in the territories concerned. Thus, as the sun set on the empire, a peculiar form of unite and rule, temporarily at least, overlay the more familiar conception of divide and rule in third world tactics.

The most glaring case of this was the Central African Federation,[2] imposed against the will of the Africans in the two Rhodesias and Nyasaland, which had the effect, while it lasted, of prolonging white settler control in all three countries. The same pattern was to be seen in the Malaysian Federation, designed to bring the Malayan rulers into play against the Communists in Singapore and the independence movements in North Borneo, Brunei and Sarawak, and in the Federation of South Arabia, which provided the central machinery through which the power of the emirs in the hinterland could be brought to bear against the Arab nationalists of Aden. The same idea lay behind the projected, but still-born East African Federation, and lies behind

[1] Philip Mason. Director of the Institute of Race Relations. *The World Today*. August, 1961.
[2] The nature and fate of this and the other Federations mentioned here are discussed in more detail below.

the new Federation of Arab Emirates set up in the Persian Gulf as recently as the beginning of 1968.

In quest of a "right relationship" with the third world, increasing emphasis has been put on financial and technical assistance to the under-developed countries, chiefly the former colonies.

In 1960, a semi-official body financed by the Ford Foundation and by British firms, the Overseas Development Institute, was set up to study the problem of assistance to the third world. The following year a new government department, the Department of Technical Co-operation, was brought into existence charged with co-ordinating and increasing technical assistance. In 1964 the Department was expanded into a fully-fledged Ministry for Overseas Development with responsibility for financial as well as technical aid. In 1966 a new Institute of Development Studies was opened at the University of Sussex with government support.

Government expenditure on financial and technical assistance still remains small—about 1/2% of the gross national product. Moreover, it includes a proportion of high-interest loans which place a heavy burden on the recipient countries. According to official estimates, in 1965 repayments of principal and interest charges on previous loans amounted to about £50,000,000 and were expected to be higher still in subsequent years.[1] Nevertheless, government disbursements rose (see Table 8) and the terms on which aid was given were lightened.

Table 8[2]
Government Expenditure on Economic Aid to Developing Countries
(£ million)

1957–58*	1960–61*	1963	1964	1965	1966	1967
18	151	163	191	195	215	208

* Financial year.

In 1965, more than half of all economic aid was given in the form of grants. In that year a new category was introduced in the shape of interest-free loans, which by the end of 1966 amounted to £80,000,000.

A high priority was given to the recruitment of British personnel for employment by the governments of the developing countries, chiefly in administration and teaching. Part of the remuneration

[1] *Overseas Development: The Work in Hand.* Command 3180. January 1967.
[2] *Commonwealth Survey.* August 17, 1965. *Survey of British and Commonwealth Affairs.* May 12, 1967. September 27, 1968.

of the great majority of these specialists, who at the end of 1967 numbered over 20,000, is paid for out of British Government funds.

The Government also encouraged the flow into Britain of students and trainees from the third world. In 1961–1962 they numbered 46,000 and occupied 9% of all places in technical colleges and 8% of all university places in the country. 3,000 received financial support from British Government funds, the rest being maintained by other bodies in Britain, their own governments or private means.[1] In the 1966–1967 academic year the total number had risen to 56,000, of whom some 5,600 were financed from British public funds.

The evolution of tactics also eventually included a change in the attitude of the policy-makers towards the United Nations.

I say "eventually" because well into the sixties the Government continued to regard the activities of the United Nations on third world questions with undisguised enmity. In a speech in December 1961, Lord Home, then Foreign Secretary, complained that resolutions had been passed by the Assembly, which could only be described as "reckless and careless of peace and security". A large number of new countries were putting their campaign for the acceleration of independence for the remaining colonies before the main purpose of the Charter. The British Government, he said, was in consequence considering whether from its point of view the United Nations had not "had its day".[2]

But in due course, and particularly after the return of the Labour Party to power, the Government came more and more to regard the United Nations as a useful bridge between "North" and "South" and as a buffer lessening the shock of collision with the Asian and African independence movements.

The Labour Party's election manifesto of 1964 sharply criticised the Conservative Government for aligning Britain with the colonial block in the United Nations, alongside Portugal, South Africa, France and Spain and in opposition to the anti-colonial majority. It promised that a Labour Government would work for greater representation for the new Asian and African members in the Security Council and Economic and Social Council.

Immediately after its election, the Wilson Government as an onus of its good intentions, appointed as its representative to the United Nations Sir Hugh Foot (now Lord Caradon), a popular figure in the third world owing to his previous resignation from the public service in

---

[1] *British Aid—1*. Overseas Development Institute. London. 1963. pp. 57–58.
[2] Speech at Berwick-on-Tweed. *Documents* . . . 1961. pp. 514–519.

protest against the policy pursued by the Conservative Government in Southern Rhodesia.[1]

The desirability of co-operating with the third world countries in the United Nations was one of the leading themes in the first major foreign policy statement by the new Labour Prime Minister. The chief concerns and aspirations of the new nations, which more and more dominate discussions in the United Nations, he said, are very different from those of the organisation's original members. Some people may regard the United Nations as an organisation for preserving the existing order, he went on, but "we do not; and the majority of its members see it as an instrument of peaceful revolution".[2]

In practice, when confronted with colonial problems of peculiar difficulty, the Government on more than one occasion departed from its former attitude that colonial affairs are internal affairs and that the United Nations therefore has no right to interfere in them.

This applied to Rhodesia following the unilateral declaration of independence by the Smith régime in November 1965. Reversing its previous attitude, London in the new circumstances voted in favour of, and itself initiated, resolutions in the Security Council directed against the rebels in Salisbury. It also applied to Aden and Southern Arabia. Until the end of 1965 the British representatives voted against UN resolutions on these territories and refused to allow a UN mission to visit them. In August 1966, however, the Government announced that, subject to certain reservations, it would "welcome the assistance and participation of the United Nations" in bringing South Arabia to independence.[3]

The New Commonwealth[4]

In their efforts to solve the North-South problem, successive Conservative and Labour Governments have placed high hopes in the Commonwealth in its new form.

In the course of the period under review, the composition of the Commonwealth underwent a radical change. The former and existing semi-colonies in the Arab world—Egypt, Iraq, the Sudan, Jordan, Kuwait, and other sheikdoms of the Persian Gulf and Southern

---

[1] Foot's account of his resignation (in October 1962) is given in Hugh Foot. *A Start in Freedom*. London. 1964. pp. 215–227.
[2] Speech at Guildhall on November 16, 1964. *The Times*. November 17, 1964.
[3] Note addressed to the UN Secretary-General of August 1, 1966. *Commonwealth Survey*. August 19, 1966.
[4] The term as used here does not include surviving colonies.

Arabia—are not and never have been members. But in the rest of Asia and Africa and in the Western hemisphere every colony, except Burma, joined the Commonwealth on attaining sovereignty.[1] In 1956 the Commonwealth consisted of Britain, Canada, Australia, New Zealand and South Africa, plus three Asian and no African members. Ten years later there were no fewer than twenty-one third-world members.[2]

At the beginning of the fifties, Churchill was still talking about Britain "gathering her Commonwealth around her" in order to revive her influence in world affairs,[3] or warning the United States and the rest of the world that they should not "underestimate the abiding power of the British Commonwealth and Empire",[4] as if it were a monolithic power bloc of which he was the undisputed spokesman. By the sixties, his successors had come to regard the new Commonwealth, with its overwhelmingly Afro-Asian membership, as primarily an instrument of policy towards the third world.

In a speech in 1961, Lord Home, then Foreign Secretary, described the political purpose of the new Commonwealth, as seen by the Conservative Party, as follows. In our Empire building, he said, we came to grips at close quarters with the problem of race and colour, in which there was the certainty of conflict unless by some bold act the danger could be laid. "The way we chose, with our eyes open to the risks," he continued, "was to bring the Asian and African colonies to independence, and then into the Commonwealth as equal partners . . . The Association is young and has its imperfections, but it is possible that by that act of faith we ensured the ultimate defeat of Communism."[5]

A report on the future of the Commonwealth put out in 1963 by an impressive gathering of representatives of the Government, business and finance, the universities, the trade unions, research institutes, the Press, etc., put the point as follows. "The Commonwealth sits astride the world problem of the developed and the under-developed nations," it said. ". . . The Commonwealth therefore represents one means by which this huge problem can be tackled, and for Britain it represents perhaps the best means."[6]

[1] Not counting British Somaliland, which became part of Somalia, and the British Cameroons, which was divided between Nigeria and the Cameroon Republic.
[2] India, Pakistan, Ceylon, Ghana, Malaysia, Nigeria, Cyprus, Sierra Leone, Tanzania, Jamaica, Trinidad, Uganda, Kenya, Malawi, Malta, Zambia, The Gambia, Guyana, Botswana, Lesotho and Barbados.
[3] *Documents* . . . 1951. p. 137.
[4] *Documents* . . . 1952. p. 47.
[5] The Earl of Home. *Great Britain's Foreign Policy*. Conservative Political Centre. London. 1961. p. 9.
[6] *The Future of the Commonwealth. A British View.* H.M.S.O. London. 1963. p. 11.

In a speech in 1965 Arthur Bottomley, the Labour Commonwealth Secretary of the day, declared that the Commonwealth is "a unique political, social and economic bridge which straddles . . . political divisions between aligned and non-aligned, divisions on grounds of race and colour, economic divisions between rich nations and poor ones". Of all international groupings, he said, the Commonwealth offers, perhaps, "the best forum for continuous compromise".[1]

Some of the policy-makers, particularly those who consider that in the conduct of foreign policy absolute priority should be given to strengthening British influence in Western Europe, doubt the viability of the modern Commonwealth and deprecate any special effort to keep it in being.

At the beginning of 1966 Enoch Powell, then still a member of the Conservative Shadow Cabinet, complained that none of the members of the Commonwealth recognised "any common interest with Britain where it would override or conflict with their own" and suggested that it would be best to let it break up.[2]

On the Labour side, one of the right-wing leaders, Mayhew, wrote that "if a hard-headed examination were made of the profit and loss to us of our relations with all Commonwealth countries, it would show plainly that we give more than we receive". He goes on to argue that the balance of political advantage is also doubtful, since the Commonwealth seldom acts together in world politics, and some members have delivered violent attacks on the British Government in the United Nations and elsewhere.[3]

However, in the period under review, the Powells and the Mayhews were in the minority.

The prevailing view that the Commonwealth is still a valuable asset particularly as regards relations with the third world, while no doubt containing elements of wish-fulfilment, is based on fairly realistic considerations.

It is true that, as shown in more detail below, centrifugal tendencies predominate within the Commonwealth. There has been perpetual conflict between London and the third-world members over colonial and racial questions. Australia, New Zealand and Canada have moved further and further into the politico-military sphere of influence of the United States. The relative importance, both to Britain and to the other members, of Commonwealth trade

---

[1] Speech at London House. February 3, 1965. *Commonwealth Survey*. February 16, 1965.
[2] *The Times*. January 15, 1966.
[3] Christopher Mayhew. *Britain's Role Tomorrow*. London. 1967. pp. 111–112.

and Commonwealth preference has steadily diminished. Nevertheless, both the economic underpinning of the Commonwealth and its political superstructure have remained in being.

In every Commonwealth country British private capital occupies an important, and in some cases dominating, position in the economy and in all, except Canada, the British share of total foreign investment is greater than that of any other country, including the United States. At the beginning of the sixties British investments in Australia totalled about £1,000,000,000 and in New Zealand about £200,000,000. In both cases the figure was more than double that for the United States, despite the long-term tendency for American investments to increase at a higher rate than British. This is not the exception but the rule. Figures for the Asian and African members of the Commonwealth are given in subsequent chapters. They show that everywhere the picture is much the same, whether in India or Pakistan, Malaysia or Singapore, Nigeria or Ghana, Kenya or Tanzania, Zambia or Malawi.

Moreover, throughout the sixties British private capital continued to flow in a steady stream into the Commonwealth countries. According to Board of Trade statistics, out of a total of £262,000,000 invested by private British companies overseas in 1964, which was not an exceptional year, 58% went to the sterling area, i.e., chiefly the Commonwealth plus South Africa, which for economic and financial purposes is still treated by London as a member.[1]

The relative significance of trade between Britain and the Commonwealth has substantially diminished. Nevertheless, the Commonwealth has remained an important market for British exports and Britain an important market for those of the Commonwealth. In 1966 32% of all British exports went to the sterling area, while the sterling area's share of the British market was 30%.

It is one of the weaknesses of the modern Commonwealth that Britain supplies only part, and not even the main part, of the foreign governmental grants, loans and credits received by the third world members. The expanded programme of British economic aid discussed above, though limited in scope, has been, however, almost entirely (as to 90%) concentrated on the Commonwealth. In Kenya, Malawi, Zambia, Uganda and Tanzania British financial assistance and the provision of British technical, administrative and in some cases military personnel still plays a key role in the economy and in the functioning of the state apparatus.

Despite the marked disparity in the political outlook of the British

[1] *Board of Trade Journal.* June 10, 1966. The figures exclude investment by oil companies.

Government and many of its new Commonwealth partners, the political structure survived and evolved in response to the new circumstances.

Conferences of Commonwealth Prime Ministers, which stand at the apex of the structure, became more frequent. The special system of diplomatic relations between Britain and the other members — with its intensified flow of information and consultation centred on the Commonwealth Relations Office in London — expanded as the Commonwealth itself expanded.

In order to increase the effectiveness of this system, it became the frequent practice to appoint specially selected political figures, rather than career officials, to represent Britain in the Commonwealth. The archetype of this new breed of Commonwealth politician-diplomatist is Malcolm MacDonald, who after having served in his father's, Baldwin's and Neville Chamberlain's Governments, in the course of the last twenty-five years has acted as High Commissioner, Governor-General, Commissioner-General or Special Representative successively in Canada, South-East Asia, India, and East and Central Africa. Geoffrey de Freitas, a member of the first post-war Labour Government, was selected by a Conservative Government as High Commissioner first in Ghana and then in Kenya. Lord Head, Minister of Defence in Eden's Government, subsequently served as High Commissioner in Nigeria and Malaysia. John Freeman, a former member of the Attlee Government, was High Commissioner in India before taking up his present post as Ambassador in Washington.

Under pressure from its partners, the Government agreed to relax the monopoly control which, through the Commonwealth Relations Office, it had previously exercised over the organisational side of all Commonwealth affairs. Part of this function is now carried out by the new Commonwealth Secretariat, headed by a Canadian, set up by decision of the Prime Ministers' Conference of 1965. In the following year the Prime Ministers' Conference was, for the first time in its history, convened not by the British Government but by the new Secretariat, held not in London, but in Lagos, and presided over not by the British, but by the Nigerian Prime Minister.

Notwithstanding the now overwhelming preponderance of Asian and African members, the cultural-linguistic bond between Britain and her partners, though much weakened, has not altogether disappeared. A very large proportion of the recent and present generation of leaders of the third-world members of the Commonwealth received part or all of their education in British schools and universities either in Britain itself or in their own countries. This applies to, among others, Nehru and Mrs Gandhi (India), Kenyatta (Kenya), Kaunda (Zambia), Banda (Malawi), Obote (Uganda), Abdul Rahman (Malaysia), Lee Kuan Yew (Singapore), Ayub Khan (Pakistan), Nkrumah and Ankrah (Ghana) and Ironsi, Gowon and Ojukwu (Nigeria).

It is likely, moreover, that this form of link will continue for some time, since the overwhelming majority of third-world students and trainees in Britain come from the Commonwealth.

In addition there are special arrangements for training certain categories of Commonwealth cadres. In 1963 there were 750 Commonwealth officers and men taking courses at various military establishments in Britain with the assistance of funds supplied by the Government. Every year a certain number of Commonwealth personnel receive special training in Britain for future employment in the diplomatic service, government departments, radio and press services, trade unions, etc., of their own countries.[1]

The foregoing takes no account of the very considerable influence still exercised by schools and universities in Asian and African Commonwealth countries staffed and financed wholly or in part from Britain.

At the time of writing the Commonwealth is thus still a working mechanism to the preservation of which the decision-makers, for understandable reasons, attach considerable importance. It is nevertheless highly unstable.

In the period under review, the most serious threat to its cohesion arose from the Macmillan Government's attempt in 1961–1963 to secure entry into the European Economic Community, which caused an unprecedented crisis in Britain's relations with practically every member of the Commonwealth, both old and new.

While a number of other problems arose, the central question for practically all Commonwealth countries was the long-term effect on their export trade of British membership of the EEC. Since the latter has a common tariff barrier against imports from third countries and in principle no tariff against its own members, the prospect was not only that the advantage enjoyed on the British market by Commonwealth exports under the imperial preference system would disappear, but that new tariffs would be raised against them, while exports from the EEC would enter duty-free. In other words, the existing situation would be reversed. Preference on the British market would be enjoyed not by the Commonwealth, but by the Six, while discrimination

[1] For more details, see *The Future of the Commonwealth.* pp. 43–46.

would be practised not against the Six, but against the Commonwealth. Owing to the high degree of dependence on the British market of most Commonwealth countries, this perspective was fraught with a grave threat to their interests.

In 1960, Britain took 53% of New Zealand's exports, 48% of Nigeria's, about 25% of Australia's, India's, Ceylon's and Ghana's and 17% of Canada's and Pakistan's.[1] For certain key commodities in the economies of the Commonwealth countries, this dependence was even greater, particularly as regards food-stuffs in the case of New Zealand and Australia and tea in that of India and Ceylon. Furthermore, Canada's, India's and Pakistan's exports of manufactured goods to Britain were particularly dependent on the tariff preference which they enjoyed.

The British Government by no means denied that this was one of the most important problems arising in the negotiations with the Six. Indeed they, and British business and financial circles generally, had good reasons, both political and economic, for trying to find a compromise solution. However urgent the desire to join the Common Market, they had a strong interest in protecting British export trade with the Commonwealth and British influence upon its members, the fate of both of which was bound up directly or indirectly with that of Commonwealth exports to Britain.

Accordingly, the Government's aim was to join the EEC on terms permitting the retention of as much as possible of the existing structure of intra-Commonwealth trade. The point was clearly put to the Six by the leader of the British negotiators, Edward Heath, at an early stage. After explaining to them the importance of the British market to the Commonwealth countries, he said: "I am sure you will understand that Britain could not join the EEC under conditions in which this trade connection was cut, with grave loss and even ruin for some of the Commonwealth countries."[2]

It follows that to a certain extent there was common ground between the British and other Commonwealth Governments on this question. But only to a certain extent. In practice, it was obvious from the first, and confirmed by the course of the negotiations at Brussels, that the Government could only obtain entry into the EEC at the cost of considerable damage to the interests of its Commonwealth partners and that it intended, if it could, to strike a bargain at Brussels at the latters' expense. Hence the open quarrel which broke

[1] *Britain and the European Communities.* H.M.S.O. London. 1962.
[2] Statement on October 10, 1961, published in *The Times* and elsewhere on November 28, 1961.

out between London on one side, and practically all the other members of the Commonwealth on the other. In September 1960, at the London meeting of the Commonwealth Economic Consultative Council, the Ministers of Finance of New Zealand and Canada expressed the strongest objections to the provisional plans in relation to the EEC set forth by the British representatives.

When in June 1961 the British Government had privately made up its mind to apply for membership of EEC, it despatched special high-level emissaries to the Commonwealth Governments in an effort to secure their agreement before the decision was publicly announced. Duncan Sandys, the Secretary of State for Commonwealth Relations, was sent to New Zealand, Australia and Canada. Peter Thorneycroft, the Minister of Aviation, was sent to India, Pakistan, Ceylon and Malaya, and John Hare, the Minister of Labour, to Ghana, Nigeria and Sierra Leone.

As even the official communiqués showed, these emissaries almost everywhere failed to achieve their objective. In Ottawa "the Canadian Ministers indicated that their Government's assessment of the situation was different from that put forward by Mr Sandys" and "expressed grave concern . . . about the political and economic effects which British membership in the European Economic Community would have on Canada and on the Commonwealth as a whole".[1] In Delhi, "Indian Ministers suggested that the accession of the United Kingdom to the Treaty of Rome might weaken existing Commonwealth links and injure the economies of the developing countries of the Commonwealth in particular".[2] In Ghana, the President declared in Parliament immediately after Hare's visit that British membership of the EEC would have "a disruptive effect" on the Commonwealth.[3] The reaction of the Australian, New Zealand and Pakistani Governments was also openly unfavourable.

The British Government, ignoring this almost unanimous opposition, on July 31 announced its decision to apply for membership of the EEC. Its Commonwealth partners, besides separate statements of anxiety and disapproval, then took the opportunity of the September 1961 meeting of the Commonwealth Economic Consultative Council in Accra to express their attitude collectively. In the discussion of the British application to join the EEC, which dominated the proceedings, the British representatives (the Chancellor of the Exchequer and the President of the Board of Trade) found themselves

[1] Nicholas Mansergh. *Documents and Speeches on Commonwealth Affairs. 1952–1962*. London. 1963. p. 635.
[2] *Ibid*. p. 639.   [3] *The Times*. 5 July. 1961.

isolated. As the communiqué states, after they had explained the reasons for Britain's application, "all other Commonwealth representatives expressed grave apprehension and concern regarding the possible results of the initiative taken by the United Kingdom ... Most Commonwealth Governments questioned whether the United Kingdom ... could possibly secure in the proposed negotiations an agreement which would protect Commonwealth interests adequately and effectively".[1]

In September 1962, while the Brussels negotiations were still in progress, the Government summoned a Conference of Commonwealth Prime Ministers in another effort to secure their acquiescence in the bargain it was hoping to make with the Six. In this Macmillan and his colleagues were also unsuccessful. Among other expressions of disagreement from all quarters of the Commonwealth, the Australian Prime Minister, Sir Robert Menzies, commented bitterly that, while Britain had evidently decided that for her the gains would outweigh the losses if she entered the Common Market, it seemed that the price was to be paid by the Commonwealth. For his part the Indian Prime Minister, Nehru, remarked that he did not see "how the Commonwealth will survive unless a radical change is made in the present proposals".[2]

This crisis in Britain's relations with her Commonwealth partners was brought to an abrupt end in January 1963 by the French veto on British membership of EEC and recent developments make it unlikely that it will recur in quite such an acute form. For one thing, the dependence of the other Commonwealth members on the British market has steadily declined. For another, some of the African members (Nigeria, Kenya, Tanzania and Uganda) have meanwhile concluded separate trade agreements with the EEC. It is obvious, however, that if serious negotiations over British membership once more get going, strains within the Commonwealth will recur. Moreover, if negotiations are eventually successful, it seems almost certain that the Commonwealth in its present form will begin to break up.

Surviving ultra-colonialist tendencies in British policy, discussed below, have also tended to weaken the Commonwealth. The desire of practically all the Asian, African and Caribbean members for an early end everywhere to European and American colonialism, racial oppression and racial discrimination caused a whole series of collisions with London,[3] whose only reliable Commonwealth allies on

---

[1] Mansergh. *op. cit.* pp. 650–651. [2] *The Times.* September 12, 1962.
[3] Anglo-Indian and certain other intra-Commonwealth conflicts over colonial questions are dealt with in more detail below.

these occasions were Australia and New Zealand, Canada usually occupying the middle ground.

In 1956, when there were as yet only three third-world members, the British attack on Egypt aroused such opposition and condemnation in India, Pakistan and Ceylon that the question of leaving the Commonwealth was raised in the Parliaments of all three countries. The prevailing mood was expressed by Nehru, who denounced the behaviour of the Eden Government as "unabashed aggression and deception . . . dangerous to the freedom of Asian and African countries and to world peace itself".[1] The Canadian Prime Minister, who was himself critical of British policy, stated publicly at the time that the Commonwealth was "badly and dangerously split. At one stage after the fighting on land began it was on the verge of dissolution".[2]

Almost the whole of the Commonwealth was ranged against London when in 1961 the latter attempted to sabotage UN military operations against the Katanga separatists in the Congo. When in December the Acting Secretary-General's Advisory Committee on the Congo discussed the British proposal for an immediate cease-fire designed to save Tshombe and his henchmen, all seven Commonwealth members of the Committee — India, Pakistan, Ceylon, Malaya, Nigeria, Ghana and Canada — opposed it.[3] Two months later, Commonwealth members, including the two newest recruits — Tanganyika and Sierra Leone — joined with the majority of the UN Assembly in rejecting British attempts to prevent the UN Special Committee on colonialism from investigating the question of racial oppression in Southern Rhodesia.[4] This pattern of Commonwealth opposition to British policy in the United Nations was repeated over a number of other colonial and racial problems, notably those concerning South Africa, South-West Africa, and the Portuguese colonies.

In 1961, against the opposition of the Macmillan Government, the Afro-Asian members put an end to South Africa's membership of the Commonwealth.

Particularly after the Sharpeville massacre,[5] anger and anxiety at the racial terror in South Africa had been steadily growing in all parts of the world, not least in the Asian and African countries of the

[1] Mansergh. *op. cit.* p. 522.
[2] *Ibid.* p. 515.
[3] *The Times.* December 18, 1961.
[4] *The Times.* February 24, 1962.
[5] On March 21, 1960, the South African police opened fire on an unarmed African demonstration, killing 70 and wounding 200.

Commonwealth. On the insistence of the latter, the Commonwealth Prime Ministers at their meeting in May 1960, in the tactful words of the communiqué, had informal discussions with the South African representative about the racial situation in his country.[1]

The following year the South African Government (and the British Government) did not get off so lightly. Since the former was then in the process of giving South Africa a new Republican constitution, tradition required that at the Commonwealth Prime Ministers' Conference in March 1961 the other members should give their consent to her continued membership. The question thus arose inescapably of whether the Asian and African members, who now numbered six — India, Pakistan, Ceylon, Malaya, Ghana and Nigeria — would any longer tolerate an openly racialist Government among their partners.

From the first, the British Government set itself the goal of securing continued South African membership, despite the opposition of the majority of the other members.

The essence of the tactics adopted was to try to separate the question of membership from that of the situation in South Africa. Under arrangements previously agreed between Macmillan and Dr Verwoerd, South Africa's membership was to be discussed first and, using the precedent established when India, Pakistan and Ghana became republics, treated, under the Chairman's (Macmillan's) guidance, as a technical matter automatically requiring an affirmative decision. The other members were to be persuaded to agree to this by a promise that they would be free to criticise South African racialism later in the Conference in the course of a general discussion on Africa. Verwoerd and Macmillan would thus have bought continued South African membership at the relatively cheap price of having to listen to a few hours of vehement, but ineffective, denunciation of apartheid.

This plan did not, however, work. When the time came the majority of Prime Ministers refused to accept the separation of the two questions. The British negotiators, again by arrangement with the South Africans, then attempted to achieve the same result by dividing the draft communiqué into two parts, one accepting South Africa's continued membership and the other recording the conflicting views of Verwoerd and his opponents on the racial question in South Africa. This manœuvre also failed.

In rejecting this solution, the Prime Ministers of Ghana and Nigeria stated that, if it were nevertheless adopted, their countries

[1] Mansergh. *op. cit.* p. 362.

would have to consider the question of their own future membership of the Commonwealth. The same view was taken by Nehru, who in his report on the Conference to the Indian Parliament said that "it seemed quite improper for us to be a member of an organisation which itself tolerated the kind of racial policies which are pursued by the South African Union Government".[1] Moreover, Nyerere, the Chief Minister of Tanganyika, which was about to attain independence, had already made known that his country would not join the Commonwealth if South Africa were still a member.[2]

Macmillan and his team, who had been supported by Australian Prime Minister, Menzies, but opposed by the Canadian Prime Minister, John Diefenbaker, were thus brought face to face with the fact that if they persisted on their chosen course, some of the existing Asian and African members would leave the Commonwealth and at least one and probably more of the remaining African colonies would refuse to join it on attaining independence. In the circumstances they decided to give way. This led in turn to the withdrawal by Verwoerd of his application for continued membership of the Commonwealth and the automatic cancellation of that membership on May 31, 1961, the day on which the new South African Republic came into existence.[3]

In 1964–1968 there was persistent conflict over the Rhodesian question between London and the African and Asian members of the Commonwealth, which at times came near to bringing about the withdrawal of some its members.

Throughout the post-war period it had been the practice for the Prime Minister of Southern Rhodesia (and later, while it was in existence, the Prime Minister of the Federation of Rhodesia and Nyasaland) to attend Commonwealth Prime Ministers' Conferences, although the representatives of other colonial governments did not normally do so. In this way, in accordance with London's policy, the settler régime, though not yet sovereign, was singled out for special treatment as heir apparent. In 1964 the third-world members put a stop to this arrangement by refusing their consent to the attendance of the Southern Rhodesian Premier at the Conference held in July of that year.

At the Conference itself, as the communiqué makes clear, pressure

---

[1] Mansergh. *op. cit.* p. 390.
[2] *The Observer*. March 12, 1961.
[3] The above account is based on Verwoerd's subsequent frank exposition of the moves and counter-moves made at the Conference, checked against the more cautious, but also detailed, versions given by Macmillan, Menzies, Diefenbaker and Nehru. Mansergh. *op. cit.* pp. 365–399.

was put on London to take practical steps towards giving Southern Rhodesia independence on the basis of majority, i.e., African, rule. The British Government at this stage evidently felt strong enough to disregard the views of its fellow members, for it made no binding promises, boldly alleged that "the Government of Southern Rhodesia was constitutionally responsible for the internal affairs of that territory" and emphasised that the granting of independence was a matter for the British Parliament.[1]

At the Prime Ministers' Conference in June of the following year this pressure was heavily increased. The British representatives adopted a more conciliatory attitude, but it proved impossible to secure unanimous agreement on the terms of the communiqué.

The third-world members demanded specific undertakings from London to convene a constitutional conference of all Rhodesian political leaders within three months with a view to the early establishment of majority rule and to use its sovereign powers to evict the settler régime if it refused to attend such a conference. The British Government, while making no definite commitment, did not reject the idea of a constitutional conference. Even so Tanzania dissociated itself from the Rhodesian section of the communiqué on the ground that London's assurances on majority rule were not adequate.[2]

In the course of 1966 the Rhodesian question occupied the whole of the Commonwealth Prime Ministers' Conference at Lagos in January and nine out of eleven days at the London Conference in September and led to open conflict between Britain and other Commonwealth members at the autumn session of the United Nations Assembly.

Ghana and Tanzania refused to attend the Lagos Conference, having already broken off diplomatic relations with Britain in protest against London's refusal to remove the settler régime. The Australian Prime Minister also refused to attend, but for the opposite reason, namely that he disapproved of attempts to interfere in London's handling of the Rhodesian situation.

By the time of the Lagos Conference, the Rhodesian settlers, led by Smith, had already made their unilateral declaration of independence and Britain, the United States and certain other countries had applied limited economic and financial sanctions. In the course of the proceedings, Wilson, in the face of openly expressed scepticism from his Commonwealth partners, clung to the proposition that "econo-

---

[1] *Commonwealth Survey.* July 21, 1964.
[2] *Ibid.* July 6, 1965.

mic and financial sanctions might well bring the rebellion to an end within a matter of weeks rather than months". By this means he averted demands for stronger action, but was nonetheless forced into making a number of concessions. He agreed to the creation of Commonwealth Committees to keep the effect of sanctions under review and to assist in the training of Rhodesian Africans for service in a lawfully constituted government. He also agreed that if the rebellion had not ended before then, the Prime Ministers should meet again in July.[1]

With the Smith régime still in power when July came round, Wilson succeeded in securing a postponement of a further meeting of Commonwealth Prime Ministers, but only over the bitter protests of, among others, the President of Zambia. Kaunda declared that while the British Government might be able to persuade other members of the Commonwealth to postpone the meeting, it had no means of forcing Zambia to stay in the Commonwealth and it might prove necessary for her to leave it.[2]

When the Conference finally convened in London in September, it was marked by open divergence between Britain, on one side, and the majority of the other members on the other. In opposition to the point of view of Wilson and his colleagues, the majority recorded their opinion that force was the only sure means of bringing down the Smith régime, that the British Government ought to declare categorically that independence would not be granted until majority rule was established and that it should enter into no further talks or negotiations with the Smith régime.

While not accepting any of these propositions, the British side secured a breathing space by promising, first, that if the Smith régime did not terminate its rebellion, Britain would withdraw all previous proposals for a constitutional settlement and would not thereafter sponsor any settlement which involved independence before majority rule;[3] and secondly, that if the rebellion was not terminated by the end of the year, Britain would support a resolution in the Security Council of the United Nations, imposing mandatory sanctions against Rhodesia.[4]

In October and November the Commonwealth majority carried its quarrel with London to the United Nations, its principal spokesmen being Tanzania and Zambia. The former introduced a resolution, overwhelmingly adopted by the Assembly, condemning the

[1] *Ibid.* January 21, 1966.
[2] *Ibid.* July 22, 1966.
[3] The so-called NIBMAR pledge—No Independence Before Majority Rule.
[4] *Ibid.* September 30, 1966.

6

British Government for conducting further talks with the Smith régime. Kaunda, in a speech to the Assembly on November 15, accused the Wilson Government of deliberate procrastination and of seeking to leave the African majority in Rhodesia at the mercy of the white minority.

When in December Wilson's efforts to reach a compromise with Smith on board H.M.S. *Tiger* at Gibraltar failed, the Government found itself obliged to implement the second of the above-mentioned promises, evidently fearing a break-up of the Commonwealth if it failed to do so. Faced by Conservative criticism of the decision to ask the Security Council to impose selective sanctions against the Smith régime, the Prime Minister said that the Commonwealth had very nearly broken up over the Rhodesian question and that he was not prepared to let this happen for the sake of a small minority in Salisbury.[1]

Thereafter the main focus of third-world pressure on London over Rhodesia shifted from the Commonwealth to the United Nations.

In the spring of 1968 Wilson and his colleagues were confronted by a draft Security Council resolution sponsored by, among others, India and Pakistan, urging the use of armed force by Britain against the Smith régime. In order to forestall this, the Government, repeating its previous manœuvre, itself proposed the imposition of comprehensive, as distinct from selective, economic sanctions, to which the Security Council agreed unanimously at the end of May.

At the time of writing the issue remains a time-bomb capable, if it explodes, of doing considerable damage to the Commonwealth. It has not yet gone off for two main reasons. First, the Government by agreeing to the imposition and subsequent strengthening of UN sanctions went a good way to meet the demands of the African and Asian members. Secondly, its efforts to make a deal with Salisbury in breach of the NIBMAR pledge, such as that proposed by Wilson at his second meeting with Smith on board H.M.S. *Fearless* in October 1968, have so far broken on the rock of settler intransigence. But it is still possible that Smuts's old prediction that "the experiment of Commonwealth may be smashed to pieces in the cockpit of Southern Africa"[2] may yet come true.

Ultra-Colonialism

If, despite all the zigzags, the prevailing tendency in the evolution

[1] *Ibid.* December 23, 1966.
[2] Quoted in *The Future of the Commonwealth.* p. 15.

of British policy has been towards acceptance of, and adaptation to, the new situation in the third world, there have, nevertheless, been substantial forces working in the opposite direction. The zigzags themselves have in very large measure arisen as a result of the strong resistance to change put up by specific ultra-colonialist interests.

It is sometimes asserted on the left that ultra-colonialism does not exist as a distinct, identifiable political and economic force, that there is no such thing as an ultra-colonialist group of companies whose interests in important respects diverge from those of financial and industrial circles as a whole. Similarly, the European settlers in Africa are sometimes considered not as a social group with aims which may run counter to those of the home Government, but as auxiliaries or mercenaries of the latter. According to this approach, basically there is only a convenient division of function between the metropolitan Government and the settlers, the latter providing part of the forces of repression on the spot, while the former looks after the rest. This may have been a correct picture in the past, but the developments of the last ten years and more have shown that it is nowadays, to say the least, misleading.

The term "ultra-colonialism" is usually associated with those French political, business and financial circles, military cadres and a large mass of settlers — "les ultras" — who in the fifties stood for a war to the death with the Algerian independence movement, and, when Paris finally accepted the necessity of recognising the independence of Algeria, turned their guns on the French Government. Ultra-colonialism is, however, an international phenomenon resulting from a divergence and polarisation, peculiar to the final phase of the colonial system, of formerly allied interest groups. It takes various forms, but its main sources are everywhere the same — certain powerful companies whose profitability is to an exceptional degree bound up with the preservation of colonial rule, and the settlers whose incomes and whole way of life depend absolutely upon it.

As the winds of change reached gale force and the colonial powers began to steer a new course, these groups remained frozen by their peculiar circumstances in the old attitudes, like so many dinosaurs surviving from a past epoch. Despite their relatively narrow social base, in Britain at any rate they turned out to be capable of exercising prolonged and at times effective pressure on official policy. Part of their strength lay and lies in their ability to appeal to the master-race, born-to-rule mentality handed on from generation to generation in a wide section of the population, which lingers on long after colonialism has been seen to be no longer a practical proposition.

British ultra-colonialism in its most distinctive and virulent form has drawn its strength chiefly from settlers in the African colonies, who in 1961 numbered 215,000 in Southern Rhodesia, 75,000 in Northern Rhodesia, and 65,000 in Kenya, and from certain British companies operating in Northern and Southern Rhodesia, the Congo, the Portuguese colonies and South Africa.

The ultra-colonialism of the settlers has its own cruel and rather obvious logic. Their privileged position and way of life was, and in Southern Rhodesia still is, wholly dependent on the preservation not only of the economic, but also the political subordination of the Africans and is incompatible with "coming to terms with nationalism".

This applies particularly to the European landowners and farmers, whose tenure arises directly from the seizure of land from the Africans and has no chance of surviving unless the state machine (police, armed forces, law courts, prisons, etc.) are in European and not African hands. Similarly, in the towns a system under which all the best-paid jobs in mining, industry, communications, commerce, banking, insurance, etc., and all the best housing and educational and cultural amenities are the monopoly of the whites is unworkable unless state power is also held by the whites.

Without relapsing into a mechanistic view of human behaviour, it is to be expected that the attitude of the beneficiaries of this racial order to a transfer of sovereignty to the Africans would be different from that of their fellow-countrymen living and working in Britain.

In practice the settlers formed one of the main props of the racialist régimes in Kenya and Northern and Southern Rhodesia and one of the main forces braking, modifying and even at times preventing the application in Central and East Africa of the new conceptions developing in London. Among their leading spokesmen have been Sir Godfrey Huggins (Lord Malvern), the first Prime Minister of the now defunct Central African Federation, to whom belongs the statement that the only proper relationship between European and African is "the partnership of rider and horse"; Sir Roy Welensky, his successor, who declared that "even in a hundred or two hundred years' time, the African shall never hope to dominate the Federation"; and Ian Smith, who in November 1965 unilaterally declared the settler Government of Southern

Rhodesia to be independent of the Government in London rather than accept the latter's wish for relatively minor political concessions to the Africans. There have been, it is true, groups of settlers who, as the tide of independence advanced, came out in favour of more moderate courses. They have, however, been in a minority.[1]

The position as regards the ultra-colonialist companies is more complex. As we shall see, the mere fact that a company such as Unilever has vast investments in Africa has not meant that it opposes greater flexibility in British colonial policy there. Much evidently depends on whether the business of a particular firm is such that it can or cannot adapt itself to a transfer of political power. Moreover, some other giants such as Shell or British Petroleum may favour continued diehard tactics in one part of the world, where they require guaranteed control of their raw material, while having no motive for ultra-colonialist attitudes in areas where they operate primarily as sellers, refiners, and shippers. For obvious reasons they must have welcomed the despatch of an expeditionary force to Kuwait in 1961, but they are not for that reason necessarily more sympathetic than big business generally to extreme racialism in Southern Africa.

There are, nevertheless, specifically ultra-colonialist companies, the chief of them being the Oppenheimer Group, the British South African Company (now reorganised under the name of Charter Consolidated) and Tanganyika Concessions. The first two inherited the major part of Cecil Rhodes's empire.

The Oppenheimer group has its main base in South Africa, Northern Rhodesia (Zambia) and Southern Rhodesia. Its principal company, the Anglo-American Corporation, in 1958 produced 30% of South Africa's gold, 22% of its uranium, and 40% of its coal, and 58% of Northern Rhodesia's copper. In Southern Rhodesia, it owns, among other properties, the Wankie coalmines. Its other main company, De Beers, in the sixties produced 40% of the world's diamonds and controlled the sales of most of the rest.

The British South Africa Company, which at one time governed Northern and Southern Rhodesia under a Royal Charter, drew its main income from royalties on every ton of copper produced in Northern Rhodesia, amounting in 1957 to nearly £9,000,000. It then also owned the Rhodesian Railway Trust and 134,000 acres of land in Southern Rhodesia.

Tanganyika Concessions derives most of its income from its large

[1] For details of these groups, see Jack Woddis. *Africa. The Lion Awakes*. London. 1961. pp. 176–180.

block of shares in the Belgian Union Minière of Katanga fame. The other main part of its profits comes from ownership of the Benguela Railway (in which the Portuguese Government has a 10% holding), which carries the output of the Katanga mines through Angola to the Atlantic. In 1961 Tanganyika Concessions received an income of over £3,000,000 from these two sources.

The members of this trio, while until recently independent of each other,[1] were linked through interlocking directorships and cross-holding of shares. Harry Oppenheimer, in addition to being head of his own group, was a director of both the British South Africa Company and Tanganyika Concessions, while Lord Robins, president of the British South Africa Company was also a director of the Anglo-American Corporation and Tanganyika Concessions. In December 1964, the British South Africa Company amalgamated with two subsidiaries of the Oppenheimer group to form Charter Consolidated.

The rate of profit of these companies has been dependent upon the retention of European political control in Africa to a far greater extent than that of the general run of British companies doing business in the third world. The Oppenheimer group's wealth is based upon the South African system of rigid and extreme racial oppression, a system which it sought, with some modifications, to impose in Southern and Northern Rhodesia. The British South Africa Company's copper royalties, being purely parasitic even by capitalist standards, could not and did not survive the passage of political sovereignty in Northern Rhodesia into African hands. Tanganyika Concessions' profits depend on the retention of Katanga as an enclave of Union Minière and upon the continued survival of the Portuguese colonial empire in Africa.

These companies have made no secret of where their sympathies lie. In the first half of the sixties Harry Oppenheimer regularly blazoned across the pages of the British press appeals for understanding of the problems facing the racialist régimes in South Africa and the Central African Federation. It is true that in South Africa Oppenheimer favoured some modification of the doctrine of apartheid, which he regarded as unrealistic, but in the Federation he was an all-out supporter of the Malvern and Welensky régimes, to which his group made loans of several million pounds in 1956 and again in 1961. On racial questions he consistently occupied a more

---

[1] An analysis of the main groupings in the British financial world at the beginning of the sixties placed the Oppenheimer group and the British South Africa Company in the grouping headed by Rothschilds, and Tanganyika Concessions in that headed by Lloyds Bank. S. Aaronovitch. *The Ruling Class*. London. 1961. pp. 166, 170.

extreme position than either the American-controlled Rhodesian copper companies or the British Government.

The Chairman of Tanganyika Concessions, Captain Charles Waterhouse, in a speech to his shareholders in 1962, warmly praised the Tshombe régime in Katanga, accused the United Nations of arbitrarily disturbing conditions there, demanded compensation for damage done to Union Minière's property by UN troops, and congratulated the Portuguese Government on the suppression of disturbances in Angola.[1]

Lord Robins, in his statement to the shareholders of the British South Africa Company in March, 1962, demanded that whatever constitutional changes the British Government introduced in Northern Rhodesia should ensure the retention of government in "responsible hands" and adequately protect the mining industry in which, he pointed out, the Company had a large stake.[2] The company participated in the above-mentioned loans to the Malvern and Welensky régimes in 1956 and 1961.

The British South Africa Company and Tanganyika Concessions have had close connections with the ultra-colonialist leaders in the Conservative Party. Captain Charles Waterhouse, who became Chairman of the latter company in 1957, had previously been leader of the so-called Suez group of Conservative Members of Parliament who revolted against the leadership of their own party in protest against the Anglo-Egyptian Agreement of 1954, providing for the evacuation of the Suez base. The present (1968) Chairman, Lord Colyton, is that same Henry Hopkinson, who as Conservative Minister of State at the Colonial Office, once declared that Cyprus could "never" be fully independent. Julian Amery, a member of the Suez group and subsequently leader of the ultra-colonialists in the House of Commons, was a director of the British South Africa Company until 1957. The elder statesman of ultra-colonialism, the Marquess of Salisbury, who in 1957 resigned from the Macmillan Government in protest against the release from prison of Archbishop Makarios of Cyprus, was also a director of that company until 1961.

It is not suggested that these gentlemen and others like them hold the views they do because they are or have been directors of these companies or in other ways draw income from ultra-colonialist sources. On the contrary, they were no doubt invited to become directors because they already held ultra-colonialist views and could

[1] *The Times.* January 26, 1962.
[2] *The Economist.* March 3, 1962.

therefore be expected the more effectively to advance the companies' interests. The result is, however, the same. A firm link exists between ultra-colonialist business and financial groups (and the settlers) and the die-hard wing of the Conservative Party and by this means they have been able to exert a direct influence on the African policy of successive Conservative Governments.

The practical consequences as regards British policy in the Central and East African colonies are examined separately. Here, by way of example, we will only recall briefly the Congo crisis of 1960–1962.

Although the Congo was a Belgian colony and its economy was mainly in the hands of the Société Générale and other Belgian companies, its fate was of the closest interest to Tanganyika Concessions, the Oppenheimer group, the British South Africa Company, the Rhodesian settlers and the die-hard wing of the Conservative Party.

As we have seen, the first-named company had a £3,000,000 a year stake in the retention of Belgian control, direct or indirect, over Katanga. Immediately adjoining Katanga on its southern border lies Northern Rhodesia, one of the main sources of wealth of the Oppenheimer group and the British South Africa Company, and at that time subjected to settler rule through the mechanism of the Central African Federation, led by Welensky.

Welensky and his backers with some reason feared the consequences to themselves of the advance of the African independence movement to their very door. From the first they regarded the retention of the Belgian and British hold on Katanga as their own direct concern and treated the defence of the northern, Katanga, sector of the copper belt as part of the defence of its southern, Rhodesian, sector.

On this basis there came into existence a powerful Katanga lobby, represented on the scene of operations by Welensky, who from his point of vantage on the Katanga frontier, gave every kind of support to the Belgian-inspired separatists, led by Tshombe with his white and black mercenaries. In London the lobby was by no means confined to the spokesmen of Tanganyika Concessions, the party most directly interested, but included the whole of the ultra-colonialist group in the House of Commons.

Government policy from first to last showed the clear imprint of the influence of these special interests. Even though the United States, nearly all the members of the Commonwealth and the overwhelming majority of the United Nations, however varied their aims and motives, were at one in opposing Katanga separatism, Macmillan, Home and their colleagues obstinately sought to shield the Tshombe régime.

This line was apparent at the beginning of the crisis, when Britain refused to vote for the Security Council resolution of July 14, 1960, arising from the reoccupation of the Congo by Belgian troops immediately after the country attained independence. Macmillan primly explained to the House of Commons that "Her Majesty's Government did not feel that it would be right . . . to call for Belgian troops to withdraw without qualification".[1]

In the autumn of 1961 the Government came to Tshombe's rescue by delaying the transit through Uganda of Ethiopian fighter aircraft destined for the UN troops in the Congo and by promoting a cease-fire before UN objectives had been attained. Part of this latter manœuvre was executed jointly by a member of the Government, Lansdowne, and Welensky, who was unofficial host at the proposed talks between Tshombe, Lansdowne and UN Secretary-General Hammerskjöld, at Ndola, on the Rhodesian side of the Katanga frontier, on the way to which the latter met his death.

The same tactics were employed in December 1961, after UN operations against Tshombe had been renewed. The Government reversed a previous undertaking to supply bombs for British-made bombers being employed by the UN forces and, to save Tshombe's skin, appealed to the UN Acting Secretary-General, this time unsuccessfully, for an immediate cease-fire.[2]

Persistent ultra-colonialist tendencies have not, however, been confined to British policy in Africa, the home of the settlers and stamping ground of the Oppenheimer and similar groups. In other parts of the third world, the Government, whether Conservative or Labour, moved by considerations of military strategy, have also clung to the rule of the gun long after political and economic factors appeared to dictate more flexible tactics. Moreover, "military strategy" here has meant mainly, though not exclusively, retention of the ability to intervene in the Middle East in defence of British oil interests there. In this case the original source of ultra-colonialist behaviour can be traced back not only to the oil companies, but to the Government itself, which owns half the shares of British Petroleum.

The prolonged and fruitless attempt to suppress the independence movement in Cyprus by force, the imprisonment of Archbishop

---

[1] *Documents . . .* 1960. pp. 277–278.
[2] *Documents . . .* 1961. p. 769.

6*

Makarios, and the ministerial statement that Cyprus could "never" be fully independent all arose directly from the strategic importance of the island in London's military plans. It was required as the new home of GHQ, Middle East, following the decision in 1954 to evacuate the Suez base. It was used as one of the main jumping-off grounds both for the attack on Egypt in 1956 and for the lifting of British and American troops into the Lebanon and Jordan in 1958. It was also required as a nuclear base in case of war with the Soviet Union. Under the compromise finally reached with Makarios in 1960, nuclear weapons remained based in special British enclaves on the island.

By the beginning of the sixties, Aden had in its turn become the site of GHQ, Middle East, and the main base and nerve centre of British military dispositions in the Persian Gulf and East Africa. Its importance as a staging post to the Far East had also increased. In these circumstances, until 1966 the Government clung obstinately to the view that, come what may, a military base must be retained there. And indeed, the pursuit of this aim led to the use until quite recently of measures of repression against the Arabs of Aden of a kind supposedly long since withdrawn from Whitehall's rule book.

As regards Singapore and Malaysia, it may seem far-fetched to apply the term "ultra-colonialist" to official policy. Once massive military operations against the independence movement were successfully concluded by the end of the fifties, British troops, though still present in large numbers, were used more in defensive operations against Indonesia than against the local population. Nonetheless, as in the case of Aden, until the mid-sixties military requirements delayed the application of the general tactics of bending to the winds of change and brought in their train repressive police operations in Brunei, Sarawak and North Borneo of the classical colonial kind.

The Government's insistence for so long on maintaining bases and troops on the Malayan mainland and in Singapore is partly to be explained by the exceptionally large British business interests in the area, but wider strategic considerations played an even more important role. Singapore, in particular, has been a nuclear base intended for use against targets far afield, and has played a key role in British, American and Australian military dispositions throughout East Asia, the Western Pacific and the Indian Ocean. The Government's position was explained bluntly by Duncan Sandys, the then Minister of Defence, in 1959, and remained unchanged for the next seven years. "There is no doubt about the continuation of the British base in Singapore," he said. "It is the pivot of our military situation in the Far East and we have no thought of changing it."[1]

British ultra-colonialism has on the whole grown steadily weaker. In Africa, in the course of the sixties, the settlers and their financial and business allies lost ground heavily. In particular, the transfer of political power into African hands in Northern Rhodesia, Kenya and Nyasaland, all once areas of white supremacy, proved to be irreversible. In 1966 the Government found itself obliged to abandon the position that key overseas bases would be maintained in all circumstances. The Defence White Paper of that year declared that in future bases would only be maintained in countries where their presence was welcome. As a corollary, it was announced that the Aden base would be evacuated by 1968, and it was in fact abandoned even sooner. In 1967 came the decision to evacuate British troops from Malaysia, Singapore and the Persian Gulf by 1971.

On the other hand ultra-colonialism is not dead. The lobby in the House of Commons, now led by Duncan Sandys, is in full cry, demanding recognition of the Smith régime in Southern Rhodesia and the retention of British control over the Persian Gulf. There is no guarantee that the views of the dinosaurs will not still from time to time get the upper hand, particularly if the Conservatives return to power.

[1] Quoted in Saul Rose. *Britain and South-East Asia.* London. 1962. p. 145.

CHAPTER FIVE

The Middle East

Collapse of the British Caliphate

In the period we are considering, the break-up of the Middle Eastern empire proceeded at a particularly fast pace, with a loss of British influence on a scale without parallel anywhere else in the third world. The catastrophic failure of the attack on Egypt in 1956 marked the opening of a new phase in British policy in the area, but, in contrast to other parts of Africa and Asia, British diplomacy proved to be singularly unsuccessful in adapting itself to changing circumstances in the Arab countries.

While Britain's relations with India or Ceylon, Kenya or Zambia, have been at least temporarily stabilised on a new basis, the same cannot be said of Egypt and Iraq or the Arab East as a whole. There being no breakwater in the shape of the Commonwealth or other strong economic and cultural ties to moderate the force of the tide, Britain's old privileged position has been washed away quickly and almost completely.

True, most of the holdings of the British oil companies have survived. In Kuwait British Petroleum has a 50% share in the on-shore concession and in 1961 Shell acquired 100% control of the off-shore rights. In Iran the combined holding of the two companies is 54%, and in Iraq 47·5%. British Petroleum has a 75% holding in the important offshore oil-field at Abu Dhabi (one of the Trucial sheikdoms in the Persian Gulf), which came into operation in 1962.

On the southern and eastern perimeter of the Arabian peninsula (Aden and the Aden Protectorates, Muscat and Oman, the Persian Gulf sheikdoms), there survived until the end of 1966 a Lilliput remnant of the old system of treaties, military bases, political and military advisers, through which London once controlled most of the Arab countries of the Middle East.

But with the abandonment of the Aden base in November 1967 and the decision to abandon the Persian Gulf bases by the end of

1971, the collapse of the caliphate inherited from Turkey at the end of the First World War entered its final phase.

Until the winter of 1956, despite a major contraction of British power during the first post-war decade,[1] the Middle East was still recognisably a British sphere of influence. Today London's ability to determine the course of events is very limited, a fact thrown into sharp relief by the gun flash which lit up this part of the world in June 1967 — the six-day Arab-Israeli war.

The British Government, which only a dozen years earlier would, for better or for worse, have been a leading actor, found itself in the wings. Its diplomacy was active enough, but in practice, so far as the great powers were concerned, the main decisions were taken in Washington, Moscow and Paris. At the height of the crisis, the U.S. President, the Soviet Prime Minister and the French President had personal meetings, but none of the three thought it necessary to invite the British Prime Minister to the high table.

Among the factors contributing to this transformation first place belongs to the exceptional power of the Arab independence movement (reinforced on its flanks by similar movements in Cyprus and, in the early fifties, Iran). The policy-makers have been faced here with an opponent comparable in strength and experience, not with the relatively unorganised anti-colonialism of Tropical Africa, but with the Indian independence movement at its peak.

This is not the place to attempt to analyse the social forces behind Arab nationalism. It is, however, common ground among most specialists that in nearly every Arab country the independence movement has behind it the mass of the town-dwellers and peasants and the great majority of the technical, administrative, military and cultural cadres from whom its leadership is drawn. Its only consistent opponent has been the class of feudal and semi-feudal landlords, headed by the royal and sheikly dynasties and their political entourages, who regarded the presence of foreign troops as an essential condition of their own continued rule.

In terms of the balance of internal social forces, the opponents of independence, except in the Arab peninsula, have had little more real weight than the Indian maharajas. This was shown fairly clearly in the Egyptian revolution of 1952 and the Iraqi revolution of 1958, when the monarchical régimes were easily overthrown and immediately sank without trace.

[1] Saudi Arabia passed from the British to the U.S. sphere of influence towards the end of the Second World War. Palestine was lost in 1948. Sovereignty over the Sudan and possession of the Suez military base were abandoned under Anglo-Egyptian agreements of 1953 and 1954.

Furthermore, despite perennial quarrels between the Arab states, solidarity and co-operation between them in the fight for independence has been at a higher level than that so far achieved in Africa south of the Sahara, Latin America or South-East Asia. The idea of Arab unity is often written off either as a mask for Egyptian ambitions or as mere words. In fact, consciousness of a common bond between the Arabic-speaking Moslem peoples of the Middle East has deep roots in nearly every part of the area and has played an important part in all the main political and military engagements between the independence movement and the Western powers.

Secondly, Britain's capacity to maintain her hold on the Middle East was for many years complicated to an unusual degree by the incursion of the United States into the area and by its attitude to the power in possession.

Before the Second World War the British share of Middle East oil production was about 70% and the American 15%. By the mid-fifties the position had been reversed, the corresponding figures being 30% and 60%.[1] This sweeping advance of the U.S. oil companies was accompanied by a parallel politico-military penetration. During and after the Second World War, the United States acquired military bases in Turkey, Saudi Arabia, and Libya and has ever since also regularly deployed its naval forces in the Eastern Mediterranean. After the collapse of the Anglo-French attack on Egypt, it became the leading Western power in the whole area, its political influence being particularly strong in Turkey, Iran, Saudi Arabia, the Lebanon and Israel.

In establishing and developing their influence in the Middle East, as we have already pointed out, U.S. leaders until the late fifties not only refused to make common cause with London against the independence movement, but posed as the latter's sympathetic friend in the struggle against colonialism. This tactical line was ruthlessly pursued during the Iranian oil crisis of 1951–54, in Egypt before, during and immediately after the Suez crisis of 1956, and throughout Britain's prolonged quarrel with Saudi Arabia over the Buraimi Oasis.

The joint Anglo-American landings in the Lebanon and Jordan in 1958 marked the end of this feature of Washington's tactics in the Middle East, a shift brought about chiefly by increasing awareness of the shakiness of its own positions in the area. By then, however, Britain's key positions in Egypt and Iraq had been lost.

---

[1] The reversal came about mainly through the immense new output in the first post-war decade of Saudi Arabia (100% U.S.) and Kuwait (50% U.S.) and the acquisition by U.S. companies in 1954 of a 40% share in the former British monopoly of Iranian production.

Thirdly, from the mid-fifties onwards British influence has been progressively weakened by the development of military, economic and political co-operation between the European socialist states, principally the Soviet Union, and the Arab countries on a scale not to be found anywhere else in the third world.

As already mentioned, the Czechoslovak-Egyptian arms agreement of 1955 signified the beginning of the end of the stranglehold of the Western powers, particularly Britain, on the supply of modern weapons to the Arab states. This was immediately understood in Whitehall, which reacted as if bitten by a particularly poisonous snake. The provision by the socialist countries of massive financial and technical assistance and the rapid development of trade between them and the Arab countries also greatly reduced the economic leverage which the Government and the oil companies were formerly able to exercise.

Besides helping with the building of the Aswan high dam, the Soviet Union has provided very large long-term credits at low interest for the industrial and agricultural development of Egypt, Iraq, Syria and the Yemen, provided Soviet experts on the spot, and made available training facilities for large numbers of Arab students and specialists in the Soviet Union. The same is true of Czechoslovakia and a number of other socialist countries.

In the political field diplomatic support given by the Soviet Union and the other socialist countries inside and outside the United Nations to the cause of Arab independence has played its part in the upshot of every clash between the latter and Britain and the other Western powers. We need only mention here the Suez crisis of 1956, the threatened intervention against Syria in 1957, the Anglo-American landings in the Lebanon and Jordan in 1958, British (and Saudi-Arabian) efforts to overthrow the Yemeni Republic since 1962 and the Arab-Israeli six-day war in 1967.

Fourthly, with the creation of the state of Israel in 1948, Arab-Israeli hostility, which had previously created difficulties for London mainly in Palestine itself, seriously hampered attainment of its aims in all parts of the Arab world.

Some experts on the Middle East seem to me to exaggerate the importance of this factor. Michael Ionides, for example, comes near to saying in his exceptionally interesting book that, if only the Eden Government had taken a firm stand against Israel in 1955–1956, Nuri es-Said, the Hashemites and the Baghdad Pact would have been saved from destruction two years later.[1] This contradicts his own

[1] Michael Ionides. *Divide and Lose*. London. 1960. pp. 133, 247.

well-founded contention that the root cause of the collapse of British influence and pro-British rulers and politicians was Arab opposition to foreign rule, or as he puts it, opposition to treaties under which "the Arab states were independent only so long as they did not want to act independently".[1] I agree on this point with one of his fellow specialists, who writes that "to argue that, had it not been for Palestine, a special Anglo-Arab relationship would have lasted . . . for several generations is to underrate the other ingredients of anti-imperialism".[2]

All the same, the fact that Whitehall, willingly or not, fathered Israel and adopted a highly ambiguous attitude towards Arab fears of, and grievances against, the new state cast its shadow over all attempts by British diplomacy to present Britain to the Arab states as their friend and protector.

Finally, one cannot leave out of account the subjective factor, the extent to which the policy-makers miscalculated the real balance of forces in the Middle East and were blinded by their own misconceptions. This can be briefly illustrated by the 1956 attack on Egypt which, apart from its other aspects, takes the palm for sheer folly in the deplorable history of British post-war policy in this area.

In the first place, the Government gravely underestimated the resistance to be expected from the Arab independence movement and the effect on Arab opinion of concerting the Anglo-French attack with that of the Israelis. The Arab states were confronted not only with undisguised aggression against one of their number by their two former masters, but by the occupation by Israel of an enormous slab of Egyptian territory. Although the details of Anglo-French-Israeli collusion are only now reaching the light of day,[3] the Arabs rightly assumed from the first that their opponents had combined and that there was a double stake at hazard—freedom from Western domination and the prevention of Israeli territorial expansion. The total effect was to bring about a defensive coalition of all sections of Arab society.

In his memoirs, Eden tells us of his hope that Nasser, whose removal he frankly declares to have been one of his main objectives, would be overthrown by "enemies at home".[4] In fact no quisling movement made itself felt in Cairo. He also writes that after the

---

[1] *Ibid.* p. 12.
[2] Elisabeth Monroe. *Britain's Moment in the Middle East.* 1914–1956. London. 1965. p. 123.
[3] See, for example, Terence Robertson. *op. cit.* pp. 157–163 and Anthony Nutting. *No End of a Lesson.* London. 1967.
[4] Eden. *op. cit.* pp. 559 and 577.

attack "not a mouse moved in the Arab lands".[1] He forgets, however, that Syria reacted by blowing up the Iraq Petroleum Company's pipeline crossing their territory, that Saudi Arabia forbade the pumping of oil to British tankers and to the Bahrein refinery, that both countries broke off diplomatic relations with Britain, that Jordan banned the use of British bases on its soil, and that the Iraqi Government had no choice but to join the other Moslem members of the Baghdad Pact in temporarily excluding Britain from their consultations and in publicly denouncing British aggression.

The Government, despite many previous lessons, also gravely underestimated Washington's determination to play its own hand and pursue its own objectives in the Middle East, whatever the consequences for its British ally. It was assumed, correctly, that the Soviet Union would support Egypt, and, incorrectly, that the United States, though unwillingly to be directly associated with military intervention, would stand aside. In fact the attack on Egypt evoked in the Security Council a temporary alliance against the aggressors between the Soviet Union and the United States. Moreover, after the attack, on top of the pressure exerted by the socialist states and the third world, the United States was in a position to use and did use Britain's financial difficulties and shortage of oil to force an unconditional withdrawal from Egyptian territory.

London's misreading of Washington's aims and intentions right up to the last minute may be illustrated by Eden's reactions to Eisenhower's personal telegrams to him just before the Anglo-French landings, details of which have been published.[2] In reply to an urgent appeal on October 30 for an immediate and frank Anglo-American exchange of views, Eden blandly evaded this proposal, saying with fatuous condescension that "when the dust settles there may well be a chance for our doing a really constructive piece of work together". When later the same day Eisenhower protested against the Anglo-French ultimatum to Egypt, Eden, in his own words, saw no reason "at this moment to suppose that the United States would oppose us at the United Nations on almost every point".[3]

It cannot be said that Britain's political leaders drew no conclusions from the series of defeats they suffered in the Middle East. In particular, the Suez débâcle convinced them that concerted action with the United States was no longer merely desirable, but essential; i.e., that no major

[1] *Ibid.* p. 543.
[2] Dwight D. Eisenhower. *The White House Years 1956–61.* London. 1966. pp. 75–78,
[3] Eden. *op. cit.* pp. 525–528.

British political or military operation could be successful, unless it had American blessing. The old objective of somehow perpetuating a British-controlled politico-military system covering the whole area was perforce abandoned, and replaced by more localised and less ambitious aims.

On the other hand, for the last ten years and more it has been difficult to discern anything which can be dignified by the name of a new Middle Eastern policy. What we have instead is a variety of expedients adopted in different parts of the area, which taken together fall short of any coherent attempt to come to terms with the new situation.

Broadly speaking, in the period under review, the main scene of active British dipomacy was the Arabian peninsula, where the old policy of attempting to maintain indirect rule in partnership with the Arab feudal class was continued. In Egypt and Iraq, formerly the chief centres of British power, no consistent tactical line was evolved to meet the new situation. Pro-Israel tendencies on the whole increased, though no definite policy towards the Israeli-Arab problem took shape. Towards the end of the period, the Central Treaty Organisation (CENTO) being almost defunct, there were signs of an attempt to knock together an "Islamic Pact", with Saudi Arabia and Iran as its main pillars, with the function, from London's point of view, of protecting British oil interests in the Persian Gulf.

In the last year or so a new factor has entered the picture, the long-term effect of which on Middle Eastern policy is at present difficult to assess, namely the redisposition of military forces now in progress resulting from the run-down of forces and bases in South-East Asia and the Persian Gulf.

Elements of the land, air and naval forces becoming available for re-allocation which, as we have already noted, are being assigned to NATO, are being used in particular to strengthen the British component in NATO's forces in the Mediterranean.

It was announced in July 1968 that a squadron of long-range maritime-reconnaissance aircraft was to be transferred from the United Kingdom to Malta, and in 1970 a guided-missile destroyer would be added to the frigate force in the Mediterranean and a commando ship temporarily stationed there.[1] It was subsequently made known that this squadron would form part of the new NATO command (Maritime Air Forces, Mediterranean) set up in November 1968 to keep watch on Soviet naval forces in the Mediterranean.[2] In

---

[1] *Supplementary Statement on Defence Policy 1968.* Command 3701. July 1968.
[2] *Survey of British and Commonwealth Affairs.* January 3, 1969.

the same month, the Government stated that the above-mentioned commando ship, or an aircraft carrier or an assault ship would be kept in the Mediterranean almost continuously from January 1969.[1]

So far as London's capacity to exert military pressure on the Middle East is concerned, the effect of this process is that, while with the abandonment of first Aden and then the Persian Gulf bases it is diminishing on the south-eastern flank, it is increasing on the north-western, Mediterranean flank, where it is exercised jointly with the United States through NATO machinery.

This development does not alter the fact that the caliphate has collapsed. But it suggests that the policy-makers intend to maintain a Mediterranean-Middle Eastern front of a new and different kind for some years to come.

The Arabian Peninsula

The shifting of the main focus of Middle Eastern policy to the Arabian peninsula was not of London's choosing, but came about as the result of the sharp decline in British influence and near paralysis of British diplomacy in the rest of the area. British politico-military positions in the peninsula, like a group of low-storied buildings which alone have survived an earthquake, owed their new prominence to the surrounding destruction.

The idea of concentrating henceforth mainly on preserving the perimeter empire in the Arabian peninsula appears to have arisen immediately after the Suez disaster. At any rate this conception, and its corollary—a special concern over Kuwait and future relations with Saudi Arabia—figured prominently at the Macmillan-Eisenhower discussion on Middle Eastern affairs in March 1957.

According to Eisenhower's account "Macmillan felt that Kuwait was really the key to the overall Middle East oil production problem . . . By itself it could produce oil enough for all Western Europe for years to come. The problem then would become that of retaining access to Kuwait and an adequate flow of oil therefrom. One of the requirements for success in this would be to achieve better relationships with the surrounding nations, most importantly Saudi Arabia."[2]

In practice British diplomacy has been concerned in the peninsula primarily with three closely inter-connected problems, that of the

[1] *Hansard. Written Answers.* November 14, 1968. Col. 147.
[2] Eisenhower. *op. cit.* p. 123.

Aden base, of the oil companies' interests in the Persian Gulf and of relations with Saudi Arabia, which are dealt with in that order below.

Aden, besides being one of the main bunkering ports of the world, served a triple military purpose. Army, navy and air force units and the high command stationed there[1] provided the military force, in support of the smaller advance base in Bahrein, to keep control of Kuwait, Abu Dhabi and the other sheikdoms of the Persian Gulf. This function was exercised for all the world to see in 1961 when, in the face of renewed territorial claims by Iraq, a substantial force was despatched to Kuwait. Secondly, Aden served as a base for military activities in East and Central Africa, particularly after sovereignty was lost over the major base in Kenya. Forces were sent from Aden to Tanganyika, Kenya, and Uganda at the time of the army revolts in 1964, and more recently to Zambia in connection with events in Rhodesia. Thirdly, Aden was an important staging post for British forces deployed in South-East Asia and Hong Kong.

Until well into the sixties, Government policy turned on the central idea that the base must at all costs be held indefinitely. This can be seen from, for example, the following statement by Duncan Sandys, the minister responsible at the beginning of the decade. British interests, he said, must be safeguarded: "Our military base at Aden is a vital stepping stone on the way to Singapore. It is also indispensable for the safety of the States within the Arab Peninsula whom we are pledged by treaty to defend." As for the movement in Aden for union with the Yemen, "One must regard this cry," he declared, "as no more than an emotional expression of Arab nationalism by people who know that there is no risk of Britain agreeing to it."[2]

But Aden, a fairly highly industrialised city and port, had by the late fifties become a centre of the Arab liberation movement and a hot-bed of opposition to British rule in any part of Southern Arabia. Moreover, a third of its population and the great majority of the labour force were immigrants from the Yemen, with strong ties with their homeland and no sense of an Aden identity. When, therefore, the Yemeni Imamate was overthrown and a nationalist-minded Yemeni Republic established in 1962, the pressure for liquidation of the colonial régime and evacuation of the base sharply increased.

As the then Governor of Aden put it, "so far the problems of Aden and the Protectorate had been mainly parochial ones. Sheltered

---

[1] At the beginning of 1966 the Commander-in-Chief, Middle East, had 17,500 land forces under his command mostly quartered in Aden, along with several operational air squadrons and a Royal Marine Commando.

[2] *Hansard.* November 13, 1962. Cols. 247–251.

from the rest of Arabia by the dense curtain of the Imam's Yemen, we had been spared the full blast of Pan-Arab nationalism. The Yemeni revolution brought its bugles to our doorstep".[1]

From then on, British sovereignty was maintained only by the continuous use of troops and the arrest and imprisonment of political and trade union leaders. According to official statistics, between 1963 and the middle of 1967 over 1,500 people, Arab and British, were killed or wounded in the colony.[2]

The political tactics employed were to set up a Federation in which the sultans and emirs of the Protectorates would provide an Arab façade for the suppression of the independence movement in Aden itself and the preservation of the base there. To quote the Governor of Aden once more, the aim was "a merger of the Colony and the Federation into a single unit, having a special relationship with Britain which would ensure us the retention of our strategic facilities for as long as we needed them".[3]

The first step in this direction was taken in 1959, when London set up the Federation of Arab Amirates of the South and concluded with it a Treaty of Friendship and Protection under which the British Government retained responsibility for foreign relations and defence. The second step came in 1963 when Aden colony, against the known wishes of the great majority of its inhabitants, was merged with the Federation, re-christened the Federation of South Arabia. As an extra precaution, London retained special powers in Aden even after the merger.

Before long, however, it was realised in London that these tactics were not going to work and, in particular, that the cost in money, men and political prestige of trying to hold the base against determined resistance in Aden, supported from the Yemen, Egypt and other parts of the Arab world, was too great.

There followed an effort to save the sheik-dominated Federal Government as a future partner and owner of the base, while giving up British occupation and control of the latter. It was announced in the 1966 Defence White Paper that British forces would be withdrawn by the time the South Arabian Federation attained independence in 1968, as was then planned. In June 1967, when the Federal Government's hold was visibly crumbling, London announced that, after withdrawal, strong naval and air forces would be stationed nearby to give it support.[4]

[1] Johnston. *op. cit.* p. 125.
[2] *Survey of British and Commonwealth Affairs.* April 28, 1967. July 7, 1967.
[3] Johnston. *op. cit.* p. 36.
[4] *Hansard.* June 19, 1967. Cols. 1127–1136.

But this volte-face came too late to achieve its object. In the course of 1967 more and more of the locally-recruited, British-trained armed forces upon which rested the power of the Federal Government transferred their allegiance to the National Liberation Front. The Federal Government itself, minister by minister, vanished into thin air. What had been meant by London to be an orderly tactical retreat then turned into a rush to get out as quickly as possible. The day of independence was advanced to November 30, 1967, by which date the last British soldier had been hastily embarked.

The end result of all these manœuvres was the establishment of the People's Republic of South Yemen, headed by the leaders of the Arab resistance movement, which aligned itself with Egypt and the Yemen and which so far has shown no inclination to maintain more than correct relations with Britain.

In the Persian Gulf the basic situation has been the same as in Aden and southern Arabia and the same tactics have been employed to deal with it. Whether they will lead to the same result—near extinction of British political influence—remains to be seen.

The decision in the winter of 1967–1968 to withdraw from the Gulf bases by the end of 1971 was taken and announced before internal opposition to British domination had reached boiling-point and left a four-year breathing space in the course of which some new and more realistic policy may evolve.

The movement against domestic feudal rulers and their foreign backers has roots in the region as in every other part of the Arab world, its main centres so far being Bahrein and Kuwait. In the former, there was serious unrest in 1956 both before and after the attack on Suez, leading to clashes between British troops and the local population and the exile to St Helena of several Arab nationalist leaders in British custody. These events also led to the enforced retirement of Sir Charles Belgrave, the Ruler's chief British Adviser. In Kuwait there were also demonstrations during the Suez crisis and attempts to damage British oil installations. But the movement has not so far gained the momentum which it achieved on the other side of the peninsula.

Tactics hinged, and at the moment still hinge, on alliances with the sheiks and emirs who, in return for military and political support against their internal and external opponents, have provided London with what it wants, in this case security of tenure for British Petroleum and Shell.

The alliance has been underpinned by permanent army, navy and air force garrisons and bases at Bahrein and more recently also at

Sharjah, and by locally recruited forces commanded by British officers.

As late as 1966 the policy was to retain the bases indefinitely and strengthen the garrisons. The Defence White Paper of that year announced that, in connection with the proposed abandonment of the Aden base, forces stationed in the Persian Gulf would be increased. In May of that year, the Government concluded an agreement with the Sheik of Bahrein, increasing annual subsidies to him "in consideration of the continued and increased use by British forces" of the existing naval and air bases on the island.[1]

Until recently, the only major political manœuvre affected Kuwait. In 1961, in order the better to fend off Iraqi claims to the territory, Britain's formal relationship with the Ruler was put on a new footing. The Anglo-Kuwait Treaty of 1899 was abrogated and replaced by another, which omitted explicit limitations on Kuwait's sovereignty. Britain's role as protector of the Ruler's power in practice remained unchanged, but Kuwait was thereby enabled to become a member of the Arab League (1961) and of the United Nations (1963).

A considerable effort was made to persuade the rulers of the oil-producing sheikdoms — Kuwait, Bahrein, Qatar and Abu Dhabi — to stabilise their régimes by using part of their vast oil incomes on social services and amenities and to contribute funds for the same purpose to their poorer neighbours. In 1965 a Trucial States Development Fund was established to which London pledged capital aid of £1,000,000 and the Ruler of Abu Dhabi £500,000. The latter was, nevertheless, on British insistence deposed in 1966 because he refused, in the words of the official account, "to use the country's increased wealth in the interests of the people of the Sheikdom".[2]

One of the effects of the decision to evacuate the bases was to make more likely increasing competition for influence in, and in some cases acquisition of, the Gulf sheikdoms between Saudi Arabia, Iran and Iraq. In this situation British diplomacy has placed its hopes on reaching an understanding with the first two, Saudi Arabia and Iran. But it has also taken steps to consolidate its own influence in the area, embarking, as we have mentioned elsewhere, on the latest in a long and rather inglorious line of British-sponsored federations in various parts of the world.

The agreement setting up the new Federation of Arab Amirates was signed on February 27, 1968. The Federation includes among its nine members three oil-producing states, Abu Dhabi, Qatar and

[1] *Commonwealth Survey.* July 8, 1966.
[2] *Ibid.* August 19, 1966.

Bahrein, to the last of which, incidentally, Iran has a long-standing claim.

The Minister of Defence, in greeting this event, said it was an important and constructive step towards ensuring the future peace and stability of the area after British forces were withdrawn, that the Government would give the Federation all possible help and was discussing with its members Britain's future treaty relations with them. Although he did not say so, the idea evidently is that, as in the case of Kuwait, the Federation should in due course become a sovereign state, a member of the Arab League and of the United Nations, but still in practice remain within the British orbit.

As regards Saudi Arabia, the task of restoring the old alliance or at least close co-operation was not an easy one. The deterioration in the relations between the two countries dated from the replacement of Britain by the United States as the dominating foreign power towards the end of the Second World War. The acute discord which subsequently developed arose from a clash of interests not only between London and the Saudi régime, but also, as we have already seen, between London and Washington.

The Anglo/Saudi Arabian quarrel revolved chiefly around the Buraimi oasis, which lies at the junction of Saudi Arabia, the Sheikdom of Abu Dhabi and the Sultanate of Muscat and Oman (both British semi-colonies) and had considerable potential significance in the struggle for the control of oil deposits in all three territories.

In 1952, despite British protests, Saudi Arabia occupied the oasis. In 1955 a military force, officered, equipped and paid for by Britain, seized it back in the name of the rulers of Abu Dhabi and Muscat and Oman, and successfully resisted determined Saudi attempts to dislodge it in 1957 and 1959.[1] The quarrel was thus already in full swing when Saudi Arabia broke off diplomatic relations with Britain at the time of the attack on Egypt and explains why they were not re-established until 1963, long after Egypt herself had renewed relations with London.

The turning point in Anglo/Saudi Arabian relations came in 1962, when the two governments were brought together by a common interest in suppressing the Yemeni revolution. Both from the first intervened in favour of the Imam, the Saudis from their own territory to the north and east and the British from the South Arabian Federation to the south. In April 1964 Britain was reprimanded by

[1] For details of this struggle see John Marlowe. *The Persian Gulf in the Twentieth Century.* London. 1962. pp. 177–178, 193–196.

the Security Council for an attack by RAF aircraft on Harib on the Yemeni side of the border.

Diplomatic relations between Britain and Saudi Arabia were renewed in January 1963, when it was stated that "the two Governments had agreed that discussion of the Buraimi issue and other problems connected with it should proceed without delay under the personal supervision of the Secretary-General of the United Nations".[1] A British trade mission visited Saudi Arabia in December 1963 and a Saudi Arabian trade mission went to Britain in May 1964. In 1965 the Wilson Government, as a result of U.S. intervention, was enabled sharply to increase its influence in Saudi Arabia in the military field.

This latter development had a complicated background connected with separate bilateral arrangements between London and Washington designed to compensate the British Treasury for heavy dollar expenditure on the proposed purchase of American F-111 military aircraft. Briefly, since 1962 British interests had been trying to secure the contract for a new air defence system (aircraft, radar communications and surface-to-air missiles) required by the Saudi Arabian Government. By October 1965 the latter was on the point of accepting a rival American tender, but the U.S. Government then decided to divert a major part of the contract to Britain as part of the above-mentioned arrangements. A joint Anglo-American tender was accepted by the Saudi Government in December 1965, the British share amounting to over £100,000,000.

The Government, with U.S. assistance, thus had some success in mending its fences with the royal house of Saud, upon an alliance with whom its long-term plans for protecting British oil interests in the Persian Gulf are now partly dependent.

Egypt, Iraq, Jordan, Israel

Two main and closely interwoven problems confronted British diplomacy in this area after the Suez débâcle. First, once the direct armed attack on the main citadel of the Arab independence movement had failed, some *modus vivendi* with the Arab states had to be worked out. Secondly, following the disastrous experiment of military collusion with Israel against Egypt, some coherent policy towards the unresolved Arab-Israeli conflict was required. Though a variety of expedients were resorted to, no effective solution to either problem has been found.

[1] *Commonwealth Survey.* January 29, 1963.

As regards Egypt, the Government decided early in 1957 to cut its losses and, making the best of a bad job, sought the establishment of normal relations. This made possible the settlement in due course of claims and counter-claims arising from the attack on Egypt and the conclusion of certain other bi-lateral agreements.

After protracted negotiations, an Anglo-Egyptian Financial Agreement was signed in February 1958.[1] Its main feature was London's acquiescence in the acquisition by Egypt of its immense military property in the Suez base as compensation for the damage caused in the military operations of 1956. Egypt, for her part, agreed to pay £27,500,000 in compensation for British property that had been nationalised or compulsorily acquired and to return certain other property to its owners. Diplomatic relations were restored in December of the same year. In August 1962 negotiations were successfully concluded on outstanding financial questions arising under the 1959 Agreement. At the same time Britain made a loan to Egypt of £3½ million on commercial terms. An Anglo-Egyptian Cultural Convention was signed in Cairo in September 1965.

But there was no political rapprochement with Egypt. The policy of the Government may have been correct enough over most strictly Anglo-Egyptian questions, but its attempts to hold on to the remnants of empire in the Arabian peninsula, not to mention other aspects of its policy in the Middle East and in Africa and Asia generally, cut directly across such half-hearted efforts as London made to put relations on a closer footing.

This became particularly apparent after the Yemeni revolution of 1962. The two governments immediately became heavily engaged on opposite sides in the civil war in the Yemen and in the connected struggle further south to end British rule in Aden and the Aden Protectorates.

The policy-makers, with an all-too-familiar over-estimation of Britain's weight in Middle Eastern affairs, seem to have believed that it was possible to secure a closer relationship with Cairo on terms dictated by themselves. Thus the Labour Government as soon as it came to power in October 1964 started what it called "a dialogue" with the Egyptian Ambassador in London aimed at improving Anglo-Egyptian relations. But only a few months later the Prime Minister publicly declared that "there is one condition on which we have insisted and must continue to insist, and that is that any really significant improvement is ruled out as long as the UAR itself, or

[1] Command 723.

UAR-inspired individuals or organisations, continue to endanger stability, indeed to endanger life itself, in South Arabia".[1]

When in September 1965 George Thomson, Minister of State at the Foreign Office, visited Cairo for the express purpose of talking over Anglo-Egyptian relations personally with Nasser, he and his advisers blandly ignored the fact that British actions in other parts of the Arab world might affect the success or failure of his mission. At the very moment of his visit London suspended the colonial constitution in Aden and carried out mass arrests of the leaders of the independence movement. Nasser thereupon cancelled the proposed talks.

At the end of 1965 Anglo-Egyptian diplomatic relations, already hanging by a thread, were broken off by Egypt, the occasion being a decision by the Organisation for African Unity that its members should take this step in protest against the British Government's failure to dislodge the Smith régime in Rhodesia.

The diplomatic support given by London to Israel during the Arab-Israeli war in 1967, coupled with its continued efforts to keep its own men in power in South Arabia after independence brought Anglo-Egyptian relations back to a state of embitterment which had not been seen since the aftermath of the Suez aggression ten years before. They are still strained today.

As regards Iraq, the tactics adopted by the Macmillan Government towards the revolution of 1958 were strongly influenced by the disastrous experience of the attack on Egypt eighteen months before.

As part of a joint Anglo-American operation, British troops were flown into Jordan to prevent the spread of the revolution beyond Iraq's frontiers, but no counter-measures were taken against Iraq itself.

Anxious to save whatever could be saved, London recognised the new régime within two weeks of its formation. This action was, indeed, taken with such speed that Macmillan and his colleagues were accused in some quarters of failing to show even the minimum of respect for their dead friends and allies, Nuri and the Iraqi royal family.[2]

In accordance with the wishes of the new régime, which had withdrawn from the Baghdad Pact and abrogated the Anglo-Iraqi Defence Agreement of 1955, all British forces were evacuated from their main base at Habbaniya by May 1959.

[1] *Hansard.* April 1, 1965. Col. 1976.
[2] See Eden. *op. cit.* p. 423. Elisabeth Monroe. *op. cit.* p. 212, John Marlowe. *Arab Nationalism and British Imperialism.* London. 1961. p. 186.

The supply of British arms to Iraq was continued, both under old contracts concluded by the former Hashemite government and under new contracts placed by its successor. An Anglo-Iraqi Cultural Agreement was concluded in December 1959.

However, as in the case of Egypt, once the Arab nationalists had come to power, the settlement of bilateral questions proved to be too narrow a base upon which to construct a stable relationship. Successive régimes in Baghdad, like the Nasser Government in Cairo, judged British policy not only by its attitude towards themselves, but by its general line in the Arab world as a whole, particularly in the Arab peninsula and over the question of Israel. By the same token, the only moment when British diplomacy in Iraq seemed likely to produce results was the brief spell when the nationalists were temporarily driven from power in 1963–64.

Relations between London and Baghdad remained tense throughout the four and a half years of the Qasim régime, conflict centring upon the oil question both in Iraq itself and Kuwait, which borders Iraq at the head of the Persian Gulf.

British control of the Iraqi Petroleum Company survived, but its freedom of action was much restricted. After protracted but unsuccessful negotiations regarding revision of the company's concession, the new régime, by a law passed in December 1961, reduced the area of IPC's operations to less than 1% of its original concession.

Less than a week after the signing of the new Anglo-Kuwait agreement of June 1961, the Iraqi Government claimed sovereignty over Kuwait and mustered troops on the border. This was met by a massive and immediate concentration of British troops in Kuwait, drawn from Aden, Bahrein, Kenya and further afield, with orders to defend its frontiers. The British position was eased by the fact that Iraq's claim was not supported by the other Arab states. Hostilities between Britain and Iraq did not break out, though there were minor clashes including the capture of a British reconnaissance party on Iraqi territory.

Not without some reason, hopes rose high in London when, in February 1963, the Qasim Government was overthrown, power passing temporarily into the hands of the right wing of the Ba'ath Party which immediately launched a campaign of mass terror against the left, particularly the Communists. From the first, the new régime showed signs of wishing to establish a close relationship with London, to which the latter responded with alacrity.

A senior member of the Government (Frederick Erroll, President of the Board of Trade) paid a goodwill visit to Baghdad only a month after the *coup d'état*, a visit which was returned by the Iraqi Minister of Trade the following July. In June 1963 a settlement was reached over the question of Kuwait. Iraq recognised the sheikdom as an independent state. Kuwait, for its part, made a loan to Iraq of £30 million repayable over twenty years. At about the same time, an Iraqi Ambassador was appointed to London, a post which, owing to the uncertain state of Anglo-Iraqi relations, had been left vacant during the five years since the revolution.

This short honeymoon was brought to an end when the right-wing Ba'athists were overthrown in 1964. Under their successors, Anglo-Iraqi relations once more became as uneasy as they had been in Qasim's day. Diplomatic and trade relations were broken off by Baghdad in 1967 in protest against London's policy during the six-day Arab-Israeli war. In the same year, IPC, in its dispute with Syria over royalties payable on its pipeline carrying Iraqi oil through Syria to the Mediterranean, found itself faced with a common front between Baghdad and Damascus and had to give way.

Jordan is the one Arab country in this part of the world where London has retained some perceptible influence in the years since the attack on Suez. It cannot be said, however, either that this has been due to any particular virtuosity on the part of British diplomacy, or that the present situation is likely to last much longer.

The survival of the Hashemite régime, and with it British (and American) influence, in the face of intense nationalist feeling among the ex-Palestinian part of the population is something of a freak, arising mainly from a peculiar side-effect of the Arab-Israeli confrontation.

At any time during the decade following the Suez events, a nationalist revolution in Jordan would almost certainly have been met by an Israeli seizure, with Anglo-American support, of the left bank of the Jordan. Thus the nationalist leaders had to reckon with the fact that the overthrow of the pro-Western Hussein would bring about not the establishment of an independent Jordan under nationalist leadership, but the situation which, as a result of the Six-day war, we have today, namely the expansion of Israel up to the Jordan river and the contraction of Jordan to its old Transjordanian boundaries.

It follows that, until the Six-day war, the Hashemite régime was being held in position by outside pressures not only from Britain and the United States, but Israel as well.

Furthermore, Hussein understood his own interests and those of his patrons better than the latter did themselves. When in 1956 he suddenly deprived General Glubb and other British officers of their commands in Jordan's armed forces, there was considerable resentment in high quarters in London. Eden, who was Prime Minister at the time, told Hussein that his action was "a severe blow to confidence on which good relations are based" and demanded that he make a public statement of loyalty to friendship with Britain and to the Anglo-Jordan Treaty.[1]

In fact Hussein's own contention at the time that his action would prove in the long run to be to London's advantage as well as his own was entirely correct. Hussein and his entourage got rid of Glubb in a hurry not because they had suddenly become converted to the ideals of the Arab independence movement, nor, as Eden suggests, out of personal pique, but because this was at the time the only way of keeping the independence movement at bay. By sacrificing Glubb and his fellow-commanders, the régime was able to promote, and thus ensure the loyalty of, the Jordanian officer corps, and by this means prolong its own existence.

The occupation by Israel of the left bank of the Jordan in the course of the Arab-Israeli war of 1967 altered the peculiar parallelogram of forces on which Hussein's régime rested. The immediate effect was to drive it into closer alliance with the other Arab states and even into seeking support from the Soviet Union which Hussein visited later that year. The régime has by this means so far secured its own survival. At the same time its old ties with Britain have, of course, grown weaker still.

One of the corollaries of the final loss of British hegemony in Egypt and Iraq after the Suez catastrophe was an increase in the importance attached in London to maintaining good relations with Israel, though there were marked fluctuations dictated by the requirements of the moment.

In 1955, when British diplomacy was actively trying to tie the Arab states to Britain through the mechanism of the Baghdad Pact, Eden, then Prime Minister, went out of his way to redefine policy towards the question of Israel's frontiers in terms likely to appeal to Arab opinion. In his Guildhall speech in November of that year he declared in cautious, but unambiguous, terms that negotiations should take place to secure a revision of those frontiers in favour of the neighbouring Arab states.[2]

The purely tactical nature of this declaration was exposed at the time of the Suez crisis only a year later, when the same Eden, as part of his attempt to overthrow Nasser and his régime, openly and,

[1] Eden. *op. cit.* p. 349.   [2] *Documents* . . . 1955. pp. 382–385.

as it turned out, unsuccessfully, supported a massive expansion of Israel's territory at Egypt's expense.

In early 1958 the Macmillan Government was once more seeking to curry favour with Arab opinion by suggesting a contraction of Israel's territory. In a statement in February, Foreign Secretary Selwyn Lloyd specifically reaffirmed the line taken by Eden in his Guildhall speech three years before and declared that "a guarantee of the existing frontiers would be bitterly resented and resisted by all the Arab neighbours of Israel".[1]

The line was again reversed at the time of the Iraqi revolution. In August 1958, immediately after it had taken place, the Israeli Foreign Minister was invited to London to discuss the situation. Two months later an agreement was concluded between the two Governments for the sale of two submarines, the first to be acquired by Israel. In the years since then, as Britain and the chief Arab states in the area have drifted further and further apart, British diplomacy has, on the whole, remained on an openly pro-Israeli tack.

Shortly after coming to power, Harold Wilson declared that, while he would like to see an improvement in relations with Egypt, "we are not going to change the general basis of our policy in the Middle East, for example, by sacrificing our ties with Israel".[2] During a visit to Israel in October 1965, the Minister of State at the Foreign Office told his hosts that "no development of Anglo-Arab relations was to be expected at the expense of relations with Israel".[3]

This general tactic was applied in practice during the Arab-Israeli war of 1967. Keeping carefully in the wake of American diplomacy, the Wilson Government gave political support to Israel before, during, and immediately after the fighting.

This course of action no doubt did something to cement the Anglo-American special relationship in Middle Eastern affairs and in world politics generally. Whether it raised British diplomatic stock in Israel is more doubtful, since, when the first stage of the crisis was over, the Government, in the interests once more of fence-mending in the Arab world, again resorted to its familiar balancing act between Israeli and Arab. Britain was the principal author and sponsor of the Security Council resolution, adopted unanimously on November 22, 1967, contemplating, among other things, the "withdrawal of Israeli armed forces from territories occupied in the recent conflict".

[1] *Hansard.* February 20, 1958. Col. 1428.
[2] *Hansard.* April 1, 1965. Col. 1976.
[3] *Commonwealth Survey.* November 9, 1965.

As to the damage done to London's influence in the Middle East generally by its support of Israel during the fighting, it is unlikely that it can be repaired short of a general shift of tactics towards recognition of the legitimacy of the Arab independence movement as a whole, such as that successfully executed by France following the end of the Algerian war. French experience suggests that a change of this sort is not incompatible with continued support for the legitimate rights of Israel.

Pact-Making, Past and Present

NATO, CENTO and SEATO are usually regarded, especially on the left, as being parts of one system of military alliances dominated by the United States and directed against the Communist powers—the Soviet Union in the case of the first two and China in the case of SEATO.

This view is certainly correct as far as it goes. All three pacts came into existence for declared anti-Communist purposes and are today still publicly justified as a necessary shield against Communist aggression. The decisive voice in all three has belonged and still belongs to Washington.

As regards CENTO, the one which concerns us here, the British Foreign Secretary could be heard declaiming at the 1966 Council meeting that the organisation was still concerned with the threat of Communist aggression and pressure, still made a valuable contribution towards the stability of a vital area of the free world and that the British Government pledged continuation of their full support.

But for British diplomacy, CENTO and its predecessor, the Baghdad Pact, from the very beginning had another and equally important purpose, namely to provide a new and more viable form of political cover for British military occupation of the Arab states, an occupation directed not against Arab Communism, the influence of which was weak, but against Arab nationalism, the influence of which was very great.

The need for such a change arose precisely from the strength of Arab nationalist feeling, which made the old system of bilateral military treaties with the Egyptian, Iraqi and Jordanian monarchies politically anachronistic. It was thought that, while Arab opinion would no longer put up with one-sided treaties, which simply legalised the presence of British garrisons in the Canal Zone, at Habbaniya, Shaiba and in Jordan, it might accept these same garrisons if they were presented as Britain's contribution to a Middle Eastern Defence Organisation directed against the Soviet Union, in which Britain and the Arab states were equal partners.

It was also thought that such an organisation would be more firmly based, if not only the Arab states, but also Turkey, Iran and Pakistan were members of it. In the first place, the governments of these three countries were, and to a now smaller degree still are, more responsive than the Arab governments to appeals for unity with the capitalist West against the socialist East. Secondly, it was hoped that the participation of these fellow-Moslem countries would to the Arab eye make Western inspiration and control of the organisation more acceptable and thus tilt the balance in the Arab capitals in favour of joining.

Finally, from London's point of view the establishment of a multilateral pact offered the prospect of tying the United States into a politico-military mechanism run by Britain, thereby harnessing American power to British aims and damping down, if not reconciling, the running conflict between American and British Middle Eastern policies.

London's plans were not in the end realised, but the considerations underlying them have retained their significance even today. A brief look at what has so far happened to British pact-making in this part of the world may, therefore, help to elucidate what its future, if any, is likely to be.

The first attempt to create an overall Middle Eastern military organisation misfired. When in 1951 Britain, the United States, France and Turkey proposed a plan for a "Middle East Command" based on Egypt, the Arab governments rejected it outright and no more was heard of it.

But when in 1955 Turkey and Iraq signed a bilateral defence agreement, the opportunity for pulling off the great project seemed to have arrived. Britain quickly adhered to what became known as the Baghdad Pact and, using it as an umbrella, concluded an agreement with Iraq, prolonging British tenure of the Habbaniya and Shaiba bases. By the end of the year Iran (and Pakistan) had also joined. Expectations were high that the Pact would, in Eden's words, "grow into a NATO for the Middle East".[1]

Turkey, Iraq and Iran faithfully played their parts, but the other, and more important, members of the cast refused to obey the directions of the impresario.

During the first phase of the Pact's existence from 1955 till 1958,

[1] Eden. *op. cit.* p. 220.

7

the United States, having encouraged its formation, and from 1957 onwards taking part in its activities, nevertheless declined to become a full member, since to have done so would have meant underwriting British ambitions in the Arab world and thereby crossing the wires of the State Department's own Arab policy. Moreover, since the United States already had a firm foothold in Turkey and Iran, and since it had already concluded a bilateral military agreement with Pakistan, it had no particular need for the Pact as a means of keeping its grip on the non-Arab members.

With the exception of Iraq, the Arab states, seeing clearly enough that the Pact was in essence simply another elaborate device for perpetuating the presence of British forces on their territory, obstinately refused to join. Even when, in March 1956, the stage seemed set for Jordan's adhesion, Hussein and his government had at the last moment to back away in the face of mass demonstrations of protest. Following the revolution of July 1958, Iraq, the headquarters and linch-pin of the Pact, fell away and the organisation was left with no Arab members at all.

From then on the Pact, renamed the Central Treaty Organisation (CENTO) with headquarters in Ankara instead of Baghdad, became, formally speaking, a military alliance between Britain, Turkey, Iran and Pakistan. At this point, however, Washington, through bilateral agreements concluded simultaneously with the three Asian partners in March 1959, became a member in all but name and the dominating power in the organisation.

In the new circumstances, the British role in CENTO and practical contribution to its activities were sharply reduced. When in 1961–1962 the establishment of a CENTO military command was under consideration, the proposal of the Macmillan Government that it should be headed by a British general was rejected by Iran and Pakistan, who insisted that the post must be filled by an American. Since 1955, British economic assistance in the CENTO framework to the other three members has totalled only some £6,500,000 and in 1968 was running at about £1,000,000 a year, including the cost of exports, equipment and training programmes.[1]

Today, the Government still declares fealty to CENTO. At the 1968 Council meeting in London, the Foreign Secretary, rejecting the idea that the organisation had no further function, urged that alliances between countries of the non-Communist world should be maintained as firmly as ever. One of his Ministerial assistants on the same occasion announced categorically that the proposed with-

[1] *Survey of British and Commonwealth Affairs.* May 10, 1968.

drawal of forces from the area East of Suez by 1971 did not affect the Government's policy towards CENTO.[1]

It seems likely, however, that CENTO now occupies a relatively humble position in British policy in the Middle East, as indicated, for example, by the independent but almost identical assessments of Kenneth Younger and Christopher Mayhew, both right-wing Labour former ministers directly concerned with these problems.

Younger remarks that it has been difficult to take CENTO seriously ever since it lost all Arab support. He discounts claims that the organisation has important achievements to its credit as regards economic co-operation and countering Communist subversion, points out that it has no unified military command and duplicates Britain's relationship with Turkey in NATO and with Pakistan in the Commonwealth and declares that "its role appears to be at best marginal for all purposes".[2]

Mayhew also stresses that CENTO has no command structure and no forces assigned to it and notes the anomaly that its main source of armaments and its most powerful supporter is the United States, which formally speaking is not a member. He complains that all the members except Britain try hard to involve the organisation in their own particular aims, citing Pakistani attempts to use CENTO against India over Kashmir and Turkish attempts to use it against Greece over Cyprus. He winds up by saying that CENTO provides a useful target for Communist political warfare and subversion, but provides no effective weapons for fighting them.[3]

On the other hand, I do not think that British pact-making in the Middle East, despite its dismal history, can be regarded as entirely a thing of the past.

As pointed out early in this chapter, there are now fairly clear signs that the policy-makers intend to strengthen British forces on the Mediterranean flank of the Arab world, expanding for this purpose the military mechanism of an already existing pact, namely NATO.

This manner of proceeding satisfies, in its own way, one of the constant long-term desiderata of British policy in the Middle East, since it presupposes a high degree of harmonisation of American and British policy. It also partially satisfies another, since it facilitates co-operation with Turkey, which is a member of NATO as well as CENTO.

[1] *Ibid.*
[2] Younger. *op. cit.* p. 58.
[3] Mayhew. *op. cit.* pp. 30–31.

On the south-western flank of the Arab world, in 1966–1967, there appeared to be developing under British prompting a new grouping, this time based on Saudi Arabia and Iran, with the familiar purpose of providing new political cover for the continued presence of British garrisons on Arab soil, namely those in the Arab sheikdoms of the Persian Gulf.

Besides much talk in the press of a new Islamic Pact, London at this period, with American help, became a major supplier of arms to both these countries. On top of the very large Anglo-Saudi arms deal mentioned above, in the summer of 1966 a contract was concluded with the Iranian Government to the value of £35,000,000 covering the supply of land-to-air missiles and naval vessels.[1] At the same time the garrisons at Bahrein and Sharjah were being increased as a defence force for what is now the above-mentioned Federation of Arab Amirates, which in turn seemed a likely candidate for membership of a local Islamic Pact.

The decision to evacuate these bases by the end of 1971 has very much altered this perspective. If there are no garrisons, the main reason, from London's point of view, for umbrella pact-building disappears, as does the means of controlling the activities of any new military organisation that may come into existence.

It seems probable, therefore, that if a new pact, based on Saudi Arabia and Iran is set up, it will not be British-run. But until the troops have actually left, one cannot be sure that those responsible will not have a last fling at wedging their conglomeration of emirs into an alliance, however unstable, with the Saudi and Iranian monarchies.

[1] *The Times*. August 26, 1966.

CHAPTER SIX

Africa South of the Sahara

The Last British Sphere of Influence?

Some fifteen years ago there were three recognisable British spheres of influence in the third world – the Middle East, a corner of South-East Asia and Southern Africa. The first, as we have seen, has disintegrated since the attack on Suez in 1956, the second, as suggested below, is unlikely to hold much longer, but the third is still fairly firmly based.

To a remarkable degree, economic, cultural and even military links formed in the years when British rule extended from Capetown to Lusaka and from Nairobi to Accra, survived the break-up of the colonial system and today constitute a grid through which London is still able to play a major part in determining the course of events.

With the exception of the South African Republic and Rhodesia, all the other states south of the Sahara which once formed part of the empire, twelve in number,[1] are independent members of the Commonwealth, of the imperial preference system and of the sterling area.

Political relations with London have varied a good deal from country to country and from time to time, but the governments of all twelve, besides taking part in numerous forms of intra-Commonwealth co-operation, still turn in the first place to Britain for financial and technical aid, and draw from Britain the great majority of their foreign cadres – teachers, civil servants, financial, agricultural and other specialists, and military and police missions.

British industrial, financial and trading capital still plays a major, and in some cases dominating, role in all the countries of the area, without exception.

British investment in the South African Republic has grown

---

[1] Nigeria, Ghana, Sierra Leone, Gambia, Zambia, Malawi, Kenya, Uganda, Tanzania, Botswana, Lesotho, Swaziland.

throughout almost the whole post-war period and by the mid-sixties amounted to over £900,000,000.[1] The bulk of this vast sum is invested in key sectors—gold, diamond, uranium and coal mining, manufacturing, oil refining and distribution, banking, shipping and insurance—and, despite the rapid advance of native Afrikaner capital, is a major factor in the South African economy. The British share of foreign investment is, moreover, still several times larger than that of any other country. In 1962, it was about 60% as compared with a U.S. share of 11%, the next largest.

A substantial part of the South African gold-mining industry, by far the biggest in the capitalist world, is controlled by British capital, over 30% of South African production being accounted for by the Anglo-American Corporation alone. By arrangement with the South African authorities, the bulk of all South African gold—about 80% —was still being sold in London at the end of 1966 and providing the main source of the gold reserve.

In Ghana the total British investment was in 1962–1963 put at £230,000,000 and in Nigeria at £150,000,000 (industry and agriculture only).[2] Owing to heavy further investment in the oil industry, this second figure is now considerably higher. In 1965 the joint investment in Nigeria of Shell and British Petroleum alone was about £150,000,000.

Unilever, which in 1960 had over £100,000,000 invested in Africa, mainly on the West coast, through its subsidiary, the United Africa Company, operates a colossal network of plantations, purchasing agencies, warehouses, shops, shipping lines, saw-mills, textile mills, soap factories, breweries and auto assembly plants in these two countries. Barclays Bank D.C.O. alone has more than fifty branches in Ghana.

The third main stronghold is the copper-belt, centring in Zambia and lapping over into the Katanga province of the Congo and Rhodesia. The main interests here are the Oppenheimer group and Tanganyika Concessions, which has an investment of £29,000,000 in Union Minière du Haut Katanga.[3]

The dominating position still occupied by Britain in the foreign trade of the whole area can be seen from Table 9.

British influence in this part of the world has been, and will

---

[1] Official statistics suggest that in 1965 the total of direct British investments in the Republic was greater than in any other single foreign country except Australia, Canada and the United States and about the same as the total in the whole of the European Economic Community. *Board of Trade Journal.* January 26, 1968.

[2] *The New Commonwealth.* December 1962. October 1963.

[3] *The Times.* June 10, 1968.

Table 9
British Share of Foreign Trade (%)
(figures for 1965)

	Imports	Exports
South African Republic	28	33*
Rhodesia	30	26
Zambia	20	38
Malawi	23	45
Nigeria	31	38
Ghana	26	21
Sierra Leone	33	67
Kenya†	28	21
Uganda†	38	17
Tanzania†	33	31

* Excluding gold.
† Excluding trade with the East African Common Market.

continue to be, eroded by the same factors as elsewhere in Africa and Asia, but they have so far acted with much less force.

In the first place, as Pan-Africanism is still much less deeply rooted than Pan-Arabism, the independence movement has been fragmented and localised and easier to handle and steer. Moreover, since, at the time when British rule was imposed, the cultural level of the African peoples was relatively low, British cultural penetration has been much deeper. Having no al-Azhar as a counterweight, the present generation of African leaders is culturally British-orientated in a way that the Arab leaders are not.

Secondly, American penetration is at present in its initial stages and is a good deal shallower than, for example, in the Middle East. The strength which the United States can already exercise was shown during the Congo crisis of 1960–1961, when, as we have seen, Washington's line on the whole prevailed over that of London, Brussels and Paris. Moreover, American capital occupies a substantial position in the South African Republic, the copper belt and West Africa.[1] The United States is not, however, yet within striking distance of dislodging Britain as the leading Western power in the area.

Thirdly, the general tendency of the third-world countries to make common cause with the socialist states over various aspects of foreign affairs and to turn to the Soviet Union as well as the West for financial and technical aid, both civil and military, has not yet

[1] Some 40% of the Zambian copper industry has long been controlled by American Metal. The Volta aluminium-power-irrigation complex is jointly owned by the Kaiser group and the Ghanaian Government.

made itself deeply felt. It is certainly present, as several years of close economic and political relations between Ghana and the Soviet Union showed, but it is so far a long way from being as strong as in the case, say, of India or the Arab states.

On the other hand, the policy-makers have been confronted here with a peculiar dilemma not to be found in other parts of the third world and arising from the past history of large-scale European settlement in southern, and to a smaller extent, central and eastern Africa.

As suggested in the discussion of ultra-colonialism, the break-up of the colonial system brought with it a polarisation of formerly allied groups, which in turn introduced a new and complicating factor into British foreign policy.

So long as British policy was aimed at preserving white rule in the African colonies, exercised either directly, as in West Africa, or jointly with the settlers, as in Central and East Africa, a common front of rulers against ruled, despite considerable internal strains, remained fairly firm. But as London veered round towards recognising and co-operating with the African independence movements deep fissures began to appear, principally between the British Government and the South African Government and also between the former and a now distinct ultra-colonialist bloc consisting of the settlers and their allies in the City and the Conservative Party.

A situation has developed in which the policy-makers cannot pursue their relatively flexible and realistic tactics in Black Africa without placing an increasingly severe strain on their relations with the main bastion of White Africa, the South African Republic. Equally, they cannot continue their alliance with the latter without endangering the new relationship built up with the twelve former colonies and also without getting at cross-purposes both with Washington and the Asian members of the Commonwealth.

The dilemma has been at its most acute in Rhodesia, where at the moment of writing the Smith régime owes its continued existence to support from South Africa, including oil supplied in breach of the UN embargo, financial loans and police and military reinforcements. On the one hand, decisive measures to push Smith and his fellow-rebels out would bring a major collision with Pretoria nearer. On the other, making peace with him and his like would set off a wave of anti-British feeling in Black Africa, where London has no less important interests to protect.

The quandary in which British diplomacy now finds itself was discussed by a group of experts, government officials and representatives of the business world in 1964–1965 under the auspices of Chatham House.

One fruit of its work was a study by one of its members of British interests in the South African Republic, seeking to show that, in so far as London is forced to choose between Black and White Africa, the verdict on the whole should be in favour of the present rulers of South Africa and their Rhodesian and Portuguese allies.[1]

The author contends that the balance of economic interest is pretty even. As regards political factors, he suggests that if Britain, ignoring the apartheid issue, continues to trade with South Africa, refuses to impose embargoes against her and maintains normal relations with her generally, in practice retaliation by the independent African states might not follow and, if it did, the consequences might not be particularly serious, even if some of them left the Commonwealth. He emphasises, moreover, the difficulties and disadvantages for Britain, as he sees them, of co-operating in UN measures of coercion against the South African Government aimed at putting an end to racialism.

This point of view is, however, more one-sided than that usually to be found in informed discussion of this issue. We may note here the author's own comment that there was no consensus of opinion in the group with which he worked except perhaps on one point, namely that the Government was faced with a peculiarly difficult problem.[2]

It is also more one-sided than the highly contradictory attitude in practice adopted by successive Governments. As shown below, many of its actions suggest that it is deeply anxious to avoid a head-on collision with Pretoria. But it has also to be remembered that when the Macmillan Government was in 1961 finally faced with an unavoidable choice between losing either South Africa or some of the African and Asian members from the Commonwealth, it chose to lose the former as the lesser evil. When in 1964 the Labour Government had to give a clear "yes" or "no" on the question of an arms embargo against South Africa, it chose, however reluctantly, to say "yes". In 1966, it was again in the end forced to say "yes" to mandatory UN sanctions against the Smith régime in Rhodesia, even though this decision contained within it the seeds of further conflict with the South African Government.

The question facing British foreign policy in Africa south of the Sahara and its attempts to deal with them are discussed region by region below.

[1] Dennis Austin. *Britain and South Africa*. London. 1966. pp. 37–57.
[2] *Ibid.* p. vii.

7*

It emerges that, from the point of view of those in authority, probably the most difficult problem of all is that of future relations with the South African Republic, an increasingly powerful—and menacing—factor in the balance of forces in the whole area.

The general picture also suggests that London's diplomacy, under heavy pressure, has undergone a considerable evolution to meet a rapidly changing situation. It may thereby have ensured that this part of the world, despite a long-term tendency for the grip of the former master to grow weaker, will remain a predominantly British sphere of influence for some time to come.

Anglo-Afrikaner Co-operation and Conflict

As we have already seen, the degree of inter-penetration of British and Afrikaner economic interests is very high. British financial and industrial groups still retain a considerable weight in key sectors of the South African economy: Britain is the chief purchaser of South African gold, South Africa is a valuable market for British exports and vice versa.

There is also a long-standing British-South African military link, which, although it has in recent years grown weaker, is still in existence, its formal framework being the Simonstown Agreement of 1955 as modified by a later understanding reached in 1967.

Under the 1955 Agreement,[1] control of the Simonstown base in peace time passed from the Royal Navy to the South African authorities. But Britain retained the right to use the base in peace and war, even if South Africa were not a belligerent. The British Commander-in-Chief, South Atlantic, with a staff of over a hundred naval and civilian personnel, remained on the spot, near, but not in, the base.

South Africa undertook to operate the existing naval communications system in accordance with the requirements of the Royal Navy and to return control into the latter's hands, should Britain be involved in war.

The two governments agreed to make joint preparations for regional defence against external aggression and for the defence of the sea route round the Cape, and to take steps to expand the South African navy for this purpose by the purchase of a large number of naval vessels in Britain.[2]

[1] Command 9520. Part of the text is given in Mansergh. *op. cit.* pp. 456–457.

[2] 6 anti-submarine frigates, 10 coastal minesweepers and 4 seaward defence boats, all except two of which had been delivered by the end of 1966. *Survey of British and Commonwealth Affairs*. March 3, 1967.

In April 1967 the two governments reached an understanding under which the Simonstown Agreement remained in force, but the British naval establishment in South Africa was reduced and the role of the South African navy in joint operational arrangements increased.

The post of British Commander-in-Chief, South Atlantic, was abolished, his local functions being transferred to the British Naval Attaché resident in Capetown, and the British naval vessel permanently stationed at Simonstown was withdrawn. It was agreed that the Chief of the South African Navy would take greater responsibility for the South African area in time of war.[1]

Until recently, not only the South African navy, but the army and air force as well have been mainly equipped with British armaments. In 1963 South African arms orders in Britain totalled nearly £90,000,000, including naval vessels, aircraft, radar and other electronic equipment. A large part of South Africa's own munitions industry has been built up and recently expanded by Imperial Chemicals and De Beers through their joint subsidiary, African Explosives and Chemical Industries.[2]

In the political field, until the beginning of the sixties and over some questions later still, London bent over backwards to remain on good terms with Pretoria.

Over apartheid, the Government for many years (until 1961) supported the South African contention that racial policy is a domestic matter and as such cannot be discussed by the United Nations. Over South-West Africa, it refused to support UN resolutions of December 1960 and April 1961 against South African annexation of the territory and refused permission to the UN South-West Africa Committee to enter the neighbouring territory of Bechuanaland, lest offence be caused to Verwoerd and his colleagues. In December 1965 the British representative spoke out strongly against a UN resolution (passed by a majority of 85 to 2, with 19 abstentions) calling for various forms of practical action in defence of the right of the people of South-West Africa to self-determination.

In 1961 the Government, having failed in its attempt to persuade the other members to accept continued South African membership of the Commonwealth, immediately rushed through legislation granting South Africa tariff preferences and other privileges which it would otherwise have lost with the loss of Commonwealth membership.

[1] *Ibid.*
[2] *Labour Research.* June 1963 and April 1964.

The Home Government evaded the UN resolution of November 1963 recommending the cessation of arms supplies to South Africa by claiming that the latter's requirements for external defence must continue to be met. This line was reversed in November 1964 after the Labour Party came to power. Even then, on Pretoria's insistence, an exception was made for 16 naval jet aircraft (Buccaneers) on order in Britain and for the subsequent supply of spares and training facilities.[1]

But despite the policy of appeasement of the South African authorities pursued by the Government, conflicts between London and Pretoria have tended on the whole to multiply and deepen during the last decade, the root cause being the gathering strength and momentum of a specifically Afrikaner imperialism, independent of, and opposed to, British capital, British policy and things British generally.

For some forty years following the Boer War, political power was in the hands of Afrikaner leaders, chief among them Smuts, inclined towards close political, military and economic co-operation with Britain and towards reconciliation and equality between South Africans of Dutch and British descent.[2] This period came to an end in 1948 with the advent to power of the Nationalist Party, the party of the Afrikaner extremists.

The Nationalists are best known for their extreme ruthlessness in enforcing a ghetto system for Africans, "coloureds" and Asians, which is what apartheid amounts to. But their programme has also included the attainment of Afrikaner supremacy over the English-speaking community, the dissolution of all links with the British Crown and the establishment of Afrikaner hegemony in adjacent British colonial territories.

During the twenty-year reign of the Nationalists under Malan, Strijdom, Verwoerd and Vorster, the state machine, social and cultural institutions of the white community — government departments, armed services, the judiciary, the educational system, religion, the Press and radio — have been progressively Afrikanerised by the squeezing out of people of British descent, by restricting the use of the English language, and by the spread of specifically Afrikaner racialist-chauvinist ideas. As part of this process, in 1961, after conducting a referendum of the white population in the previous year,[3] the Nationalist Government declared South Africa a republic, thus

---

[1] *Hansard.* November 25, 1964. Col. 1281.
[2] In 1963 the two groups made up 63% and 37% of the white population respectively.
[3] The result was close, 48% of the votes cast being negative.

putting an end to the remaining formal prerogatives of the British Crown.

In their external policy, the Nationalists have steadily pursued their aim of replacing Britain as the dominant power in the colonial territories on their northern border. By the end of the fifties there were signs that these territorial ambitions were beginning to arouse serious concern in London. Thus *The Economist* warned that, unless counter-measures were taken "an Afrikaner-dominated Southern African state" might come into existence, including Southern Rhodesia, Bechuanaland, Swaziland and Basutoland. It also prophesied that the Afrikaners might then resume their northward march.[1]

In the case of the three protectorates, the South African Government, with increasing insistence, repeated the claims of its predecessors that they should be incorporated in South Africa, while the British Government continued as before to reject these claims. At the end of 1966 the issue entered a new phase when London conceded sovereignty to Bechuanaland (Botswana) and Basutoland (Lesotho) and both countries became members of the United Nations. It so happens that in 1968 the same course was adopted in respect of Swaziland.

The long-term significance of this move remains to be seen. However, as regards Lesotho, which is surrounded on all sides by South African territory and where political power passed into the hands of Chief Jonathan and other tribal leaders willing to act as stooges for Pretoria, the initial effect was to open the way to an increase in South African influence.

As regards Rhodesia, in the mid-sixties the formerly subterranean struggle between London and Pretoria came into the light of day, South Africa emerging as the main ally of the settlers in its defiance of the British Government.

When, following the unilateral declaration of independence by the Smith régime in November 1965, London organised a voluntary system of selective economic sanctions designed to recall the settlers to obedience, the South African Government not only refused to take part, but did its best to frustrate the whole undertaking. In particular, supplies of oil from across the South African border blunted what was, potentially at least, the most effective form of pressure on Smith and his colleagues, namely the Anglo-American oil embargo.

[1] *The Economist.* March 7, 1959.

In November 1966 a member of the South African Government, Schoeman, gave notice that if the British Government invited the United Nations to impose mandatory sanctions against the Smith régime, South Africa would continue to maintain her normal relationship with Rhodesia, and went on to read the British Prime Minister a public lecture on the dire consequences for Britain of taking such a course.[1] The day after Wilson had announced that the Government had finally decided to take this step (December 5, 1966), the South African Prime Minister declared that South Africa could not "as a matter of principle" take part in sanctions against Rhodesia.[2]

There are, however, powerful political forces on the British side determined on reversing the present deterioration in relations and securing a rapprochement. This has emerged clearly in the continuing controversy over the question of arms supplies for Vorster and his friends.

At the end of 1967 the Labour Government, confirming its 1964 decision to abide by the Security Council resolution of that year, rejected a renewed South African attempt to purchase military equipment in Britain. It maintained that British trade with South Africa would not be jeopardised by this action, and that there was no evidence that Pretoria would denounce the Simonstown Agreement as a result of it.

The Conservative leadership, however, in the person of Heath, declared that the Government's attitude was "damaging to our national interest in finance, in trade and in defence, and a Conservative administration would reverse it".[3]

It seems to me, nonetheless, that tension in Anglo-Afrikaner relations is likely, on the whole, to increase. As in the case of Chamberlain's policy of appeasing the Nazis, appeasement of Pretoria has not prevented the latter from pursuing its own peculiar form of Boer War against its old opponent, sometimes by stealth and sometimes quite openly.

In other words, the vision of stable relations and mutual understanding with the Afrikaner extremists sought by the Homes and the Heaths is a mirage.

There are, furthermore, clearly visible limits to the concessions which London can make to Pretoria without serious damage to its wider foreign political interests. Apartheid and other forms of racial

---

[1] *Commonwealth Survey.* December 9, 1966.
[2] *Survey of British and Commonwealth Affairs.* January 20, 1967.
[3] *Hansard.* December 19, 1967. Cols. 1095–1158.

tyranny in southern Africa are now major issues in world politics. So the line which Britain takes concerning them has repercussions not only on her position in Black Africa and the Commonwealth but also in the whole third world and within the Western alliances as well.

Dilemma in Central Africa

Second only to the question of relations with South Africa, the most intractable problem facing British diplomacy has been the conflict between, on one side, the interests of the British settlers in Rhodesia and Zambia and the small, but powerful, group of British companies supporting them, and, on the other, the much wider interests by which the general course of British policy in Africa has been determined.

The two problems are, as we have seen, closely interwoven, the more so that the Oppenheimer group, which is based on South Africa, is overwhelmingly the strongest single British financial-industrial group in Rhodesia and Zambia. Besides controlling half of Zambia's copper output and the Wankie coal mines serving both territories, it has its finger in a dozen branches of the Rhodesian economy, among them banking (Rhodesian Acceptances), chemicals (African Explosives and Chemical Industries-Rhodesia), metallurgy (Rhodesia Alloys), chrome (Wankie Collieries), sugar (Lowveld), and cattle ranching (Willoughby).[1]

Afrikaner ambitions in Central Africa and the activities of Harry Oppenheimer and his partners are, however, strands in a very tangled skein, the main knot of which has been tied by the Rhodesian settlers and the British Government.

In 1923, by agreement with London, the settlers now numbering 200,000 and making up some 5% of the population, obtained control of the state apparatus of the colony, including the armed forces and police. At the beginning of the sixties, they had at their disposal ten white Rhodesian army battalions and five air squadrons and a police force containing, including reserves, 14,000 white Rhodesians.[2] Military and police strengths are now considerably larger and have been reinforced by contingents seconded from South Africa at the request of the Smith régime.

The army, police, judiciary and prison service have been used to

[1] *Labour Research*. January 1967.
[2] *Sunday Times*. March 4, 1962.

maintain a system of social, economic, and political oppression of the African population scarcely less severe than that in South Africa and, as there, have served to perpetuate a gigantic land robbery. By the end of the fifties the settlers held about 50% of all allocated land, owning 279 acres of good land per head, while the Africans had 17 acres of poor land per head.[1]

Settler autonomy suited London so long as its aim was to hold on to sovereignty in Black Africa indefinitely, but when the third-world strategists found themselves obliged to organise a retreat from this position serious difficulties began to loom up on the horizon. The home Government became more and more concerned with finding a basis for long-term partnership with African political groups and leaders after independence, while the settlers remained determined that political power should never pass into African hands.

London's first scheme for dealing with the problem was heavily weighted in favour of the settlers' point of view and was supported by all except the most extreme racialists among them. It eventually broke down owing to massive African opposition, which in turn caused a major change in the Government's tactics.

The Federation of the two Rhodesias and Nyasaland set up by London in 1953 was, in fact, though not in name, a hybrid form of colonial régime under which the three territories would in time attain independence, but under settler rule, with a sprinkling of selected Africans brought in to give the façade of the new structure a slightly off-white tinge. Its main effect was to bring in the Southern Rhodesian settlers with their army and police force for the enforcement of and perpetuation of white domination in Northern Rhodesia and Nyasaland as well as in their own territory.

For the time being, the Southern Rhodesians and their less numerous European allies in Northern Rhodesia, drawn mostly from the privileged caste of white employees of the mining companies, shared power with London. They controlled the Federal machine, situated in Salisbury, the settlers' stronghold, and headed by Sir Godfrey Huggins, until then Prime Minister of Southern Rhodesia. London retained responsibility for an interim period for the colonial administration in Northern Rhodesia and Nyasaland. But ahead beckoned the day, when, in accordance with the expressed hopes of the British Government, the Federation would "attain full membership of the Commonwealth",[2] i.e., the Federal Government would become free to decide the fate of all the peoples of the Federation as it saw fit.

---

[1] W. A. Hunton. *Decision in Africa*. London. 1959. p. 28.
[2] Mansergh. *op. cit.* p. 120.

With the sickening mixture of hypocrisy and blockheadedness characteristic of so many colonial policy statements of this period, this operation was conducted under the general slogan of "racial partnership", which was advanced as a middle way between the herrenvolk principles applied in South Africa, on one side, and the demand of the Africans for majority, i.e., African, rule, on the other.

The high claims made for this conception may be seen from a statement made by the Foreign Secretary, Selwyn Lloyd, in the United Nations in 1959 on the subject of racial problems in British colonies. "We reject the idea of an inherent superiority of one race over another," he said. "Our policy is therefore non-racialist; it offers a future in which Africans, Europeans, Asians . . . will all play their full part as citizens in the countries where they live, and in which the feelings of race will be submerged in loyalty to new nations."[1]

In intention and in practice, however, "racial partnership", far from allowing Africans to "play their full part as citizens in the countries where they live", had precisely the opposite effect of perpetuating settler domination and the denial of human rights. Not long before Selwyn Lloyd's speech, Federal elections were held in North and South Rhodesia and Nyasaland (November 1958) at which practically every white person had a vote while this privilege was granted to 747 out of a total African population of 7,000,000.

The turning point in Government tactics came in March 1959 when, with the aid of Federal forces, demonstrations against European domination, particularly in Nyasaland, were repressed with great severity, but were on such a scale as to rouse serious doubts in London about the feasibility of preserving the Federation at least in its original form.

One of the first signs of these doubts was the report of the Devlin Commission, appointed by the Macmillan Government to enquire into events in Nyasaland. It was critical of specific measures taken against the Africans, declaring that "Nyasaland is — no doubt only temporarily — a police state . . . where it is unwise to express any but the most restrained criticism of Government policy". The report admitted that opposition to the Federation was "deeply rooted and almost universally held", that the population wanted "above all else self-government for the black people in Nyasaland such as they have seen happening in other parts of Africa" and that there were a number of Nyasas no less qualified than the average European to take political decisions.[2] The Commission thus punctured several myths

---

[1] *Ibid.* p. 349.
[2] Command 814. 1959.

systematically propagated by the Federal Government and by the British Government itself.

A year later, in October 1960, there followed the report of the Monckton Commission, also appointed by the Macmillan Government, whose task was to review the Federal constitution.[1] This showed even more clearly which way the wind was blowing. Like the Devlin report, it admitted that the Federation was unpopular among the African peoples, and stated that "the strength of African opposition in the Northern Territories (Northern Rhodesia and Nyasaland) is such that Federation cannot, in our view, be maintained in its present form". Its most significant recommendation was that the component territories of the Federation should have the right, if they wished, to secede from it.

Since from the beginning the Federation's only chance of survival had rested on the forcible retention within it of the two northern members, this latter recommendation was attacked tooth and nail by the Federal Government, now headed by Welensky, and by its supporters in the Conservative Party, who launched an all-out campaign to prevent any change in official policy.

The struggle revolved mainly round the question of constitutional reform in Northern Rhodesia. In January 1961, the Colonial Secretary, Macleod, without publishing his proposals, let it be known that he favoured changes which would alter the balance in the territorial legislature in favour of the African representatives. The London conference summoned to consider these and other proposals was boycotted by Welensky's political followers in Northern Rhodesia and simultaneously the ultra-colonialists in Parliament and in the Cabinet, led by Lord Salisbury and Duncan Sandys, plus emissaries sent by the Federal Government to Britain, brought heavy pressure to bear to have the proposals withdrawn.[2]

Welensky, for his part, issued a threat to London foreshadowing that which was some four years later not merely uttered, but carried out in respect of Southern Rhodesia by the Smith régime. "The Federation is mine," he declared, "and I am prepared to fight, to go the whole hog if necessary, to keep it."[3]

This pressure was at first successful, Macleod's proposals being withdrawn, and in June 1961 replaced by others[4] acceptable to the

[1] Command 1148. 1960.
[2] W. P. Kirkman (*op. cit.* p. 92), who gives a full and authoritative account of this battle, puts the number of Conservative M.P.s opposed to Macleod's proposals at about one hundred.
[3] *Daily Worker*. February 28, 1962.
[4] Command 1423. 1961.

Federation lobby, but not to the African leaders in Northern Rhodesia. By February 1962, however, the Government, convinced at last that the Federation could not be held together by force in the face of rising African opposition, reverted to the Macleod proposals. At the same time the affairs of the Federation and its constituent territories were entrusted to the Deputy Prime Minister, Butler.

Butler's task was in effect to wind up the Federation, which he accomplished in December 1963. In the following year, both Nyasa-land (Malawi) and Northern Rhodesia (Zambia) became indepen-dent sovereign states under African leadership.

Since then the Government has attempted to pull off in Southern Rhodesia (now renamed Rhodesia) what it had failed to achieve on the larger stage of the Federation, namely transfer of sovereignty to a régime controlled by the settlers but containing an admixture of collaborationist Africans.

In pursuit of this aim, it went so far as to veto a resolution in the UN Security Council, in September 1963, calling upon it "not to transfer to its colony of Southern Rhodesia, as at present governed, any powers or attributes of sovereignty until the establishment of a Government fully representative of all the inhabitants of the colony". In doing so, it found itself almost completely isolated, eight members voting in favour of the resolution, while the United States and France abstained.

This undertaking has, however, so far proved to be no more practicable than the plan for a sovereign, settler-run Federation, the principal difficulty now being the opposition of the settlers.

As the Federation collapsed, control of the administration in Salisbury passed into the hands of the out-and-out die-hards, whose party, the Rhodesian Front, was voted into power for the first time at the all-white election in December 1962. Its leader, Winston Field, in April 1964 was replaced by Ian Smith, an even more con-vinced die-hard than himself. In November 1965 the Smith régime unilaterally declared Rhodesia independent and demanded British recognition of the *fait accompli*.

As a result London has found itself confronted with a régime in Salisbury which regards even "racial partnership" as too liberal a conception. At the same time, the Government's need for a façade behind which to transfer power to Salisbury has become greater than ever, since Commonwealth, black African and third-world opinion is now thoroughly aroused and the price which would have to be paid for an undisguised sell-out to the settlers has risen accordingly.

The nature of the tactics adopted by the Government can be seen from the deal proposed by Wilson to Smith at their meeting on H.M.S. *Tiger* in December 1966, and repeated with variations at their second meeting on H.M.S. *Fearless* in October 1968, a deal on both occasions rejected by Smith.

The settlers were to agree to a slight widening of the African franchise, paper guarantees against arbitrary changes in the constitution, the temporary inclusion in the Rhodesian Government of five nominated members drawn from outside the Rhodesian Front, two of whom would be Africans, a temporary increase in the Governor's powers and certain other even less substantial concessions. In return, London would recognise the independence of Rhodesia.

The whole arrangement was to be subject to the results of an investigation by a Royal Commission on the acceptability of the revised constitution to the people of the country, but both the composition and the terms of reference of the Royal Commission were to require the prior consent of the Rhodesian authorities. Smith himself and most of his colleagues were to remain in power throughout the transition period, unless they meanwhile lost the confidence of the Rhodesian (predominantly white) electorate.[1]

As Wilson himself said in his explanation to Parliament, this meant handing over to Smith and his partners "responsibility for a future Rhodesia" and giving him "what no Government in this country has given in our generation, and that is the right of independence without majority rule".[2]

It is possible that these tactics, coupled with the pressure on Salisbury now exercised by UN mandatory sanctions, will in due course achieve their immediate object. Disunity in the Rhodesian Front led in July 1968 to the resignation of two extremist members of Smith's team. At the same time a new party was formed representing primarily the interests of the European business community, who stand to lose less than the European landowners and farmers from political concessions to the Africans.

But a bargain struck along the lines of the *Tiger* and *Fearless* proposals cannot solve the dilemma facing London, though it might ease it. A viable long-term Anglo-Rhodesian relationship can, it seems to me, only develop on the basis of African majority rule in the country, which the bulk of the settlers, with South African backing, are determined to prevent. The outlook is, therefore, in any case one of further quadrilateral struggle between the African independence movement, the settlers, London and Pretoria for some time to come.

[1] *Rhodesia: Proposals for a Settlement 1966.* Command 3159. 1966.
[2] *Hansard.* December 5, 1966. Col. 1053–1080.

East Africa

In East Africa the policy-makers were faced with a problem similar to that in the Rhodesias, and for many years attempted to deal with it in a similar way. Here also "racial partnership" was tried out as a means of ensuring perpetual settler participation in the Government of Kenya, and the Federal gambit was played as a means of extending the influence of that Government into Uganda and Tanganyika (Tanzania).

One key element in the situation was, however, different, making possible in the end a more favourable result from London's point of view. This difference lay in the relative weakness of the settlers as an independent force.

In Kenya, where the settlers were concentrated, they in 1960 numbered only 65,000 out of a population of some 7,000,000, a considerably smaller proportion of the total than in Southern Rhodesia or even Northern Rhodesia. Unlike their Southern Rhodesian brethren, they had not established themselves as the political rulers of the country, the control of the armed forces, police and whole state apparatus having remained in the hands of the colonial administration responsible to the Colonial Office.

There were, furthermore, no ultra-colonialist giants, such as the Oppenheimer group and the British South Africa Company, forming states within the state and able, as in the Rhodesias, to power a settler-dominated Federation on the spot and lobby for it in the City and at Westminster.

In practice this meant that from the beginning the Government was able to take less account of the specific needs and demands of the settlers and, when necessary, to exercise effective pressure upon them. It also meant that when in the sixties a reversal of tactics, as in Central Africa, became unavoidable, the Government had more freedom of manoeuvre. As shown below, it ended by buying the settlers out, an operation which, though not impossible, would be far more difficult and expensive to carry out in Rhodesia.

In the fifties, the Government gave first priority to beheading the independence movement in Kenya by crushing the revolt of the Kikuyu tribe against the colonial administration and the settlers. From 1952 onwards, substantial British military and police forces for several years conducted a major campaign against the Mau Mau rebellion, imprisoning, shooting and hanging in the process more than 100,000 Africans. Kenyatta and other leaders of the independence movement were imprisoned on trumped-up charges and not finally given their freedom until 1961. As late as 1959 a group of eleven Kikuyu prisoners were beaten to death by their guards in the Hola prison camp, a crime which considerably embarrassed the then Colonial Secretary, Lennox-Boyd.

At the same time pressure was brought to bear on the Kenya settlers to get them to realise that, with the existing unfavourable balance of forces, they would have to make both political and economic concessions to the Africans if their future position in the country was to be secured.

Although the settlers did not control the machinery of government, under their influence the whole political, social and economic life of the country was based on racial discrimination, leading, among its other results, to acute land hunger among the African masses.

By law, the so-called White Highlands, the most fertile area, was reserved exclusively to European ownership. At the end of the fifties 4,000 Europeans owned 11,000,000 acres of the best land, while 6,000,000 Africans were left with 33,000,000 acres. Taking the two ethnic groups as a whole, the Europeans held 195 acres per head and the Africans 5·6 acres per head.[1]

It was part of the task of the policy-makers in London to persuade the beneficiaries of this system that it could not remain unaltered, that they would have to move on from racial supremacy to "racial partnership".

In 1952, i.e., in the same year as he and his colleagues launched their war on the Kikuyu, the Colonial Secretary, Oliver Lyttelton (Lord Chandos), warned the settlers during a visit to Kenya that "sixty thousand Europeans cannot expect to hold all the political power and to exclude Africans from the legislature and from the Government". "Besides force, which must now be used and which we will furnish," he went on, "you must turn your minds to political reform, and to measures which will gradually engage the consent and help of the governed. The security of your homes, the security of the money, hard work and skill which you have lavished on your farms . . . cannot rest upon battalions of British troops: it can only rest upon the building of a multi-racial society."[2]

The same note was struck by the report of the Royal Commission on East Africa, 1953–1955, which stressed the particular necessity of relaxing the European grip on the land in Kenya. "The historic process up to date has been one of communities for the most part living separately and not one of partnership in development," it said. ". . . A policy without the co-operation of the indigenous people

[1] Hunton, *loc. cit.*
[2] Chandos. *op. cit.* p. 398.

is no policy at all . . . It must be the first duty of statesmanship," it continued, "to seek out the possibilities and ways of making adjustments so as to avoid a clash of culture and race. Future policy needs to be associated with an ideal which can command general allegiance and inspire a new confidence in joint endeavour. In this respect the retention of land in the Highlands of Kenya for purely European use . . . has very serious limitations. It makes the Europeans appear as a tribe hanging on to their tribal territory instead of pooling it for the common territorial need."[1]

In pursuit of these ideas, the Government gave its support to the leader of the more liberal group among the settlers, Michael Blundell (since knighted), who became the principal white "partner" until the concept of a permanent political role for the settlers had finally to be given up. In the early sixties, the Government began to pay out large sums from its own resources to buy out settlers in the White Highlands in order to make way for African farmers.

In their policy towards the African population the Government combined forcible repression of the radical independence movement with encouragement of collaborationist African leaders within the framework of constitutional concessions.[2] It was able, for a time, to make effective use of ethnic, in this case tribal, factors for this purpose.

When operations against the Mau Mau movement were completed and the state of emergency ended in 1959, two rival African political parties took shape—the more radical Kenya African National Party (KANU), based on the Kikuyu and Luo tribes, and the Kenya African Democratic Party (KADU), based on the smaller tribes. In this situation, the Government's main concern was to prevent the two parties from uniting under Kenyatta, the acknowledged national leader, and to promote the political fortunes of Ngala, the KADU leader, and of Mboya, temporarily the chief figure in KANU.

In January–February 1960, while Kenyatta and some of his closest colleagues were held in prison, a constitutional conference was held in London, attended by representatives of KANU, KADU, the settlers and other ethnic groups. The result was a new constitution on strictly "racial partnership" lines, i.e., while African representation in the legislature was considerably increased, representation was guaranteed to Europeans (and Asians) on a racial basis and out of all proportion to their numbers.[3]

[1] Mansergh. *op. cit.* pp. 88–89.
[2] The first step in this direction was the so-called Lyttelton Constitution of 1954, under which for the first time one seat in the colonial government was reserved for an African (and two seats for Asians). Chandos. *op. cit.* p. 407.
[3] For a summary of the relevant provision, see Mansergh. *op. cit.* pp. 107–108.

Meanwhile, official propaganda against Kenyatta was kept going at full blast. In May 1960, by way of justification of his continued detention, the Governor of Kenya publicly denounced Kenyatta as "the African leader to darkness and death".[1] At about the same time an official report was issued repeating all the old charges concerning atrocities committed during the Kikuyu uprising and Kenyatta's responsibility for them.

At the elections held under the new constitution in January 1961, KANU returned more representatives to the legislature than KADU, but refused to participate in the government unless Kenyatta were released. Ngala and KADU were less scrupulous, to put it mildly, and entered a coalition administration in alliance with Blundell's New Kenya Party and nominees of the colonial authorities. The aim of establishing a "racial partnership" régime appeared to have been achieved. But not for long.

The pressure in Kenya for the release of Kenyatta proved to be irresistible. He was freed from all restrictions in the summer of 1961 and shortly afterwards assumed the leadership of KANU. The Government were then driven to placing their main hopes not so much on constitutionalised "multi-racialism" as on securing that, when the time came to concede sovereignty, power could be handed over to KADU rather than KANU or at least a coalition in which the former's influence was strong.

At a further constitutional conference in London in February–April 1962 the Government conceded the principle of universal adult suffrage, but in alliance with KADU against KANU insisted on a constitution giving wide powers to regional assemblies and weakening those of the central government.[2] This system, if put into practice, would have given KADU considerable advantage as compared with KANU.

The tide in Kenya in favour of early independence under Kenyatta's and KANU's undivided leadership was, however, running too fast for this manœuvre to succeed. KADU began to disintegrate, some of its representatives in the legislature going over to KANU. In October 1963 the Government, in breach of its pledges to KADU, was forced to agree to substantial changes in the constitution desired by KANU. In December Kenya became independent with Kenyatta as its undisputed leader.

The Government's plans for an eventual federation of the three

---

[1] Quoted in Kirkman. *op. cit.* p. 56.
[2] For details, see Mansergh. *op. cit.* pp. 109–113.

East African colonies turned on the development and evolution of the East Africa High Commission consisting of the Governors of Kenya, Tanganyika and Uganda. The Commission was first set up in 1948 and charged with certain economic and financial functions in all three territories. The long-term hopes nurtured in government circles were expressed by the Colonial Secretary, Lyttelton, in 1953, when he spoke of the possibility of "the evolution, as time goes on, of still larger measures of federation of the whole East African territories".[1]

By 1961 the East Africa High Commission was still an organ of the three Governors, but had the beginnings of an organic relationship with the Kenya, Tanganyika and Uganda legislatures, which by this time contained African majorities. This took the form of a central Legislative Assembly consisting, besides officials of the High Commission, of contingents from the three territorial legislatures. With the advice and consent of this Assembly, the High Commission exercised legislative powers in Kenya, Tanganyika and Uganda over a wide field, including railways and harbours, posts and telecommunications, civil aviation and the collection of income tax and customs and excise dues.[2]

The question of the future of this embryonic federal organism arose in sharp form when in March 1961 it became clear that one of the members, Tanganyika, was to become independent before the end of the year. After some hesitation the leaders of the independence movement in all three colonies determined that political federation could not be considered until after independence for all and that, in the words of the Vice-President of KANU, it was only as independent states that they could consider the forms of their association with one another.[3]

Accordingly, at discussions in London in June 1961 with representatives of the three colonies and the High Commission, the most the Government could obtain was that the latter body should be replaced by an East African Common Services Organisation to carry on its economic and financial functions and that the territorial legislatures should participate more closely in the work of the new organisation.

With the attainment of independence by Tanganyika in December 1961, by Uganda in October 1962 and by Kenya in December 1963, the question of whether or not the three countries should federate passed out of London's control.

---

[1] Chandos. *op. cit.* p. 420.
[2] Mansergh. *op. cit.* p. 113.
[3] Quoted in Jack Woddis. *Africa. The Way Ahead.* London. 1963. p. 146.

The Common Services Organisation remained, however, as a not unimportant channel for the exercise of British influence in East Africa in the future. In 1967, the three states, though not federating, formed themselves into an East African Community, with an internal common market and an external common tariff, one feature of which was to be a strengthening and expansion of existing common services.

By finally executing a tactical retreat from its original aims, particularly in Kenya, the Government made possible a fairly close relationship with the former East African colonies after independence, all of them becoming members of the Commonwealth, the sterling area and the imperial preference system.

This relationship rested and still rests very largely in the continuing need of Kenya, Tanganyika (now Tanzania) and Uganda for financial and technical assistance and London's readiness to provide it and indeed to give special priority to East Africa in this respect. In 1964–1965, Kenya, Tanzania, Uganda and the East African Common Services received sums in one form or another amounting to more than half of all government aid to the African members of the Commonwealth — in round figures £36,000,000 out of £64,000,000.[1] Part of these funds went to pay for part of the cost of British civil personnel employed by the three new states, who, as we have recalled elsewhere, in 1963–1964 numbered no less than 8,000, a large proportion being former employees of the colonial administration.

The lion's share of Government funds went and is still going to Kenya, partly owing to the increasing sums paid by London to the Kenya Government to buy out European land-holders. The total for the financial year 1964–1965 was £18,000,000, which was about twice the combined figure for the four West African members of the Commonwealth, Nigeria, Ghana, Sierra Leone and Gambia.[2] In 1968 technical assistance to Kenya was running at about £4,000,000 a year, while further land-purchase was being financed out of a British interest-free loan of £18,000,000 for the period 1966–1970.[3]

British military influence has also remained strong in Kenya and Uganda, though not in Tanganyika, the turning point coming at the beginning of 1964, only a month after British sovereignty in the area came to an end.

In Tanganyika and Uganda British officers had remained in command of the armed forces after independence, and in Kenya, the

[1] *Commonwealth Survey*. February 18, 1966.
[2] *Ibid.*
[3] *Survey of British and Commonwealth Affairs*. March 15, 1968.

site of important British military, naval and air bases, whole units remained in the country, though they were due for withdrawal by the end of 1964 under arrangements agreed between the British and Kenyan Governments.

When in January 1964 African regiments, first in Tanganyika and then in Uganda and Kenya, refused to obey their officers, both British and African, all three Governments asked London for the help of British troops in restoring order. This request was immediately met, forces already in Kenya and commandos sent from Aden being used for the purpose.

In the case of Kenya this episode led to the conclusion of an agreement providing for a considerably closer military relationship with Britain than had previously been accepted by the Kenyan leaders, and which is still intact today.

In June 1964, Sandys, then Commonwealth Secretary, announced that he had come to an understanding with Kenyatta and his colleagues under which fixed military installations, equipment and arms to the value of about £10,000,000 were to be transferred to Kenya free of charge and British personnel would be provided for training the Kenyan army, navy and air force. In return it had been agreed that "units of the British forces might return to Kenya from time to time for training and to carry out joint exercises with the Kenya forces". The RAF and Royal Navy received the right to the continued use of airfields in Kenya and the port of Mombasa.[1]

After the army mutiny, the Uganda Government, for its part, made an arrangement with London under which British officers remained temporarily in command of the country's armed forces, British officers were attached to the Uganda army for training purposes and facilities were provided at British military establishments outside Uganda for training Uganda army and air force personnel. The Tanganyikan Government, on the other hand, refused a British offer to provide a training mission for the Tanganyikan army and to provide air-training facilities for Tanganyikans.[2]

Among factors likely to weaken London's influence in East Africa, the most important seems to me to be radical tendencies in African political circles, capable, as happened for some years in Ghana, of bringing about a restriction of the freedom of action of British business interests and the development of a close relationship with the socialist world in matters of foreign policy, foreign trade and foreign financial and technical assistance.

[1] *Commonwealth Survey*. June 9, 1964.
[2] *Ibid.* March 31, 1964.

The only signs of this so far have been in Tanzania, which, under Nyerere's leadership, has in recent years taken steps to limit foreign ownership of companies operating in the country and has been one of the leading critics of British handling of the Smith régime in Rhodesia and one of the main supporters of the guerrilla movement in Southern Africa generally.

In Kenya, on the other hand, the right wing is at present in the ascendant. In 1966 the radicals in KANU were expelled both from the party and the Government, Oginga Odinga was replaced as Vice-President of KANU by the Colonial Office's old protégé, Ngala, and a witch-hunt was begun, and at the moment is still continuing, against all those considered to harbour dangerous thoughts.

British influence in the area is also vulnerable from another quarter, namely the activities of the United States and the other capitalist powers. In particular the association agreement concluded by the new East African Community with the European Economic Community in July 1968 helps to clear the road for an expansion of the operations of West German, French, Italian and Benelux firms at the expense of their British competitors.

All in all, however, Britain is still by a long way the dominant foreign power, and the Government, judging by its performances to date, intends to ensure, so far as it can, that it remains so.

West Africa: The House that Jack Built

The foregoing shows, I think, that not only in the Middle East, but also in Africa the general picture has been not of a wise and far-sighted government conducting a liberal experiment in freeing the subject peoples, but of men compelled reluctantly to retreat farther and farther along a road upon which they did not want to travel. In the case of Southern Rhodesia, precisely because the Conservative administrations of the fifties refused to recognise the new balance of forces taking shape, the policy-makers have landed themselves in a blind alley from which they are still trying to escape.

But there is one region in which something resembling a consistent, long-term policy of bringing the colonies to independence was applied, namely West Africa. Here the authorities decided at the beginning of the fifties that a complete transfer of political power was inevitable and necessary in the not-too-distant future[1] and a process of deliberate preparation for independence took place.

---

[1] Nkrumah, the leading advocate of early independence, was released from jail and appointed Chief Minister in Ghana as early as 1951.

In the third volume of his study of African problems, Woddis raises the question of the aim of the tactics of preparing the colonies for independence, and suggests that it was not simply a device for putting off the evil day, but a means of ensuring that, when the change-over took place, it did so under British guidance.[1] This is certainly right, but a clear distinction also has to be made between different meanings attached by the Government to independence in different parts of Africa.

In the two Rhodesias, Nyasaland and Kenya, it seems to me that London into the early sixties really was trying to put off the evil day by substituting independence under settler rule (the Central African Federation) or with built-in settler influence (the 1954 and 1960 Kenya constitutions) for independence under African rule, while in West Africa colonial tactics were designed to lead to independence in the ordinary sense of the word.

Independent Ghana (1957), Nigeria (1960), Sierra Leone (1961) and Gambia (1965) were slowly and methodically constructed from British blueprints under the guidance of British officials and constituted the nearest thing to a house that Jack built in the whole continent, except perhaps the Sudan.

There were no doubt a variety of reasons for the difference, including the foresight and goodwill of some of the key colonial administrators and officials concerned, but the main causes are not far to seek.

There were here neither a body of settlers with a special interest in the indefinite prolongation of white rule, nor military bases so important that London tried to hang on to them at all costs. The main British industrial, commercial and financial groups operating in the area were not the inheritors of Cecil Rhodes's empire with roots in South Africa, but companies, some primarily concerned with Africa and some not, able to, and in varying degrees willing to, adapt themselves to a transfer of political power to African hands.

This applies in the first place to Unilever, the group with the largest stake and most pervasive influence in the region. In his report to his shareholders for 1960, the Chairman expressed himself as well satisfied with the company's affairs in Africa, despite the rapid disappearance of colonial rule. Noting that Nigeria had just achieved independence, he said: "Our business here had a most successful year and we continue to find new outlets for our enterprise and our management skills." Remarking that Ghana had in that year become a republic, thus severing its last constitutional link with the

[1] Woddis. *op. cit.* pp. 59–60.

British Crown, he said: "We have been able to adapt ourselves to the changing patterns of commerce in this country and our business has done well."[1]

In 1961 the Chairman of Amalgamated Tin Mines of Nigeria, a subsidiary of the London Tin Corporation, was fulsome in his compliments to independent Nigeria. "Since Nigeria achieved independence within the Commonwealth," he told his shareholders, "relations with the Federal and Northern Regional Governments have been most satisfactory and I look forward with confidence to a continuation of the excellent co-operation we have always enjoyed."[2] It was the policy of the company, he added, to appoint senior Africans to responsible positions.

Barclays Bank D.C.O., which has close connections with the ultra-colonialist companies, gave only cautious approval to the emergence of independent African states in its annual report for 1961. As if, however, to emphasize the Bank's willingness to bow to the inevitable, the Chairman at the same time announced that four prominent Nigerians had been appointed to its board in Lagos, with another Nigerian as Chairman, and that two Ghanaians had been appointed to the board in Accra.[3]

Shell and British Petroleum were also able to adapt themselves to the winds of change in Nigeria, where, as we have seen, they control by far the greater part of the new oil Eldorado, so far the only one in Africa south of the Sahara. They granted the Nigerian Government a half share in their refinery near Port Harcourt and a fairly large share of the profits of the new industry. The two companies far outpaced the American Gulf Oil Co., which not only came late into the field, but ran into serious difficulties in coming to terms with the Nigerian authorities.

The two principal problems so far encountered by British diplomacy have been different in origin, but similar in their effect.

First, for some eight years until Nkrumah was overthrown at the beginning of 1966, the Government of Ghana pursued an increasingly radical internal and external policy, which threatened in due course to lead to a major weakening of British political and economic influence in the country.

Secondly, the elaborate federal structure built up by the colonial authorities in Nigeria before they left began to break up only some six years later, leading to the war at present (1969) still being

[1] *The Times.* April 28, 1961.
[2] *New Commonwealth.* December, 1961.
[3] *The Times.* December 11, 1961.

fought between the Federal forces and the Ibo people, who have regrouped in their home territory and set up the new state of Biafra. In the case of Ghana, the Government's general tactical line was to remain on as good terms as possible with Nkrumah and his colleagues with the aim of keeping the country within the British orbit and preventing a firm alignment with the socialist states. Anglo-Ghanaian relations at times became very strained, but never broke down, even when formal diplomatic relations were discontinued on Accra's insistence in 1965. These tactics, from London's point of view, in the end paid off, when the balance of internal forces swung against the radicals, bringing General Anksah and his men to power in their stead.

In its economic policy the Nkrumah Government placed heavy emphasis on the development of the public sector at the expense of the private sector, thereby weakening the dominating position of British firms in the economy, a few of which were, indeed, bought out and nationalised, among them five gold-mining companies and BOAC's subsidiary, Ghana Airways. The process was, moreover, accompanied by measures to staunch the outflow of profits from foreign businesses, including exchange control, a tax on exported profits and a limit on remittances abroad by insurances companies.

At the same time opponents of this policy, such as the Finance Minister, Gbedemah, much favoured in British business circles, were removed from office. Nkrumah explicitly justified this action on anti-capitalist grounds. It was undesirable, he said, that "men with varied business connections should be members of a government, which must from now on be increasingly animated by socialist ideals",[1] In December 1961 a White Paper was published in Accra, accusing foreign business interests and foreign government agencies of complicity in attempts to reduce Ghana to quasi-colonial status.

In the military field, the Nkrumah Government broke most, though not all, of the fairly strong links with London surviving into the independence period.

There was no Anglo-Ghanaian Defence Agreement, but in the first four years of independence the country's Chief of the Defence Staff was General Alexander of the British Army, and the Chief of Naval Staff and Chief of Air Force were also British. Altogether there were about 200 British officers serving in Ghana.

In September 1961 the Ghanaian authorities abruptly dismissed Alexander and other senior officers, appointing Ghanaians in their

[1] *Commonwealth Survey*. October 10, 1961.

place. A considerable number of other British officers were also relieved of their duties. While Nkrumah asked that a British military team should remain for training duties, he announced that the dismissals should be regarded as a decisive step in the direction of the complete Africanisation of the country's armed forces.

Over foreign policy questions, Ghana, as one of the leaders of the world anti-colonial movement, as an active opponent of the nuclear arms race, foreign bases and military blocs and as a proponent of non-alignment, was a constant thorn in London's side. During the Congo crisis, in an attempt to defeat the efforts of the British Government to save Tshombe and his mercenaries, Accra protested to the United Nations against the halting of UN military operations and accused "certain powers from outside the African continent, who are intent on destroying the prestige of the United Nations and on maintaining colonial rule and exploitation in Africa".[1] In 1965, Ghana broke off diplomatic relations with Britain in protest against the Government's appeasement of the Smith régime in Rhodesia.

Ghana's policies were persistently attacked in Conservative circles and by the Conservative Press. The events of 1961 in particular touched off a violent Press campaign in which even the staider newspapers joined. Its flavour can be gauged from the *Sunday Times* statement that "the sudden dismissal of General Alexander from command of the Ghana Army is racialism" (!) And its suggestion that the Queen's visit to Ghana, then about to take place, should be cancelled.[2]

The Government, for its part, was more cautious. It made representations to the Ghana Government about the latter's White Paper of December 1961, but did not enter into open polemics. A member of the Cabinet (Duncan Sandys) was despatched to Accra to pour oil on the waters before the Queen's visit, which duly took place.

The conciliatory character of the official line emerges particularly clearly from its attitude to the Volta scheme.

The idea of building the Volta dam as a source of electric power for a new aluminium industry based on Ghanaian bauxite (and other purposes) dated from the colonial period and was originally to have been carried out with credits from the British Government and private capital from British and Canadian aluminium companies. Owing, however, to London's inability to find the large sums required, by 1960, on the initiative of the Ghana Government, the project was under active consideration by the U.S. Government and

---

[1] *The Times*. September 22, 1961.
[2] *Sunday Times*. October 1, 1961.

Kaiser Industries. Following a visit by Nkrumah to Washington, the U.S. President (Kennedy), informed him in July 1961 that the United States was ready to co-operate.[1]

Later in the year, owing to the Nkrumah Government's increasingly close relations with the socialist states, its criticism of the Western powers and multiplying signs that it wished to start building a socialist society in Ghana itself, the U.S. Government began to think seriously of withdrawing from the project. This in turn caused the British Government to intervene in Washington against such a move.

According to Schlesinger's account, which reads as if it were based on documentary evidence, Macmillan wrote to Kennedy in November 1961 strongly urging him to continue participation in the Volta scheme. In Macmillan's opinion, Nkrumah had not yet "gone over to the Russians". If the United States were now to withdraw, the Africans would regard this as an attempt to use financial power to dictate the national policy of independent African states. The Russians would move in. Cancellation might have the same effect in West Africa that Dulles's repudiation of the Aswan dam had had in Egypt in 1956. On the other hand, continued Macmillan, if the West backed the Volta dam, it would be convincing proof to the Africans that industrial development could be combined with freedom.[2]

This point of view coincided with Kennedy's own and the U.S.-Ghanaian agreement concerning the scheme was signed in Accra in January 1962.

As we have remarked, the Government's (and Washington's) patience, at any rate in the short run, had its reward. The fall of the Nkrumah Government in 1966 meant a sharp swing to the right in Ghana's internal and external policies, the jailing of the most radical elements in the country and the return to power of exiled or imprisoned politicians known for their close contacts with British and Western business interests.[3] One of the first acts of the new régime was to restore diplomatic relations with London, with which it has so far remained on cordial terms.

For six years after Nigeria obtained independence, British diplomacy had to contend with almost none of the problems confronting

---

[1] Schlesinger. *op. cit.* p. 498.
[2] *Ibid.* p. 499.
[3] In 1967 the Chairman of the British-owned Ashanti Goldfields Corporation remarked with satisfaction that General Anksah's régime was "pro-West, pro-capital and pro-private enterprise. The Nkrumah brand of half-baked socialism has been discarded." Quoted in *Comment.* April 15, 1967.

it in Ghana, and where they arose at all, they did so in attenuated form.

The factor immediately responsible for this apparently idyllic situation was the British-made, long-evolved independence constitution, which was heavily weighted in favour of the Northern Region, the stronghold of London's old allies, the Moslem feudal rulers.

From 1960 to 1966 the Federation was run by a coalition government, led by the nominee of the northern potentates, Abubakar Tafawa Balewa. Azikiwe, who had once occupied a position in Nigerian political life similar to that of Nkrumah in Ghana, faded into the background in the honorific post of President.

The Balewa Government pursued a policy of open house to foreign, particularly British, capital and showed no inclination to favour the public over the private sector of the economy. The sharpest Anglo-Nigerian conflict in the economic field arose out of Britain's attempt to join the European Economic Community in 1961–1963.

This British move presented a considerable danger to Nigerian interests. Her export trade with the EEC, which then took some 40% of her total exports, was already threatened by the privileged status enjoyed by the exports of EEC's associated states in Africa (the former French, Belgian and Italian colonies). If Britain joined the EEC, this threat would be extended to Nigerian exports to Britain also, another 35% of the total.

The solution proposed by the British Government, namely that Nigeria should herself become an associated state, was at the time rejected by Accra.[1] The question, however, receded into the background when France vetoed British membership in January 1963. Nigeria subsequently opened trade negotiations with the EEC which led to a bilateral agreement in May 1966 providing for a form of associate membership of the EEC involving reciprocal tariff concessions. The agreement tends in the long run to increase the competitive position on the Nigerian market of EEC as compared with British exports, but was designed, on the Nigerian side, as far as possible to minimise this effect.[2]

On attaining independence, Nigeria, alone of the African colonies, concluded a formal military agreement with Britain. It provided for mutual defence, the detailing of British military personnel to staff, administer and train the Nigerian armed forces, the supply to

---

[1] Nigeria's policy on this question was set out at length in a speech by Balewa on September 24, 1962, reprinted in Mansergh. *op. cit.* pp. 660–667.
[2] For a summary of the agreement, see *Commonwealth Survey.* May 27, 1966.

Nigeria of British weapons and warships, and the grant of unrestricted overflying and air staging facilities to the Royal Air Force.[1]

A year later, in January 1962, the agreement was by common consent abrogated in circumstances very different from those surrounding Ghana's dismissal of its British military commanders at about the same time. The British and Nigerian Government declared in a joint statement that the agreement was being dissolved because it had been widely misinterpreted as impairing Nigeria's freedom of action. The statement went on to say that, despite the abrogation of the agreement, the two Governments would continue to afford each other facilities in defence matters.[2]

It would not be true to say that the Nigerian Government did not oppose certain aspects of British foreign policy in the third world. In common with practically the whole of the Commonwealth, it ranged itself against London during the Congo crisis of 1960–1962 and during the years of open appeasement of the Verwoerd régime in South Africa. On the other hand, during Balewa's reign, Nigeria, unlike Ghana, Tanzania and Zambia, served on the whole as a brake upon the anti-colonial, non-alignment movement in Africa and the third world generally. At the Commonwealth Prime Ministers' Conference in Lagos in January 1966, Balewa acted as lightning conductor for his British colleague, ensuring that some of the high charge of African indignation at Wilson's policy in Rhodesia ran harmlessly into the ground.

This period of what was from London's point of view in every sense highly profitable relations with Nigeria ended with a crash in 1966, when the Balewa régime was overthrown and has been followed by several years of intense and deepening difficulties for the policy-makers. The break-up of the Federation and the Nigerian-Biafran war have seriously endangered the interests of some of the most powerful business groups in Britain, particularly those of Shell and British Petroleum, and placed British diplomacy in the highly embarrassing position of having to manœuvre between the Ibo leaders in Biafra (where most of the oil is) and the Federal Government.

It is sometimes suggested on the left, quite wrongly in my opinion, that this upheaval in Nigeria was British-inspired. Its total effect was to break up the unity of the country, the argument runs, and it is, therefore, a typical example of the old colonial tactic of divide and rule. In fact, it seems to me, the opposite is true, namely that in

[1] Mansergh. *op. cit.* pp. 581–583.
[2] *Ibid.* p. 583.

making the independence constitution Whitehall used the new tactic of unite and rule and by doing so at first reaped a good harvest in the close co-operation received from a northern-weighted Federal Government, resting on socially the most backward forces in the country. It is now suffering severely from the boomerang effects of these same tactics in the shape of the disintegration of the Federation owing to its own internal contradictions, the consequent disruption of the economy and the political dilemma in which the British Government has been placed.

At the moment of writing the Government is trying to pick up the pieces by continuing to support the central authorities by arms supplies and other means, but at the same time attempting to work out some system of guarantees for the Ibos, securing them from further massacres organised from the north.

It is hard to foresee what is going to happen, but it seems unlikely in any case that Anglo-Nigerian relations will again be as exceptionally close as they once were, or that British influence will regain all the ground that it has lost.

CHAPTER SEVEN

South and South-East Asia

Half In, Half Out

There is, I think, an important distinction to be made between the politico-military and the politico-economic aspects of British policy in the arc of countries stretching from Pakistan in the west to Singapore in the east.

As a result of fairly recent decisions taken in London, the British military role within the area is likely to decline rapidly in the near future.

On the other hand, the stake of British industrial, financial and commercial interests remains very substantial. In India, Pakistan, Ceylon, Malaysia and Singapore, Britain's share of private capital investment is a great deal larger than that of any foreign power, including the United States. British firms have more capital invested in India or Malaysia than in any other single country of the third world, except the South African Republic. Britain still has a leading position in the foreign trade of all five states.

All five are members of the Commonwealth, the imperial preference system and the sterling area, and through these and other politico-economic links have on the whole maintained a closer relationship with Britain than any of the other Western powers, a relationship which London continues to do its best to maintain.

The two aspects are inter-connected. In particular, the decision to withdraw from the bases in Malaysia and Singapore undermines the peculiar father-son relationship between London and these two states. But it does not follow that British political and economic influence there will shortly be eliminated, and still less that British influence in the Indian sub-continent, in which the military factor plays a relatively small part, will be directly and adversely affected.

There is, moreover, a further distinction to be made between Britain's nuclear and non-nuclear role.

British nuclear strategy in the face of the acquisition by China of a nuclear capacity is discussed in detail in Part III of this book. But here, too, it must be borne in mind that so far as Anglo-Indian relations in particular are concerned, what is most important is not whether Britain retains conventional forces on the Asian mainland, but whether she retains part of her nuclear striking force in the Indian and Pacific Oceans, a question which does not necessarily depend on the fate of the South-East Asian bases.

One should not, therefore, jump to the conclusion that, because a major diminution in Britain's military role is taking place, Britain, by analogy with France after her withdrawal from Indo-China, will soon cease to play more than a marginal part in the affairs of South and South-East Asia. Owing principally to the strength of her economic and political links, it seems more likely that she will remain half in and half out for several years to come.

For all that, there has been a change of emphasis in military policy, which is of central significance in considering British policy in this part of the world.

Up to 1966–1967 the Government and its advisers, like their predecessors, were intending to hold the South-East Asian bases indefinitely.

The residual military privileges in the Indian sub-continent obtained during the independence negotiations at the end of the forties were soon annulled, in 1954 in the case of Burma and in 1957 in the case of Ceylon, when the major naval base at Trincomalee was abandoned. But the great complex of bases and garrisons in Singapore and Malaya remained.

The importance attached by the strategists in London to the benefits supposedly derived from this nowadays unique *place d'armes* can be seen from the extraordinarily large share of Britain's total military resources absorbed by it up to only two or three years ago.

According to the Defence Estimates for 1966–1967, the break-down of overseas military expenditure by geographical area was as follows:

Far East (excluding Hong Kong)	£235,000,000
West Germany and Berlin	103,000,000
Mediterranean	67,000,000
Middle East	66,000,000

A break-down of the distribution of service personnel gave a similar picture, the figure for the Far and Middle East being 80,900; for Western Europe — 64,800; and for the Mediterranean and Near East — 22,200.[1]

[1] *Defence Estimates 1966–67.* Command 2902. 1966.

In the mid-sixties it was very much in the minds of the present Prime Minister and the present Minister of Defence to maintain something like an even balance between Asia and Europe in the disposition of Britain's military strength. In June 1964, shortly before coming to power, Wilson said that "the peace-keeping role, which will, over the next generation, be the main contribution of this country to world affairs . . . will mean a very big role for this country East of Suez" and that "at the margin, 1,000 troops deployed East of Suez is a bigger contribution to peace than 1,000 in Germany". [1]

Healey's 1966 Defence Review did not go as far as this, but it did say that "it is in the Far East and Southern Asia that the greatest danger to peace may lie in the next decade, and some of our partners in the Commonwealth may be directly threatened. We believe it is right that Britain should continue to maintain a military presence in the area". It also said that the Government intended to retain its important military facilities in Malaysia and Singapore for as long as the Governments of the two states agreed. [2]

There was a great deal more to the East of Suez doctrine, first formulated by Wilson as above, than the future of the South-East Asian bases. It contained within it as it developed the idea of British participation in a nuclear counter-force directed against China, a question discussed elsewhere. In its original version it also provided for the maintenance of permanent bases in Aden and the Persian Gulf, an aspect which we have already discussed. It was, nevertheless, part and parcel of the doctrine that land, air and naval forces should remain in Singapore and Malaysia and that the whole network of bases there should be held in order to serve them.

It was possible to glimpse the shape of things to come in 1966, when the Government, besides reaffirming its intention to keep the bases, also said that, against the day when it might no longer be possible to use them freely, it had begun to discuss with the Government of Australia the possibility of alternative facilities there, if necessary. But the real turning point came in 1967, when in two jumps in quick succession the policy-makers reversed their position. [3]

A Defence White Paper issued in July 1967, concluding the overall review of defence policy started by the Labour Government when it came to power in 1964, made the first jump.

The intention was here announced of withdrawing altogether from the Singapore and Malaysia bases "in the middle 1970s", the

[1] *Hansard.* June 17, 1964. Cols. 1396–1412.
[2] *The Defence Review.* Command 2901. 1966.
[3] *Ibid.*

precise timing being made conditional "on progress made in achieving a new basis for stability in South-East Asia and in resolving other problems in the Far East". Meanwhile, the armed forces stationed there and the civilian personnel, then together numbering some 80,000, would be reduced to about 40,000 by 1970–1971.[1]

The second jump came as a direct result of the devaluation crisis in November of the same year. As the first item in the Government's programme of cuts in public expenditure, the Prime Minister announced the acceleration of the withdrawal from the Malaysian and Singapore bases, which would now unconditionally be completed by the end of 1971. The two Governments concerned had been informed, he said, that Britain did not intend to retain a special military capability for use in the area after that date.[2]

This decision is unlikely, in my opinion, to be reversed, though the time-table might be made more elastic. It is true that withdrawal has been opposed by the Conservative leadership. As soon as it was decided, Heath denounced it as premature and said that Britain should maintain a military presence in Malaysia and Singapore "so long as our friends want us to remain there".[3] Since then he has several times promised that, if his Party is returned to power, British forces will stay for an indefinite period. But abandonment of the bases enjoys not only the support of almost all shades of opinion in the Labour Party, but of the out-and-out Europeans among the Conservatives, who in their turn include representatives of the extreme right. As long ago as 1965, Enoch Powell, speaking at the Conservative Party Annual Conference, urged that priority be given to military strength in Europe and cast doubt on the whole conception of an East of Suez strategy, a view to which he has subsequently adhered.

The effect of this decision also has to be looked at in the context of British policy towards SEATO, the main Western military alliance in the area.

From London's point of view this organisation has had one, and it can almost be said only one, attractive feature, namely that it has provided an extra link between Britain and her main military allies in the Pacific area, the United States, Australia and New Zealand. But in other respects it has not at all suited the needs of British diplomacy.

When SEATO was in the process of formation, the Government publicly expressed the view that "there will never be any real

---

[1] *Supplementary Statement on Defence Policy.* Command 3357. July 1967.
[2] Statement in the House of Commons on January 16, 1968. Command 3515, 1968.
[3] *Hansard.* March 5, 1968. Col. 257.

security in South-East Asia without the good-will of the free Asian countries" and that if a permanent South-East Asia defence organisation came into existence "it will not be fully effective without the understanding and support of the Colombo Powers", i.e., India, Pakistan, Ceylon, Burma and Indonesia.[1] This requirement, which with time made itself more and more acutely felt, has never been fulfilled.

From its inception SEATO was regarded with suspicion and even hostility by all except one of the Asian states of the area with which Britain is primarily concerned. Neither India, Ceylon and Burma nor Malaysia and Singapore became members and none of them has shown any serious signs of changing its attitude. Moreover, the only Asian member of the Commonwealth which is a member of SEATO, Pakistan, has become a dissident voice within it. At the SEATO Council meeting in 1965, Pakistan dissociated herself from the Council's views on Vietnam and the Indonesian-Malaysian dispute, and in 1966 again dissented over Vietnam.

Every year at the Council meeting the Foreign Secretary has sworn allegiance to SEATO and sung its praises. It seems likely, however, that for some years the real attitude of the Government has been closer to that expressed by Christopher Mayhew, when, following his resignation in 1966, he acquired freedom to speak openly on such matters. "SEATO has been an almost total failure," he writes. "It was the child—a sickly child—of Mr Foster Dulles's passion for anti-Communist pacts . . . It was far too white and far too Western . . . The Organisation has never yet acted collectively on any military question. It is safe to forecast that it never will."[2]

In the new situation, the Government has stated that it will remain a member of SEATO, as one way of demonstrating its interest in the stability of the Far East. But it at the same time said that forces ear-marked for use by the organisation will be reduced as British forces are withdrawn from Singapore and Malaysia,[3] which presumably means that by the end of 1971 no British forces will be so ear-marked.

From this it can be concluded that the significance attached in London to SEATO is now approaching zero. It should also be noted that its liquidation is an essential feature of the British plans for a reorganisation of the anti-Communist alliances in the Pacific and Indian Oceans discussed in Part III.

---

[1] *Hansard.* June 23, 1954. Col. 432.
[2] Mayhew. *op. cit.* pp. 29–30.
[3] *Statement on the Defence Estimates 1968.* February 1968.

"Our Frontiers are on the Himalayas"

It is perhaps unfair to pick out this Wilsonian flight into hyperbole, since the statement is on the face of it absurd. While British troops did once stand on the Himalayan passes, with the present world balance of power Britain is no more able to defend India's frontiers, except as an auxiliary of the United States, than Portugal can defend the frontiers of Brazil.

But in its context, which was political and economic, and not military,[1] I think this catchpenny phrase more nearly expresses the established attitude in high quarters to India than appears at first sight. The full text said that the future of Asia today, and more than the future of Asia, depended on the result of the competitive struggle between the democratic way, exemplified by India, and the Communist way; that the modern Commonwealth derives directly from India's decision to become a member of it; and that for reasons not only of idealism, but also self-interest, "our frontiers are on the Himalayas and in the standard of living of the people of India".

Over the twenty years since India became independent, this point of view has been dominant in the policy towards her of successive governments, from Attlee's and Churchill's to Macmillan's and Wilson's. All, despite moments of considerable strain, have endeavoured to keep a London–New Delhi special relationship in being, all have regarded India as the corner-stone of the modern Commonwealth and all have hoped, so far in vain, that eventually a South and South-East Asian security system will take shape, guaranteed by Britain and the United States, but pivoted on India, potentially by far the strongest of the non-Communist powers in the area.

In the period we are considering, the general tendency has been for the economic underpinning of British influence in India to grow weaker, but at the same time there has been a certain political rapprochement between London and New Delhi.

The role of British private capital in India remains very considerable. At the beginning of the sixties, the British share of all private foreign investment was almost 80% and was estimated at about £300,000,000, more than double the figure of 1948. Britain also retains a large share of India's foreign trade, in 1965 taking 19% of her exports and providing 12% of her imports. But the picture is entirely different when it comes to governmental financial aid for India's economic development.

---

[1] Speech on June 10, 1965, inaugurating the Nehru Memorial Exhibition in London. *Commonwealth Survey.* July 6, 1965.

It is not that official, financial and policy-making circles generally attach little importance to this question. This can be seen from Wilson's statement above and many others of the same kind. If one turns to one of the chief British studies of India's problems, one finds that its central thesis is the necessity of a full-scale Marshall Plan for India to save her, Asia and, indeed, the whole world, from socialism.[1]

The fact is that over the last decade the Indian Government's need for foreign financial aid has grown more and more acute, while the weakening of Britain's position in the world economy as a whole and her own chronic balance of payments difficulties have severely limited her capacity to meet it.

During the years immediately following independence, India relied heavily on her large sterling balance accumulated in London during the Second World War. When this reserve was used up and the British Government had refused requests for large long-term loans, she turned elsewhere for help. The Soviet Union provided large credits on easy terms for industrial projects. In the consortium of Western powers formed to co-ordinate foreign loans to India far and away the biggest role is played by the United States Government and by the International Bank for Reconstruction and Development (IBRD) and the International Development Association (IDA), of both of which the United States is the leading member.

As can be seen from the following table, the British contribution in the first half of the sixties was less even than that of West Germany

Table 10[2]

| | (Million dollars) | | | | | |
	1961–2	1962–3	1963–4	1964–5	1965–6	Total
United States	545	435	435	435	435	2285
IBRD and IDA	250	200	245	245	245	1185
West Germany	225	139	99·5	95	86	644·5
Britain	182	84	84	84	84	518
Japan	50	55	65	60	60	290
Canada	28	33	30·5	41	41	173·5
France	15	45	20	20	20	120

NOTE : *Smaller contributions by Italy, the Netherlands, Belgium and Austria are not shown.*

[1] Barbara Ward. *op. cit.* See in particular pp. 11–12, 197, 205–206, 213–214, 218–219.
[2] *Commonwealth Survey.* May 11, 1965.

On the political front, in the fifties and early sixties the factor which most disturbed Anglo-Indian relations was the wide gap between the positions of London and New Delhi on two key questions, that of colonialism and racialism in the third world and that of the arms race, military blocs and East-West relations generally. Though for different reasons, the gap has in both areas tended to grow narrower in the most recent period.

The acuteness of the conflict on colonial matters can best be illustrated by the events of 1961, when Anglo-Indian relations reached their lowest ebb in the years since independence.

As recalled elsewhere, at this period London was giving active support to Tshombe's foreign mercenaries and gendarmes in Katanga in direct opposition both to the Congolese Central Government and to the United Nations. India, on the other hand, not only supported the line laid down by the United Nations, but provided the bulk of the latter's military force in the Congo. In practice, this meant that when in September 1961 London deliberately delayed the arrival of fighter aircraft for the United Nations force and refused to supply the latter with bombs, it was sabotaging the military operations of a large body of Indian troops.

The Indian reaction, not surprisingly, was sharp; the more so that, by way of a smoke-screen, reports were put out by the BBC and the British Press that Indian troops were behaving with brutality in the Congo. Nehru declared at a Press conference that the British Government's attitude to UN activity in the Congo had affinities with that of the Verwoerd and Welensky régimes in South Africa and Rhodesia and showed how deep the roots of British colonialism were.[1] The Indian Defence Minister said that India's armed forces would never forget the disgraceful accusations made against them in Britain.

Fuel was added to the flames by the markedly hostile reaction of the British Government when, in December 1961, India put an end to Portuguese rule in Goa and other enclaves on Indian territory. India's action was at once denounced by the Government (and the Leader of the Opposition, Gaitskell) in the House of Commons. In the Security Council, Britain voted in favour of a resolution, blocked by a Soviet veto, condemning India. India's anti-colonialism in general and her behaviour over Goa were attacked with unconcealed venom in a major public speech by the Foreign Secretary.[2] On the same day Nehru bitterly remarked at a Press conference that "it is

[1] *The Times.* September 18, 1961.
[2] Home's above-quoted speech at Berwick-on-Tweed on December 28, 1961.

only when India goes to Goa they say we are hitting at the United Nations. When the UN is in the open field challenged and obstructed in its work in the Congo, in Katanga, when all this is done, this is fair play".[1]

In the years since this major collision, there has been no quarrel over colonial questions of comparable intensity, the underlying reason being the rapid dissolution of the colonial empires, including the British. As, with some exaggeration, the Zinkins put it in their study of Anglo-Indian relations "the occasions on which India, as the leader of the anti-colonial bloc, and Britain, as the leader of the colonial powers, are likely to confront each other have therefore now become negligible".[2]

This formula goes too far, since there are still some essentially colonial, racial questions, such as policy towards Rhodesia, South African apartheid and Commonwealth immigration into Britain towards which the British and Indian approach is different, and others may still arise. But it is certainly true that as the colonial system has disintegrated what has been one of the main causes of Anglo-Indian friction has faded with it.

As regards the problem of relations between the capitalist and socialist worlds, of military blocs and of the arms race, relations between London and New Delhi have undergone a similar evolution, the turning point coming with the Chinese attack on India in 1962.

Up to the beginning of the sixties, the positions of the two powers were opposed.

India, in pursuit of her policy of non-alignment, refused to join any military alliances, while Britain became a member of all the main Western blocs. India was a persistent opponent of the nuclear arms race, while London supported and participated in the building up of the Western nuclear force. India was an early advocate of the principle of peaceful co-existence when Britain was still heavily engaged in the cold war.

Conflict between the two Governments over these issues was, it is true, never as severe as that between New Delhi and Washington. In the first half of the fifties, Britain, unlike the United States, followed India in recognising the Chinese People's Republic. The Indian and British Governments, though in different degrees, were both concerned to limit the scope of the Korean War and to prevent a major conflagration in Indo-China. The United States and not Britain was

[1] *Documents* . . . 1961. p. 725.
[2] *Op. cit.* p. 171.

the mainspring of SEATO, a particular target of Indian criticism.[1]

Moreover, London had its own long-term reasons for trying to avoid a head-on collision with India. The point is well put by Northedge. "To attempt to bully India into a pro-Western alignment," he points out, "would have been to invite serious consequences for the Commonwealth. It would have defeated Mr Nehru's efforts . . . to show that Commonwealth membership left India entirely free to pursue her own foreign policy without being forced into an unwelcome military alliance. It would have discouraged those British colonies which were soon to attain their independence from following India's example and remaining in the Commonwealth."[2]

Nevertheless, when the Indian Government denounced military pacts, NATO as well as SEATO, and warned that in the nuclear age war spelled destruction for both the attacker and the attacked and put forward the principles of peaceful co-existence (Panch Shila, as "a challenge of Asia to the rest of the world",[3] it was challenging British as well as American foreign policy.

More recently Anglo-Indian differences in this field have tended to diminish. In the first place, British policy has advanced a considerable way towards the positions already occupied by the Indian leaders in the fifties. This applies particularly to the Indian theses on the suicidal character of nuclear war, and on the futility and danger of the cold war. Secondly a major change has come over India's attitude towards part of the socialist world. Her relations with the Soviet Union and the other European socialist states have continued to develop normally and, indeed, become closer. But there has been a drastic deterioration in her relations with China — China with whom the principles of Panch Shila were originally jointly worked out and announced to the world.

Following the Indian-Chinese armed clash of 1962, the Indian Government has been forced to give a high priority to the defence of her northern and north-eastern frontiers. With the acquisition by China of nuclear weapons, the question has arisen of possible Indian counter-measures in this field also. These developments have brought with them a change in the Indian attitude towards closer military co-operation with Britain and the United States.

An Indian appeal for urgent military assistance against China was considered by Macmillan and Kennedy at the Nassau Conference in December 1962, when they had before them the reports of the high-

---

[1] See for example Nehru's speech in the Indian Parliament of September 29, 1954. Mansergh. *op. cit.* pp. 461–466.

[2] Northedge. *op. cit.* p. 188.

[3] Speech by Nehru in the Indian Parliament. March 31, 1955. Mansergh. *op. cit.*, p. 468.

level British and American missions despatched to New Delhi in November immediately on receipt of the Indian request.[1] It was then decided that Britain (with other members of the Commonwealth) and the United States would provide emergency military aid to the value of some £20,000,000 each.[2] In January a joint Anglo-American air defence mission (in which Canada and Australia were also represented) visited India, which led to the provision of radar and other equipment for India's frontier defences and an agreement that British and U.S. fighter squadrons would from time to time be based in India for joint training exercises with the Indian Air Force. The first of these exercises, "Exercise Shiksa", took place in November, 1963.[3]

In the wider strategic field, the situation has remained more fluid. But, as shown in Part III of this book, the question of nuclear protection for India, and the possibility of some form of Indian participation in a reorganised system of alliances, now figure openly in British plans, something that would have been hard to imagine ten years ago.

The long-term perspective depends on a number of variable quantities, not least political developments within India and future Chinese policy towards India. Moreover, Britain's capacity to play a substantial role in India's defences is strictly limited. The Indian Armed Forces are already to a large extent equipped with aircraft, missiles, radar, tanks, etc., from countries other than Britain, chief among them the United States, the Soviet Union and France.[4] Even if Britain does retain a nuclear force in the Indian and Pacific Oceans, it can never have more than marginal significance compared with those of the United States and the Soviet Union.

It seems likely, nevertheless, that the present closer politico-military relationship between Britain and India will continue in being for some time to come.

Pakistan

The British role in the economy of Pakistan is much the same as in the case of India, i.e., it is very considerable in the private sector, but

[1] The British mission was headed by Duncan Sandys, Commonwealth Secretary, and General Hull, Chief of the Imperial General Staff, and the American by Averell Harriman and General Adams, Chief of the U.S. Strike Command.

[2] *Commonwealth Survey.* April 9, 1963. pp. 353–354.

[3] *Ibid.* March 31, 1964. p. 357.

[4] For details, see *The Military Balance 1968–1969.* Institute of Strategic Studies. London. 1968. pp. 47–48.

relatively minor when it comes to government loans, credits and grants.

British private investment at the beginning of the sixties was estimated at £60,000,000 (and has continued to grow since then). This was 52% of all foreign private investment, compared with 15% for U.S. firms. The British lead in foreign trade is not so large. In 1965 Britain took 14% of Pakistan's exports and provided 15% of her imports. The first figure is higher than that for the United States, but the second is a good deal lower.

As regards governmental financial aid, the following table shows that, so far as the Western consortium is concerned, the contribution of the United States leaves all others far behind and that Britain's share is less than that of both West Germany and Japan.

Table 11[1]

	(Million dollars)					
	1960–1	1961–2	1962–3	1963–4	1964–5	Total
United States	129·6	150	350	212·5	212·5	1054·6
IBRD and IDA	—	77·4	132	80	80	369·4
West Germany	37·5	25	55	40	38·1	195·6
Japan	20	20	25	30	30	125
Britain	22·4	19·6	28	22·4	22·4	114·8
France	—	10	15	10	10	45

NOTE: *Smaller contributions by Italy, the Netherlands and Belgium are not shown.*

As regards political relations, in the fifties the Government of Pakistan, not least in the hope of strengthening its hand in its conflict with India over Kashmir and other questions, pursued a strongly pro-Western foreign policy. Alone of the Asian members of the Commonwealth, Pakistan became a member of SEATO and the Baghdad Pact (CENTO). In 1954 she concluded a bilateral military agreement with the United States, providing for the supply of U.S. arms in return for promises by Karachi to contribute to "the defensive strength of the free world", "to control trade with nations which threaten the maintenance of world peace" and other cold war commitments generally then demanded by Washington of its client states.[2]

The course adopted by Pakistan's leaders, besides leading to a

[1] *Commonwealth Survey.* November 24, 1964. p. 1160.
[2] Mutual Defence Assistance Agreement of May 19, 1954. Mansergh. *op. cit.* pp. 440–443.

large increase in U.S. influence in the military field, ensured a considerable measure of harmony with London. The questions which particularly disturbed Anglo-Indian relations — colonialism, the nuclear arms race and the cold war generally — caused scarcely a ripple in Anglo-Pakistan relations. For its part, the British Government leant over backwards to avoid giving the impression of sympathy for the Indian case in Indian-Pakistani disputes.

In the sixties this situation changed. Closer military co-operation between India and Britain and the United States resulting from the Indian-Chinese border conflict caused a revulsion in Karachi against the Anglo-Saxon powers and in favour of improving relations with the Soviet Union and China.[1]

In an angry speech in November 1962 the Pakistani Minister for Foreign Affairs said that Pakistan had lodged strong protests with her allies who were supplying arms to India, which he described as "an act of gross unfriendliness towards Pakistan". He particularly deplored that a fellow member of the Commonwealth, of SEATO and CENTO, namely the United Kingdom, should by its actions increase the threat to the security of his country and commit "an act hostile to Pakistan". He went on to warn that his Government might find it necessary to withdraw from SEATO and CENTO.[2]

British dipomacy, of course, attempted to soothe Pakistani anxieties. Written assurances were obtained from the Indian Government, and announced to the world, that arms supplied for use against China would not be used against Pakistan. The Minister of Defence, Sandys, went so far as to declare publicly that he had, in effect, tried to use India's need for arms to force her to come to terms with Pakistan. When he and Harriman were in New Delhi, he said, they had promised emergency help, but had pointed out to Nehru that "when we came to consider longer-term military aid, the British and American peoples would be unhappy to see that an appreciable part of the Indian Army was being deployed not for defence against China but for defence against Pakistan". It was to be hoped, therefore, that a new attempt would be made by India to settle her differences with Pakistan.[3] These manœuvres had, however, little effect in Pakistan (or in India).

It would be wrong to suggest that the events of 1962–1963 brought

---

[1] In the course of 1963 Pakistan signed agreements with China concerning frontier disputes (covering the northern frontier of Kashmir), the development of trade, and the opening of air services between the two countries.

[2] Speech in the National Assembly on November 22, 1962. Mansergh. *op. cit.* pp. 622–624.

[3] *Hansard.* December 3, 1962. Col. 935.

about a permanent breach in Anglo-Pakistani relations. Nonetheless, since then Pakistan's foreign policy has not been anything like as tightly tied to that of London and Washington as it once was.

This has shown itself in various ways, not least, as recalled above, in Pakistan's refusal since 1965 to be associated with SEATO's support of the U.S. invasion of Vietnam. But perhaps the clearest evidence of the decline of British (and American) political influence in Pakistan is provided by the denouement of the major military conflict between Pakistan and India in the winter of 1965. In the critical situation in which it then found itself, the Pakistani Government, instead of trusting as usual to the mediation of its Anglo-Saxon allies, accepted the suggestion of the Soviet Government that the Pakistani and Indian leaders should meet on Soviet soil to discuss a settlement. As a result of negotiations conducted under the auspices of Soviet Prime Minister Kosygin, the conflict was ended by the Indian-Pakistani Tashkent Declaration of January 10, 1966.

Transition in Malaysia and Singapore

British policy towards these two states is now undergoing a major change. Until 1966–1967 its central aim was to ensure indefinite possession of the network of permanently garrisoned bases. It is now being readjusted to ensure the maximum degree of influence in the situation which will arise in 1971, when, according to present plans, the bases will have been given up and the garrisons withdrawn.

The problems now facing British diplomacy are likely to prove by no means easy. As the following account shows, the present unique structure of British-Malaysian-Singapore relations has required manœuvres of Byzantine complexity and massive military expenditure to build and, even more, to shore up against imminent collapse. When the main prop, the British garrisons, is withdrawn, the resulting changes in the balance of internal and external forces are almost bound to cause far-reaching, and at present unpredictable, political changes.

The present rulers of Malaysia were placed in power by British bayonets in order to outflank the Communist-led independence movement, which in the late forties and early fifties was the most powerful political force in the country. In recent years, particularly after the end of hostilities with Indonesia in 1965, the Government has shown an increasing tendency to ignore London's wishes. All the same, its continued existence has remained very much dependent on a close understanding with its British patrons. The social basis of the Kuala Lumpur Government—the Malay feudal landowners and a small Malayan, Chinese and Indian business upper crust—is very narrow. Moreover, owing to its systematic discrimination against the main mass of Malaysians of Chinese extraction, who make up over 40% of the population of Malaya, it is sitting on a volcano so far as racial conflicts are concerned.

In Singapore the position is different, since power is in the hands of a political party, somewhat similar in its composition and outlook to the British Labour Party, which, besides enjoying the support of the business community, also has a considerable following among the mass of the population. Moreover, since the population of the island is overwhelmingly of Chinese origin, the ethnic problem is not as acute here as it is in Malaya. It is a fact, nonetheless, that the People's Action Party owes its predominance to nearly twenty years of un-remitting effort by the colonial authorities since the war to destroy the powerful Communist movement in Singapore, and that the balance of political forces in the island is to this day affected by the presence of the British bases.

The extent to which the economies of Malaysia and Singapore are still dominated by British business interests is greater than in any other sovereign state in Asia.

According to official statistics, in 1964 the earnings of British companies here were £22,400,000, which is only slightly less than the equivalent figure for the whole of Western Europe (£23,500,000) and larger than that for India (£21,500,000).[1]

Most of these earnings came from the rubber and tin industries, more than half of which are in the hands of British firms, among them the London Tin Corporation, Harrison and Crosfield, Guthrie and Dunlop. When one considers that, apart from agriculture, these two industries provide the means by which the people of Malaysia chiefly live[2] and that British capital occupies a similar position in banking, insurance, shipping and the oil industry, it is no exaggera-tion to say that the keys to the economies of the two states have so far remained in British keeping.

Britain also still has a considerable share of the foreign trade of Malaysia and Singapore, though it is diminishing. In 1964 it was 16·6%, compared with 12·1% for Japan and about 6% for the United States and Australia.

The scale of the military establishments maintained and the

---

[1] *Board of Trade Journal*. June 10, 1966. The figures exclude oil companies.
[2] In 1965 rubber plantations occupied 60% of the total cultivated area, and the rubber industry accounted for one-third of budget revenue and 45% of the value of all exports.

military rights enjoyed by the British Government have also been without parallel in Asia, and indeed anywhere in the former colonial empire.

Singapore has been the site of three military airfields, at which part of the nuclear striking force was based, of a naval base and dockyard capable of serving the largest warships, of an army base with supplies for 60,000 men, and of GHQ, Far East. In West Malaysia (Malaya), the Commonwealth Strategic Reserve has been quartered near Malacca at a new base opened in 1960 and built at the joint expense of the British, Australian and New Zealand Governments. There has been a major air base at Butterworth in the north-west, used mainly by the Australian air force, and a British jungle-training school in the south. In the mid-sixties the number of British service personnel serving in Singapore and Malaysia was between 40,000 and 50,000 (about the same number as were stationed in West Germany).

The presence of this very considerable military machine was provided for under the Anglo-Malayan Defence Agreement of 1957, with which the Australian and New Zealand Governments were associated and which was extended to cover Singapore, Sarawak and North Borneo in 1963, when Malaysia was established.

This agreement, much like the Anglo-Egyptian and Anglo-Iraqi treaties of the thirties, granted the British Government the right to maintain "naval, land and air forces including a Commonwealth Strategic Reserve" on Malaysian territory and to "have, maintain and use bases and facilities" there.[1]

The treaty placed a certain limitation on the uses to which British bases might be put. The effect of Articles VII and VIII was that, if it was desired to use them for purposes other than the defence of Malaysia and British possessions in the Far East, this could only be done with the prior agreement of the Malaysian Government. This meant that they could not automatically be used as SEATO bases. The restriction was, however, more apparent than real, since it did not apply to the bases where London particularly required fuller freedom of action, namely those in Singapore.

This was made clear in the 1963 agreement between Britain, Malaya, Singapore, Sarawak and Sabah establishing Malaysia. The Government of Malaysia, it said, will allow the British Government to use bases in Singapore in such manner as the latter might consider necessary to defend Malaysia and the Commonwealth and "to preserve peace in South-East Asia".[2] When Singapore ceased

[1] Mansergh. *op. cit.* pp. 571–573.
[2] *Commonwealth Survey.* July 30, 1963.

to be part of Malaysia in 1965, the Governments of both states announced that they continued to recognise Britain's extended military rights in Singapore as thus defined.[1]

Although the political, economic and military levers in London's hands have thus been exceptionally powerful, the relationship between Britain and Malaysia and Singapore has been far from stable. The edifice so carefully built, rebuilt and built on to by successive Conservative and Labour Governments has remained standing, but only just.

In the early post-war years, when the mass movement to end British colonial rule was at its height, Singapore, owing to its military importance and because it was the main centre of the independence movement, was torn from its Malayan hinterland and, regardless of the attainment of sovereignty by Malaya in 1957, was ruled as a separate colony until 1963.

This tactic had the full support of the Malay oligarchy in Kuala Lumpur, which feared that union with Singapore would carry a threat not only to the archaic social and political structure of Malaya, but to the system of discrimination against Malayans of Chinese origin embodied both in the Malayan franchise laws introduced by the colonial authorities before independence and in the 1957 constitution with which the latter endowed the new state.[2]

This on the whole successful manœuvre had a built-in hazard, which soon made itself felt. By separating off Singapore, the tacticians in London had eased the path of Tunku Abdul Rahman[3] and his friends on the mainland, but they had also left themselves face to face with a militant independence movement, with strong Communist tendencies, on the island, threatening tenure of the bases.

In order to avert a head-on clash, the Macmillan Government in 1959 brought into existence the pseudo-state of Singapore. The franchise was widened, the powers of elected ministers were increased, a local "head of state" was appointed, but defence and foreign affairs remained in the hands of the British High Commissioner. Moreover, internal security, i.e., control over Communists and left-wing Socialists, was placed in the hands of a special council on which the British and Singapore Governments were represented by three representatives each and the Malayan Government by one.

[1] *Ibid.* August 31, 1965.

[2] The terms of reference of the Reid Commission which drew up the constitution specifically laid down that the latter must safeguard "the position and prestige of Their Highnesses as constitutional rulers of their respective states" and "the special position of the Malays". Mansergh. *op. cit.* p. 189.

[3] The Tunku, the leading figure in the Malayan and Malaysian Governments, is a British-educated son of the Sultan of Kedah.

The mainland régime was thus brought in by the back-door to help keep the island's political development on a safe course. As one of the leading experts on these matters put it, Kuala Lumpur thus obtained the casting vote and "access to all information relating to internal security in Singapore".[1]

However, pressure for the end of colonial rule in any form continued to mount in Singapore, particularly after the formation in 1961 of the Socialist Front, standing to the left of the People's Action Party (PAP), led by Lee Kuan Yew, which formed (and still forms) the Government. This produced a volte-face in London's tactics on the question of relations between Singapore and Malaya.

Other factors played their part, but in the new circumstances the basic idea was to outflank the left in Singapore by granting her independence within in a new Malaysian Federation dominated by the Tunku's régime in Kuala Lumpur. Since colonial rule would be ended, the wind would be taken out of the sails of the Socialist Front, and the position of Lee Kuan Yew and the PAP strengthened. At the same time, through the Federal machinery, Kuala Lumpur would, if necessary, now be able to intervene in Singapore through the front-door and not the back-door.

The case for this change of front was clearly put by, among others, the late John Strachey, an expert on the question, since as Labour Secretary of State for War in the Attlee Government he had earlier been directly concerned with suppressing the Malayan partisans. "Democratic government in the city-state of Singapore is tending to become impossible . . . the present Government, founded on the PAP . . . is facing increasing difficulties," he wrote after a visit there in 1961. "Public men in Singapore will have to declare themselves in favour of some such federal scheme or accept the leadership of the Chinese Government and its powerful agency in Singapore, the illegal, but formidable Communist Party." "Unless this wide federation . . . can be realised", he went on, "Britain may well be faced with the necessity of either reverting to direct colonial rule [i.e., abolish the 1959 reforms—D.M.] or evacuating the Singapore base."[2]

The policy-makers also saw an opportunity of solving their problems in the three British territories of Sarawak, Brunei, and Sabah (North Borneo), which formed an awkward colonial enclave on the northern coast of the Indonesian island of Kalimantan (Borneo). In all three the movement to get rid of colonial rule was getting stronger

[1] Saul Rose. *op. cit.* p. 141.
[2] *New Statesman.* August 18, 1961.

and at the same time both the Indonesian and Philippine Governments were showing an uncomfortably close interest in their future.

The inclusion of these territories in the new Malaysian Federation meant that, while British colonial rule would end, they would in practice be subordinated to London's friends in Kuala Lumpur and also be brought within the scope of the Anglo-Malayan Defence Agreement of 1957, i.e., British troops could remain there as long as the British Government wished.

From the point of view of the Malayan Government, the creation of Malaysia had two main advantages. First, by weakening the left in Singapore, it would stave off the main long-term threat to the position of the Malay oligarchy. Secondly, the inclusion of Sarawak, Brunei and Sabah appealed to the empire-building proclivities of the Tunku and his supporters and also tipped the ethnic balance in the new Federation against the Chinese community.

On the other hand, reunion with Singapore, even though power there were firmly in anti-Communist hands, carried with it a risk that in time Singapore business interests and, even more important, the PAP, with its slogan of equal rights for the Chinese community and a relatively more advanced political and social programme generally, would extend their influence into Malaya itself and upset the status quo. It was for this reason that Malaysia as originally conceived by the Tunku was at first to be confined to Malaya, Sarawak, Sabah and Brunei.

There was thus from the beginning an underlying conflict of interest between London and Kuala Lumpur regarding Malaysia, the former, with its eye chiefly on the future of its main base in the Far East, requiring the inclusion of Singapore, while the latter, concerned chiefly with preserving its own power, regarded the proposed marriage with misgiving. On the other hand, the points of view of the British and Singapore Governments on this question in the main coincided.

Under strong British pressure and after tortuous negotiations involving not only the three principal dramatis personae, but also the Indonesian and Philippine Governments and the United Nations, Malaysia was brought into being in September 1963.[1] Its life as a form of union between Malaya and Singapore was, however, to prove a short one.

The immediate result of the creation of Malaysia was to precipitate a crisis in the relations between Indonesia on one side, and Britain

---

[1] The Sultan of Brunei, desiring to keep undivided **control of his large oil revenues** from Shell, decided in the end to stay out.

and the new state on the other. The Sukarno Government, until its break-up in September 1965, imposed an economic boycott of the whole of Malaysia, and sequestrated the very substantial property of British oil, rubber, tea, banking, insurance and other companies in Indonesia,[1] and despatched military detachments into Sabah, Sarawak and, on a smaller scale, Malaya.

Sukarno's policy of "confrontation", since it threatened the interests of all three of Malaysia's founding fathers—the British, Malayan and Singapore Governments—temporarily muffled conflicts between them. These conflicts, however, proved to be so sharp that Malaysia disintegrated before even the end of "confrontation" was in sight.

In August 1965, suddenly and without warning to London, the Malaysian Government, still entirely in the hands of the Malay oligarchy and its allies, expelled Singapore from the Federation. This event arose from a whole complex of political, economic and financial disputes, all reflecting in one way or another the struggle for power between Kuala Lumpur and Singapore and the different class forces and ethnic communities on which they are based.

Abdul Rahman himself appears to have had his hand forced by the extremist wing of his own party.[2] This at any rate is the most likely explanation of the confidential letter which he wrote at the time to the Singapore Government and which the latter, for its own purposes, published. "If I were strong enough and able to exercise complete control," he wrote, "I might perhaps have delayed action, but I am not and so I think this is the only possible way out."[3]

Since the rift, the Singapore Government, in its somewhat isolated position, has kept close to its British ally, but London's relations with the Malaysian Government have deteriorated.

Despite British efforts to prevent this, in the course of 1965–1966, owing to the intransigence of Kuala Lumpur, the Malaysian-Singapore split widened still further. The joint Central Bank, the common currency and the Joint Defence Board went out of existence and plans for a common-market were shelved.

The Malaysian Government began actively seeking supplementary financial and military support from the United States, France, Japan, the International Bank for Reconstruction and Development and elsewhere. In November 1965 the IBRD announced that it was making a loan of 45 million dollars to Malaysia.

[1] Officially valued in 1963 at £160,000,000.
[2] The United Malays' National Organisation, of which the extremist wing was led by the secretary-general, Dato Syed Jaafar Albur.
[3] Published in the *Financial Times* and the Press generally on August 11, 1965.

When in May 1966 the Wilson Government, then in the throes of a financial crisis, refused a Malaysian demand for an extra military subsidy of £75,000,000, the Tunku and his colleagues embarked on a number of retaliatory measures. In August they declared that in future the parity of the Malaysian dollar would be fixed in gold instead of sterling. This move, while it had no immediate consequences, implied that the Malaysian Central Bank might at its own discretion convert its sterling balances into gold, thus weakening Britain's balance of payments position and the sterling area generally. In the same month, the Malaysian authorities abolished Commonwealth preferences on a wide range of goods making up about one-fifth of all British exports to the country.[1]

In the new situation created by the decision on military withdrawal, which was given a cool reception by both the Malaysian and Singapore régimes, the Government has been endeavouring to safeguard the future of the large British politico-economic stake in the area in two main ways.

First, it has made available fairly large sums to cushion the impact of the withdrawal of British military forces on the economies of the two states, which will be considerable in the case of Singapore.

In June 1968 it was announced that £50,000,000 had been allocated to Singapore and £25,000,000 to Malaysia, to be spent on projects put forward by the two Governments and approved by the British Government, with the proviso that these sums should as far as possible be spent on British goods and services.[2]

It was announced at the same time that all defence lands, fixed assets and certain movable equipment required by the two Governments for civil or military purposes would be handed over free of charge. In accordance with this decision, the naval dockyard at Singapore was transferred to a company owned by the Singapore Government in December 1968 and will be operated as a commercial ship-repairing yard under the management of a British firm and with the assistance during the transition period of 150 British personnel, naval and civilian.[3]

Secondly, against the day of departure, London has been fostering the development of joint Malaysian-Singapore air and naval defence systems, using British weapons and equipment and operated by British-trained personnel, advised by British military specialists on secondment.

---

[1] For details, see *Keesing's Contemporary Archives.* 1966. p. 1621.
[2] *Survey of British and Commonwealth Affairs.* June 21, 1968. 25% of these sums will be grants and the rest interest-free loans, repayable over 25 years.
[3] *Ibid.* January 3, 1969.

Proposals on these lines have been put forward bilaterally and also at the five-power defence conference of Britain, Australia, New Zealand, Malaysia and Singapore, held at Kuala Lumpur in June 1968, where they were in principle approved.[1]

While the Government has so far held firmly to its decision that no British units should be permanently stationed in the area after 1971, at the same conference it stated that the training and exercising of British forces there would continue after that date and also that the British contribution to the five-power military exercises planned for 1970 would include a major reinforcement exercise from the United Kingdom.[2]

These bridge-building activities will help to stabilise Britain's relations with Malaysia and Singapore on a new basis. But old conflicts, so far held in check by the British military presence, are already coming to the surface in acute form, both between the Malayan and Chinese ethnic groups in Malaysia, and between the latter and Singapore, Indonesia and the Philippines. The tendency for the Malayan oligarchy in Kuala Lumpur to seek friends other than Britain among the powers is also increasing. There is, moreover, an unresolved conflict between London, Canberra and Washington over the future cost, in men and money, of maintaining Western control over the area, in which the Australian and American Governments are closely interested, but which has hitherto been achieved mainly at British expense on a scale which the exchequer can no longer bear.

All in all, despite the stiff upper-lip of the Government and the bold promises of the Conservative leaders, it seems to me almost inevitable that there will be a marked falling away in British political as well as military influence in South-East Asia during the next few years.

Looking once again at the situation in the third world as a whole, it seems probable that during the seventies southern Africa will be the only recognisable predominantly British sphere of influence, that the British role in South-East Asia will be radically reduced and that in the Middle East, while Shell and British Petroleum will find ways of continuing to operate, the last remnants of the caliphate in the Persian Gulf will crumble away.

[1] See paragraphs 8 and 9 of the communiqué. *Ibid.* June 21, 1968.
[2] *Ibid.* paragraph 11.

PART III
POLICY TOWARDS THE COMMUNIST POWERS

Policy Towards the Communist Powers

As has been seen in Parts I and II of this book, the question of policy towards the Communist powers enters into all the main problems of British foreign policy.

As shown in Chapter 2, politico-military dispositions and agreements concerning the Soviet Union have formed the core of the Anglo-American "special relationship" in the post-war period. British policy in Western Europe and Anglo-West German relations depend to a major degree on the Government's attitude to the wider question of relations between the capitalist and socialist halves of Europe as a whole (Chapter 3). Chapters 4–7 show that British policy in the third world, and particularly in the Middle East, has been to a very considerable extent determined by the development of a new and much closer relationship between the Soviet Union and the new sovereign states of Asia and Africa. As recalled in Chapter 7 the Chinese factor plays a part in British policy in the whole Commonwealth arc stretching from Pakistan in the West, through India, Ceylon, Malaysia, and Singapore to Australia and New Zealand in the East.

This phenomenon reflects, of course, the fundamental change in the balance of forces between the capitalist and Communist states which followed the Second World War. The whole of Eastern and most of Central Europe (including one-third of Germany) and China plus half of Korea and Vietnam, moved from one side to the other. In terms of economic, political and military strength and influence, the Soviet Union emerged in the post-war period as a super-power of the same order as the United States. In East Asia and the Pacific the military balance is undergoing a radical transformation owing to the development by China of its own nuclear weapons and delivery systems.

One of the principal effects of this change, taken together with the general trend towards political independence in the third world, has been that the influence of the Communist powers on the course of international affairs as a whole is now no less than, and is likely to become greater than, that of the Western powers, a fact with which the latter, including Britain, were and are compelled to reckon at every step.

There is no point in re-examining here those aspects of British policy towards the Soviet Union and China, which have already been discussed in Parts I and II. There remains, however, the question of the general evolution of that policy and of the factors underlying it.

There are, I think, two main dangers lying in wait for students of this problem. One is exaggerating the influence of anti-Communism in British diplomacy towards the socialist states, thereby reducing it to a series of variations on a single theme. The other is treating London's policy in this field almost entirely in terms of traditional great power manœuvring, leaving only a marginal role to the anti-Communist factor.

The fact is that, taking the whole period since the establishment of the first socialist state in 1917, the extent of the influence of anti-Communism on British diplomacy has varied enormously in relation to that of other factors. British policy towards the Soviet Union has always been determined by a mixture of hostility towards Communism as such and of considerations having nothing to do with the socialist structure of Soviet society, but in widely different proportions at different historical periods.

Here one has only to remind oneself that, at one extreme, in 1918–1920 the British Government conducted a war of intervention in Russia for the express purpose of overthrowing the Communist régime, and that, at the other extreme, in 1941–1945 it allied itself with that same régime for the purpose of defeating the principal anti-Communist force in Europe, Nazi Germany. The moving spirit was, as it happens, in both cases the same man, and one whose attitude to Communism as such was just as hostile in the second period as it was in the first, namely Winston Churchill.

In the post-war period, there has not been as wide a swing between one extreme and the other, but it needs no argument to show that the relative weight of anti-Communist considerations in British foreign policy was far greater in, say, 1950, at the height of the cold war, than it is now at the beginning of the seventies.

Moreover, the influence of the anti-Communist factor has varied not only in time, but also in space. Ever since the formation of the Chinese People's Republic in 1949, British diplomacy has pursued markedly different policies towards the two chief Communist powers, the Soviet Union and China.

The basic reason for this is not to be found in the peculiarities of Soviet and Chinese Communism, but in the facts of political, economic and military geography. From the point of view of the Government and its advisers, notwithstanding the world-wide scope of British financial and commercial interests, Communism in Europe — on Britain's door-step — is one thing, and Communism on the other side of the world another.

It is true that innumerable statements by the practitioners and theoreticians of British foreign policy on the danger of Communism give the impression that they regard it as a single enemy, one and undivided, from whatever quarter it may threaten. In this respect, the following statement by Lord Home in 1962 is typical: "Communism as a total system was and is a menace to ours," he said. ". . . The main assault has been transferred to Africa and Asia — except for Berlin — but it is still with us and directed against our interests."[1]

But in practice British diplomacy has been much more empirical than such statements imply. Relations with the European Communist states and with the Asian Communist states have been dealt with not as two aspects of a single problem, but as essentially different, though to some extent inter-connected, problems.

With the deep rift which developed between Moscow and Peking in the sixties and the consequent reduction to nil of Sino-Soviet co-operation in international affairs, this differentiation in policy towards the two Communist world powers became more marked than ever. But it existed before the rift and is likely to remain for years to come, even if co-operation between the Soviet and Chinese Governments and Party leaderships is meanwhile restored.

This differentiation has made necessary a distinction in the following chapters between British policy towards the Soviet Union and the other European Communist states on one hand, and towards China and the other Asian Communist states on the other.

It is sometimes suggested or implied on the left that there is also an important distinction to be made between British policy towards the Soviet Union and policy towards the other European socialist states (except the GDR), namely Poland, Czechoslovakia, Yugoslavia, Hungary, Rumania and Bulgaria. This thesis rests on the undoubted fact that the policy-makers were and remain on the look-out for opportunities of driving a wedge between the Soviet Union and its allies, of weakening the latter's political, military and economic links with Moscow and, when the wind has been fair, have trimmed their diplomatic sails in Eastern Europe accordingly.

But, looking at the picture as a whole, the history of the last fifteen years or so shows a major swing in British diplomacy towards the

[1] Interview in the *The Observer*, September 16, 1962.

Soviet Union and its allies alike, arising from the same basic causes and producing the same characteristic results. Moreover, as regards time scale, except in the case of Yugoslavia, the new approach was applied first towards the Soviet Union and then towards the Eastern European states. If the right proportions are to be observed, therefore, such differences of tactics as there have been are best considered in the context of this general evolution.

The same is, I believe, true of British policy towards events in Vietnam and Laos, which has had its special features, but is essentially a derivative of British policy towards China and Communism in East Asia generally.

CHAPTER EIGHT

The Soviet Union and the Other European Communist States

General Evolution of Policy towards the Soviet Union

Looking back over the period under review, I think that two main features of British policy stand out fairly clearly. Firstly, it was assumed throughout that, whatever else might change, Britain's guns and those of her allies must still be trained on the Soviet Union. Secondly, there was a strong and persistent tendency to seek a *modus vivendi* with her.

Since the arrangements between London and Washington for joint targeting of their nuclear striking forces on Communist Europe and the high priority given by the policy-makers to the perpetuation of NATO are discussed elsewhere in this book, it is the second feature which concerns us here.

One has, however, to bear in mind that these two aspects of British policy are closely interlocked. The *modus vivendi* sought by successive Governments has been an expanding system of negotiations, understandings, agreements and exchanges between Britain and the Soviet Union developing within the existing system of opposing military alliances. There has been a substantial difference here between recent French policy, which has not proceeded from permanently functioning military arrangements with the United States inside and outside NATO, and British policy, which has.

Furthermore, it is not possible to speak of a steady movement away from a policy of pressure on the Soviet Union towards a policy of stabilisation and normalisation of relations with her. The course of Anglo-Soviet relations has been very uneven, having been punctuated with crises connected with developments both inside the Communist system (Hungary in 1956 and Czechoslovakia in 1968) and at sensitive points on the frontier between the two systems (Berlin in 1958–1961 and Cuba in 1962).

As a result, the attitude of those in authority has oscillated between

9   257

positive and negative poles, sometimes favouring far-reaching schemes for constructive co-operation and sometimes while still admitting the necessity of co-existence, calling for a precautionary sharpening of swords.

By way of illustration, we may contrast here the optimistic line at the time of Kosygin's visit to London in February 1967 and the grim tone to be heard following the Czechoslovak crisis in August 1968, only a year and a half later.

On the former occasion, the Government spoke of the evident desire of the Soviet Government, which it shared itself, for the best possible relations between the two countries, of the prospect of a new Anglo-Soviet treaty of friendship and co-operation, of a developing bilateral relationship on European security and of expanding commercial, technological and cultural exchanges, and described the visit as "a landmark in Anglo-Soviet history".[1]

On the latter occasion, Labour and Conservative leaders alike, while warning against relapsing into what Wilson called the frozen immobilism of the cold war and recognising that efforts to reduce tension in Europe must continue, called with one voice for the preservation and strengthening of NATO.

Heath, for example, said that Soviet dominion over the Soviet empire could only be challenged by the use of nuclear weapons and the direct involvement of the United States. The West had not been prepared to face this over Hungary in the past and was not prepared today to face it over Czechoslovakia or any other part of Eastern Europe under Soviet sway. On the other hand, what could and must be done was to ensure the security of Western Europe, particularly through NATO.[2]

Nevertheless, through all the freezes and thaws in East-West and Anglo-Soviet relations over the last fifteen years or so, it seems to me that a combination of deep-seated factors impelled British policy to move by fits and starts along the road leading towards and not away from a stable *modus vivendi*. The factors responsible for this are discussed separately below. Here an attempt is made to identify the main milestones on the way.

The process of reassessment in high quarters of the international scene and of the priorities of British foreign policy lying behind this evolution began a good deal earlier than the period we are considering, the turning point being the first Soviet atomic test in 1949. This

---

[1] Statement by the Prime Minister on February 13, 1967. *Survey of British and Commonwealth Affairs.* March 3, 1967.
[2] Statement on August 26, 1968. *The Times.* August 27, 1968.

can be briefly illustrated by sharply contrasting pronouncements by Churchill before and after that event.

In 1948 Churchill quite openly urged that the Soviet Union be forced to give way to the will of the Western powers while the military balance was in their favour. "The Western nations," he said, "will be far more likely to reach a lasting settlement, without bloodshed, if they formulate their just demands while they have the atomic power and before the Russian Communists have it, too."[1]

In 1950, the same speaker, while still recommending a military approach, had already grasped that, in the new circumstances, it was unlikely to produce the desired results and was already setting his sights on a political dialogue between East and West. "Our whole position in the atomic sphere has been worsened . . . by the fact that the Russians, unexpectedly . . . have acquired the secrets of the atomic bomb, and are said to have begun its manufacture," he said. "Let us therefore labour for peace, not only by gathering our defensive strength, but also by making sure that no door is closed upon any hope of reaching a settlement."[2] From the same year dates the first of his many public appeals for talks with the Soviet Union at the highest level, for "a parley at the summit".[3]

Five years later the idea of a stable East-West relationship in Europe based not only on a balance of armed force, but also the negotiated settlement of disputed issues, had taken deep enough root to give rise to a group of inter-connected *démarches* by London in 1955 and the first half of 1956 designed to start a general rapprochement with the Soviet Union.

Of the Western Governments concerned, the British Government was the most active in bringing about the Geneva Summit Conference in July 1955, the first meeting of its kind since the Second World War and a major turning point in the relations between the capitalist and Communist systems as a whole.

Incidentally, Anthony Eden's determination that the conference should be held appears to have been dictated, at least in part, by what subsequently turned out to be the correct calculation that the bargaining position of the West was likely in future to deteriorate, both militarily and politically. In a paper circulated to his Cabinet colleagues in March 1955, urging the early opening of discussions with the Soviet Union, he argued that the passage of time was unlikely to improve the relative position of the Western powers. On the

---

[1] Speech at the Conservative Party Conference at Llandudno on October 9, 1948. *Keesing's Contemporary Archives.* 1948. p. 9572.
[2] Winston Churchill. *Speeches. In the Balance.* London. 1951. p. 243.
[3] *Ibid.* p. 207.

contrary, he wrote, once saturation in thermonuclear weapons was reached, the relative military strength of the West would decline. The ratification of the Paris Agreements of the previous year (legalising West Germany rearmament) might, he said, prove to be the high point of Western political cohesion.[1]

At the Geneva Conference itself, the British Prime Minister, alone of the Western representatives, put forward a proposal regarding the inspection of military forces in Germany which went a considerable way to meet the Soviet point of view on the German question. As shown in Chapter 3, this step marked the beginning of the end of British support for the official Western thesis that the road to European security lay through the absorption of the German Democratic Republic by the Federal Republic.

At the end of the Geneva Conference, Eden, again alone among the Western heads of government, invited the Soviet leaders to visit the West for bilateral talks. The visit took place in April 1956 and was the first in the series of visits exchanged between the Soviet and British Prime Ministers, which subsequently became, and still is, a familiar feature of the international landscape.

The visit, while it produced no very important concrete results, had the general effect of deepening already existing doubts in London about the utility of a predominantly military approach to relations with the Soviet Union. This can be seen from a minute sent by Eden to members of his Cabinet on April 30, 1956. Now that the Russian visit was over, he said, it was necessary to review Government policy. "Our main weapons of resistance to Soviet encroachment have hitherto been military. But do they meet the needs of the present time? I do not believe that the Russians have any plans at present for military aggression in the West. On the other hand are we prepared with other weapons to meet the new challenge?"[2]

A new note regarding Anglo-Soviet relations was also struck in the communiqué of the Commonwealth Prime Ministers' Conference in July 1956, shortly before the Hungarian and Suez storms broke. A new element has been introduced into international relations by the devastating power of thermonuclear weapons, it said. "A progressive improvement in the relations between the Soviet Union and the other great powers would help to remove the fear of war."[3]

A number of diplomatic moves made by the Macmillan Government in 1959–1960 form, it seems to me, a second milestone further

[1] Eden. *op. cit.* p. 289.
[2] *Ibid.* p. 363.
[3] *Documents* . . . 1956. pp. 662–663.

along the same road. Despite the temporary paralysis caused by the Hungarian and Suez crises, British efforts to bring about a rapprochement with the Soviet Union were not only resumed, but were now directed towards specific forms of co-operation over a wide range of central problems.

The key event here was the Prime Minister's visit to the Soviet Union at the beginning of 1959 (February 21 to March 3), made under the formal pretext of returning Bulganin and Khrushchev's visit to Britain three years before, but which was intended to, and did, accomplish far more than a mere renewal of contact.

The Government, in the first place, reaffirmed the principles lying behind Eden's earlier initiative, namely that, from the point of view of British diplomacy, even major differences between the capitalist and Communist powers are negotiable and should, when necessary, be discussed personally between the heads of government of the two sides. Both points were enshrined in the Macmillan-Khrushchev communiqué, which said that "the Prime Ministers endorsed the principle that differences between nations should be resolved by negotiation and not by force" and that their meeting had made it easier for each side to understand the point of view of the other.[1]

Incidentally, though this did not appear in the communiqué or in British and Soviet public statements at the time, it seems likely that the two sides also informally agreed to work for a second Soviet-American-British-French summit meeting. Throughout the rest of 1959 and the first half of 1960,[2] Macmillan, though keeping up unrelenting pressure on Eisenhower to agree to such a meeting, said nothing about any prior commitment to the Soviet leaders, but Eisenhower, who put up a prolonged resistance, tells us that in June 1959, after a number of exchanges with Macmillan had already taken place, he was shocked to learn from Christian Herter, then Secretary of State, that the Prime Minister "while in Moscow, had definitely agreed to press for a summit, regardless of conditions".[3]

The two Prime Ministers also jointly sponsored a proposal regarding European security going considerably further than Eden's unilateral suggestion in 1955 for mutual military inspection along the East-West border. As recalled in Chapter 3, their basic idea was the same as that of the Rapacki plan, namely that there should not only

---

[1] *Documents* . . . 1959. pp. 11–13.
[2] Until May 1960, when the second summit in Paris collapsed in the smoke and dust of the U.2 affair.
[3] Eisenhower. *Waging Peace.* p. 401. For ealier and later Anglo-American exchanges on the same subject, see pp. 355, 399, 402, 409–410, 423 (footnote 8).

be inspection, but also limitation of nuclear and conventional forces in an agreed area in Europe.

Correctly as it later turned out, Macmillan and Khrushchev picked out the conclusion of a test ban treaty as the key at that stage to further progress with disarmament. British anxiety to secure an agreement on this subject was expressed not only in general phrases, but also in a number of *démarches* by the Prime Minister in 1959 and 1960 designed to secure a compromise between the Soviet and American points of view.

In particular, during his Moscow visit, Macmillan, despite a request from Washington not to do so, put forward a compromise proposal regarding on-site inspection of explosions, which was accepted by the Soviet Government, but blocked by the U.S. Government until the following year.[1] The Government continued to prod its American partner even at the final negotiations in Moscow in July 1963, at which the text of the Partial Test Ban Treaty signed in the following month was at last agreed. The British delegate, Lord Hailsham (Quintin Hogg), protested to London at what he considered to be the rigidity of his U.S. colleague, Averell Harriman, which in turn led to last-minute representations by Macmillan to Kennedy.[2]

So far as Anglo-Soviet trade and cultural relations are concerned, the visit marked what proved to be a decisive turn away from the embargoes and bans of the cold war period. As a result of understandings then reached, a five-year Anglo-Soviet Trade Agreement was signed on May 24, 1959, and the first of a series of annual and bi-annual agreements on cultural, educational, scientific and technical exchanges was signed on March 28 of the same year.

In the sixties, as we have already remarked, the quest for a *modus vivendi* with the Soviet Union and its European allies, until then an idiosyncrasy of British diplomacy, step by step became a common feature of the foreign policy of all the Western powers, the main turning point being the advent of the Kennedy Administration in 1961, when the American decision-takers, putting aside their golf-clubs, took out their slide-rules and, impressed by what they saw, at last abandoned messianic anti-Communism as a guiding principle in international affairs.

One result of this general shift in Western diplomacy was that London no longer stood out clearly as the trail-blazer in improving East-West relations in Europe. Indeed in the mid-sixties this role was

---

[1] For details of this and other similar episodes, see Michael Wright. *op. cit.* pp. 136–138.
[2] Schlesinger. *op. cit.* pp. 773–775.

taken over by Paris. It is possible, nevertheless, to discern a third milestone in a number of crucial decisions affecting relations with the Soviet Union taken by the Labour Government shortly after its accession to power in 1964.

The most important of these were of a politico-military character and were all adumbrated in the Wilson Government's first annual White Paper on Defence, which contained, among others, the following three theses: first, deliberate aggression, even on a limited scale, is unlikely in Europe; secondly, agreements to prevent the dissemination or acquisition of nuclear weapons must be an urgent aim of British foreign policy; and thirdly, the principal military purpose of allied forces in Europe should be to deter and suppress local conflicts first and foremost by conventional and not nuclear forces, before they can escalate into major war.[1]

The first proposition represented the first recognition in a Defence White Paper of a truth privately accepted,[2] but publicly denied by the policy-makers for the previous ten years and more, and now won a prominent place in official military doctrine. Thereafter, similar, formerly heretical, assertions that "the danger of deliberate war in Europe at any level is small",[3] that "the whole Soviet attitude towards Western Europe has changed decisively"[4] and that "tension in Europe has relaxed and there is little danger of aggression at present"[5] figured in a whole series of major statements on defence policy.

Since the conception of the cold war had from the first been built round the central myth that the Soviet Union was about to attack Western Europe at any moment, the significance of this public change of front needs no stressing. Moreover, in practice the Government, while unwavering in its support of NATO, used its influence to bring about a corresponding change in the military doctrine of the alliance.

This was made particularly clear in a speech by the Minister of Defence in October 1966, the main theme of which was that "NATO strategy is hopelessly out of date" and should in future take account not only of the military capacity of the Soviet Union, but also of its real intentions—of the fact that "the Soviet Government has shown itself much less ready than it was before to contemplate the use of

---

[1] *Statement on the Defence Estimates, 1965.* Command 2592. February 1965.
[2] See, for example, Eden's minute to the Cabinet of April 1956 quoted above.
[3] *The Defence Review.* Command 2901. February 1966.
[4] Speech by Minister of Defence. October 27, 1966. *Commonwealth Survey.* November 11, 1966. p. 1146.
[5] *Statement on the Defence Estimates 1967.* Command 3203. February 16, 1967.

force even on a small scale and for limited objectives, anywhere on the long frontier of NATO from the North Cape to the Caucasus.[1] At its Council meeting in December 1967, NATO as a whole finally accepted a now strategic concept based on this point of view.[2] The chief influence here was, no doubt, that of the United States, but with Britain as her chief partner.

The second proposition meant in practice that, on the Western side, London played much the same catalysing role in the negotiations leading up to the Treaty on the Non-Proliferation of Nuclear Weapons, signing on July 1, 1968, as it had in the negotiations culminating in the Test Ban Treaty of August 1963.

British policy on the central issue in these negotiations — the future nuclear status of West Germany — was discussed in detail in Chapter 2. But it is worth recalling once again two crucial decisions taken by the Wilson Government: first, its outright refusal, made plain in the winter of 1964–1965, to participate in the multi-lateral nuclear force proposed by Washington and Bonn; and secondly, its refusal in the summer of 1965 to sponsor the American draft of a non-proliferation treaty unless, as desired by the Soviet Union, it was amended to exclude the possibility of West German co-ownership of a multi-lateral force.

The third proposition marked the official public funeral of the ridiculous and already discredited, but nevertheless dangerous, doctrine, promulgated by Duncan Sandys in his capacity of Minister of Defence in 1957–1958, that in the event of any military conflict in Europe, great or small, Britain would at once resort to nuclear weapons.[3] It also reflected the Government's desire to defuse NATO's military plans and dispositions by an upgrading of the role assigned to conventional forces and a downgrading of that of nuclear forces, an object which was finally achieved also at the above-mentioned NATO Council meeting in December 1967.

Here again, presumably the decisive influence was exercised by the United States. There is, however, no reason to doubt the Government's claim to a share of the credit. We may note in this connection that, with the air of a proud father, the Minister of Defence singled out this particular change as the most important of those agreed at the NATO December 1967 session, since, as he put it, in the event of a major conflict, victory, or even the survival of the human race,

---

[1] Speech to the British Atlantic Committee. *Commonwealth Survey*. November 11, 1966.
[2] This emerges only in muffled language in the NATO communiqués, but is spelled out in detail in the passage on NATO defence planning in *Statement on the Defence Estimates 1968*. Command 3540. February 22, 1968.
[3] See below, p. 275.

might depend on prolonging the period of conventional resistance.[1]

Throughout the sixties successive Governments encouraged the further development of commercial, scientific, technological and cultural exchanges with the Soviet Union and concluded a whole network of agreements for this purpose.

As regards trade, in April 1964 the Anglo-Soviet Trade Agreement of 1959 was extended for another five years. In September of that year, despite heavy pressure from the United States, the Douglas-Home Government, in order to clinch a Soviet order for Terylene plant from Polyspinners worth some £30,000,000, drove a coach and horses through the NATO system of control over export credits for the Communist countries.[2] During Kosygin's visit to Britain in February 1967, he and Wilson agreed that preparations should start for the conclusion of a long-term (not merely five-year) trade agreement. In April 1968, an Anglo-Soviet Navigation Agreement was signed, designed mainly to promote Anglo-Soviet sea-borne trade.

In May 1964 a British agricultural exhibition took place in Moscow, the first of its kind to be organised by British agricultural exporters, and was followed in July 1966 by a British industrial exhibition, opened by the President of the Board of Trade and later visited by the Prime Minister. A Soviet industrial exhibition was held in London in August 1968, the largest ever organised by the Soviet authorities.

It cannot be said that there was a particularly sharp rise in the total volume of Anglo-Soviet trade. Nevertheless, as can be seen from the following table, the figure climbed at a steady rate and almost without a break.

Table 12
Anglo-Soviet Trade

(£ Million)

1959	1961	1962	1963	1964	1965	1966	1967	1968
98	128	142	155	137	165	176	188	262

As regards other forms of exchange and co-operation, the original agreement on cultural, educational, scientific and technological exchanges of March 1959 was renewed and expanded in December 1959,

---

[1] *Hansard.* March 4, 1968. Cols. 50–72.

[2] Under NATO rules export credits were supposed to be limited to a period of five years, whereas on this occasion the Export Credit Guarantee Department of the Board of Trade gave cover for a Midland Bank loan for fifteen years.

9*

January 1961, January 1963, February 1965 and February 1967. In the particular case of scientific and technological co-operation, there was a big move forward as a result of an understanding between Wilson and Kosygin during the latter's 1967 visit to Britain, which led to the conclusion of an Anglo-Soviet Technological Agreement in January 1968, providing for co-operation between Government departments, private and state firms, scientists and engineers over a wide range of technological problems.

Variations on the Same Theme in Eastern Europe

British policy towards Poland, Czechoslovakia, Hungary, Rumania and Bulgaria underwent a similar evolution, though with a considerable time-lag, and, by the end of the period we are considering, in all its main features resembled British policy towards the Soviet Union, both as regards the development of trade, technological, scientific, cultural and other exchanges and, particularly in the case of Poland and Czechoslovakia, the willingness to recognise the legitimacy of their interest in a European settlement and, indeed, in other international problems.

The extent of the advance from London's original position that these countries were mere pilot-fish on the back of the Soviet whale, and as such should be boycotted and ignored, can be seen clearly in Gordon Walker's announcement to the world, shortly before he became Foreign Secretary in 1964, that in his opinion they were "true nations, not satellites".[1]

In the diplomatic field, the turn of the tide came in 1957, when, as we have seen, London entered into negotiations with the Polish Government regarding the Rapacki plan for a denuclearised zone in Central Europe.

Exchanges of visits at Foreign Minister level date from 1963, when, on the initiative of the Macmillan Government the Czechoslovak Minister for Foreign Affairs paid an official visit to London, the first Foreign Minister from any of these countries to do so for almost twenty years. The British Foreign Secretary returned the visit in 1965.

In 1963 the Bulgarian Foreign Minister called on the Foreign Secretary on his way through London. In 1965, on the invitation of the British Government, he was followed by an official delegation, headed by Todorov, one of the Bulgarian Deputy Prime Ministers, who was received by the Prime Minister. In the same year the

[1] *The Times.* June 17, 1964.

Hungarian Foreign Minister paid an official visit to London at the invitation of the Foreign Secretary.

In 1964 the Polish Foreign Minister, on his way through London, had talks with the Prime Minister and the Foreign Secretary. The latter paid an official visit to Warsaw in 1965, the first British Foreign Secretary to do so since Bevin's visit eighteen years earlier.

Official delegations from Rumania visited London in 1966 and 1968, on both occasions headed by a Deputy Prime Minister and including a deputy Minister for Foreign Affairs. A return visit to Bucharest was paid by the British Foreign Secretary in 1968.

The development of normal diplomatic relations with Poland and to a lesser extent with Czechoslovakia was hampered by the Government's equivocal attitude on the question of Germany's eastern frontiers, though in 1967–1968 it moved some way towards meeting the Polish and Czechoslovak point of view.

Whereas the French Government, in a public statement by de Gaulle in 1959, recognised the Oder-Neisse line as the frontier between Germany and Poland, Conservative and Labour Governments alike, in concert with Washington and Bonn, continued to maintain that the question could only be settled at some future hypothetical German Peace Conference. The Foreign Secretary repeated this thesis during his visit to Warsaw in 1965, adding only that, when the time came for a decision, the wishes of the inhabitants of the disputed territory (who are now overwhelmingly Polish) would certainly be taken into account.[1]

In 1968, however, the official line became rather less non-committal, the House of Commons being informed that the wishes of the inhabitants would be "of fundamental importance" when the time came to make a final settlement and that, since Poland had been in possession of the territory for over twenty years, there was "nothing to stop these changes being ratified in a peace settlement."[2]

It is useless to try to guess when an end will be put to this havering, which is out of keeping with the present-day general tactics of British diplomacy in Eastern Europe. One cannot help wondering, however, whether some Foreign Secretary, taking his courage in both hands, will not soon follow the French example. If Franco-West German relations were able to stand the strain, it is hard to see why Anglo-West German relations cannot do so also.

Although the Government did not accept the Czechoslovak contention that the Munich Agreement of 1938 was null and void *ab*

[1] *Commonwealth Survey.* September 28, 1965. p. 932.
[2] *Survey of British and Commonwealth Affairs.* June 21, 1968.

initio, its attitude towards the validity of the present Czechoslovak-German frontier was and is less ambiguous than in the case of the Polish-German frontier. Here also it maintained that a final settlement must await a German Peace Conference, but publicly stated in 1967 that the fact that the Munich Agreement was once made could not justify any future claims against Czechoslovakia, and that no consideration should be given to any changes of frontier effected in or after 1938.[1] In 1968 Parliament was told that, so far as Britain was concerned, when the time came for a final determination of Germany's frontiers by a peace treaty, the treaty discussions would start from the basis that Czechoslovak frontiers were not in question.[2]

In the first half of the sixties, the Government, among other measures to expand exports to Eastern Europe, replaced its short-term with medium-term, five-year trade agreements, as it had already done with the Soviet Union. A five-year agreement was signed with Czechoslovakia at the end of 1962, which in 1967 was replaced by another similar agreement for the period 1968–1972. Five-year agreements were signed with Poland and Rumania in 1963 and with Hungary in 1964. In that year the Minister of State, Board of Trade, included Rumania, Hungary and Bulgaria in a trade-promotion tour, and in doing so was the first member of the Government at any level to visit these three countries since the end of the war. The steady, if undramatic, upward trend in British trade with Eastern Europe can be seen from the following table.

Table 13
British Trade with Eastern Europe[3]

(£ Million)

	1959	1962	1963	1964	1965	1966	1967	1968
Poland	49	71	68	73	74	90	105	105
Czechoslovakia	17	27	28	30	32	38	38	42
Rumania	5	16	19	17	21	26	36	58
Yugoslavia	25	38	33	41	34	40	n.a.	n.a.
GDR	9	16	16	17	20	30	29	30
Hungary	7	12	13	16	15	18	22	23
Bulgaria	4	5	6	7	9	14	13	12

In 1967 and 1968 agreements on technological exchanges were

[1] *Hansard*. April 22, 1967. Cols. 207–208.
[2] *Survey of British and Commonwealth Affairs*. June 21, 1968.
[3] *Commonwealth Survey*. September 1, 1964, December 23, 1966. *UN Year book of International Trade Statistics*. 1966. *Survey of British and Commonwealth Affairs*. February 16, 1968; February 28, 1969.

signed with Rumania, Hungary, Poland and Czechoslovakia, similar to the above-mentioned agreement with the Soviet Union.

In 1967 the Government opened a Great Britain-East Europe Centre in London, charged with fostering cultural, economic, political and social contacts with Bulgaria, Czechoslovakia, Hungary and Rumania.

As regards Yugoslavia, from the time of the break with the Soviet Union in 1948 until the restoration of relations in 1955, she received far more favourable treatment at London's hands than any other Communist country in Europe.

In 1949–1950 a five-year Anglo-Yugoslav trade agreement was concluded and Yugoslavia was granted credits of some £8,000,000. In 1951 the Attlee Government joined the U.S. and French Governments in an agreement with Belgrade to provide grants totalling £50,000,000 to cover the country's estimated trade deficit in the period 1951–1954.

Besides economic measures of this kind, Yugoslavia was also given political support.

In February 1951 the Government defined its position on the security of Yugoslavia in a public statement, which ran as follows: "His Majesty's Government are alive to the potential threat to Yugoslavia from the swollen armed forces of the satellites which has been emphasised by hostile Soviet and satellite propaganda," it said. "Any threat to Yugoslavia, who played a heroic part in resistance to Hitler's aggression, is naturally of concern to His Majesty's Government and we are in touch with other Governments."[1]

In July of that year, in a statement on emergency economic aid to Yugoslavia, the Foreign Secretary declared that the greatest importance was attached "to strengthening Yugoslav resistance to pressure from the Cominform states".[2] During a visit to Belgrade in September, the President of the Board of Trade (Sir Hartley Shawcross), in promising maximum technical aid, said that it was in Britain's interests to see Yugoslavia a stable, independent country able to "work out its own future without fear of interference or domination from outside".[3]

In 1952–1953 a high level exchange of visits took place. Eden, then Foreign Secretary, visited Belgrade in September 1952, and Tito paid a return visit to London in March 1953. As can be seen from the communiqués, the main purpose of the British side was in both cases

---

[1] *Documents . . .* 1951. p. 379.
[2] *Ibid.* p. 382.
[3] *The Times.* September 17, 1951.

to demonstrate support for the Yugoslav Government in its resistance
to the pressure exercised against it by the then Soviet leadership.

Ministerial exchanges of visits continued after the restoration of
Soviet-Yugoslav relations, Kardelj, a senior member of the Yugoslav
party leadership, came to London in November 1955 and Popovic,
Minister of Foreign Affairs, did so in October 1958. Selwyn Lloyd,
while Foreign Secretary in the Macmillan Government, and Michael
Stewart, during his first spell as Foreign Secretary in the Wilson
Government, visited Belgrade in September 1957 and April 1965
respectively. Stewart again visited Yugoslavia in June 1968.

At the other end of the spectrum, the German Democratic
Republic throughout the period under review was officially classified
as a non-person among the European Communist countries, the
Government maintaining the agreed formal position of all the NATO
powers, adopted at Bonn's behest, that no such state existed. In 1966,
for example, the Wilson Government, in oral and written statements
issued jointly with the United States and French Governments and
designed to frustrate the GDR's application for membership of the
United Nations, declared that only the government of the Federal
Republic of Germany was entitled to speak on behalf of Germany in
international affairs, that the so-called German Democratic Republic
was not a state and that attempts to establish it as such could only
make more difficult a peaceful settlement in Europe.[1]

As the process of détente in Europe proceeded, this attitude involved the Foreign Office lawyers in increasingly uncomfortable
contortions. Thus in 1963, when for understandable reasons the
Government wished both German states to sign the test ban treaty, it
tacitly agreed with the other two sponsoring powers, the Soviet
Union and the United States, that the GDR would sign the copy
deposited in Moscow and the FRG the copy held in Washington or
London. But, when called to account for its conduct by Bonn, found
itself obliged to advance the extraordinary thesis that, when the
GDR affixed its signature, as a non-state it acquired no rights to
require observance of the treaty by other parties including Britain,
but at the same time itself became obliged to observe its provisions.[2]

But although, contortions or no contortions, this attitude was
maintained up to the end of the period under review, this does not
mean that there was no evolution in British policy towards the GDR
similar in substance to that affecting the other European Communist

---

[1] *Commonwealth Survey*. April 29, 1966. pp. 478–479.
[2] Anglo-West German communiqué following the London visit of the West German
Foreign Minister on August 14–15, 1963. *Commonwealth Survey*. October 8, 1963.

states. On the contrary, as we have seen, from the mid-fifties onwards British diplomacy on questions of European security in practice assumed the indefinite existence of two Germanys and of the present frontier between them and, provided the special status of West Berlin and Allied rights of access to it were recognised, showed less and less disposition to quibble over the legal powers of the East German Government to control the movement of civil and military traffic over its own territory.

Cultural exchanges and the flow of tourists remained at a lower level than in the case of the other European Communist states, but as can be seen from Table 13, British trade developed at much the same rate with the GDR as with her neighbours. In order to get round the difficulty presented by non-recognition, trade agreements similar to those negotiated with Poland, Czechoslovakia, Rumania, Hungary and Bulgaria were concluded not between governments but between the Federation of British Industries (or, as it is now called, the Confederation of British Industry) and the East German Chamber of Foreign Trade.

It would be over-simplifying matters to regard the above-described evolution of British diplomacy in Eastern Europe only as a process of normalisation and stabilisation of relations. As part of their new approach, the policy-makers, whenever internal developments within the socialist system appeared to offer opportunities, tried to encourage centrifugal tendencies within it and, in particular, to weaken the links between the Soviet Union and its allies and to draw the latter into closer and separate understandings with the West.

In his above-mentioned treatise on co-existence in 1957, Gaitskell held out the hope to his readers that, against a background of continuing instability and fluidity within the socialist system, his plan for East-West military disengagement would lead to the political disengagement of the Eastern European states from the Soviet Union, since, as he put it, the withdrawal of the Red Army to Russia would weaken the position of the Communist Parties of Eastern Europe. "We wish to see the satellite states regain their freedom without war," he wrote. "We owe it to the peoples of the satellite countries at least to examine what can be done to win freedom for them by diplomatic means."[1]

Sir Leslie Rowan, an influential figure in the establishment, advanced a similar argument in favour of developing trade with Communist Europe, one of the main theses of his Lees Knowles Lectures in 1960. Trade could become a real bridge between the

[1] Gaitskell. *op. cit.* pp. 54–58.

Communists and the West, and in the process fundamentally alter
the Communist outlook, he said. Trade and travel could help to
bring about the liberation of the People's Democracies from the
absolute power of the centre.[1]

Lord Butler, during his term as Foreign Secretary, claimed quite
openly that by its bridge-building efforts the Government was helping to steer the course of events in Eastern Europe in the desired
direction. Having raised the status of its diplomatic missions in this
part of the world,[2] liberalised trade and increased cultural exchanges,
the Government would, he said, "continue to encourage the evolu-
tionary trends apparent in Eastern Europe".[3]

During the Czechoslovak crisis of 1968, Foreign Secretary
Stewart thought the moment appropriate to show special favour to
Rumania. He pointedly cancelled his visits to Budapest and Sofia,
but continued on his way to Bucharest.

Such manœuvres, however, must, as we have said, be looked at
against the wider background of British policy towards the Soviet
Union and Communist Europe as a whole, in which they form the
grace notes and not the tune itself. Whether this will continue to be
so remains to be seen, but the factors responsible for the main line
of evolution of British diplomacy towards the Soviet Union and other
European Communist states are deep-seated and powerful and unlikely, in my opinion, to alter much in the foreseeable future.

The Strategic Factor

Among these factors, first place, it seems to me, belongs to changes
in the strategic picture unfavourable to the West and giving rise to
unavoidable adjustments and adaptations in the policy-makers'
attitude to East-West relations in Europe as a whole.

Perhaps the first thing to be said is that, since the end of the Second
World War, no British Government or its American and other allies
have yet seriously contemplated a purely conventional war with the
Soviet Union, i.e., one in which the use of nuclear weapons was
excluded. Since the Soviet conventional forces were and are overwhelmingly stronger than those of NATO, both in London and in
Washington war with the Soviet Union has so far all along meant
nuclear war.

[1] Leslie Rowan. *Arms and Economics. The Changing Challenge.* Cambridge. 1960. pp. 59–63.
Before becoming head of Vickers in 1958, Rowan was Private Secretary to Churchill and
Attlee and then Second Secretary at the Treasury.
[2] The British Legations in Sofia, Budapest and Bucharest were raised to Embassy
status at the end of 1963.
[3] *Hansard.* June 16, 1964. Col. 1127.

So far as Britain's strategic situation is concerned, the key developments, therefore, were those in the nuclear field, of which the following is a brief chronology.

The first U.S. A-bomb test took place in 1945. U.S. nuclear bombers targeted on the Soviet Union were first stationed in Britain in 1948. The first Soviet A-bomb test was carried out in 1949 and the first British one in 1952. The U.S. and the Soviet Union conducted their first H-bomb tests in November 1952 and August 1953 respectively, a difference of only eight months. The Soviet H-bomb was constructed by cheaper and quicker methods, later adopted by the Americans. The first British H-bomb test took place in 1957. The first sputnik, indicating the possession by the Soviet Union of rockets capable of direct counter-strike against the territory of the United States (ICBMs), was launched in 1957.

This order of events meant that for a short time, from 1948 until the beginning of the fifties, Britain as a provider of bases and the United States as the provider of the striking force threatened the Soviet Union with nuclear attack without much risk of providing a response in kind. But in the early fifties the strategic situation radically altered. Britain, though not yet the United States, was now exposed to Soviet bomber and medium-range rocket counter-attack first with A-bombs and by the middle of the decade with H-bombs.

During this period Britain continued to provide bases for the U.S. striking force and also contributed a small striking force of her own, which was fused with that of the Americans for purposes of operations against the Soviet Union. She thus assumed the uniquely dangerous posture of preparing with the United States to strike a nuclear blow at a more powerful adversary, while she, but not the United States, presented a priority and wide-open target to obliterating counter-attack.

From about 1958 down to the present day the situation of the two allies has been essentially similar, American territory having become vulnerable to a Soviet nuclear response delivered by ICBMs, against which there is so far no known defence. One may also note that the strategic significance of the quantitative lead held by the United States in the manufacture of A-bombs was nullified in the mid-fifties by the almost simultaneous Soviet and American production of the H-bomb.[1]

[1] This rough periodisation is based on estimates by the two leading British scientists concerned with strategic questions, Blackett and Zuckerman. P. M. S. Blackett. *Studies of War*. London, 1962. pp. 90, 141. Sir Solly Zuckerman. *Scientists and War*. London. 1966. pp. 36, 62. It provides for a necessary time-lag between the testing of new weapons and their operational availability in quantity.

It follows that from the early fifties the Government was not in a position to participate in nuclear war against the Soviet Union without bringing about the destruction of the country. Owing to the small size of the British Isles, to its high population density and, in terms of modern bomber ranges, its proximity to the Soviet Union, this was true before the latter acquired H-bombs. After that event the fact became more obvious than ever to anyone concerned with these matters.

It also follows that, notwithstanding the British commitment to act jointly with the United States, for some six or seven years, say 1952 to 1958, given the then differing strategic situations of the two countries, the angle from which Washington and London viewed the prospect of nuclear war was also different. To Britain's leaders, pressing the button meant automatically destroying their own country, to the American leaders it did not, since the degree of vulnerability of U.S. territory was still uncertain.

There is plenty of evidence that the Government and its advisers were well aware of and seriously worried by the situation in which they found themselves.

In a number of speeches at the beginning of the fifties Churchill pointed out the danger to which Britain was exposed by the presence on her territory of American nuclear bombers targeted on the Soviet Union. The Conservative Party, like the Attlee Government, agreed, he said, that the United States should have bases in East Anglia "from which they could use the atom bomb upon the Russian cities and keypoints". But the decision to provide these bases presented an "extraordinary risk", placed Britain in the front line of targets in the event of war, and made especially necessary an understanding with the U.S. Government regarding the use of atomic weapons.[1]

In the mid-fifties, when it had become clear that the Soviet Union was in a position to retaliate with H-bombs as well as A-bombs, the Government, from the Prime Minister downwards, publicly advanced the thesis, by no means then as generally accepted as it is today, that war between the two systems meant annihilation. Thus, Eden told the U.S. Senate in early 1956 that, since the most powerful nations on earth now commanded weapons of unheard-of destructiveness, war can never bring victory "when oblivion confronts aggressor and victim alike".[2]

There was also to be heard in Government statements a note of relief that the Soviet Union, by catching up with the Americans in

---

[1] Churchill. *In the Balance*. pp. 339–340, 354, 454.
[2] Speech to the U.S. Senate. February 2, 1956. Eden. *op. cit.* p. 338.

the nuclear field, had diminished the risk that the latter would start a nuclear war.

Eden's repeated assurances to the British public at this period that "it becomes increasingly unlikely that any country possessing the hydrogen bomb would deliberately use it against a rival power that owns it also" and that "if there is less fear of world conflict today, this is due to the deterrent of nuclear weapons",[1] if read out of their historical context, are susceptible of various interpretations. But the change in the situation, the new factor, to which he was referring and from which he drew comfort was not, of course, that the United States had acquired the capacity to deter the Soviet Union (which it had always had), but that the Soviet Union had acquired the capacity to deter the United States.

For some years, roughly between 1954 and 1958, there opened up a yawning gap between such realistic assessments of the strategic situation and official military policy as propounded by the Ministry of Defence.

What can fairly be described as a doctrine of nuclear suicide reached full flower in the 1958 Defence White Paper, which stated that if the Russians launched an attack on the Western powers "even with conventional forces only, they would have to hit back with strategic nuclear weapons". But the White Paper at the same time admitted that the resulting nuclear war would result in the destruction of Britain, since it was "not practicable to attempt to defend the country as a whole against nuclear attack".[2] Some readers will remember that at the time Vicky neatly summed up the situation in a cartoon of Duncan Sandys, the Minister responsible, facing a Russian bear and holding a pistol to his own temple, over the caption "One Step and I Shoot".[3]

This weird doctrine certainly reflected the dangerously low intellectual ceiling of its authors, but its temporary adoption was almost certainly due not to ignorance of the real strategic situation, but to other factors having only an indirect bearing on a possible conflict between East and West.

As suggested below, the decision-makers at that time laboured under the illusion that they could secure a long-term easement of the economic burden of military expenditure by altering the balance in the country's armed forces in favour of nuclear, as opposed to conventional, methods of warfare. Moreover, faced with a choice of

[1] Speech at Bradford. January 18, 1956. *Keesing's Contemporary Archives.* 1956. p. 14640.
[2] *Report on Defence. Britain's Contribution to Peace and Security.* February 1958. Command 363.
[3] *New Statesman.* March 1, 1958.

priorities, both external and internal political considerations inclined them towards an official strategy, which would provide them
with a rationale, however flimsy, for maintaining Britain's nuclear
status among the Western powers and at the same time gain them
credit at home for the abolition of conscription.

One cannot say that even today the doctrine of nuclear suicide,
or rather modifications of it, are completely buried. In the period
following the Czechoslovak crisis of 1968, the Minister of Defence
more than once spoke of a possible early, though not immediate, use
of tactical nuclear weapons in the event of war in Europe. In its
extreme form, it was, however, abandoned in 1959 and its chief
author shunted off to another ministry.

In November of that year a highly-placed British general, Sir
John Cowley, with the Government's consent, admitted publicly
that for Britain to take part in a nuclear war was tantamount to
suicide. If nuclear weapons were used against the Soviet Union, he
said, "there can be little doubt that it would result in the destruction
of Britain. If general war broke out, the only alternatives would be
either to stop fighting or destroy the world". He then went on to
question whether it could ever be morally right for a government to
choose a course leading to the complete destruction of the population.[1] From then on these obvious truths slowly but surely won an
increasingly prominent place in official military pronouncements.

In 1961 Sir Solly Zuckerman, then Chairman of the Defence
Research Policy Committee, also with the Government's consent,
contributed a paper to a symposium held at NATO Headquarters,
suggesting that there were no circumstances in which nuclear
weapons, including tactical nuclear weapons with which NATO's
forces were armed, could rationally be used. "One may fairly ask,"
he wrote, "what meaning there is in the idea of using nuclear
weapons 'to defend our territories and people'. One can deter with
nuclear weapons. Can one defend?"[2]

In 1962 Lord Home, then Foreign Secretary, gave the Government's endorsement of this thesis. "Nuclear power," he said, "cannot
be used unless it is by a man so mad and so blind that he is prepared
to blow the world to bits and himself and his country with it."[3] He
also said in the same year, with some gnashing of teeth, that this
meant recognising the status quo. "It is degrading beyond words," he
told the UN Assembly, "that in these days the peace should depend

[1] Address to the Royal United Service Institution. *The Times.* November 4, 1959.
[2] This paper was subsequently published in *Foreign Affairs.* New York, January, 1962,
and reproduced in Zuckerman. *op. cit.* pp. 101–121.
[3] Speech at the 1962 Conservative Party Conference. *The Times.* October 13, 1962.

on the balance of terror, but it is better than destruction. And therefore, we must decide at once not to disturb the balance of power."[1]

In 1965 Zuckerman, by then Chief Scientific Adviser to the Labour
Government, with the latter's authorisation, launched another and
even more trenchant attack on a Western strategy based on the use of
either strategic or tactical nuclear weapons, and on American theoreticians attempting to justify such a strategy, particularly Herman
Kahn and Thomas Schelling.

As regards strategic weapons, the plain fact was, Zuckerman said,
that neither the Western nor the Soviet blocs could ever afford to put
the concept of strategic nuclear war to experimental test, since the
smallest experiment might cost millions of lives. An all-out nuclear
exchange could never be a rational action, justified by any set of
conceivable political gains. Tactical nuclear weapons employed in
direct support of forces in the field were not there for use like conventional weapons, but only for deterrence. "The consequences of
their being used are so fearful that a primary purpose of all the nuclear
powers has become that of seeing that the weapons are never used."[2]

By the end of 1967, as we have already seen, not least owing
to the prolonged efforts of Healey, Zuckerman and the rest of
the British politico-military machine, NATO was at last persuaded to take serious account of these ideas in its revised strategy.

I think it is also worth calling attention to the views of one of the
leading strategic experts in the country, Blackett, who, though in the
fifties among the Government's most stringent critics, enjoyed and
enjoys considerable respect in policy-making circles and whose ideas,
though heretical at the time they were uttered, later became part of
the official canon.

In 1954, in an analysis of the consequences of the Soviet acquisition
of the H-bomb, Blackett pointed out that, with the new relation of
forces, the West certainly could not now attack targets in the Soviet
Union without bringing about the destruction of London, Paris and
other big European cities. If a crisis arose, the European members of
NATO would be bound to try to prevent the use of nuclear weapons
in order to save their own cities from destruction. So far as Britain
was concerned, a military policy based on the use of nuclear weapons
was, therefore, bluff. He thus anticipated General Cowley's less
bluntly worded statement in the same sense by about five years.[3]

---

[1] *Commonwealth Survey.* November 6, 1962.
[2] The Lees Knowles Lectures, 1965, republished in Zuckerman. *op. cit.* See in particular
pp. 51–76.
[3] First published in the *New Statesman and Nation* in August 1954. Republished in
Blackett. *op. cit.* pp. 27–46.

In 1958 the same author published his conclusion that, with the existing effective nuclear parity between the Soviet Union and the West, the latter could also not use tactical nuclear weapons on the battlefield in a war with the Soviet Union without risking the destruction of Western Europe. For this reason, despite official NATO military doctrine, Britain and the United States would not in fact be able to initiate the use of tactical nuclear weapons if a limited war broke out in Europe, and, if they were used, the British Government would immediately have to dissociate itself from this action in order to prevent Britain being destroyed. Here Blackett anticipated the official point of view as expressed by Zuckerman by about three years.[1]

As the foregoing shows, throughout the period under review the powers that be, though they continued actively to prepare for nuclear war with the Soviet Union, at the same time, owing to changes in the nuclear balance leading to a catastrophic deterioration in Britain's strategic situation, became increasingly anxious, one might almost say determined, that such a war should not take place.

Here, I think, is the main reason why in the fifties Britain emerged as the main advocate among the Western powers of acceptance of the status quo between East and West in Europe, the first among them actively to seek a *modus vivendi* with the Soviet Union. In particular Eden's pioneering moves in this direction in 1955 and early 1956 and Macmillan's initiatives in 1959–1960 cannot be fully understood except in the context of the radical strategic changes which immediately preceded them.

By the same token, the subsequent more or less consistent adherence by both Conservative and Labour Governments throughout the sixties to a policy of stabilisation of relations with Communist Europe was and is organically connected with a continuing strategic situation in which the only alternative to peaceful co-existence was and is peaceful non-existence.

The Costs of Confrontation

Throughout the period under review, successive Governments were also pushed willy-nilly away from cold war attitudes and towards attempts to bring about a relaxation of East-West tension in Europe by the pressure of economic factors.

Since one of the effects of the scientific and technological revolution

---

[1] "Nuclear Weapons and Defence". First published in *International Affairs*. London. October 1958. Republished in Blackett. *op. cit.* pp. 54–72.

has been enormously to increase the cost of armaments, it has brought about a situation in which only the two giant powers, the United States and the Soviet Union, are able to afford a full range of weapons, a full set of clubs.

This is partly because modern weapon systems require the backing of the most advanced and largest nuclear, chemical, electronic, metallurgical, aeronautical and other industries and the most advanced and numerous scientific and technological cadres, and partly because the momentum of the revolution is so great that over the last twenty years many, if not most, new weapons have been out-of-date, strategically obsolete, by the time they reached serial production. This in turn means that development costs have been not only vast, but recurrent. Moreover, so far there has been a tendency for each new generation of weapons to be more expensive than the last.

Britain has an advanced modern industry and first-class scientists and technologists, but not on a scale to sustain the cracking pace of the contemporary arms race without going bankrupt.

Bankruptcy is not used here as a mere figure of speech. Throughout the post-war period, the specific disease of the British economy has not been, as before the war, catastrophic falls in production accompanied by long-term mass unemployment, but a chronic deficit in the balance of payments. The main problem has not been how to avoid a slump in the classical sense, but how to balance the country's foreign account, the main items in which are exports and imports.

In these circumstances, heavy military expenditure, far from acting as a necessary stimulant to the economy, makes a bad situation worse, mainly by causing a huge diversion of industrial resources, skilled man-power and scientific research from civil production for export to purposes which are irrelevant to the central economic problem.

Some idea of the size of the diversion is given by the following figures relating to the end of the fifties. Military expenditure then accounted for rather more than 7% of the gross national product (GNP), the highest figure for any capitalist country, except the United States. The number of persons employed on defence inside and outside the armed forces was 1,118,000, or 4·5% of the working population. 49% of all expenditure on research and development was used for military purposes. 25% of all qualified scientists and engineers engaged in research and development were employed on defence work.[1]

[1] *The Economic Effects of Disarmament.* Economist Intelligence Unit. London. 1963. pp. 7, 11, 26, 30.

By the mid-sixties the situation had improved, but only slightly and not in all respects. The military share of the GNP was a little below 7%,[1] of the labour force — 5·6%, of research and development expenditure — 40%, and of qualified research and development personnel — 20%.[2]

On top of this indirect effect on Britain's solvency, or rather insolvency, an astronomically high rate of military expenditure has also exercised a direct adverse influence on the balance of payments owing to heavy recurrent foreign exchange losses arising from overseas military expenditure. Table 14 below shows net overseas military expenditure, i.e., it allows for Government receipts on military account from foreign sources. It will be seen that in recent years the balance of payments has been burdened with an annual deficit of around £250,000,000 on this account.

Table 14
Net Overseas Military Expenditure[3]

(£ Million)

1959	1960	1961	1963	1964	1965	1966	1967*
130	163	187	236	268	267	273	258

* Provisional.

It cannot be said that any Government has yet faced up squarely to the economic consequences of massive military expenditure. This can be seen from the following annual totals, which, even allowing for price increases, show a general upward curve, the only break being towards the end of the fifties. Behind these figures lies a determination that Britain should remain a nuclear power next only to the two super-powers and, until the final crash of sterling in 1967, also a military force in the Far and Middle East as well as Europe.

Table 15
Annual Military Expenditure[4]

(£ Million)

'56–57	'57–58	'58–59	'59–60	'60–61	'61–62	'62–63	'63–64	'65–66	'66–67	'67–68
1525	1430	1468	1476	1596	1689	1767	1792	1909	2055	2205

[1] By 1967–1968, it had dropped to 6.5%.
[2] Zuckerman. *op. cit.* p. 45.
[3] Command 1671, 1962; Command 2966, 1966; Command 3571, 1968.
[4] Labour Research. April 1968. p. 59.

The failure of the political leaders of both parties to grasp this nettle firmly is also shown by the fact that they have more than once been painfully stung by it.

This happened to the Macmillan Government which in the late fifties declared to all the world, and particularly to its jingo supporters in the Conservative Party, that the British-built Blue Streak ballistic nuclear rocket was to be the future keystone of the country's military might, but in April 1960 was forced to admit that it was after all proving to be too expensive and had to be abandoned.

The next much advertised centre-piece of the armaments programme, the TSR-2 aircraft, suffered the same fate for the same reason, though on this occasion the Labour Government, which cancelled the project in April 1965, was able to put the blame on its Conservative predecessors.

But Wilson and his colleagues then fell into the same trap themselves. In cancelling further work on the TSR-2, they announced that they had obtained an option to buy American F111s in its place, and at far less cost, and in 1966 gave a firm order for 50. But as part of the economies imposed by the crisis and devaluation of sterling in November 1967, this scheme had to be abandoned also.

Moreover, as a result of that same crisis, the Labour Government, having with much fanfare proclaimed that in British military dispositions the accent would be shifted to the Middle East, the Indian Ocean and the Far East, found itself obliged drastically and hurriedly to cut back its commitments in the whole area East of Suez.

On the other hand, throughout the period under review, the Government was conscious, and at times acutely concious, of the conflict between its military and economic policies, between its efforts to maintain and constantly renew a costly military establishment and its efforts to put an end to recurrent balance of payments crises and consequent threats to the stability of the pound.

This can be seen from the far-reaching changes in military policy made in the mid-fifties. Their most striking feature was a shift of emphasis in favour of nuclear as against conventional forces, a change arising primarily from politico-economic and not strategic considerations.

From the strategic point of view, as we have already noted, the new policy made no sense since, by its sponsors' own admission, nuclear war could only lead to the destruction of the country. But the Government, from the Prime Minister downwards, rested its case primarily on other non-strategic considerations and above all on the necessity, if Britain was to retain her rightful place in the world, of cutting down the military burden on her economy.

The main features of the new policy were set out in the Defence White Paper of 1957, which announced the forthcoming abolition of conscription, a substantial reduction in the size of British forces in West Germany and other cuts in conventional forces, to be combined with greater concentration on the development of nuclear weapons systems. One can find there no rational military justification for this course, but a good deal of convincing argument of another kind.

Britain, said the White Paper, had been bearing a disproportionately large share of the total burden of Western defence. Her influence in the world depended first and foremost on the health of her internal economy and the success of her export trade. Without these, military power could not in the long run be supported. Too many of the working population, and in particular too many qualified scientists and engineers, were engaged on military work. Too much of the output of the metal-using industries, upon which export trade largely depended, was devoted to defence. Too big a strain was put on the balance of payments by the retention of large forces abroad.[1]

As we have seen from the fate of Blue Streak and the TSR-2, the idea that the development of the latest nuclear weapons systems was, in economic terms, within Britain's capacity soon proved to be a delusion. Nevertheless, as shown in Table 15, the 1957 reforms did produce a temporary dip in the level of military expenditure.

A fresh attack on the problem was made by the Labour Government immediately upon assuming power in 1964, spurred on by the monumental deficit in the balance of payments which it inherited from the Conservatives. Indeed, Denis Healey gave first place to the economic factors in his first major speech in the House of Commons as Defence Minister. He called for extreme vigilance in controlling the impact of military policy on the balance of payments and, even more important, on the country's production resources, particularly in scientists and skilled manpower. "Unless we are to allow our defence expenditure to rise continually not only in absolute terms but also as a percentage of our rising material wealth," he said, "we must be prepared to reduce the calls on our military resources."[2]

The Wilson Government's first Defence White Paper defined the same question as one of the two central problems of defence policy, pointing out that it was particularly formidable in an era when the

[1] Command 124. April 5, 1957.
[2] *Hansard.* November 23, 1964. Col. 1029.

cost of weapons tended to rise much faster than the nation's wealth.[1] In his speech introducing the White Paper, the Defence Secretary, insisting that military expenditure must be cut, urged very much the same well-founded economic arguments as Sandys had done seven years before. "We are still spending a higher proportion of our national wealth on our defence forces than any other country of our size," he said, "and this expenditure bears particularly heavily on our balance of payments and on the type of resources, both in man-power and manufacturing capacity, which we need most of all to get our economic situation right."[2]

Later the same year Healey announced that the Government's long-term aim was by 1969–1970 to achieve a defence bill not greater than £2,000,000,000 at 1964 prices and to reduce the military share of the GNP from 7% to 6%.[3] Since the Government's programme then still included the maintenance of strong forces and bases East of Suez and the purchase of F111s and other highly expensive features, this target was probably at the time unrealistic. But since the heavy cuts later forced upon the Government by the 1967 devaluation crisis, it seems not impossible that it may be attained.

The Government's concern over the economic effects of high and rising military expenditure both reflected and evoked similar concern in industrial and financial circles, or at least in the top echelon, which is able, and indeed bound, to judge the question in relation not only to immediate profit and loss, but also to the wider problem of restoring the country's competitive position on the world market and of balancing her foreign account.

This is not to ignore the existence of powerful companies which, since a large part of their profits are derived from Government arms contracts, are directly interested in maintaining certain forms of military expenditure at a high level. The hair-raising disclosures in 1964 and 1967 concerning Ferranti's contract for manufacturing the Bloodhound missile and Bristol Siddeley's contract covering the overhaul of aircraft engines indicate that such profits can be very high indeed.[4]

But the traditional stereotype of the sinister and all-pervading influence of the merchants of death does not correspond to the situation in the country in the fifties and sixties. There is here, I think, an important difference between the United States and Britain.

---

[1] *Statement on the Defence Estimates, 1965.* Command 2592.
[2] *Hansard.* March 3, 1965. Col. 1341.
[3] *Commonwealth Survey.* August 31, 1965.
[4] Both companies found themselves obliged in the end to return large sums to the Treasury, Ferranti £4,250,000 and Bristol Siddeley £3,900,000.

In his well-known farewell address, President Eisenhower warned his countrymen, with every justification, against "the acquisition of unwarranted influence, whether sought or unsought, by the military-industrial complex", i.e., the immense military establishment and arms industry, whose economic, political and even spiritual influence, he said, could be felt in every American city and state and in every office of the Federal Government.[1] Such a situation could arise in Britain, but has not so far done so.

In this connection, it is worth glancing again at the views expressed at the beginning of the sixties by Sir Leslie Rowan, head of Vickers, a company lying near the heart of the British military-industrial complex. The central idea of his book was that the threat from the Communist states is now economic rather than military. The Communists still sought to destroy the institutions of the West, he wrote, but "in the present phase they place first priority on the economic weapon . . . this threat could be more dangerous to us in the long run than the military threat".[2]

Britain could no longer aspire to be among the greatest military powers, Rowan continued. If she kept up her guard in conventional weapons and the United States maintained the power of effective nuclear retaliation against the Soviet Union, the danger of war was remote. Since Russia and the other Communist states had declared war in the fields of trade, Britain should take up the challenge and seek to expand her trade relations with them. "Does it make economic sense, in our own interests, to disregard or restrict our trade with countries which contain one-third of the population of the world . . . ?"[3]

We may also note the study of the probable economic effects of disarmament by the Economist Intelligence Unit, which is based on information supplied by the firms who would be most directly affected by a radical reduction in arms expenditure, i.e., those working on military contracts.

The general drift is indicated by the authors' thesis, substantiated in the second part of the book, that, as there are many competing claims on the economy which cannot at present be satisfied fully, the removal of the need for defence expenditure would provide considerable scope for current and new civil projects, both in the public and the private sector.[4] The situation would vary from industry to

---

[1] *Public Papers of the President 1960–1961*. Washington. 1961. p. 1038.
[2] Rowan. *op. cit.* p. 56.
[3] *Ibid.* p. 57.
[4] Economist Intelligence Unit. *op. cit.* p. viii.

industry and firm to firm, the aircraft industry being the most vulnerable, but the study suggests that in the event of general disarmament "the transition period should pass without any major setback being experienced by the economy as a whole".[1]

It is obvious, of course, that the whole of the costs of British military policy do not arise from the contest between the capitalist and Communist halves of Europe, between NATO and Warsaw Pact countries. It is difficult to draw any exact dividing lines, but until recently a major part of them were attributable to a mixture of neo-colonial and anti-Communist aims in the Middle East and South-East Asia.

Moreover, there is plenty of evidence that the insistence of the policy-makers that Britain should become and remain a nuclear power arises from considerations by no means confined to the possibility of war with the Soviet Union (or China). Macmillan, for example, when pressed to explain why Britain needed to have the H-bomb when America already had it, replied quite frankly that the possession of an independent nuclear force "gives us a better position . . . with respect to the United States. It puts us where we ought to be, in the position of a Great Power".[2]

Nevertheless, the interaction between the economic pressure exercised by the military budget and the evolution of British policy towards the Soviet Union and Communist Europe generally has been close and continuous.

This is clearest in the field of NATO strategy and tactics. As we have seen, from the mid-fifties until very recently successive Governments were forced by the prick of dire necessity to keep down and cut back the size of the British forces deployed on the continent and to avoid situations in which they would be compelled to increase them. As the Ministry of Defence put it not so long ago, "NATO is essential to our security . . . But the foreign exchange problem has added urgency to the reappraisal of NATO strategy."[3]

The main effect of the economic factor, however, has been greatly to increase the anxiety of the authorities to secure a halt to the nuclear arms race.

No Government, Conservative or Labour, has so far shown any inclination to abandon Britain's nuclear status, but throughout the sixties they have been aware that the country cannot keep up with the race except at ruinous cost. They have had, therefore, a

[1] *Ibid.* p. 141.
[2] *The Times.* February 24, 1958.
[3] *Statement on the Defence Estimates.* February 1967. Command 3203.

major economic as well as strategic interest in at least freezing the situation as it now is by agreements such as the ban on nuclear tests and on the dissemination of nuclear weapons and also in the attainment of an understanding between the Soviet and U.S. Governments, which will forfend further escalation of the nuclear arms race during the seventies.

The Domestic Political Climate

Throughout the past fifteen years and more the British political climate has been unfavourable to aggressive and rigid attitudes in East-West relations, and has tended to push British policy in the same direction as strategic and economic factors.

The subject of the influence of internal political changes on policy towards the Soviet Union is beset by pitfalls. It is easy, for example, to exaggerate the effect upon British diplomacy of such dramatic mass movements as the Campaign for Nuclear Disarmament at the end of the fifties and the beginning of the sixties. The Baldwin and Chamberlain Governments ignored the results of the even bigger and more representative Peace Ballot, in which 11,000,000 citizens showed a three to one majority in favour of military sanctions against aggressor states. It must be noted that when the CND captured the 1960 Labour Party Conference, Gaitskell and his friends refused point-blank to be bound by its decision and got it reversed the following year.

Moreover, those concerned with international affairs sometimes suffer from the professional disease of thinking that foreign policy questions occupy a larger place in the public mind and particularly the voter's mind than they really do. The central issues in all British general elections since the war have been domestic and not foreign.

But for all that, British diplomacy is not conducted in a special compartment isolated from the political tides sweeping the country and from the struggle for power between the two main parties.

Firstly, ministers and party leaders are no more immune from popular, particularly electoral, pressures on foreign policy issues than they are on domestic issues. Hoare in 1935, Chamberlain in 1940 and Eden in 1957 were all driven from office by hostile waves of opinion, inside and outside Parliament, set off by foreign policy catastrophes for which they were principally responsible.

These were extreme cases, but every government is aware that sooner or later it has to answer to Parliament and the electorate for its conduct of foreign affairs, and every opposition leadership knows that its chances of regaining power depend to some extent on what foreign policy programme it presents to the voters.

Secondly, it is not true, as used to be alleged on the left, that there are no significant differences between the foreign policies of the Labour and Conservative leaderships. On the contrary, they have a built-in tendency to diverge, arising from the different social bases of the two parties and from the different internal political pressures to which their leaders are subjected. What is true is that the differences are tactical and not strategic and that their extent has varied widely at different historical periods.

During the twenties, relations with the Soviet Union were a major issue between the two parties, particularly at the general elections of 1924 and 1929. The victory of Labour in 1924 led directly to *de jure* recognition and in 1929 to the restoration of diplomatic relations meanwhile broken off by the preceding Conservative Government. Similarly, in the late thirties the Labour leadership ranged itself with the Churchill group of Conservatives against the Chamberlain Government's appeasement of Nazi Germany. It voted against the Munich Agreement, and in 1940 brought Churchill to power by refusing to join a coalition government unless it was led by him and not Chamberlain or Halifax.

During the early post-war years there was an open alliance between the two front benches against the left-wing of the Labour Party on all the key aspects of East-West relations in Europe.[1] But as suggested below, in the period under review the differences once more made themselves felt.

Thirdly, although the Foreign Office, like the Ministry of Defence, the Treasury and the whole state machine exercises a considerable influence on policy, it cannot, despite popular legend, pursue its own way regardless of what Government is in power or of what the Prime Minister, the Foreign Secretary and the Cabinet want.

Before the war the initiative in the almost fatal policy of appeasing the Axis powers lay throughout with Chamberlain, who pursued it in the face of scepticism and divided opinions in the upper echelons of the Foreign Office and executed it chiefly with the help of an official, Sir Horace Wilson, drawn from outside its ranks. In more recent times a group of senior Foreign Office officials were, by all accounts, opposed to the attack on Egypt in 1956, but were unable to prevent Eden and Selwyn Lloyd from plunging into disaster.[2]

[1] See on this subject Eden. *op. cit.* p. 5, Kilmuir *op. cit.* pp. 145–146.
[2] See, for example, Anthony Nutting. *No End of a Lesson.* p. 138.

In the period with which we are concerned, British policy towards Communist Europe has, I think, been mainly influenced by two different internal political factors, one operating throughout the last twenty years and affecting the leaderships of both parties alike and the other touching primarily the Labour Party and coming directly into the picture only in the sixties.

Ever since the strategic balance began to change to the disadvantage of the West at the end of the forties, the central question in East-West relations, the question whether or not the world is to slide into a nuclear holocaust, has, at one time or another, disturbed every thinking man and woman in the country.

This does not mean that the public at large has eagerly followed the ins and outs of the German and Berlin questions, of disarmament negotiations, or of intra-NATO quarrels over nuclear weapons. But it does mean that millions of people are politically sensitive to the general drift of British diplomacy in this area and to the attitude adopted by the two party leaderships.

The result has been that both the Conservative and Labour leaders have engaged in a contest, particularly during the run-up to general elections, to convince the voters that they and not their opponents can best be trusted to steer away from nuclear war and towards a détente with the Soviet Union. The contest has thrown up a lot of unfulfilled promises and disingenuous proposals, but it has also acted as an extra spur to diplomatic moves genuinely designed to reduce tension in East-West relations.

Churchill's first public suggestion for "a parley at the summit", referred to earlier, was launched in the middle of the 1950 election campaign and caused something like panic in the Labour leadership, which tried unsuccessfully to brush off the idea as an electoral stunt. He again sought to gain credit from this suggestion in his broadcast election address at the height of the election campaign in 1951.[1]

In the spring of 1955 the Conservative Government, by then faced with public pressure from the Labour leadership to initiate a summit meeting, so contrived matters as to make this cause securely their own in good time for the May general election. At the cost of flurrying its American partners, it announced on April 25, some two weeks before the official Western invitation to the Soviet Union was issued, its unconditional agreement to take part in a four-power conference at any level and as soon as possible.[2]

Eisenhower, who had been holding out for a preliminary Foreign

---

[1] *Keesing's Contemporary Archives.* 1951. pp. 11781–11282.
[2] *Keesing's Contemporary Archives.* 1955. p. 14191.

Ministers' meeting, says rather sourly in his memoirs that presumably domestic political exigencies had something to do with the behaviour of the new Prime Minister, Eden.[1] James Reston, then the best informed of Washington correspondents, reported quite flatly that the American decision in the end to fall in with Eden's wishes was due to the desire to help him win the election.[2]

Macmillan's visit to Moscow in February–March 1959 was undertaken at a time when, against the background of the Berlin crisis, public anxiety over nuclear tests, American nuclear bomber patrols over Britain, American nuclear bases and the danger of nuclear war generally, was at its height, and when the October general election was looming up on the horizon. While his initiative was greeted by a chorus of abuse from Bonn, personally led by Adenauer, it was bound to and did receive all-round approval at home.

In terms of party politics, the Conservatives had to reckon with the fact that Gaitskell and the Labour leadership, as recalled in Chapter 3, had already come out as advocates of far-reaching measures of disengagement as the prescription for a European détente. The results of the Moscow visit trumped this card in Gaitskell's hand, even though he, in an effort to establish himself as the better East-West bridge-builder, paid a visit to the Soviet Union in August during the run-up to the election campaign.

The Labour leadership was equally unsuccessful in its endeavours to present itself to its own party and to the public generally as the champions of nuclear disarmament.

In June 1959 the National Executive of the Labour Party and the General Council of the TUC launched a proposal for a so-called non-nuclear club with British membership, which, owing to French opposition, was known in advance by its authors to be unrealisable.[3] This disingenuous manœuvre not only failed to stem the onrush of the unilateral disarmers within the Labour Party, but confirmed the general impression in the country that in these matters Gaitskell would be a poor alternative to Macmillan.

The opinion polls showed that by the time of the October election there was widespread belief even among Labour supporters that the Conservatives were better able to handle East-West relations than their opponents.[4]

Thus, throughout the fifties the Conservatives, at first when in opposition and then when in power, held the whip-hand over the

---

[1] *Mandate for Change.* p. 505.
[2] *New York Times.* May 11, 1955.
[3] For text, see *Labour Research.* August 1959. p. 121.
[4] D. E. Butler and Richard Rose. *The British General Election of 1959.* London. 1960. p. 71.

Labour leadership on the question of defusing East-West relations. Paradoxical though it may seem, although mass opposition to American bases, to West German military ambitions and to all forms of nuclear strategy was much stronger among Labour than Conservative supporters (see Chapters 2 and 3), Attlee and Gaitskell, while responding in some degree to pressure from below, for the most part trotted at the heels of Churchill, Eden and Macmillan, and never succeeded in wresting the initiative from them.

In the sixties this situation altered, the main reason being a change in the balance of forces within the Labour Party itself, a shift to the left, narrowing the gap between the mass of party supporters in the trade unions, local organisations and among the public generally, on one side, and the leader and his circle, on the other.

It would take us far from the theme of this book to attempt to analyse this shift, the main causes of which lay outside the field of foreign affairs. We will only mention that its history runs back to 1956, when the hold of the right wing on the trade unions began to slip, that by 1960 Gaitskell and his friends were in serious trouble, suffering a double defeat, first on the question of nuclear strategy and then in their attempt to remove Clause 4 from the Constitution of the Party,[1] and that the new balance of strength showed itself for all to see in 1963 when, on Gaitskell's death, the candidate of the centre and left, Harold Wilson, defeated the candidate of the right, George Brown, in the contest for the leadership of the Party.

From this moment on, party alignments on the central question of East-West relations in Europe resumed what I think it is fair to call their natural configuration.

As the October 1964 general election approached, both party leaderships once again attempted to present themselves to the voters as the authentic champions of a peaceful settlement, but this time the initiative was seized by the new Labour leadership under Wilson as regards both concrete proposals and direct contacts with the Soviet Government.

In their election literature on foreign affairs, the Conservatives gave first place to what they called the tireless efforts of their leaders "to seek common ground and reasonable solutions in negotiation with the Soviet Union" and made play with Eden's role in the 1955 Summit, with his initiative in inviting the Soviet leaders to Britain in 1956 and with Macmillan's pilgrimage to Moscow in 1959.[2] In an

---

[1] The clause looking to "common ownership of the means of production, distribution and exchange".

[2] *The Election Campaign Guide 1964*. The Conservative and Unionist Central Office. London. 1964. p. 401.

effort to maintain this image, R. A. Butler, then Foreign Secretary, was despatched on a visit to Moscow at the end of July, two months before the dissolution.

The Conservatives were, however, outbid by their opponents. Wilson and the Shadow Foreign Secretary, Gordon Walker, visited the Soviet Union in June 1963 and again in June 1964. Arriving hot-foot from the latter visit, Gordon Walker claimed, quite justifiably as it turned out, that in their talks with the Soviet leaders he and Wilson had marked out a promising line of advance. If, as the Labour Party recommended, the proposed multilateral nuclear force with West German participation were dropped, he said, there was a good chance of reaching a non-proliferation agreement, and also, possibly, some form of nuclear freeze in Central Europe.[1] This line was repeated in the Labour Election Manifesto, which also promised that a Labour Government would make "an all-out effort to develop East-West trade as the soundest economic basis for peaceful co-existence".[2] There is no reason to doubt that these energetic tactics appealed to the electorate and played some part in Labour's return to power.

During the following five years, owing to the general easing of East-West relations in Europe and the shift of the main focus of tension in international affairs to the Far East, the question of policy towards the Soviet Union and its European allies played a consider-ably smaller part in British internal politics.

The general election campaign of 1966 was as usual fought chiefly over domestic issues and, as far as foreign policy is concerned, more attention was paid to the question of entering the Common Market and how to handle the Smith régime in Rhodesia than to the nuclear arms race, European security or any other matter directly concerning Communist Europe. Thereafter the Government's attitude towards the American war in Vietnam overshadowed all other foreign policy issues in the minds of all political parties and groups and of the public generally.

But at the same time the very fact of the replacement of the Con-servatives at the levers of power by the new Labour leadership in 1964 and the latter's confirmation in office by a large majority in 1966 was itself favourable to a stabilisation of relations with Communist Europe.

In the first place, the arrival on the scene of Wilson and his colleagues acted as a catalyst, precipitating a number of necessary

[1] *Hansard.* June 16, 1964. Cols. 1139–1152.
[2] "The New Britain", published in full in *The Times.* September 12, 1964.

and overdue steps in this field which the preceding Conservative régime had contemplated but, owing to internal disagreements, could not bring itself to take.

The most important of these measures were described at the beginning of this chapter. Here we will only recall that both the Macmillan and Douglas-Home Governments had been divided on the merits of the Washington-Bonn proposal for a multilateral nuclear force and as a result had said neither yes nor no to British participation. The Labour Party, however, went to the polls in 1964 with a definite undertaking to refuse participation, a promise which in due course it fulfilled, thereby contributing to the demise of this proposal.

Secondly, the intensity and persistence of the Labour Government's pursuit of a personal dialogue with the Soviet leaders was carried over from Wilson's practice while in opposition and developed Anglo-Soviet summitry to a level far above that sought by its Conservative predecessors. In the first four years of the Labour administration, Wilson himself paid two visits to Moscow, in February 1966 and January 1968, and in between received the Soviet Prime Minister on an official visit to London in February 1967. The Foreign Secretary paid official visits to Moscow in November–December 1965 and in May 1968 and entertained Gromyko in London in March 1966. During the same period there was a round dozen of visits exchanged by other British and Soviet Ministers.

While the attitude of both party leaderships towards the 1968 Czechoslovak crisis was in essentials the same, Labour Ministers showed more concern than their Conservative opponents at the prospect of a general deterioration in East-West relations. As we have already recalled, both leaderships said that the actions of the Soviet Government confirmed the need to maintain the NATO alliance. But when it came to practical measures, the Conservatives urged, while the Government opposed, the immediate summoning of a high-level NATO conference, the Conservatives demanded, and the Government rejected, a deferment of the withdrawal of British forces East of Suez.

The attitude of the two leaderships to long-term policy showed the same difference of emphasis. Wilson spoke up for moderation, saying that "the future of the world depends on continuing to work for détente between East and West" and that he rejected the view that there was no choice except to relapse into the frozen immobilism of the cold war. Douglas-Home, for the Conservatives, without denying this proposition, could only bring himself to say, *pianissimo*, that if a policy of strength and conciliation was pursued it might be possible to make agreements with the Communist world which may be of benefit to all mankind.[1]

This is a bad moment to attempt to predict in what way the internal climate is likely in future to influence British policy towards Communist Europe, since all the indicators helping one to judge the general drift in domestic politics are at present distorted by the effects of the prolonged balance of payments crisis from which the country is just emerging. I would, however, like to make two guesses, one reasonably safe and the other risky.

The first, based on the experience of the last two decades, is that, while there will be sharp fluctuations in Anglo-Soviet relations, public opinion will continue to exercise steady pressure on both the Labour and Conservative leaderships in favour of a course leading towards a stabilisation of relations between the two systems.

The second, based perhaps more on hope than anything else, is that the Labour leadership will not again, as Attlee, Bevin and Gaitskell did in the fifties, run behind the Conservatives both in grasping the realities of the situation and in sensing the movement of opinion among the mass of the people.

[1] *The Times.* August 27, 1968.

CHAPTER NINE

China and the Other Asian Communist States[1]

China in British World Policy

In considering British policy towards Communist China and the other
Asian Communist states, it is, I think, necessary above all to remind
oneself that at the time of the Japanese victorious onslaught on her
positions in 1941–1942 Britain lost her great power status in the Far
East and has never regained it.

At the end of the Second World War Britain recovered her colonial
possessions in South-East Asia and Hong Kong, but was shut out by
the United States from any real say in Japanese affairs, and in
China had no influence with the Communists and almost none with
the Nationalists, the latter being entirely dependent on American
arms and money. Australia and New Zealand, which owed their
escape from subjugation by the Japanese almost solely to the United
States, continued to regard the latter, and not Britain, as their
principal military ally.

Although Churchill and his colleagues had foreseen and tried to
forestall this situation,[2] successor Governments found themselves
powerless to alter it. Compelled through weakness to distinguish
more sharply than before between areas of primary and secondary
concern, they perforce gave priority to Europe and the Middle East
over the Far East, the region geographically the most remote, the one
on which the British hold had proved in the test of war to be the
weakest and also the one in which the United States had for the time
being established, so far as the other leading capitalist powers were
concerned, an unassailable hegemony.

The policy-makers also found themselves obliged to determine
distinct priorities within the Far Eastern area, concentrating upon

---

[1] Since the period of active British engagement in Korean affairs falls outside the scope
of this book, North Korea is only touched on in passing. On the other hand, although Laos
is not a Communist state, British policy there is included, since it formed an integral part
of policy towards Vietnam and the Vietnam war.

[2] See, for example, Churchill. *The Second World War*. Vol. VI. London. 1954. pp.
129–136.

preserving the British stronghold in South-East Asia (Malaya, Singapore, Sarawak, Brunei and North Borneo) and, if possible, retaining Hong Kong, while making no serious move to restore Britain's once considerable political and military influence on the Chinese mainland. China thus became in a double sense a secondary front.

This pattern was established under the direct pressures of the war itself, emerging clearly in the Anglo-American conflict over priorities first as between the European and Pacific theatres and then as between the South-East Asian and Chinese theatres. It persisted during the early post-war years, when London launched an all-out drive to crush the Communists in Malaya and Singapore, but, in sharp contrast to the United States, played a waiting game during the Chinese Civil War. It survived the transfer of power to the Chinese Communists in 1949. Britain, again in sharp contrast to the United States and indeed all the other leading Western powers, almost immediately recognised the new Chinese People's Republic and gave every sign of desiring peaceful co-existence with it. The same pattern showed itself unmistakably during the series of Far Eastern crises during the first half of the fifties.

If one compares British policy towards the European and Asian Communist states at that period, one major difference immediately strikes the eye. As regards Europe, despite a growing desire in London for a relaxation of tension, it was (and still is) regarded as axiomatic that Britain must keep large forces, both conventional and nuclear, on the continent and at home, permanently disposed for a possible war with the Soviet Union, and that Britain must maintain permanently functioning bilateral and multilateral arrangements with the United States and other allies for this purpose. As regards Asia, on the other hand, the central idea was entirely different. It was consistently held that Britain, far from standing permanently ready for a possible war with Communist China, should do all in her power to avoid one and should use whatever influence she had to prevent the United States from becoming involved in one either.

At a critical moment during the Korean war, when a full-scale Sino-American war seemed imminent, the Prime Minister (Clement Attlee) urged upon President Truman that, as the West was engaged in a global struggle against Communist expansion, "it would be suicidal to allow our forces to be bogged down in China ... To try to attack China — a huge amorphous mass — was folly".[1]

Churchill also made his views on this point perfectly clear. Expressing his disquiet at the diversion of attention and resources from

[1] Francis Williams. *op. cit.* p. 236.

Europe, he said that "when the main dangers are so much nearer home, we do not want to see ourselves tied down or entangled in a war in Korea—still less in a war in China".[1] In his opinion nothing could be more foolish than for the armies of the United States and the United Nations to be engulfed in the vast areas of China or for Generalissimo Chiang Kai-shek to plunge on to the mainland.[2]

This latter danger increased the following year, when the U.S. Government announced that, while the U.S. 7th Fleet would continue to guard Formosa from attack from the mainland, it would no longer shield Communist China from attack by Chiang's forces in Formosa. Even the official British reaction to this was uncompromisingly unfavourable, the Foreign Secretary saying publicly in February 1953 that the Government could not approve of this step, which it feared might have unfortunate political repercussions without compensating military advantages.[3]

Unwillingness to contemplate war with China played a major part in determining British policy during the Indo-China crisis of 1954. As early as May 1952, in reply to American suggestions that it might prove necessary to blockade China's coasts and disrupt her internal communications, the Foreign Secretary stated that "Her Majesty's Government were strongly opposed to any course of action in South-East Asia, which would be likely to result in a war with China".[4]

When in April 1954 the Cabinet, despite the heaviest American pressure, finally rejected Dulles's plan for military intervention in Vietnam, it did so in the belief that such intervention would probably lead eventually to action against the Chinese mainland and that, in Eden's words, Britain would find herself involved in the wrong war, against the wrong man in the wrong place.[5]

The same line was pursued in the subsequent crisis over the Nationalist-held off-shore islands (Quemoy and the Matsus) in 1954–1955.

The Government took the position in public statements that the islands "undoubtedly form part of the territory of the People's Republic of China" and that the Nationalists should withdraw from them.[6]

Behind the scenes, Churchill privately expressed his fears to Eisenhower that during the next two or three years the United States

[1] Statement on January 30, 1952. *Documents* . . . 1952. pp. 56–57.
[2] Statement on February 26, 1952. *Survey of International Affairs.* 1952. London. 1955. p. 306.
[3] *Documents* . . . 1953. pp. 440–441.
[4] Eden. *op. cit.* p. 83
[5] *Ibid.* pp. 106 and 102.
[6] *Hansard.* February 4, 1955. Cols. 159–160.

might be drawn into a Chinese war.[1] Eden, for his part, spent a good deal of energy at the Geneva Summit in July 1955 in trying to persuade his American and Soviet colleagues to bring about a peaceful solution.[2]

It is true that, when in 1958 the Chinese Government once more started military operations to regain the islands and the danger of a direct Sino-American clash once more loomed up, the Government, though pressed hard by the Labour leadership, this time refused to be drawn into public opposition to Washington and Chiang.

The reason for this, however, lay in a change not in British policy towards China but in Anglo-American relations, one which worked strongly against open polemics. As shown in Chapter 2, the special relationship had at this time recently entered a new and, from London's point of view, favourable phase, bringing with it, among other things, a renewal of Anglo-American co-operation in the nuclear field and joint Anglo-American landings in the Lebanon and Jordan.

In this situation, as their public statements showed, Macmillan and his colleagues leant over backwards to avoid giving offence in Washington, but at the same time maintained the established British position on the conflict itself.

A Foreign Office statement of September 12, 1958, said that "we have no obligations or commitments of any kind to take military action for the defence of Quemoy, Matsu or Formosa . . . The United States Government have neither sought nor received promises of British support in the event of war over the Chinese offshore islands". At the same time it went on to say that the immediate question was whether a dispute of this nature should be settled by force and that on this point the British Government strongly supported the United States and not the Chinese position.[3]

In a published exchange of letters with Gaitskell on September 15, Macmillan repeated this formula, adding that in its relations with Washington on the matter the Government preferred to proceed by way of "unfettered consultations and honest advice between partners in private", and not by taking public attitudes.[3]

Since then, the order of priorities in British world policy has remained the same and London's hold in the Far East has become more tenuous than ever. If the Government's plans are carried out, the last British soldier will have left Malaysia and Singapore by the end of 1971 and, short of a major reversal of policy, Britain will no longer

[1] Eisenhower. *op. cit.* pp. 609.
[2] Eden. *op. cit.* pp. 308–311.
[3] *Keesing's Contemporary Archives.* 1958. p. 16391.

have a Far Eastern base from which to conduct a land war not only in China but in South-East Asia as well.

As shown in more detail below, despite the Maoist upheaval and despite the connivance of the Conservative and Labour leaderships at the American invasion of Vietnam, British diplomacy towards China has continued to pursue the limited objectives of developing normal political and economic relations and of ending her isolation from the mainstream of international discussion and negotiation. In this period Britain played the pioneer role in breaking up the Western economic embargo against China, just as she had earlier been the first and only Western power to reject the American-imposed diplomatic boycott of Peking. London also resumed its efforts to secure the admission of the People's Republic to its proper place in the United Nations.

On the other hand, from the beginning of the sixties onwards, signs appeared of an intention to play a role, if only a subordinate one, in the new balance of power taking shape in the Pacific and Indian Ocean areas as a result of the emergence of a new and much stronger China, one armed with nuclear weapons.

The policy-makers cannot be accused of harbouring wild dreams of restoring Britain's bygone position in the Far East and still less in China itself. But they have been far from indifferent to the reverberations of increased Chinese power in the arc of Commonwealth countries, stretching from India and Pakistan in the north-west, through Malaysia and Singapore to Australia and New Zealand in the south-east.

The acquisition by China of nuclear weapons is not the only new element in the new relation of forces, but, as can be seen from the following remark by Prime Minister Wilson, its central significance was immediately recognised. "Any approach to world affairs," he said, "that does not recognise the problem created by the Chinese detonation of a nuclear device is unreal and already outdated."[1]

As has been recalled in the second part of this book, Harold Macmillan's Government's reaction to the Chinese attack on India's north-east frontier in the year 1962 was immediately to enter into military arrangements with the United States of America. This move made provision for Britain's participation, if only in a minor way, in the air defence of India against China. After the Chinese breakthrough in the nuclear field, special arrangements were put in hand,

[1] *Hansard.* December 16, 1964. Cols. 418–419.

though not in the end completed, for the establishment jointly with the Americans of a new nuclear base in the Indian Ocean and discussions were opened with the Australians regarding a possible new base in Australia.

In the Indian Ocean, where the RAF already maintained an important staging post at Gan in the Maldive Islands, a new colonial administrative unit, British Indian Ocean Territory, was created in November 1966, which, in the words of the official announcement, would "be available for the construction of defence facilities by the British and United States Governments".[1] We have it on the authority of Mayhew, who was Minister for the Navy until 1966, that the Government's purpose was to make available the islands of Aldabra and Diego Garcia as possible airfields, communications centres and refuelling and supply points.[2]

In April 1967 an Anglo-American Agreement was published providing a framework for consultation and apportionment of costs should military installations be built there. It was also stated that representatives of the U.S. Navy and the British Ministry of Defence representatives would thereafter visit Aldabra also.[3]

As one result of the devaluation crisis of November 1967, the Government announced that it would not proceed with the proposed staging post at Aldabra, which, it said, would have cost £4,000,000 in 1968 and a great deal more in later years.[4] But it cannot be assumed that the United States will not set up a nuclear base in British Indian Ocean Territory, nor that, if one is built, it will not be used by the RAF and the British Navy.

As regards Australia, the Government's plans, about which it was a good deal more secretive, at one time evidently included a base not only for its nuclear striking force, but also for conventional forces transferred from Singapore and Malaysia.

In 1965, when the air was thick with rumours on the subject, the Ministry of Defence denied that a new base was to be built, but confirmed that British V-bombers (part of the nuclear striking force) were flying from Singapore to carry out joint exercises with the Australian air force at Darwin in Northern Australia.[5]

A year later, however, it was disclosed in the 1966 Defence White Paper that discussions had already begun with the Australian Government about the possibility of acquiring permanent military

---

[1] *Commonwealth Survey.* September 2, 1966.
[2] Mayhew. *op. cit.* p. 19.
[3] *Survey of British and Commonwealth Affairs.* June 9, 1967.
[4] *Hansard.* November 27, 1967. Cols. 50–77.
[5] *The Guardian.* January 14, 1965.

facilities in Australia.[1] The 1967 White Paper said that these discussions were continuing.[2] No specific mention was made of the matter in official statements on Far Eastern military policy in 1968, but the Government declared in general terms that, once withdrawal from Malaysia and Singapore had been completed by the end of 1971, Britain would not maintain a special capability for operations outside Europe.[3]

All in all it seems likely that, while the Government has abandoned whatever thoughts it may have had of transferring part of the permanent garrisons in Malaysia and Singapore to a new base in Australia,[4] it intends to make increasing use of Australian territory and Australian facilities for elements of the British nuclear striking force, both naval and air, visiting or patrolling in the Pacific and Indian Oceans.

In 1966–1967 both the Conservative and Labour leaderships came out with proposals for re-organising the system of Western alliances in the Indian and Pacific Oceans to permit Britain to join the United States, Australia and New Zealand in providing a strategic nuclear shield against China.

Sir Alec Douglas-Home was first in the field with a plan for "an Asian SEATO" with exclusively Asian membership, which would be responsible for land defence, while the present United States-Australia-New Zealand groupings, ANZUS, would be expanded to include Britain and would "guarantee the lifelines of Asia by keeping open the Pacific, Indonesian and Indian seas".[5] A few months later, the Labour Minister of Defence, without spelling out the details, advanced a similar idea. The ideal solution, he said, would be one in which Britain, the United States, Australia and New Zealand, while no longer belonging to an Asian regional defence association, would provide it with "an external guarantee".[6]

The preoccupation with China lying behind these plans showed itself clearly in what was perhaps the frankest of all the Labour Government's many attempts to justify its East of Suez doctrine, forced out of the Prime Minister by the critical probings of his own

[1] Command 2901. February 1966.
[2] Command 3203. February 1967.
[3] *Survey of British and Commonwealth Affairs.* March 15, 1968.
[4] According to Mayhew, transferring the full facilities of the Singapore base to Australia might have cost well over £100,000,000 and would have been received with mixed feelings by the Australian authorities, who regarded British forces stationed in Australia as a poor substitute for British forces stationed on the Asian mainland. *op. cit.* p. 89.
[5] Speech at the Conservative Party Annual Conference, 1966. *The Times.* October 15, 1966.
[6] Speech at the Royal Commonwealth Society. *Survey of British and Commonwealth Affairs.* May 26, 1967.

supporters. "Did anyone think," Wilson asked, "that India wanted them to leave her to become a cockpit, forced to choose between Russia and America to protect her against China? If you are going to ask countries such as India to renounce their right to develop or acquire nuclear power . . . when the dominating fact is that a hostile neighbour has already got it—then you have got to give them security . . ."[1]

Whether Britain will for long be a participant in a Western, predominantly American, nuclear counter-force pointed at China is doubtful, despite the evident intention in high quarters that she should.

In the first place, experience of the devaluation crisis in 1967 suggests that to do so may prove to be literally beyond her means. As a result of the crisis, the Government found itself on financial grounds obliged to cancel its order for fifty U.S. F111 aircraft on which the future British air striking force in Asia and the Pacific was to have been based, and, as we have seen, to withdraw from participation in the construction of the proposed new base on Aldabra. Secondly, the pressures working in favour of an even more marked European bias in British policy are powerful and may lead to an even more drastic diminution in the British military role East of Suez than is at present planned.

But for the time being, while in tactical terms Britain, except in the special case of Hong Kong (see below), has all but disengaged herself from China, strategically she has not yet done so.

The Impact of Maoism

Although the strengthening of the personal dictatorship of Mao Tse-tung and his entourage and the mounting chauvinism and megalomania of Chinese foreign policy connected therewith brought about major changes in the international scene during the sixties, the effect on British policy towards China has been remarkably small.

Maoism imported its own peculiar complications into Anglo-Chinese relations. The "cultural revolution" overflowed into a series of incidents in 1966–1968, including the sacking of the British Embassy in Peking and clashes on the Chinese–Hong Kong border and in Hong Kong itself. For a much longer period, both particular vagaries of Maoist policy such as the "great leap forward" launched in 1958 and the general economic disorganisation resulting from the

[1] *The Times.* June 16, 1966.

struggle for power at the top hampered the development of commercial relations.[1] But the essentially conciliatory character of British diplomacy has remained unchanged.

The basic reason for this has been that, despite the violent anti-imperialist slogans shouted from Peking, Maoist foreign policy has so far been directed less against the capitalist great powers than against the other Communist states, above all the Soviet Union, and against the strongest and most influential of the third-world countries — India.

As regards military matters, a distinction must be drawn here between China's testing of nuclear weapons, which presented all the powers, capitalist and Communist alike, with a new long-term problem, and her military dispositions and actions, which did not.

During the sixties, as a result of military pressure exercised by Peking, both the Soviet Union and India were forced to look to the security of their frontiers with China and to take costly and large-scale counter-measures. The Western powers, on the other hand, were confronted with no direct challenge of this kind.

The only military engagements fought by China in the last decade with a foreign country have been the border clashes with India in 1962 and with the Soviet Union in the last few years. There has been no armed conflict with the United States in connection with either Formosa or the Vietnam war. Even British sovereignty in Hong Kong, geographically, ethnically and historically part of China and militarily defenceless against Chinese attack, has not as yet been challenged.

In the economic field, again as the direct result of Maoist policy, there was a major switch in the direction of China's foreign trade away from the Soviet Union and towards the leading capitalist powers. China continued a high rate of exports to the Soviet Union in payment of her debts, but, as can be seen from Table 16, there has been a clear tendency for advanced capitalist countries to replace the Soviet Union as China's main source of imports.

It cannot be said that the political strategists in London were particularly quick in taking the measure of Maoism or that even today they have fully grasped its nature and significance in world affairs. It would, indeed, be surprising if they had, since, so far as I know, no one in the capitalist or Communist world has yet succeeded in producing a satisfactory analysis of it.

For several years after the Moscow-Peking conflict became common knowledge, the Government and the opinion-formers remained

[1] See on this subject Pauline Lewin. *The Foreign Trade of Communist China*. New York. 1964. pp. 54–58.

Table 16[1]

Exports to China

($ Million)

	1960	1961	1962	1963	1964	1965	1966	1967
Soviet Union	817	367	233	187	135	192	175	n.a.
Western Europe[2]	276	133	118	131	143	263	378	472
Japan	3	17	39	62	153	245	315	288
Australia and Canada[3]	33	284	236	307	278	266	257	287

cautious in suggesting how, if at all, British and Western diplomacy generally should react to it.

As late as July 1963, Edward Heath, then the Government's chief spokesman on foreign affairs in the House of Commons, after reviewing differences between Chinese and Soviet views on peaceful co-existence and the role of the national-liberation movement, told his hearers that it would be wishful thinking to make too much of these differences. "Surely what we must realise," he said, "is that both sides will have an undeniable interest in maintaining the ties which bind them."[4]

Floyd, a leading specialist on Communist affairs, in a massive work on the subject published in 1964, noted with approval that "Communism as an idea, as a policy and as an organisation, is divided, and because it is divided it is weaker". But, without himself making any concrete proposals, merely complained that advantage was not being taken of this situation. "The Sino-Soviet split is a serious challenge to Western policy-makers," he wrote, "and one which they still have not taken up."[5]

Edward Crankshaw, in a study written at about the same time, was equally positive that there was a critical breach and not a passing quarrel between the Soviet and Chinese leaderships, but was equally at a loss when it came to drawing practical conclusions about the future. There were too many imponderables, he said. He claimed to have a shrewd idea of how the Soviet Union would develop, "but who can tell how Communist China will develop?"[6]

It is true that in high quarters some advantage to the West has

---

[1] *UN Yearbook of International Trade Statistics*; Pauline Lewin. *op. cit.*; *Far Eastern Economic Review*. July 18, 1968.
[2] Britain, West Germany, France and Italy only.
[3] Mainly wheat and Australian wool.
[4] *Hansard*. July 2, 1963. Col. 226.
[5] David Floyd. *Mao against Khrushchev*. London. 1964. pp. 207–208.
[6] Edward Crankshaw. *The New Cold War. Moscow v. Pekin*. London 1963. pp. 7, 157.

been seen in the extreme anti-Russianism of the present Chinese Government.

One proponent of this thesis was, and perhaps still is, Sir Alec Douglas-Home. In a speech shortly after he became Prime Minister, having noted with satisfaction that the Communist world had split in half, he asserted that the presence of China on the eastern frontier of the Soviet Union was now a permanent factor compelling the latter to pursue a foreign policy more acceptable to the West.[1] An echo of this same idea appeared in the 1967 Defence White Paper, which, in explaining why NATO could now take a more sanguine view of Soviet intentions, mentioned, among other things, that "China has become a factor which the Soviet Government cannot ignore".[2]

One has to remember, however, that whatever advantages may be thought to have accrued to British world strategy by the split between Moscow and Peking, its particular form and particular consequences have also brought obvious disadvantages.

The breakdown in Sino-Soviet co-operation in the nuclear field and the development of an independent Chinese nuclear capacity has certainly set up new pressures on the Soviet Union, but they have also presented the Western powers with new and awkward problems. Apart from anything else, the Maoist position has contributed to the frustration of one of the main broad aims of British diplomacy in the present period, namely a stabilisation and reduction of arms levels and a universal ban on the spread of nuclear weapons.

Similarly, Chinese aversion to all forms of co-operation with the Soviet Union over the Vietnam war (including sabotage of the Soviet supply line to Hanoi) has certainly handicapped the Soviet Union and eased the path of the Americans, but it at the same time effectively jammed the machinery established under the Geneva Agreements by which Britain and the Soviet Union were supposed to act as honest brokers in the Vietnamese and Laos conflicts.

In these circumstances there has been no firm consensus of opinion in policy-making circles as to whether, taking in the whole world picture, the conflict between Peking and Moscow in the form it has so far taken has been a blessing, a mixed blessing or no blessing at all. We may note in this connection Alistair Buchan's conclusion, in summing up the views of the experts in 1965, that "the Sino-Soviet rift may by no means be to the advantage of the West".[3]

---

[1] Speech at the Conservative Party Annual Conference 1963. *The Times*. October 12, 1963.

[2] *Statement on the Defence Estimates*. Command 3203. February 1967.

[3] Buchan (Ed.) *China and the Peace of Asia*. New York. 1965. p. 10.

However, by the mid-sixties one central idea had taken firm hold, namely that, from Britain's point of view, Mao's bark was worse than his bite, despite his claim to be the chief scourge of the imperialists, and that, while his ultra-revolutionary slogans suggested world-wide ambitions, his immediate aims, potentially dangerous though they were, chiefly concerned the creation of a Chinese sphere of influence on China's own borders and the rectification of those borders themselves.

The Government and its advisers are not so foolish as to regard Mao and his henchmen as paper tigers. But to misuse another of his figures of speech, while strategically respecting China owing to her increasing strength and future nuclear capacity, tactically, i.e., in the short run, they have not been disposed to take Peking's threats at face value.

Thus the Minister of Defence in a speech in April 1966 said that the actions of the Chinese, and not their words, should be the clue to British interpretations of their intentions. In recent years, he continued, China had been far more cautious in the military field than the Soviet Union, witness the Cuban crisis. Communism had been spread in Eastern Europe by the Red Army, whereas he did not foresee the expansion of Chinese military power in this sense in South-East Asia. It was clear, however, that the Chinese Government would exploit instability and local conflict anywhere on its borders in order to promote its influence.[1]

Much the same opinion was expressed by the Leader of the Opposition, Edward Heath. On returning from a tour of Asia, he said in December 1965 that the general feeling was that China did not wish to enter on a campaign for the military domination of Asia, but that she would support subversion where it was found and in some cases encourage it.[2]

The same conception can be found in the statements of the Government's advisers on Far Eastern and Chinese affairs.

Robert Scott, British Commissioner-General in South-East Asia at the end of the fifties and thereafter Commandant of the Imperial Defence College and Permanent Secretary to the Ministry of Defence, wrote in 1965 that he did not believe that "Communist China is expansionist in the sense of conventional military aggression. It is not territorial gains that she seeks, but a ring of Communist buffer states, vassals of China, not of Russia." China's aim was to drive Europeans and Americans out of East Asia by all means short

[1] *Commonwealth Survey.* July 8, 1966,
[2] *Ibid,*

of war—"she will avoid direct military involvement if she can".[1]

W. A. C. Adie, a former Foreign Office specialist on Far Eastern affairs, in articles published in 1966 and 1967, stressed "the dichotomy between what China seems to be saying and what she seems to be doing" and suggested that for the time being there was little likelihood of Chinese expansion in the literal sense—"only subversion, provocation and above all propaganda and bluff".

Writing after the "cultural revolution" had got into its stride, Adie suggested that, owing to continuing internal disorder, China would for some time be too isolated, weak and divided to be dangerously aggressive. He also held that while the line of Lin Piao (Mao's second-in-command) stressed world-wide guerrilla war and sounded militaristic, it was basically defensive. Liu Shao-ch'i and the anti-Maoist opposition, he wrote, would probably have turned China into something more like a Stalinist state with more capability for conventional and nuclear offensive action, and were therefore potentially more dangerous to the outside world in the long-run.[2]

It is also of some interest that *The Economist*, I suppose the most influential of establishment journals, early on came to the conclusion that China under its present leadership did not represent such a danger as appeared at first sight.

As regards questions of Marxist theory, it wrote, the Soviet point of view was obviously preferable to that of Peking. But the Soviet Union and not China remained "the present menace to the West in terms of present power". In a prediction which has so far turned out to be correct, it said that attempts by the Chinese to win the non-white world to their side could probably be defeated "because they are a traditional master race themselves; because their ruling group takes little trouble to understand other peoples or to know the rest of the world; because the idea that war is inevitable is the last idea that the non-aligned nations are disposed, by their position, to accept".[3]

A Diplomacy of Limited Objectives

As we have already suggested, the main aims of British diplomacy towards Communist China have been to maintain normal diplomatic

---

[1] Alastair Buchan (Ed.) *op. cit.* pp. 52–53.
[2] *International Affairs.* London. April 1966 and July 1967.
[3] *The Economist.* August 3, 1963.

realations with her, to draw her into the normal process of international discussion and negotiation and, within this framework, to develop Sino-British trade and to prolong the British tenure of Hong Kong for as long as possible.

Owing to American opposition, which was at times very strong, there have been major deviations from this course, and, owing also in part to the volatile attitude of Peking, it has not produced any very striking results. Nevertheless, it is possible, I think, to discern one general line, running back to the foundation of the People's Republic and, to judge by present signs, likely to continue unchanged into the immediate future.

The attempt to maintain normal diplomatic relations met with difficulties from the first, since the Chinese Government held that, until various demands were satisfied, it could not agree to the establishment of diplomatic relations, but only to negotiations regarding their establishment. In practice this meant for some four years a British chargé d'affaires was uneasily perched in Peking with indeterminate status and there was no Chinese diplomatic representation in London at all.

Following a personal appeal by Eden to Chou En-lai in the course of the 1954 Geneva Conference,[1] this situation was ended in that year, when a Chinese chargé d'affaires was appointed to London. Even then the Chinese Government would not agree, and still has not agreed, to an exchange of ambassadors.

In 1966–1967, as we have already mentioned, the Government's determination to maintain diplomatic relations with Peking was severely tested by the ricochets of the "cultural revolution", the climax coming in August 1967, when in Peking the British mission was sacked and in London the staff of the Chinese mission staged a pitched battle with police outside their Embassy.

These events led to the imposition of temporary restrictions on the movements of Chinese diplomatic personnel in Britain similar to those imposed on British personnel in Peking, but brought no change in the Government's desire to keep open its channel of communication with the Chinese. When tension over these incidents was at its highest, the Foreign Office issued a statement saying that Her Majesty's Government had no wish to exacerbate the already unhappy relations between themselves and the People's Republic. "They are willing," it said, "at any time to discuss with the Chinese Government, on a rational and businesslike basis, the mutual relaxation of all these restrictions and the return to conditions between

[1] Eden. *op. cit.* p. 123.

them and the Chinese Government conducive to the proper conduct of international affairs."[1]

On the question of Chinese representation in the United Nations, succcssive governments, though in the fifties retreating under heavy American pressure into a highly ambiguous position, have consistently maintained that China's seat belonged to the People's Republic and not to Chiang's régime in Formosa.

In 1950, after hesitation in the early part of the year, the British vote was cast in favour of the People's Republic at the UN Assembly in September. This attitude was maintained for a short period even after China joined in the Korean war. The communiqué issued after the Attlee-Truman talks in Washington in December 1950 stated that the two Governments held opposing points of view on the subject. "The United Kingdom has recognised the Central People's Government and considers that its representatives should occupy China's seat in the United Nations. The United States has opposed and continues to oppose the seating of the Chinese Communist representatives in the United Nations."[2]

The following year the Government yielded a major hostage to fortune by voting, reluctantly, for the UN's February resolution declaring the People's Republic an aggressor in the Korean war. It thereupon resorted to a manœuvre enabling it to retain its position on the question of UN representation intact without having to defend it openly in the United Nations against a hostile majority led by the United States.

These tactics were deployed by a Foreign Office spokesman in the House of Commons in June 1951. His Majesty's Government still believes, he said, "that delegates from the Central People's Government should represent China in the United Nations. In view, however, of that Government's persistence in behaviour which is inconsistent with the purposes and principles of the Charter, it now appears to His Majesty's Government that consideration of this question should be postponed for the time being".[3]

"For the time being" turned out to be ten years, despite repeated efforts behind the scenes to get Washington to see reason.

During his visit to Washington in 1956, Eden, not for the first time, sounded Eisenhower and Dulles on the possibility of reopening the question. Against his hosts' contention that, owing to the state of American opinion, "a move to get China into the United Nations

---

[1] *Survey of British and Commonwealth Affairs.* September 15, 1967.
[2] *Documents . . .* 1949–1950. p. 124.
[3] *Hansard.* June 11, 1951. Cols. 159–160.

now . . . would be fatal", he still argued, as he had often done before, the case for seating the People's Republic. There was now a truce in the Far East, he said, and the United Nations was a universal organisation in which one must expect to have unpleasant people. But he came away empty-handed.[1]

Until the end of the fifties, in order to avoid giving offence in Washington, the Government continued on one pretext or another to vote in favour of postponing the issue. But in 1961 it at last decided once more to stand up and be counted.

This was heralded by a declaration by the Foreign Secretary in February that "international life requires that Communist China should be seated in the United Nations".[2] When the matter came to a vote in the Assembly in December, the British delegate supported a Soviet resolution in this sense. On this and subsequent occasions he evaded the question of what was to happen to Chiang's representatives by saying that, in the British view, sovereignty over Formosa was undetermined and the question of who should represent Formosa in the United Nations was therefore also undetermined.[3]

This has remained the official position down to the present day, surviving both the Chinese attack on India's frontier in 1962 (launched shortly before that year's vote was taken) and the 1967 physical assaults on British diplomatic personnel and property mentioned above. In 1968 the Foreign Secretary (Michael Stewart) pointed out that the absence from the United Nations of the representatives of the People's Republic partly accounted for the former's failure to play any significant part in ending the Vietnam war, that the United Nations must be a universal organisation and that states should not be excluded from it on the ground that one disliked their Governments.[4]

The attitude of the Government towards commercial relations with Communist China has been similar to its attitude towards political relations, and its policy has run a similar course.

Again under heavy pressure from Washington, London was obliged to give a draconian interpretation to the UN Assembly resolution of May 1951, calling for an embargo on the shipment of strategic materials to the People's Republic. But Britain took the lead among the Western powers in trying to break down this barrier and, when it was down, despite setbacks and disappointments, the

[1] *Eden. op. cit.* p. 333.
[2] *The Times.* February 9, 1961.
[3] *Commonwealth Survey.* February 12, 1963.
[4] *Survey of British and Commonwealth Affairs.* October 25, 1968.

Government set its sights on the maximalisation of Sino-British trade and has continued to do so down to the present day.

In pursuing this line, the policy-makers have been prompted and supported by British business interests specially concerned with the Chinese market. These firms, grouped together in the China Association,[1] not only favour recognition of, and the maintenance of normal relations with, the People's Republic, but have shown considerable realism in assessing their own prospects under a Communist régime and in adapting themselves to it.

The key move here was made soon after the Communists came to power and was made necessary by the particular nature of the stake built up by British firms in China. To a great extent, this took the form of profits not from external trade, but from large capital investments in China itself which were highly vulnerable under a régime dedicated to breaking the power within the country of private capital. These investments, chiefly concentrated in Shanghai, were in 1952 officially estimated at between £200,000,000 and £250,000,000.[2]

After some two years of vain effort to resume business operations inside China, the firms principally concerned decided to cut their losses and to concentrate thenceforth on obtaining as large a share of China's external trade as possible. In 1952, the Government, at the request of the China Association, informed the Chinese Government that nearly all the firms involved, since they could no longer operate satisfactorily in China, had decided to wind up their affairs and to set up a new form of organisation better suited to current conditions.[3] Thereafter, practically all British holdings in China were liquidated with major capital losses.[4]

The question of restrictions on trade with China came to a head in 1956–1957. As regards the economic side of the matter, British firms suffered as sellers, buyers, shippers, insurers and bankers both in direct British-Chinese trade and in trade between China and Hong Kong, Malaya, Singapore, Ceylon and Indonesia, a great deal of which was in their hands. Politically, the restrictions not only cut across the general line of British policy towards China, but were unacceptable to the Government of Ceylon and caused acute complications in Malaya, both countries being major exporters of

---

[1] For some details of the China Association and its policy, see Brian Porter. *Britain and the Rise of Communist China*. London. 1957. p. 153, and Evan Luard. *Britain and China*. London. 1962. pp. 145–147.

[2] *Hansard*. May 20, 1952. Col. 267.

[3] Note of April 12, 1952. *Documents* . . . 1952. p. 460.

[4] Jardine Matheson, for example, are said to have abandoned assets worth £30,000,000. Luard. *op. cit.* p. 141.

rubber to China. The restrictions were, moreover, unpopular with all sections of public opinion at home.

The Government, with the active support of the firms concerned, waged a long battle inside and outside the so-called China Committee (part of the Western machinery set up in Paris for operating trade embargoes against all parts of the socialist world) to secure a relaxation of the restrictions by consent, its chief opponent being the United States. During his visit to Washington in February 1956, Eden pressed the issue with Eisenhower and his advisers, making play chiefly with the undesirable political effects of the existing restrictions in Malaya, Ceylon and other Asian countries.[1]

These efforts having failed, the Government decided to proceed unilaterally. In May 1957 the Foreign Secretary announced in the House of Commons that in future Britain would apply the same controls to exports to China as it applied to exports to the Soviet Union, i.e., substantially reduce them. Other members of the China Committee, he said, had not yet defined their position, but he expected (correctly as it turned out) that, now that Britain had shown the way, the majority would follow suit.[2]

This move cleared away the principal political obstacle on the British side to the development of trade with China. It was followed in the sixties by a move on the Chinese side which worked in the same direction. As we have already recalled, owing to the Chinese-Soviet conflict, Peking switched a major part of its foreign purchases from the Soviet Union to the Western powers, including Britain.

The combined result was to place the commercial relations between the two countries on a new and more promising footing.

In the spring of 1963 the Chinese Vice-Minister of Foreign Trade came to Britain as the guest of the Government, the first Minister of the People's Republic to do so, and with his accompanying officials visited the works of a number of leading British firms, including ICI, Vickers-Armstrong, Courtaulds and Rootes. In November 1964, at the invitation of the Chinese, the President of the Board of Trade (Douglas Jay) returned this visit, and in the course of it opened a British Industrial Fair in Peking, the largest to be held in China by any Western country since 1949. There followed several smaller exhibitions, one of which was opened in Tientsin in September 1967 less than a month after the sacking of the British Embassy in Peking by the "cultural revolutionaries".

[1] Eden. *op. cit.* pp. 332, 337–338.
[2] *Hansard.* May 30, 1957. Cols. 622–624.

There were, on the other hand, countervailing factors, holding back the development of Sino-British trade.

In point of time, the first of these was the general seize-up in China's foreign trade at the beginning of the sixties, caused by blunders by the Chinese leaders in their internal economic policy combined with catastrophic crop failures. For this reason, in 1961 and 1962 the rising trend in British exports following the relaxation of restrictions was sharply, though temporarily, reversed.

Secondly, as time went on British companies faced increasingly severe competition for Chinese orders from rival firms in Western Europe and Japan, particularly the latter. A glance back at Table 16 shows that Japanese exports to China, which were almost nothing in 1960, in the second half of the decade were running at about 75% of those of Britain, West Germany, France and Italy put together.

The switch-back course of British exports to China in the last ten years or so is shown in Table 17. It will be seen that they have regained and passed the level reached in 1960. They still, however, make up an insignificant proportion (less than 1%) of British exports as a whole.

Table 17

British Exports to China[1]

(£ Million)

1956	1957	1958	1959	1960	1961	1962	1963	1964	1965	1966	1967
11	12	27	24	32	13	9	13	18	25	33	37

The Hong Kong Anomaly

There has been one major exception to the policy-makers' general line of tactical disengagement from China, namely the preservation of British sovereignty in Hong Kong.

Here still survives the last working model of a nineteenth-century British colony, situated on Chinese territory, inhabited by some 4,000,000 souls almost all of whom are Chinese and not British citizens, ruled autocratically by a British Governor responsible only to London, and garrisoned by some 10,000 British troops.

The colony is in every way highly vulnerable—politically, owing to the close ties of the population with the People's Republic, economically, became of its dependence on the latter for food and

[1] *UN Yearbook of International Trade Statistics. Far Eastern Economic Review.* July 18, 1968.

water supplies, and militarily, since it is indefensible against attack from that quarter.

By continuing to hold Hong Kong the Government has embroiled itself in a whole series of conflicts with Peking, which have placed a heavy strain on Anglo-Chinese relations as a whole.

To take only recent years, in 1965–1966, by allowing the colony to be used by U.S. combat forces engaged in the Vietnam war, the Government called down on its head protests from the Chinese (and North Vietnamese) Government that it was helping American aggression and endangering Chinese security. As a result, the air shuttle between South Vietnam and Hong Kong for American servicemen on leave had to be suspended.[1]

In 1967 armed clashes between the Hong Kong police and garrison and Chinese demonstrators inside the colony and on the Hong Kong-China border, in which some 50 people were killed and 800 injured, and the arrest of Communist leaders, police raids on Communist organisations and the closing of Communist newspapers in Hong Kong were the immediate cause of the near breakdown in diplomatic relations between London and Peking in August of that year.[2]

The Government, nonetheless, has so far shown no sign of wishing to disengage from Hong Kong. On the contrary, while on a visit to the colony following the disturbances just referred to, one of its members publicly reaffirmed its intention of holding on. The Government, he said, desired a good working relationship between China and Hong Kong and between China and Britain, "but I must make clear that we cannot consider any abdication of our authority and responsibilities in Hong Kong".[3]

This apparently atavistic attitude arises in part from the unwillingness, common to all the colonial powers, to give up what does not belong to them until the eleventh, and sometimes the twelfth, hour has struck.

It also arises from the profitability of the colony. As we have remarked before, the absolute figures given by official statistics have little meaning by themselves, but have some significance for purposes of comparison. In 1965 earnings on direct British capital investment in Hong Kong's four hundred square miles, estimated at £7,400,000,

---

[1] *Commonwealth Survey.* July 8, 1966.

[2] The sacking of the British Embassy on August 22 followed an ultimatum delivered by the Chinese Ministry of Foreign Affairs on August 20 that, if the suspension of Communist newspapers in Hong Kong were not lifted within 48 hours, the British Government must take the consequences. *Survey of British and Commonwealth Affairs.* September 15, 1967.

[3] *Ibid.* December 8, 1967.

were not much less than those from the whole of Nigeria and more than those from Ghana.[1] Moreover, only part of the cost of military forces maintained in the colony falls on the British exchequer. Under an arrangement made at the end of 1966, the colonial administration contributes £5,000,000 a year from its own resources for this purpose.[2]

The main factor, however, has been that the leaders of Communist China for both political and economic reasons have not yet directly challenged British sovereignty. They have said that Hong Kong will in due course return to China, they have at times used their political and economic leverage there to cause acute difficulties for the colonial administration, but they have not so far attempted to recover the colony either by force or by negotiation.

On the political side, China's policy over Hong Kong has, it seems to me, been dictated primarily by the desire to avoid consolidating a Western coalition against her and in particular to play off London against Washington. By using Fabian tactics, the Communist leaders have successfully encouraged already existing conciliatory tendencies in British policy and contributed to the isolation of the United States from its Western allies in Far Eastern matters.

On the economic side, the Chinese leaders could not and cannot put an end to the Hong Kong anomaly without endangering China's main source of foreign exchange. In 1967 it was estimated that Peking's total receipts from the colony were running at no less than £250,000,000 a year. The main part of this came from China's enormous trade surplus with Hong Kong, arising chiefly from the sale of foodstuffs and amounting to nearly £170,000,000. Large sums in foreign exchange also accrued from remittances from Chinese residents and from the profits of Peking's own business interests there.[3]

Looking ahead, it is possible, perhaps even probable, that the British and Chinese Governments, each for its own different reasons, will continue to preserve Hong Kong as a freak in the natural history of both Communism and colonialism for some years to come. But even if they do, it will remain a potentially explosive factor in Anglo-Chinese relations until the day it is returned to China of which it is geographically, ethnically, culturally and historically an integral part.

---

[1] *Board of Trade Journal.* June 30, 1967.
[2] *Survey of British and Commonwealth Affairs.* March 31, 1967.
[3] *The Economist.* October 19, 1968.

The Vietnam-Laos Crises

British policy towards Vietnam and Laos has had the same basic features as British policy towards Communist China and for the same reasons.

From the point of view of British foreign political strategy as a whole, former Indo-China, like China itself, is in a double sense a secondary front. It is not only far from the areas of primary concern to British foreign policy (Europe and the Middle East), but also, unlike Thailand and Indonesia, does not abut directly on the main surviving centre of British power in East Asia (Malaysia and Singapore) and, owing to years of first French and later American domination, has never been, and is not likely to become, of even commercial interest to London.

This is not to say that the policy-makers were or are indifferent to the outcome of the internal struggle in these countries between the Communists and their opponents. Before and after having successfully crushed the Communist partisans in their own South-East Asian stronghold and establishing fairly stable anti-Communist régimes in Kuala Lumpur and Singapore, they were ready purveyors of advice and advisers to Washington on how to do the same in Vietnam and Laos.

Nevertheless the attitude of the Government and the establishment generally to Communism in Vietnam and Laos has been very similar to their attitude towards Communism in China or, for that matter, Cuba, and very different from their attitude to Communism in their own bailiwick in Malaya or on their own doorstep in Western Europe. They would have been glad if the French or the Americans had succeeded in bringing Ho Chi Min and his men to heel, but did not regard it as a major tragedy when they failed to do so.

As shown below, this attitude has been implicit in the long-term policy of the decision-makers throughout the last fifteen years and has sometimes even been made explicit by penumbral figures close to the seats of power.

Thus, when at the end of 1966 President Johnson during his Asian tour had given every sign of intending to plunge deeper still into the Vietnamese morass, William Hayter, former British Ambassador in Moscow and now an influential opinion-maker on foreign policy matters, instead of the usual hints and haverings, posed the question outright of whether it was necessary to oppose the Communisation of South Vietnam and answered definitely that it was not.

Britain and the West were not engaged in a world-wide anti-Communist crusade, he said, but in protecting themselves and their own way of life in their own countries. "We may think Communism a detestable way of life for ourselves. But it is not for us to decide whether it is right or wrong for other countries, unless its adoption by other countries imperils us."[1]

As in the case of China, Washington's highly aggressive policy forced upon London a problem far more important and acute than that presented merely by the strength of the Communists in Vietnam and Laos.

Successively in 1954, 1960–1961 and 1965–1968, the American Government threatened to escalate what was essentially a colonial war into a world conflict, involving China and possibly the Soviet Union, on one side, and at a minimum Britain, Australia and New Zealand as well as the United States, on the other. In 1954 a major role was also still allotted to France.

In other words, United States policy over Vietnam and Laos showed a persistent tendency to drag Britain into precisely the kind of war in East Asia which her leaders, as we have already seen, were bent on avoiding.

Because of the sharpening conflict between the demands of the Anglo-American special relationship, prompting support for American escalation, and the demands of London's own order of priorities, prompting search for a political settlement, the course of British diplomacy became increasingly tortuous and contradictory, so much so that at home it in the end aroused widespread opposition and contempt.

The period falls roughly into two phases — 1954–1962, when Britain's weight was thrown openly against American military intervention, and 1962–1968, when first the Conservative Government and then the Labour Government, while still refusing to commit British forces to Vietnam or Laos and still expressing certain reservations about U.S. policy, gave it their moral support.

In both phases, as we shall see, the underlying aim of the policy-makers remained the same, namely to defuse the Indo-Chinese powder barrel, even if this meant, as it did and does, recognising the permanence of Communist power in a large part of former Indo-China. What changed was not the Government's objective but, as in various aspects of the China problem, its willingness publicly to

---

[1] William Hayter. "Need the West still 'Contain' Communism?" *The Observer.* November 6, 1966.

uphold a policy running directly contrary to that of their American partners.

1954–1962

When the first world crisis over Vietnam arose in 1954, the balance of forces in the country was such that the French colonial army could no longer hope by its own efforts to bring the whole of Indo-China to heel. The essential question before Paris, Washington and London was whether the United States and Britain should come to France's assistance by direct military intervention or whether a compromise settlement should be sought with the Vietnamese Government in Hanoi, and the Chinese and Soviet Governments.

The Churchill Government chose the second alternative and in doing so appears to have been moved by three main considerations.

First, in accordance with its already established world anti-Communist strategy, it was anxious to avoid any risk of war with China and to steer Washington's policy in the same direction. As already noted above, the Foreign Secretary informed the U.S. Government as early as May 1952 that the Government were strongly opposed to any course of action in South-East Asia which would be likely to result in a war with China.

Secondly, the authorities were anxious to avoid the estrangement of India, Ceylon, Burma and Asian opinion generally, which was actively opposed to any attempt to prolong colonial rule in Indo-China. As Eden tells us in his account of the crisis, he and his colleagues considered "it was essential not to alienate India by our actions in a part of the world which concerned her closely".[1]

Thirdly, the Government, which was still engaged in major military operations against the Communist-led independence movement in Malaya of a kind very similar to those of the French in Indo-China, hoped to turn Indo-China into a buffer zone, or as Eden called it "a protective pad",[2] between China in the north and Malaya, and its immediate neighbour Thailand, in the south.

At the beginning of April 1954, over a month before the fall of Dien Bien Phu, the Government officially conveyed its opinion to the State Department that the Western powers would probably have "to accept a policy of compromise with the Communists in Indo-China" and that this compromise should take the form of the partition of Vietnam.[3]

In advocating partition, the Government had already considered

[1] Eden. *op. cit.* p. 94.
[2] *Ibid.* p. 123.
[3] *Ibid.* p. 92.

and rejected the alternative of admitting Communists to a share in the government of Indo-China as a whole, which London thought would bring Communist activity and influence dangerously close to its own stronghold to the south. As Eden puts it, "My chief concern was for Malaya. I wanted to ensure an effective barrier as far north of that country as possible."[1]

The British plan envisaged that, as soon as a compromise settlement had been reached, a Western military organisation could be set up in South-East Asia to bolster up the non-Communist régimes in Laos, Cambodia, South Vietnam, Thailand and other states, but stipulated that this should be done in such a way as to secure at least the acquiescence of the Asian members of the Commonwealth. Thus in mid-April the U.S. Secretary of State, Dulles, was informed that the British Government welcomed the idea of an organisation for collective defence in South-East Asia, but that its membership would require the most careful consideration and that "on no account should India and the other Asian Commonwealth countries be deliberately excluded".[2]

Lastly, in its attitude to the crisis the Government made a distinction between Indo-China, on the one hand, and Thailand, on the other, due to the latter's strategic position on Malaya's frontier. In a conversation with Dulles towards the end of April, Eden, while casting doubt on the usefulness of outside military intervention in Indo-China, told him that, in the event of the total collapse of the French military position there, he would favour joint Anglo-American military action to safeguard the frontiers of Thailand.[3]

This general line, pursued throughout the 1954 crisis, directly collided with U.S. plans for military intervention in Indo-China and played a considerable part in frustrating them.

What proved to be the decisive clash came when, despite heavy pressure personally exercised by Dulles and the Chairman of the U.S. Joint Chiefs of Staff Committee, Admiral Radford, the Government decided and announced publicly in the House of Commons on April 27 that it was "not prepared to give any undertakings about military action in Indo-China in advance of the results of Geneva", i.e., the conference on Korea and Indo-China, with the participation of the Soviet and Chinese as well as the United States, British and French Governments, already convened for the following month. The effect of this decision on U.S. policy is summed up by Eisen-

---

[1] *Ibid.* pp. 87 and 91.
[2] *Ibid.* p. 96.
[3] *Ibid.* p. 101.

hower, who records that "this ended for the time being our efforts to find any satisfactory method of Allied intervention".[1]

There then followed an Anglo-American battle for the support of the French Government. In May and June Washington embarked on separate negotiations with Paris behind London's back aimed at launching U.S. military intervention with or without British participation.[2] When, however, the French Government fell in mid-June and Mendès-France came to power, Paris swung definitely over to London's side.

The U.S. Government was thereby forced to abandon its plans and grudgingly to fall into line. This was reflected in an Anglo-American policy document drawn up during the visit of Churchill and Eden to Washington later in the month, contemplating a compromise at Geneva, based on the partition of Vietnam.[3] From then on, though the U.S. Government refused to sign the Geneva Agreements on Indo-China of July 1954, it ceased actively to sabotage the efforts of Mendès-France and Eden to bring about their conclusion.

British diplomacy was less successful in its attempts to draw the non-aligned powers, particularly India, into a Western military pact, which would guarantee the continuance of non-Communist régimes in Laos, Cambodia and South Vietnam. London obtained Washington's permission to invite the Colombo powers — India, Ceylon, Pakistan, Burma and Indonesia — to participate in the Manila conference in September. All except Pakistan refused on the ground that participation in such a pact would infringe their policy of non-alignment.[4] As a result the South-East Asia Treaty Organisation (SEATO) was set up on the lines desired by Washington and became an instrument of American and not British foreign policy.

The general direction of British tactics during the Laos crisis of 1960–1961 was much the same as during the Vietnam crisis of 1954.

The crisis itself arose from the sustained efforts of the U.S. authorities over several years to establish its own extreme right-wing protégés in power in Laos in preference to the neutralist coalition Government of Souvanna Phouma, containing representatives of the extreme right, the centre and the Communists. This aim was pursued with the active co-operation of the Thai Government and with funds and arms distributed largely through the CIA.[5]

---

[1] Dwight D. Eisenhower. *Mandate for Change*. London. 1963. p. 351.
[2] *Ibid*. pp. 358–361 and Eden. *op. cit*. pp. 119 and 127.
[3] The text is given in Eden. *op. cit*. pp. 132–133.
[4] *Ibid*. pp. 143–144.
[5] For detailed critique of U.S. intrigues in Laos in 1954–1960 see A. M. Schlesinger. *op. cit*. pp. 294–299.

When in August 1960 a major part of the Laotian armed forces, led by Kong Le, rose against the American puppet régime and in favour of the restoration to power of Souvanna Phouma (which was also the aim of the Communist-led Pathet Lao), Washington's thoughts turned to direct military intervention. Eisenhower tells us that by the end of December he and his advisers had concluded that the "anti-Communist government of Boun Oum would need a great measure of outside help if it was to survive" and that the time might be approaching to "make active use of the Seventh Fleet, including landing parties", and that such action might have to be taken regardless of the views of Britain and France—"with our allies or without them".[1]

This was also the burden of Eisenhower's advice to Kennedy, on handing over the presidency to the latter in January 1961. He said that "it would be fatal to permit the Communists any part in a new Laotian régime" and that the United States should, if necessary, "intervene unilaterally".[2]

The Macmillan Government supported American intrigues in Laos so long as they appeared to have any chance of success, in particular by rejecting Soviet proposals in 1958 and 1959 that the International Commission in Laos set up under the Geneva Agreements of 1954, whose activities had been suspended, should reconvene. But when in December 1960 it became clear that Washington was moving towards direct military intervention, London opposed this and came out openly in favour of a political settlement based on the Geneva Agreements and providing for Communist participation in the Laotian Government.

On December 19, 1960, just at the time when the Eisenhower Administration was actively planning to send its troops into Laos, the Foreign Secretary, Lord Home, declared in the House of Lords that "our idea of the international position of Laos is that it should be genuinely unaligned. It has been the policy of H.M. Government ever since the rebellion of Captain Kong Le's troops in August of this year to encourage the Laotians to form a government of national union. I think this is more desirable now than ever before."[3]

The thoughts of the Government were expressed more bluntly to the U.S. Government in February 1961, by which time Kennedy had taken over the presidency from Eisenhower. Using the privilege of an old personal friend, David Ormsby-Gore (now Lord Harlech), then

[1] Eisenhower. *op. cit.* pp. 609–610.
[2] Schlesinger. *op. cit.* p. 148.
[3] *Documents* . . . 1960. pp. 523, 524.

Under-Secretary of State at the Foreign Office, treated Kennedy to a scathing critique of U.S. policy in Laos. He said that the United States "had done its best to destroy Souvanna Phouma, who represented the best hope of a non-Communist Laos, and instead was backing a crooked, right-wing gang; the impression of Washington always rushing about to prop up corrupt dictators in Asia could not have happy consequences".[1]

As it turned out, Kennedy and his advisers had meanwhile reassessed the situation in Laos and drawn conclusions similar to those already drawn in London. The abandonment of the extreme measures planned by his predecessor was marked by his statement at a Press conference on March 23 that "if in the past there has been any possible ground of misunderstanding of our desire for a truly neutral Laos, there should be none now".[2]

Later the same month Kennedy and Macmillan had a hurried meeting in Florida, at which they agreed that, while joint military intervention might be necessary in the last resort, a solution should be sought on the lines recommended by London, i.e., the formation of a neutral coalition government, including both Communists and the extreme right and headed by Souvanna Phouma. The way was thus opened for the conclusion of a cease-fire in Laos and the reconvening of the 1954 Geneva Conference by its joint Soviet and British Chairmen. The reconvened Conference opened at Geneva in May 1961 and led eventually to the settlement of July 1962.

It may be noted that, as in 1954, the Government, while opposing military intervention in Laos, regarded similar action in Thailand in a different light. Thus in May 1962, when Communist-led forces in Laos were approaching the Thai border and the Thai Government, no less a "crooked, right-wing gang" than the CIA's trusties in Laos, appealed for assistance, the Macmillan Government not only approved the despatch of U.S. forces, but itself sent a squadron of Hunter jet fighters to Thailand. The Prime Minister, when questioned in the House of Commons, emphasised that this force was intended not for intervention in Laos, but for the defence of Thailand, if her territory were attacked.[3]

1962–1968

The year 1962 marked a turning point in British diplomacy in Vietnamese and Laotian affairs. From then on until the modification

[1] Schlesinger. *op. cit.* p. 304.
[2] *Ibid.* p. 303.
[3] *Commonwealth Survey.* June 5, 1962. pp. 473–474.

of American policy in 1968 there was a widening gap between what was still thought in high quarters to be in the long run the right way of tackling the situation and the words and deeds of the Government.

On the one hand, signs continued to appear that the idea of neutralising the succession states in Indo-China by agreement with Hanoi, Peking and Moscow, which underlay the 1954 and 1962 Geneva Agreements and which involved putting up with Communist influence in the area, was still very much alive. On the other, the Government and opposition leaders lent Britain's name to American actions, the avowed object of which was to crush the Communists in Vietnam by force.

In the above-mentioned paper published in 1965, Robert Scott, one of the Government's chief advisers on South-East Asia and a key figure in the military establishment, unequivocally favoured neutrality for the area "with the agreement and consent of all concerned, including China", which, he said, would be in the best interests of the countries concerned and of the rest of the world.

Similarly, Sir Alec Douglas-Home's plan for reorganising the Western system of Far Eastern alliances, put forward in 1966 (see above), specifically provided that Vietnam, Laos and Cambodia should be excluded from the proposed "Asian SEATO" forming the advanced echelon of Western military dispositions. Those three countries would make up a separate belt of non-aligned states, whose neutrality would be internationally guaranteed and supervised.

In 1967 almost the same proposal was sketched out by Christopher Mayhew, writing from the vantage point of recent membership of the Government. A belt of strictly neutral states might be formed of Cambodia, Laos, Vietnam and also Burma, he wrote, standing between China and another group of states, Thailand, Malaysia, Singapore and Indonesia, which would look more towards the West than towards China. He went on to warn that no collective non-aligned association was likely to emerge so long as some of the South-East Asian states remained heavily dependent on Western military alliances.[1]

But instead of working for a solution on these lines, as it had done in 1954 and 1960–1961, the Government, whatever advice it may have given to Washington in private, in public upheld the righteousness of the latter's cause, thereby increasing the danger of a general conflagration in East Asia, which it was anxious to avoid, and making more difficult of attainment its own long-term objectives.

[1] Mayhew. *op. cit.* p. 81.

Omens of what was to come were already visible in 1962, when the Macmillan Government, while actively promoting the neutralisation of Laos, took the opposite line over Vietnam. The Foreign Secretary welcomed the Laotian settlement of that year as evidence that "both the East and the West, who were in danger of meeting in a clash of rivalries in this area, have decided that the will of neither will prevail and that they will live with neutraility".[1] But at the time these words were spoken, the Government was already on record as giving unqualified approval to the increase in U.S. military aid to Saigon then taking place.[2]

The critical moment came in 1964–1965, when the United States, on top of massive military intervention in South Vietnam, embarked on what was to prove to be three years of heavy, though fruitless, bombardment of North Vietnam up to only a few miles from the Chinese border.

The prologue to this escalation took place in August 1964 when, following what now appears to have been a stage-managed attack on U.S. warships in the Gulf of Tonkin, American aircraft, on Johnson's orders, carried out retaliatory strikes on North Vietnamese territory. In the Security Council and in a special statement issued by the Prime Minister (Sir Alec Douglas-Home) and the Foreign Secretary (R. A. Butler), the Government supported this action as an exercise of the essential right of self-defence and as fully consistent with the UN Charter.[3]

When Washington, on February 7, 1965, began the general bombardment of the North, the Government, now headed by Wilson, took the same attitude, the Foreign Secretary (Michael Stewart) declaring against all reason that the American action did not increase the danger of the situation in Vietnam and was a legitimate reaction to the help given by the Vietnamese in the North to the Vietnamese guerrillas in the South.[4]

This remained the official British attitude for the next three years, and was publicly reaffirmed when U.S. bombers renewed their raids on the North after the Christmas truces of 1965–1966 and 1966–1967. It was adhered to after U.S. policy had come under heavy fire within the President's own party, after it had been condemned by the French Government and after the 1966 and 1967 Labour Party Annual Conferences had specifically called for the cessation of U.S.

[1] *Hansard.* House of Lords. July 25, 1962. Cols. 1029–1030.
[2] *Hansard.* February 19, 1962. Cols. 171–174.
[3] *Commonwealth Survey.* September 1, 1964.
[4] *Hansard.* February 8, 1965. Cols. 38–39 and April 1, 1965. Col. 1860.

bombing and for negotiations on the lines of the 1954 Geneva
Agreements.

During this period the Government made a number of anxiety
gestures mainly designed to still opposition at home and perhaps its
own conscience, but, with one possible exception, none of them had
any effect on the course of events. The exception was Michael
Stewart's expression of disapproval at a Press conference in Washington in March 1965 of American use of poison gas in Vietnam.[1] All the
rest were agreed with the U.S. authorities beforehand and treated
by the latter as at worst innocuous, and at best helpful, to their own
policy.

When on June 29, 1966, Wilson and his colleagues publicly
regretted that U.S. aircraft had attacked "targets touching on the
populated areas of Hanoi and Haiphong" and dissociated themselves from this action, they at the same time reaffirmed their support
for American policy in Vietnam as a whole and that they considered
that only Hanoi and not Washington bore the onus of continuing the
war. It also emerged that the issue of a statement of this kind had
been concerted with Johnson earlier.[2]

Similarly, the series of peace missions organised by London in
1965,[3] since they were all aimed at persuading Hanoi and the
Vietnamese supporters in the South to give way to American military
pressure, were mediatory only in the sense that Neville Chamberlain's activities over the Czechoslovak question in 1938 were
mediatory, i.e., their object was to persuade the victim, as the police
say, to come quietly.

Not surprisingly, these efforts met with no response in the Communist capitals, but were well received in Washington, their net effect
being to add colour to the latter's threadbare story that the aggressors
were to be found in Vietnam and not the United States. Stewart,
indeed, boasted that, as a result of these missions, the whole world
could now see that Britain and the United States wanted peace and
that it was not they who were at fault.[4]

The schizophrenic character of British diplomacy over Vietnam
in recent years is to be explained, I think, primarily by London's

---

[1] *The Times.* March 24, 1965.
[2] *Commonwealth Survey.* July 8, 1966.
[3] Gordon Walker's mission in April–May 1965, which never got off the ground as the
Chinese and North Vietnamese Governments refused to receive him; the Commonwealth
mission launched at the Commonwealth Prime Ministers' Conference in June 1965,
which also ran into the sand as the Soviet, Chinese and North Vietnamese Governments
were not willing to open discussions with it; and the mission of Harold Davies in July
1965, who succeeded in giving his views to officials in Hanoi, but nothing else.
[4] *Hansard.* July 20, 1965. Cols. 1355–1373.

pre-occupation with the far-reaching aim of developing new forms of Anglo-American co-operation in the Far East and Indian and Pacific Oceans, which, whatever the Government's misgivings over the escalation of American aggression, precluded open opposition to it.

As we have already seen, British plans for a counterforce to Chinese nuclear weapons, for strengthening the defences of India, hinged and hinge on a permanently functioning system of Anglo-American partnership similar to that which has long existed in Europe, and have no substance unless backed by American military, political and financial power. They presuppose a common Anglo-American front on all major politico-military questions in the area and are incompatible with divided counsels on what has recently been the chief of them.

We must also remember that when in 1964–1965 the Government took the critical decision to give its blessing to the American attack on North Vietnam, it was itself then deeply entangled in the Indonesian-Malaysian confrontation in Borneo and anxious to buy American help. As shown in Chapter 2 of this book, despite initial reluctance on Washington's part, Wilson and Johnson eventually struck a bargain in December 1964, in which American support for British policy in Malaysia was expressly balanced against British support for American policy in Vietnam.

Now that American policy in Vietnam has taken a more realistic turn and that the process of running down British bases on the Asian mainland is under way, it seems possible that British diplomacy, escaping from its present ignoble posture, will revert to its original conciliatory course, aimed at giving the three succession states the neutral status all along assigned to them on political maps projected in London. It is, however, alas, too late to wipe out what seems to me to have been one of the most shameful pages in the history of British foreign policy.

Conclusion

Some conclusions about the direction in which British foreign policy is moving in particular fields have already been suggested in their context in various parts of the book. Here the intention is to put forward briefly some more general ideas about what is happening, arising from the study as a whole.

Firstly, it emerges that British foreign policy is still undergoing major readjustment to a world in which Britain's part as one of the main centres of civilisation remains unchanged, but in which the capacity of her rulers to bend other peoples and other nations to their will has sharply diminished. Whichever group of states we take — the Communist countries, the other capitalist powers, or the former colonies and semi-colonies of Asia and Africa — the policy-makers have been forced, and are still being forced, to readjust their sights to nearer and more accessible targets than those previously aimed at.

Two of the three main processes underlying this change, the expansion and increased strength of the socialist system and the formation of new independent states in Asia and Africa linked with the socialist as well as the capitalist system, have reduced the effective range not only of British foreign policy, but that of all the Western powers, including the United States, and are, I think, irreversible.

On the other hand, the third process, the steady decline during the last two decades of British power as compared with that of the other leading capitalist states, is one which might well be reversed in the seventies and eighties.

This decline has, it seems to me, been brought about mainly by the boomerang effect of certain characteristics of British capitalism, which earlier contributed to its strength, but in the post-war period have had the opposite result of weakening it, chief among them an exceptionally large diversion of resources to the protection of politico-military positions overseas, an exceptionally high rate of new capital investment abroad and the free use of sterling as a reserve currency by the rest of the world.

327

These peculiarities have had multifarious harmful effects for Britain in the social and political, as well as economic fields, but, as in some forms of illness, they have been associated with one main symptom, one main focus of pain, namely a chronic weakness in the balance of payments, to which they all directly contribute, and which, in its turn, has been the cause, through the stop-go procedure, of the country's chronically low rate of industrial growth.

If this analysis is approximately correct, the authorities, under the sharp spur of recurrent crises of the pound, have, with great reluctance, been moving in the right direction, since they apparently are now at last liquidating the remaining British *places d'armes* in South-East Asia and the Middle East and have in recent years somewhat reduced the military share of the gross national product, bringing it down nearer to that for France and West Germany. There have also been signs of reconsideration of the alleged benefits to Britain of continuing massive exports of private capital and of the preservation of the sterling area.

It is quite likely, therefore, that in the present and next decade British diplomacy, while its radius of action shrinks in the world as a whole, will at the same time acquire a greater freedom of manœuvre than it at present possesses in areas of prime concern, particularly in all aspects of European affairs. What use is made of this greater manœuvrability will depend to a considerable extent on the internal political factor.

Secondly, the study shows that the scientific and technological revolution has given an entirely new twist to the question of allies and partners. Britain has an advanced modern industry, first-class scientists and engineers and a highly skilled working class, but she cannot take full advantage of current radical changes in the means of production within the existing framework of her international relations. In this respect she is at a disadvantage as compared with both the United States, with its enormous internal sources of capital accumulation and internal market, and with France and West Germany which, by joining together in the European Economic Community, have opened the road to at least a partial solution of the new problems of size with which they, like Britain, are confronted.

Here again, the peculiar structure of British capitalism inherited from former times is now in contradiction with its present needs. British industry and finance has a privileged position in an extraordinarily wide area, namely the Commonwealth, but with the exception of Canada and Australia, it consists of countries which, owing to the relative backwardness of their economies, cannot effectively act either as partners in the financing, development and application of the discoveries of modern science or as principal market for the output of the most advanced branches of British industry. In the world as it is today, this double role can only be played by either the Western European or the North American countries, which between them already take by far the greater part of Britain's exports.

It follows that, even if the decline of Britain within the hierarchy of the capitalist powers is arrested by measures which the Government has already been forced to take, in the conditions created by the scientific and technological revolution her future position is also bound up with the development of qualitatively new relations with other advanced industrial states. Herein lies, I think, the main reason why over the last ten years the policy-makers have found themselves obliged to return again and again to the thorny question of Britain's membership of the European Economic Community, and why all Commonwealth-centred conceptions of British foreign policy have faded into the background.

The desirability or otherwise of British membership of the EEC depends at any particular time on a complex of variable factors, i.e., on the concrete economic, social, political and military conditions upon which membership can be obtained in the prevailing circumstances. But there is one factor which is not variable, namely the objective demands of the contemporary revolution in the means of production, lying at the root of the process of Western European economic integration.

Thirdly, anyone who looks long and at all critically at the recent history of British foreign policy must conclude, I think, that there is a deplorably large gap between what successive Governments, their advisers, and policy-making circles generally, have conceived to be the situation and the situation itself. In other words, what may be called the error factor in foreign policy has been so big as substantially to influence the course of events for the worse. The establishment not only pursues aims and interests diverging, sometimes widely, sometimes not, from those of the public at large, but multiplies the harmful effects of doing so by its inability to estimate correctly the consequences of its own actions.

There is nothing new in this. The disastrous policy towards Nazi Germany conducted by the Conservative caucus in the thirties arose not only from political, largely anti-Communist, affinities but also from a completely wrong idea of the real intentions of Hitler and his régime. Nor are major miscalculations an idiosyncrasy of British

11*

foreign policy. The present American invasion of Vietnam was launched and persisted in partly owing to a gross under-estimation of the power of resistance of the people of Vietnam. But I think all the same that the error factor has played a particularly large part in the actions of Britain's leaders during the period considered here.

The classic example is the Eden-led attack on Egypt in 1956 which, as it was based on erroneous estimates of all the main elements in the situation, led to results exactly the opposite of those intended. But the same must be said of the first attempt, conducted by Macmillan and Heath, to gain entry into the Common Market which, proceeding in its tactics from false assumptions about both French and West German foreign policy, inadvertently accelerated precisely those bloc-building tendencies on the continent which the Government was trying to arrest. It is hard to say how many millions were unwittingly thrown away during the fifties and early sixties as a result of wildly wrong assessments of the cost of, and need for, Blue Streak, TSR-2 and other weapons-systems, and harder still to guess at the astronomic losses during the last decade flowing from the ill-founded belief in high quarters that the parity of the pound could and should be maintained. No explanation is, I think, possible of the swift rise and fall of the East of Suez doctrine, associated with the name of the present Prime Minister, without recognising a large element of sheer miscalculation.

There is one common factor in these and a large number of other blunders, namely an over-estimation of the real strength of Britain's position in the world. Bearing in mind that most of the present generation of policy-makers formed their conceptions of British power before and during the war, this strongly suggests that the particularly high rate of error is a function of the particularly rapid change in the post-war balance of forces to the disadvantage of all the imperialist systems, particularly the British. It is also seems likely that the present generation of top people, by age, training and bent, has more difficulty in grasping the foreign political consequences of the scientific and technological revolution than will the succeeding generation.

Lastly, as shown in relation to particular issues in the course of the study, changes in the domestic political climate have played a significant part in the evolution of foreign policy in two main ways.

Firstly, on the big questions, particularly the danger of nuclear war in all its many aspects, there has been a strong ground-swell of opinion in favour of sanity and good sense, which has had an indirect effect on the behaviour of both the Conservative and Labour leaderships. Secondly, the general shift to the left both among the electorate as a whole and within the labour movement has produced, as a direct result of the return of the Labour Party to power, certain distinctive tactical changes for the better in the course of British diplomacy.

Not even their best friends could reasonably claim that Wilson and his colleagues have carried out all their electoral promises and still less that they have brought about a transformation of foreign policy. But there is, I think, an analogy here with what has happened since 1964 over certain aspects of social policy.

Roy Jenkins, referring in a well-known speech to such matters as censorship, divorce, capital punishment and support for the arts, suggested, with good reason, that British society had become more civilised. I do not think that any Government which supports the American invasion of Vietnam can call itself civilised, but on a whole row of questions, from overseas bases to multilateral nuclear forces and arms for the South African Bruderbond, the Wilsons have shown more sense, and in some contexts common decency, than the Heaths and the Homes.

This phenomenon does not depend on personal qualities. As has been shown, over certain questions in the post-war period, Churchill and Macmillan were more far-sighted than Attlee and Gaitskell. Man for man, most people would, I imagine, prefer to entrust the Foreign Office to, say, Maudling, than George Brown. It arises from the difference in the social basis of the Labour and Conservative parties and corresponds to the similar phenomenon in, for example, West Germany, where the foreign policy tactics of the Social Democrats show the same sort of differences from those of the Christian Democrats.

In recent years, the slightly different angle of vision of the two Parties on foreign affairs has been most obvious in policy towards the third world, since the ultra-colonialists have a powerful and permanently functioning lobby within the Conservative Party and almost no representation in the Labour Party at all. But, as I think the study shows, the same sort of difference can be discerned today pretty well across the board, and, judging from the current statements of the Conservative leaders, is likely to persist well into the seventies.

Index